Key Account Management

Key Account Management

The Definitive Guide

Third edition

Diana Woodburn
and
Malcolm McDonald

WILEY

A John Wiley & Sons, Ltd, Publication

Library of Congress Cataloging-in-Publication Data
McDonald, Malcolm.
    Key account management : the definitive guide / Malcolm McDonald,
Diana Woodburn. — 3rd ed.
        p. cm.
    Includes bibliographical references and index.
    ISBN 978-0-470-97415-5 (pbk.)
    1. Selling—Key accounts. 2. Marketing—Key accounts. I. Woodburn, Diana.
II. Title.
    HF5438.8.K48M35 2011
    658.8′04—dc22

                                                                2010045341

ISBN 978-0-470-97415-5 (paperback), ISBN 978-0-470-97475-9 (ebk),
ISBN 978-0-470-97473-5 (ebk), ISBN 978-0-470-97472-8 (ebk)

A catalogue record for this book is available from the British Library.

Typeset in 10/12pt Palatino Roman by Thomson Digital, Noida, India.
Printed in Great Britain by TJ International Ltd, Padstow, Cornwall, UK

Contents

Foreword

I find it truly amazing that it is only in the past decade that key account management (KAM) has emerged as a major discipline in its own right. Even more surprising is that most business schools resolutely refuse to include it in their curriculum, preferring to stick with the perennial four 'Ps of marketing', which, while still relevant, are totally dependent on getting the strategy right for the new breed of powerful, global customers, who now demand seamless service from their suppliers in every country of the world where they operate.

Cranfield is a shining exception to the rule. In 1996 the first structured research was done on best practice key account management under the leadership of Professor Malcolm McDonald and Diana Woodburn. The current KAM Best Practice Research Club is a sophisticated extension of those exciting, earlier forays into best practice key account management.

The implications for suppliers of the enormous power of buyers today are felt across the entire corporate spectrum, and after a decade of research at Cranfield, we can now truly say that instigating best practice key account management implies a substantial programme of change management and simply cannot be achieved by tinkering with the salesforce.

The sequence of events is as follows:

1. Select the correct accounts to be included in the key account programme.

2. Categorize them according to their potential for helping us to grow our profits continuously.

3. Analyse their needs.

4. Develop strategic plans for and with each of them.

5. Get buy-in from all functions about their role in delivering the agreed value propositions. This involves IT, manufacturing, logistics, HR, finance, operations and R&D. This way, these functions will be customer-driven.

6. Get the right organization structure to serve the selected key accounts' needs.

7. Get the right people and skill sets in the key account team.

8. Implement the plans on an annual basis.

9. Measure the success of the plans, particularly in respect of whether they create shareholder value added.

10. Reward individuals and teams for their success.

Malcolm McDonald and Diana Woodburn have done a remarkable job in capturing all their research and practical experience in this excellent book and I commend it to you.

Martin Lamb
Chief Executive
IMI plc

Acknowledgements

We are extremely grateful to Beth Rogers, now of Portsmouth Business School, who for many years helped us with our research and our thinking. Her part in earlier versions of this book, and particularly for the mini-cases for practical learning, was invaluable. We would like to acknowledge the contribution of Professor Tony Millman on the original key account management research report, back in 1996. Special thanks are due to him for his enthusiasm for the topic. His previous work, and that of Dr Kevin Wilson, was invaluable in creating frameworks for understanding the development of supplier/customer relationships.

Our thanks are due to other colleagues for their help and support: particularly to Dr Sue Holt, for allowing us to include some of her research; to Professor Nigel Piercy of Warwick Business School, for stimulating our thinking on several topics; to Dr Nikala Lane for her contribution to the section on teams; and to Professor Lynette Ryals for her overall support. Huge thanks are due to Steve Doubleday and Peter Mouncey for their major contribution to the editing process. We should certainly not forget our spouses for their endless forbearance during the writing process.

Lastly, too numerous to mention individually, are all the practitioners and their companies who have helped to develop our understanding of key account management, shape our thinking and validate our ideas: through the Cranfield KAM Best Practice Research Club, its focus syndicates and other practitioner forums, through participation in research and in KAM development consultancy projects, and through help with the case study insights distributed throughout the book.

The purpose of this book

To help the time-starved reader, we have started each chapter with a 'Fast Track' for those who want a rapid reprise of the content before you delve deeper into the chapter or, indeed, skip to another chapter that contains material relating to your immediate priority. All the Fast Tracks have been compiled into one integrated section at the end of the book, so you can start or finish with the complete helicopter overview.

As this is a book designed for thinking practitioners, we have avoided filling the text with academic references, but we have added a list of items for further reading around each chapter, included at the end of the book.

The expression 'caveat emptor' (beware buyer) has been turned completely on its head during the past 10 years, so that 'caveat vendor' (beware seller) is now the norm. Customer power, particularly in over-supplied Western economies, is here to stay, hence the growing importance of key account management as a topic on the agendas of all companies, big or small.

This book represents state-of-the-art best practice, based on a decade of in-depth research into global best practice key account management from both supplier and customer perspectives, which has shown that, among other findings:

- Key account management is a strategic approach distinguishable from account management or key account selling. It should be used to ensure the long-term development and retention of strategic customers.

- Key account management is high profile, but difficult to do well.

- Key account management is appropriate to several types of relationships, but is most clearly manifest when supplier and customer have a mutually recognized partnership and a degree of trust.

- There are often mismatches between the way suppliers and customers perceive each other and their relationship, so careful communication and vigilance are vital.

- Regular monitoring of the profitability of individual customers by suppliers provides crucial information, but is quite rare because customer profitability is difficult to measure.

- Key account managers need a broad portfolio of business management skills to deal with interdependent or integrated customer relationships.

- Key account management has structural implications for selling companies. Interdependence and integration can only be achieved where the key account manager has a considerable degree of control over resources and decision making.

This book proposes ways of dealing with these findings, taking the reader to a level whereby he/she can implement solutions. It is intended to help key account strategists and key account managers to capture and develop a scientific basis for their company's practice. The scope of key account management is widening and it is becoming more complex. For key account management to be successfully implemented, there is an urgent need to develop reliable diagnostic tools and measures of performance that support strategic marketing decisions. The skills of professionals involved in key account management at strategic and operational levels need to be constantly updated and developed. So this book demonstrates how key account management can be implemented, and describes the elements of best practice that can be adopted by all types and sizes of organization.

Chapter 1: The crucial role of key account management

This chapter sets key account management in the context of a dramatically changing business environment where increasingly complex relationships have altered the nature of marketing, and imposed an urgent need for greater understanding and more appropriate treatment of key relationships.

Chapter 2: Selecting and categorizing key customers

We explain how to select and categorize the most appropriate accounts to target for key account management, which arguably means that this chapter is the most important in the whole book. Your KAM programme can be fatally flawed by making the wrong decisions at this stage.

Chapter 3: Relationship stages

There is a clear hierarchy of key account relationships increasing in complexity and intimacy with the customer. Understanding where you are is crucial to adopting the right behaviour towards the customer.

Chapter 4: Developing key relationships

Important relationships should not be left to develop on their own. Application of the right tools and techniques can help you get to the level to which you aspire with more speed and confidence.

Chapter 5: The buyer perspective

Needless to say, buyers have their own view of key supplier relationships, and not necessarily the one the supplier would like. Ignorance of their perspective leads to complacency, inertia and disappointment, so understanding it is mandatory, however unwelcome.

Chapter 6: Key account profitability

Profitability belongs to customers much more than to products. Since customers and customer behaviour cause cost as well as revenue, real customer profitability must be measured. It is not easy but, again, ignorance is foolhardy.

Chapter 7: Key account analysis

This chapter examines how to analyse key accounts in order to establish and prioritize their needs.

Chapter 8: Planning for key accounts

We introduce the processes for and the tools and techniques of key account planning. We describe how to set objectives and strategies for each targeted key account, and how to measure their profitability.

Chapter 9: Processes – making key account management work

While key account plans are intrinsic to key account management, a plan is only a plan until it is implemented. Most companies' processes are not set up to deliver the promises of key account management but, like many initiatives, the devil is in the implementation.

Chapter 10: The role and requirements of key account managers

Key account managers can fulfil one of four roles in managing the customer relationship, which, depending on the complexity of the relationship, may or may not involve leading a dedicated team. Each role has its own set of competences and attributes which should be understood in matching the right key account manager with each key account.

Chapter 11: Rewards and performance in key account management

KAM is designed to improve or at least maintain performance with challenging customers. This chapter gets to grips with what performance means in KAM, at the level of individual key accounts, the whole key account portfolio, and the key account manager. Most companies are determined, rightly or wrongly, to give rewards as incentives for good performance, but seek assistance on how to structure a rewards scheme and what kind of reward to offer.

Chapter 12: Organizing for key account management

There is no perfect structure for key account management as it is essentially a cross-boundary activity, though some structures are less KAM-friendly than others. This chapter looks at how key account management can be positioned in the organization and some of the issues that arise.

Chapter 13: Transitioning to key account management

The rest of the book reflects best practice KAM, but this chapter charts the journey to achieve it from the beginning. KAM is a cultural change as well as a business initiative, and a long haul, not to be undertaken lightly. Following the four-phase route that other suppliers have used will help to anticipate issues and prepare solutions for them.

Innumerable tomes have been written about the importance of customer focus and getting close to customers. There can be no closer focus than 'the segment of one'. While all customers are important, there is a danger in spreading scarce resources too thinly and achieving little of the real intimacy required by those few customers who can help us make significant progress towards our long-term objectives. The dilemma, then, is which customers to include in the key account management programme.

The growing complexity of business-to-business markets, which are in a state of metamorphosis from chains of value to integrated recipes of value, presents a great challenge.

All the indications are that in business-to-business marketing, key account management is not so much an option, but a customer expectation.

This book is designed to provide a route through this most difficult of terrains. It is a route map that has emerged from the authors' extensive research into the practice of global key account management with some of the world's leading companies. Although there is still much to learn, we believe readers will find this book representative of the very best of best practice.

Diana Woodburn
Professor Malcolm McDonald
Marketing Best Practice

Before you read this book!

Just to give you an idea of your start point, try completing the two questionnaires below before you read further. The first questionnaire is designed to establish the current position of your organization on key account management, overall and on the 10 fundamental requirements of a successful KAM programme. The score profile will show you areas of existing strength and areas in need of serious attention. Try it with other people in your organization and see if they hold the same view.

The second questionnaire is aimed at your individual position, since most readers of this book will have had at least some experience of managing key accounts. Be as honest as you can – no one is looking!

Come back to this page after you finish reading the book and repeat the questionnaires. Your view may change as you learn more about what key account management really means, in practice, and your personal scores may change too, if you have picked up some of the ideas in the book and implemented them.

1. How well developed is key account management in your organization?

Score out of 10: 0 = not at all; 10 = best practice.

Does KAM in your organization have:	Before reading the book	After reading the book
A role in achieving the strategic vision?		
High profile support from senior management?		
Buy-in from appropriate organizational framework including teams?		
Careful selection of appropriate customers?		
Deep understanding of key customers and their strategies?		
Well-grounded, analysis-based customer plans?		
Customized offers, service or costs?		
Excellent, well-rounded key account managers?		
Excellent communications?		
Supportive, effective, dependable processes?		
Total		

2. How well do you know your key accounts?

Score out of 10: 0 = not at all; 10 = best practice.

Do you know:	Before reading the book	After reading the book
Your key customer's segments/products and how you add value to them?		
The customer's strategic plan?		
The customer's financial health (ratios, etc.)?		
The customer's business processes (logistics, purchasing, production, etc.)		
What the customer values/needs from its suppliers?		
Your company's proportion of the customer's spend?		
Which of your competitors the customer uses, why, and how it rates them?		
How much attributable (interface) costs should be allocated to your customer?		
The real profitability of the account?		
How long it takes to make a profit on a major new customer?		
Total		

List of figures and tables

Tables

1 The crucial role of key account management

Fast track

For over 15 years, the authors have been researching global best practice in the domain of account management, sponsored by many of the world's leading companies. The following topics in particular have been the focus of our research:

- **Key account selection:** Only a few selected customers can be included in the key account programme.

- **Classification of key accounts:** Derogatory labels like A, B, C, or gold, silver, bronze should be avoided at all cost.

- **Key account profitability:** The power of customers and their increased purchasing power has led to greater demands on the services of their suppliers. Unfortunately, many traditional accounting systems are incapable of accurately capturing all of the associated costs of dealing with major customers. Consequently, many suppliers are acting in ignorance of which customers make or lose them money.

- **Key account needs analysis:** A deep understanding of the customer's business is essential to success.

- **Strategic planning for key accounts:** Just as a three- to five-year strategy is essential for any business, so strategic plans for selected customers, signed off by the customers themselves, are also critical to success.

- **Roles and skills of key account managers:** Selling and negotiation skills are no longer sufficient on their own.

- **Other issues:** Information technology, organization structure and internal marketing all contribute to creating successful key account programmes.

The challenges that all organizations face today are:

- **Market maturity:** In most sectors, mature markets have transferred power from suppliers to customers, as suppliers compete for a share of a decreasing number of customers.

- **Globalization:** Market maturity has led to an increasing number of industries in which only a handful of truly global companies dominate the landscape. Hence, any supplier who cannot offer a seamless service in every part of the world where the customer operates will not win the business.

- **Customer power:** With their new-found power, customers are increasingly looking to selected suppliers to give them competitive advantage by product and process development.

All these developments mean that suppliers have to be much more stringent in their key account selection criteria. They must allocate their scarce resources intelligently across their customer base, taking account of the risks associated with different kinds of customers in order to build continuous shareholder value added.

In this chapter

Introduction

Back in 1996, the authors started a research club in Cranfield University School of Management because it was obvious even then that the power had been transferred from suppliers to customers. Customers were exercising their new-found power by dropping suppliers who did not live up to their expectations and by forcing down prices from other suppliers.

This apocryphal story about the buying director of General Motors was never denied: He called his suppliers together in Detroit and announced that they were all to drop their prices by 20 per cent and asked for questions. One brave chief executive officer of a supplying company told the GM buying director that his technology was years ahead of any competitor, was already 20 per cent cheaper than his competitors and that he could not reduce his prices by 20 per cent. The GM buying director asked his commissionaires to escort this supplier out and announced that his company would never deal with GM ever again. He then asked for further questions!

While no doubt the story has been embellished over the years, you will instantly recognize this particular type of obnoxious bullying buyer and the reality is that you sometimes need to deal with them because of their size. Nonetheless, there is an appropriate way of handling such customers so that the relationship is still profitable and this will be covered in Chapter 7.

The problem back in 1996 was that no business schools anywhere in the world had bothered to do any research into the transfer of power from supplier to customer, so the authors established a research club based in Cranfield with the sole purpose of researching global best practice in the domain of key account management. By 2011, this research club has been going for 15 years and has systematically researched best practice, not just on the supply side, but also on the customer side. This dyadic research approach was essential because, even back in 1996, it was obvious that supplier delusions about customer relationships were rife. Over the intervening years, the following topics have been the focus of our research.

Selecting key accounts

The authors heard a director of a major telecommunications company claim that they had 1000 key accounts! The chief executive of a health care company claimed that they had 200 key accounts.

Such numbers are, of course, totally ridiculous. A moment's thought will reveal that any supplying company has limited capacity to commit cross-functional resources to selected customers. Each of us has hundreds of friends, but we only have capacity to devote real quality time and love to a handful – maybe four or five.

The same principle applies to companies, who must decide extremely carefully which major customers they are prepared to allocate this scarce resource to. This issue is expanded in Chapter 2.

Categorizing key accounts

Even today, the authors hear of suppliers classifying their key accounts using fatuous labels like A, B, C or gold, silver and bronze. Imagine a call centre operator letting it slip that they were dealing with a C or a bronze customer! The mind boggles over such derogatory, supplier-centric labels. A more suitable and customer-friendly type of categorization is provided in Chapter 2.

Key account profitability

Our research reveals that about 85 per cent of Western European companies do not know whether they make or lose money from their biggest customers. They *think* they know, but most do not.

One of the authors used to be marketing and sales director of Canada Dry. Thirty years ago, two major retailers used to each buy about 3 million dozen bottles of ginger ale each year. One of these customers insisted on daily, just-in-time, store-by-store delivery, resulting in major stock-holding and delivery problems. They also insisted that the salesforce called daily to carry out merchandizing. Finally, they took about 145 days' credit. The other retailer, taking a similar amount of products, asked for stocks to be delivered centrally to their warehouse for them to carry out their own deliveries. They did not insist on merchandizing and paid their accounts in 45 days. Yet, the accounting system calculated that both customers were equally profitable, as it allocated overhead costs on the basis of volume bought.

We have enjoyed activity-based costing (ABC) for over 20 years, yet most companies still have not learned the lesson that it is the cost of dealing with the customer after the 'product has left the factory' that causes either profit or loss. Even today, most companies still do product profitability and marmalade their fixed costs to customers based on turnover, thus penalizing customers who are inexpensive to service and rewarding customers who are expensive to service.

> Most companies still do product profitability and marmalade their fixed costs to customers.

Customer needs analysis

Readers would surely agree that suppliers must really understand the needs of their customers and amend their approach accordingly. Alas, this certainly was not the case back in 1996 and is still largely untrue today. When key account managers are trained to sell volume and are paid accordingly, they have little interest in giving up substantial amounts of time and energy in researching the processes, organizational intricacies, financial details, etc. of their customers. But without such an investment they will never be able to align their offers with their customers' needs.

Strategic planning for key accounts

This latter point is obviously related to the issue of preparing strategic plans for key accounts. The authors were recently running a key account management (KAM) workshop for a blue-chip supplier of expensive equipment for hospitals. On being told that one hospital had a multimillion pound budget for such equipment, we asked about the supplier's strategic plan for this hospital. Alarmingly, we were told that there was only a one-year forecast and budget. We were reminded of the famous saying that the good thing about not having a strategy is that failure comes as a complete surprise and is not preceded by a long period of worry and depression! Having strategic plans covering a period of at least three years, agreed with the customer, is a major factor in successful and profitable relationships, yet even today little exists beyond supplier-centric forecasts and budgets.

> The good thing about not having a strategy is that failure comes as a complete surprise and is not preceded by a long period of worry and depression!

Roles and skills of key account managers

It was surprising to say the least, that little was known in 1996 about the roles and required skill sets of key account managers. Among other things, we supervised a major doctoral thesis on this topic, so we can speak with great authority on what world class key account managers should be doing and what skill sets they require.

Rewards and performance

This intuitively simple topic becomes extremely complex in the context of the kinds of rewards that are appropriate for success in dealing with different types of key accounts. This is dealt with in Chapter 11.

Transitioning to KAM

The cultural and behavioural issues over time involved in changing from a product- or sales-orientated organization are extremely complex and need to be carefully planned for. This is dealt with in Chapter 13

Other issues

Other areas for our research efforts included the role of IT, organizational structures, measuring KAM effectiveness, communications and cultural issues, all of them covered extensively in this book.

The point we are making is that the material presented in this book is based on 15 years of in-depth research into global best practice KAM and is therefore unlike most other books on the topic, which tend to rely on anecdotal or second-hand evidence for the assertions that are made. This is the reason why we feel comfortable in describing this book as 'the definitive guide for practitioners', as the research club has been sponsored over the years by some of the most famous companies in the world and over 3 million euros have been invested in it.

1.1 Pressures that have led to growth in customer power

1.1.1 Summary of the pressures

The characteristics and techniques of KAM were not extensively explored apart from the need for a dedicated salesforce beyond the 1990s.

As we have indicated in our introductory comments, while sales and marketing strategists have for some time been convinced that effective KAM leads to increased sales, heightened profitability and improved sales productivity, the characteristics and techniques of KAM were not extensively explored, apart from the need for a dedicated salesforce beyond the 1990s. The impetus behind this unprecedented interest in the dynamics and mechanics of KAM comes from an awakening to the need to address changes in both the context and constructs of marketing.

The marketplace today is a different world from that which we knew before and the rules of engagement have evolved significantly. Such rapid and radical transformation warrants attention. For example, most organizations assume that KAM is an approach for the private sector, but over the last five years the public sector has become involved, seeing KAM as an approach to achieving goals independent of commercial interests. Parts of government are key customers for private companies; public sector organizations are also suppliers to private companies; and KAM has been deployed to manage the relationships between entirely public sector organizations too. Any organization, public or private, needs to respond to the constant changes in its environment, and KAM has become a popular and powerful response.

> ## Case study insight
> ### ECITB: Transitioning to KAM in the public sector
>
> The Electricity and Construction Industry Training Board is tasked with increasing competence within the Engineering Construction Industry, from apprentices through to technicians and managers. Its key customers are companies and contractors who employ trained people, but when the Board decided to embark on KAM, people inside the organization were not even all agreed about who the customers were: the Government, the employers, or the engineers and apprentices. The organization took some time to explore and understand KAM, and came to the conclusion that it was the right way to achieve the change of orientation and approach it wanted.
>
> ECITB appointed three KAM champions as a core team to drive the programme and, after three years, KAM had been implemented, customer satisfaction was up and employee engagement was up. The Board rated the programme as a great success in bridging the gap, not uncommon between public institutions and commercial businesses, which had existed between the organization and many of its customer companies. The next stage on the journey was to increase the number of customers managed through account plans and roll out a CRM system that would follow the new way of working. It had taken some time to win 'hearts and minds' to KAM but progress, initially frustratingly slow, was now accelerating.

With hindsight, we can easily recognize those pressures in the business environment that have led to the ascendancy of KAM as a separate and significant discipline. These pressures were initially identified in a research report published by Cranfield and the Chartered Institute of Marketing entitled *Marketing, the Challenge of Change* (McDonald *et al.*, 1994) and are described in the following sections (Sections 1.1.2–1.1.5).

1.1.2   Rapid change

Time has become a major determinant of competitive advantage. The drive towards lean production systems has increased interdependency in supply chains. Any company that is complacent will be quickly overtaken. Ironically, the shorter the opportunity for success, the more important it becomes for companies to think strategically and for the long term. In so doing, the potential for minimizing the risks inherent in rapidly changing markets through supply chain partnerships is often an attractive option. The symptoms and challenges in responding to rapid change are listed in Table 1.1.

Any company that is complacent will be quickly overtaken.

Managers understand that, for a product or service to be commercially advantageous to the provider, value must be added faster than cost. The concept has been labelled 'lean supply' by purchasing

Table 1.1
Responding to rapid
change

Symptoms	Challenge
Compressed time horizons	Ability to exploit markets more rapidly
Time-based competition	Process excellence and flexibility
Shorter product lifecycles	More effective new product development
Shorter technology lifecycles	More investment in skills and understanding of applications and technology
Transient customer preferences	Flexibility in approach to markets, accuracy in demand forecasting, and optimization in price setting
Increasingly diverse business area	Cultural sensitivity

professionals. Lean supply involves the study of the entire supply flow from raw materials to consumer as an integrated whole.

In theory, effective supply flow is an absolute. In practice, companies just have to keep applying continuous improvement to be leaner than the competition. Adopting an approach in which the supplier and customer are joint guardians of the value in transit is vital. Examination of the value in transit demands that both the supplier and customer open their 'books' and facilitate two-way assessment in order to optimize performance. There should be no blame and excuses.

Lean supply practice also lends itself to sharing some costs critical to mutual success.

Lean supply practice also lends itself to sharing some costs critical to mutual success. Joint research and development, joint merchandizing, integrated logistic and electronic data interchange (EDI) are just a few examples of the opportunities available for making things happen better, cheaper and faster.

This concept is equally applicable to service industries.

1.1.3 Process refinement

Companies must be flexible, not just to raise customer satisfaction but to avoid waste and loss.

Company activities have shifted away from producing predefined products or services towards having the capability to produce creative solutions for customer requirements. Companies must be flexible, not just to raise customer satisfaction, but to avoid waste and loss. The symptoms and challenges in refining the process are listed in Table 1.2.

The prerequisite for process redesign is access to information across organizational boundaries. Without that exchange of information, no streamlining can be achieved. Buyer–seller partners are increasingly sharing common databases. The obvious example is stock management. If point of sale data is transferred to commonly held databases of stock information, the suppliers of logistics services and goods can

Symptoms	Challenge
Move to flexible manufacturing and control systems	Project orientation to deal with micro-segmentation
Materials substitution	Means to shift from single transaction focus to the forging of long-term relationships
Developments in technology	More investment in skills to realize innovations (such as microelectronics and the potential of technology robotics)
Concentration on core business	Embrace opportunities for suppliers to run non-core aspects of customer's business
Quality focus	Widespread involvement in quality initiatives
Collaborative working practices	Create greater customer commitment

Table 1.2
Refining the process

make sure that retail outlets are always fully stocked with the fastest moving lines. That enables everybody to make more money through the consumers obtaining what they want when they want it. Buyers and sellers also need to examine their current activities together in order to explore and optimize processes.

The output of process redesign (or re-engineering) should be enhanced customer value. Customers want quality through attention to detail. Any customer wanting to initiate new quality indicators with a supplier is more likely to do so if there is a strong element of trust and partnership. The closeness of customer relationships can be greatly enhanced through collaboration, both across and between organizations. Joint planning initiatives and coordinated working practices can be used to create mutual understanding, benefit and commitment.

> The output of process redesign (or re-engineering) should be enhanced customer value.

Our way of depicting how organizations receive goods and services, add value and sell them into their end-user markets is Professor Michael Porter's value chain. Figure 1.1 depicts the standard Porter value chain model for a manufacturing organization and Figure 1.2 depicts a value chain for a service organization.

Within these models, companies will have functional specialists working together, ensuring a consistent and integrated approach to the development of value.

1.1.4 Redefining the marketplace and pleasing the customers

As well as the need to respond to rapid change through the refinement of processes, there is a need to recognize the changing nature of the

> A product/market lifecycle is the aggregate sales at a point in time of all goods or services which satisfy the same or similar needs in a market.

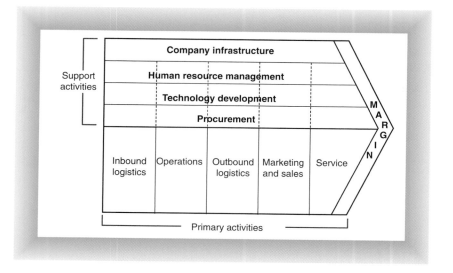

Figure 1.1
The value chain.

marketplace itself (Table 1.3). Many markets today are mature. For example, most people in Western Europe have cars, washing machines, dishwashers, televisions, calculators and so on, so competitors in these replacement markets need to innovate and to look elsewhere for growth.

Market maturity

Figure 1.3 illustrates the impact of market maturity on the key elements of business management. A product/market lifecycle is the aggregate sales at a point in time of all goods or services which satisfy the same or similar needs in a market. The final column clearly

										Reducing cost	Creating value
Infrastructure				– Legal, Accounting, Financial Management							
Human resource management				– Personnel, Pay, Recruitment, Training, Manpower Planning, etc.							
Product & Technology Development				– Product and Process Design, Market Testing, R&D, etc.							
Procurement				– Supplier Management, Funding, Subcontracting, Specification							
Recognize exchange potential	Initiate dialogue	Exchange information	Negotiate/ tailor	Commit	Exchange value	Monitor					
										Reducing cost	
										Creating value	

Figure 1.2
Internal value chain: service companies.

Symptoms	Challenge
Commoditization	Need for product/process differentiation
Lack of growth and over-capacity	Need to achieve growth within key accounts
Greater and stronger competition	Customer retention more vital than ever
Low margins	Greater pressure for cost reduction and quality improvement
Saturated markets	Need for new market creation and stimulation
Downsizing	Need to apply resource where it can deliver most value to customers

Table 1.3
Redefining the marketplace

illustrates the danger of allowing products and services to degenerate into commodities, with price availability and costs representing the only determinants of success. It is this danger more than any other that forces suppliers to pay more attention to key customers' specific requirements as a means of securing effective differentiation.

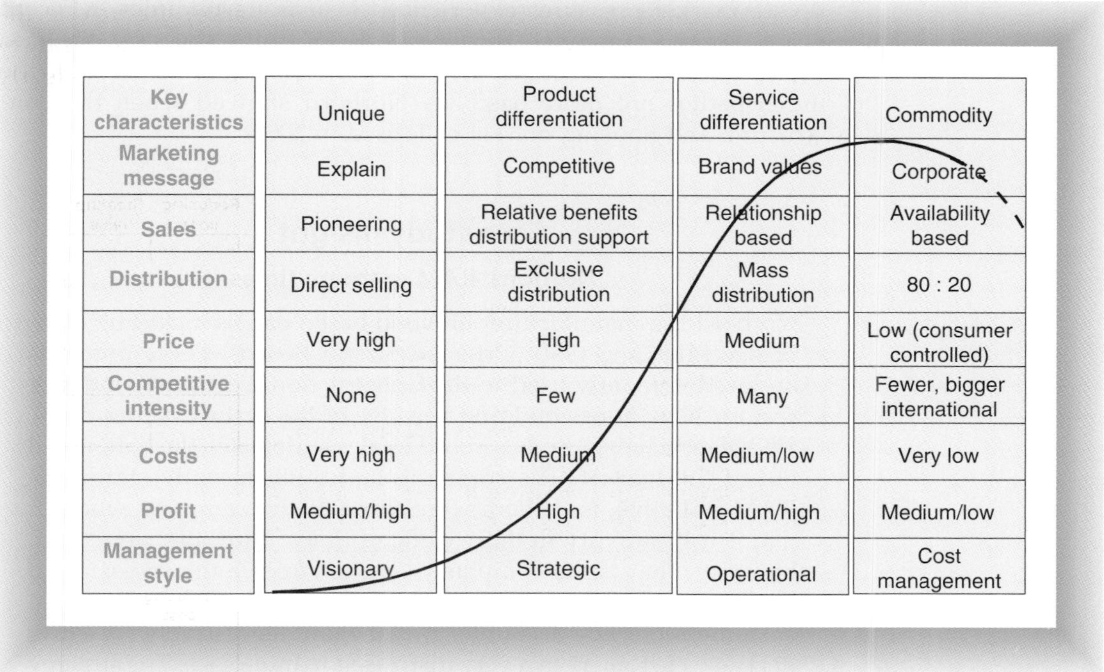

Key characteristics	Unique	Product differentiation	Service differentiation	Commodity
Marketing message	Explain	Competitive	Brand values	Corporate
Sales	Pioneering	Relative benefits distribution support	Relationship based	Availability based
Distribution	Direct selling	Exclusive distribution	Mass distribution	80 : 20
Price	Very high	High	Medium	Low (consumer controlled)
Competitive intensity	None	Few	Many	Fewer, bigger international
Costs	Very high	Medium	Medium/low	Very low
Profit	Medium/high	High	Medium/high	Medium/low
Management style	Visionary	Strategic	Operational	Cost management

Figure 1.3 The product/market lifecycle and market characteristics.

The fact that most industry-to-industry product/service markets in the developed world are mature has clearly propelled the development of

KAM. Suppliers know that they can only grow at the expense of a competitor and the obvious first option is to prise more of existing customers' business away from the opposition by means of account penetration. Highly professional KAM can facilitate the achievement of this objective.

Case study insight

IMI's response to market maturity

IMI was until recently a 'metal bashing' company based principally in the Midlands in the UK. Their Board redefined their market boundaries into five 'platform businesses' which they could dominate, put much of their manufacturing in South America and China, and began developing close relationships with selected global customers. As a result, they became one of the most profitable manufacturing companies in the world.

Business can only be won by being better than competitors and taking market share from them.

When inflation and growth were high in Western economies, companies enjoyed a comfort zone, which masked inefficiency. Now, most economies are experiencing low inflation and in many sectors across the world, prices are falling. In such a climate there is no room for complacency. Business can only be won by being better than competitors and taking market share from them. Product, process and people improvements are imperative. Under the kind of severe market pressures experienced in many economies in recent years, some companies throw out KAM with the cry 'Back to basics!' This is a mistake: in hard times, companies need to be much better, not more basic, as Norbord showed when the construction and housing market collapsed in 2009.

Case study insight

Norbord: KAM in tough times

Norbord is a manufacturer of wood based panels including chipboard, MDF and OSB (Oriented Strand Board). These products are predominantly used in the Construction, Furniture, and DIY sectors. New house building was one of the first casualties of the UK financial crisis, and Norbord's sales suffered as the bottom fell out of the market. The company had quite recently started its KAM initiative, and there were those in the company who felt that it was a luxury in those difficult times. Directors were clear, however, that if the company were to survive the recession, it would be, in part, by working even more closely with its strongest customers (its key accounts) rather than aggressively trying to find new customers in a very distressed marketplace. The strategy is paying dividends, and Norbord will come out of this recession with KAM more firmly embedded in its internal practises, and its approach to the marketplace.

Customer power

The change within the business environment that is having the most dramatic impact on the development of KAM is the new-found expertise and power of customers and consumers in exercising choice (Table 1.4). Customer empowerment is not just a cultural change emanating from the growing popularity of adopting a customer focus; it is a consequence of mature markets. Nowadays, customers know that they can demand more from suppliers because suppliers must seek to retain customers – not just to maintain profitability, but also to stay in business.

> Nowadays, customers know that they can demand more from suppliers because suppliers must seek to retain customers.

Symptoms	Challenge
Customers more demanding and more knowledgeable	Quality and traceability favour supply chain partnerships
Purchase behaviour strategic rather than tactical	A strategic and sympathetic approach to selling is required
Concentration of buying power	Selling companies need to add more value to succeed
Higher expectations	A greater investment and closer relation to the customer are required
Customer identity and role more complex	Need to better manage the complexities of multiple market channels

Table 1.4
Pleasing the customer

Customer power manifests itself in many ways. For example, there is the considerable concentration of industry, most recently on a transnational scale, which has made big customers even bigger (Figure 1.4). However, bigger customers do not necessarily mean more business

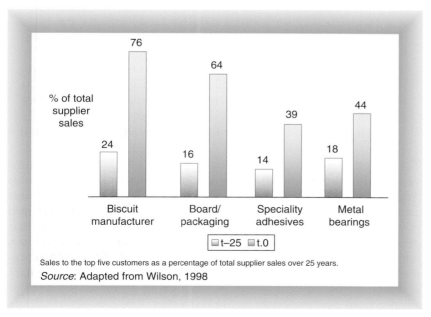

Sales to the top five customers as a percentage of total supplier sales over 25 years.
Source: Adapted from Wilson, 1998

Figure 1.4
Concentration of buying power in industries.

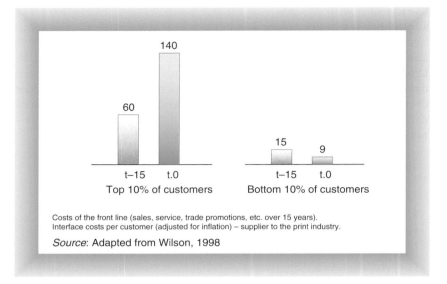

Figure 1.5
Cost of servicing the customer.

Suppliers who cannot meet the geographical scope and consistent outputs demanded by global customers are rationalized off lists of preferred suppliers.

opportunity. Suppliers who cannot meet the geographical scope and consistent outputs demanded by global customers are rationalized off lists of proposed suppliers. Customers want sophisticated solutions, which means that winning customer accounts can be very costly. It also means that retaining customers, which requires ongoing investment, is critical in achieving long-term profitability (Figure 1.5).

Case study insight
Key Industrial Equipment's response to the danger of commoditization

Key Industrial Equipment is a distributor of specialist products offering thousands of categories. In addition to offering a comprehensive range, the company has received industry recognition for innovation and service. It offers extremely rapid delivery, electronic data interchange and will take on the assembly of parts if the customer requires it. In discussions with customers, they place the emphasis on end-to-end value rather than on unit price.

Consumers will soon leap-frog any links in the supply chain that they feel do not add value.

The customer may have always been hailed as king but, not being a very well-informed monarch, the king was often at the mercy of his 'subjects' (suppliers). The rising power of consumer pressure groups and the popular media have changed all that. They have wrested power from companies and vested it in the ultimate users of their products and services. End-customers expect a great deal of respect, which is now often contractually assured in some sort of charter document. The logical extension of this consumer-driven scenario is cooperation between all organizations delivering value in the flow of supply from raw materials to the consumer. The concept of adding value is significant. Consumers will soon leap-frog any links in the supply chain that they feel do not add value.

Customers need raw materials to be converted into what they can use, taken to where they need them and presented to them for choice. Which company in the supply chain does any of these is irrelevant. Consumer champions are currently also casting a critical eye over the whole supply chain for ethical and environmental reasons. Trusted brand names have to ensure that their values are passed up the supply chain.

> Consumers today know more about supply chains than might ever have interested them 10–20 years ago.

Consumers today know more about supply chains than might ever have interested them 10–20 years ago: they see it as relevant to the end-product they obtain. The idea of companies working together with their suppliers in order to deliver more value to the end-consumer is an attractive one, a matter of common sense. This is particularly pertinent to businesses which operate across national boundaries where the value chain is exceedingly complex and cultural sensitivities must be respected.

1.1.5 Globalization

The globalization of business has had many side-effects, including a greater interdependency between global customers and suppliers who have the capability to meet each other's increasingly complex needs (Table 1.5). These suppliers also realize the extent to which they can grow with their key customers if they consistently succeed in meeting their customers' expectations cost-effectively.

Symptoms	Challenge
Industry players undifferentiated	Restructuring to achieve wider scope (restructuring of domestic operations to compete internationally)
Greater and stronger competition	Customer retention more vital than ever
Lower margins	Greater pressure for cost reduction and quality improvement
Greater customer choice	Need to customize offers
Larger and more complex markets	Need to become customer-focused in larger and more disparate markets

Table 1.5
Coping with globalization

Figure 1.6 shows that as industries mature, the end-result is often only a handful of truly global companies dominating an industry. Hence, there are only 10 car companies in the world and four firms of account-ants, while in the UK, for example, four supermarkets account for about 80 per cent of all fast-moving consumer products.

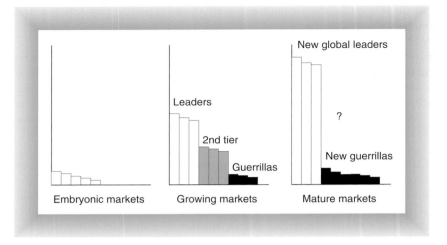

Figure 1.6
Evolution of market maturity.

1.1.6 Implications

The impact of all these changes – the imperative of keeping pace with rapid change, the requirement of refining processes, the necessity of redefining the character of the marketplace, the need for satisfying increasingly sophisticated customers/consumers and the obligation of facing the growing scope and scale of competition – has reverberated through the business relationship itself. It has encouraged KAM away from the traditional construct of a single relationship between salesperson and buyer, and towards the concept of strategic customers, where key customers command attention on vital statistics measuring more than simply their size.

CHECKPOINT

Pressures on businesses today

- Do you know how the pressures described above affect your company?

We see an increasing number of companies starting to build models of account attractiveness, matching their resources to the profit and status of any potential given customer or prospect. We also witness increasing professionalism among purchasers and decision-making units in buying companies as they evaluate the longer-term value offered by suppliers (the quality of products, processes and people) rather than solely the price deal.

1.2 Why understanding relationships is so important

The intercompany relationship is the 'glue' that binds companies together.

The relationship between two organizations has an existence beyond the obvious types of interaction, such as product and service adaptation, operational delivery and underlying strategy. All of these contribute to the nature and development of the relationship as well as depending on it (Figure 1.7). The intercompany relationship is affected by these interfaces and may also buffer turbulence arising from them. It is the 'glue' that binds companies together more or less closely and the medium through which interactions take place to deliver action.

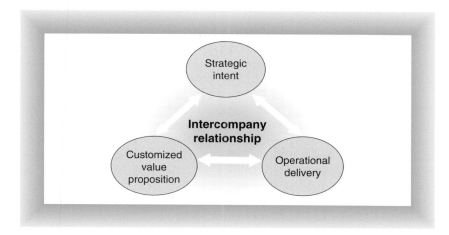

Figure 1.7
The relationship as a medium.

Clearly, understanding the nature and potential of the customer relationship is critical in assessing opportunities and managing business development. We need to know where we stand now with our customer and what further engagement might entail. We will also need a sound appreciation of their market position, and internal strengths and constraints (see Chapter 7).

Understanding key relationships is both important and challenging because:

● the risks are ambiguous and the stakes are high,

● supplier–buyer interactions are already complex and lie at the heart of major change, and

● key relationships operate at different levels which require different behaviours.

1.2.1 Relationship risks

One of the primary reasons for developing relationships is risk reduction. There are risks associated with building close relationships with key customers as well as risks associated with not building them. In theory, there should be less chance of relationship breakdown where there is joint commitment, barriers to exit and mutual understanding and trust (see Chapters 3 and 4). However, while these attributes may appear highly desirable, they actually carry risks of their own. For example:

● The risk of being vulnerable to opportunism and not obtaining a satisfactory saving or return on investment in the relationship.

- The risk of committing to one partner at the exclusion of others and 'backing the wrong horse'.

- The risk of misunderstanding the relationship and failing to achieve reciprocal security.

1.2.2 Satisfactory return

The major question must be 'If we put time, effort and money into developing closer relationships with our trading partners, will they be more profitable?' The answer is not clear-cut, though it may be summed up as 'Yes, possibly, but not automatically'.

> Traditionally, customer cost accounting has been rudimentary.

There is ample evidence from numerous sources indicating that suppliers have great difficulty in measuring the real profitability of their customers. Traditionally, accounting systems have used a geographical or business unit and/or product basis of analysis and customer cost accounting has been rudimentary. Substantial costs such as special customized developments, high-level, intercompany contacts and various additional services are very rarely allocated to individual customers. Thus, real customer profitability is difficult to analyse in practice and these intrinsic difficulties are compounded by inherent challenges to internal vested interests.

Alarmingly, although few suppliers can assess the profitability of individual key accounts accurately, many suspect that, ultimately, they lose money on them. While Chapter 6 explores this problem in greater detail, the issue is introduced here to highlight some fundamental points.

- Close relationships with key accounts have substantial cost implications.

- The mismanagement of just a few large accounts can be potentially (disastrously) loss-making.

- Customer relationships should be carefully selected and prioritized for the prudent investment of scarce resources (see Chapter 2).

CHECKPOINT

Customer profitability

- Do you know the profitability of individual customers?

> All too often the cost of pursuing a closer relationship is not anticipated and properly quantified.

The cost of building close, sophisticated, groundbreaking, new relationships should not be underestimated. Frequent, multilevel, multifunction communication alone represents a considerable expense. Further, relationships development usually entails investment in initiatives such as joint marketing, new restructuring, electronic commerce, staff retraining and stockholding. All too often the cost of pursuing a closer relationship is not anticipated and properly quantified.

Firmness can pay off handsomely: one loss-making company, admittedly with dominant shares in its core markets, implemented 'an aggressively upward pricing policy' with great success and achieved a return to excellent profits within two years.

1.2.3 Implications of joint commitment

In many cases, the commitment of the buying company is greater than that of the selling company (although the latter would not see it this way). Where it does not make sense to multisource a product or service, the buying company may be obliged to adopt a sole supplier. Meanwhile, the selling company will continue to supply other customers. The buying company must ensure that it has made the right choice, not only in relation to the matter at hand, but also because its decision will be a statement to other suppliers.

Similarly, a selling company's key customers may demand supplier exclusivity, preventing the supplier from broadening its customer base by serving the customers' competitors. The practice of exerting such pressure has generally been accepted by advertising agencies, for example, while other sectors have resisted it. However, the growth in the number of customers of considerable size has meant that this practice is increasingly tolerated.

The range of functions and initiatives involved in the relationship may reach a point where significant company-level backing is required which cannot be satisfied simply by allocating more resources, people and time. At this level of relationship, there may not be any room for parallel relationships, even for the selling company. For example, if two competing companies were developing similar new products at the same time using a shared supplier, the supplier would find it exceedingly difficult to work with both customers in the same way. Confidentiality might be hard to guarantee, as might be the origins of a research breakthrough. If the supplier and each of the buying companies were to approach the marketplace together, the fact that the company is offering products together with two different partners might confuse consumers.

> At this level of relationship, there may not be any room for parallel relationships, even for the selling company.

However, by choosing to work with a single business partner, both supplier and buyer are consciously excluding others and declaring that the decision is right for them. Both companies want a partner they can work with and benefit from. 'Backing the right horse' for a strategic-level relationship need not be as much of a gamble as backing a real horse if the pre-existing relationship is well understood and well managed.

1.2.4 Misconception and disappointment

There is a common misconception that closer relationships will automatically bring greater profits. The reality is not so simple. The inability of companies to measure profitability accurately or realistically gives cause for confusion. However, it would appear that relationship stage, maturity and business success are linked: closer key relationships are widely considered more successful than relatively distant key relationships according to a range of accepted success and financial indicators (Figure 1.8). Nevertheless, a substantial minority of relationships do not conform to this 'rule' and it would be a mistake to assume that developing any relationship will automatically bring success or that relationships which are not developed to closer levels are failures. This was clearly demonstrated in the Cranfield/*Financial Times* research report (McDonald and Woodburn, 1999).

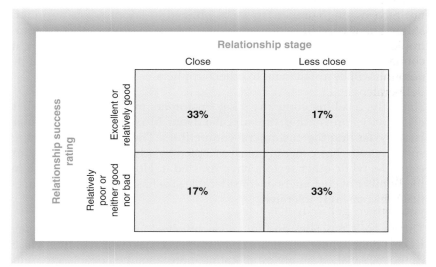

Figure 1.8
Relationship closeness versus relationship success.

From the supplier's perspective, an attempt at forced intimacy would be a mistake.

A number of these non-conformists represent successful relationships that are not particularly close for good reasons. For example, if the product or service purchased is not a core item and does not offer opportunities for deriving differential benefit, the customer may naturally decide that a simple purchase with minimal support is adequate. Any extra attention or additional services lavished on the customer might be accepted, but not necessarily valued. From the supplier's perspective, an attempt at forced intimacy would be a mistake in this case and the business should be serviced with efficiency and a positive attitude, but not much more.

Case study insight

'I do not think suppliers would benefit from getting any closer to us: quite the reverse. We are a very "taking" company and it would not do them any good.' (Retailer)

It is not uncommon for some key relationships to be close, but to be considered unsuccessful and/or unprofitable. They may be intransigent situations into which companies have been cornered, perhaps by a determined buyer, optimistic key account manager or poorly written contract.

The fact that relationships can reach higher levels of intimacy and still prove unsuccessful should make companies wary of selecting the right relationships to develop in the first place as well as managing them extremely carefully (see Chapter 2). Part of that selection process should be an assessment of the relationship's current stage of development and the buyer's and supplier's respective degrees of commitment.

There is yet a further danger: that of sliding imperceptibly, by numerous smaller steps, into a relationship that the company has failed to anticipate, which has implications that they are unprepared for or cannot recognize. Logically, the development of key customer relationships should be a strategic process linked to the design and implementation of overall business strategy. Surprisingly, this critical connection is often overlooked. Customer relationships, whether key accounts or otherwise, should be examined objectively and developed deliberately in line with company aims and capabilities.

> Customer relationships, whether key accounts or otherwise, should be examined objectively and developed deliberately in line with company aims and capabilities.

1.3 Increasing complexity of key account relationships

Relationships with key customers are not only complex, but increasingly so. For top customers, the simple model of 'I, salesperson, sell; you, buyer, get' only applies in certain circumstances. Few, if any, major business initiatives are now developed on this axiom. So why have things changed and how has this made key account relationships more complex?

1.3.1 The consolidation of customers

Key customer relationships often involve major corporations as both suppliers and customers. Because an amorphous mass is impossible to motivate and measure, most large companies introduce subdivisions into their businesses and the larger these companies become, the more entities they will contain. In many cases, a supplier will do business with more than one entity within the client company. While such a multiple interface offers potential benefits in terms of developing an inside track to new business with other parts of the organization, it may also incur undesirable costs. For example, there may be an obligation to service uneconomical parts of the business, involvement in internal competition, downward price levelling and additional communication costs.

1.3.2 Dual roles: the customer may be 'competitor' as well as 'client'

As companies consolidate, the situation in which a customer is both a competitor and sometimes a supplier arises more frequently. Obviously, this intertwining of relationships and roles complicates behaviour. Takeovers that juxtapose competitors inappropriately are a common cause of terminated key account relationships. However,

> The situation in which a customer is both a competitor and sometimes a supplier arises more frequently.

some companies struggle on and learn to live with ambivalence, perhaps because industry consolidation leaves them with very little choice of customer or supplier. The potential for internal and external conflict is heightened and management of the relationship becomes evidently more strained.

1.3.3 The development of global businesses that demand global supply

Global customers requiring global supply and service add additional complexity to the task of managing relationships effectively. Problems which are easily identified but not easily resolved originate from differences in terms of language, culture, zone and geography, making the servicing of pan-global operations a tough challenge for even the fittest of suppliers. The prevalence of knowledgeable and powerful country managers helps somewhat, but the scope and size of the task remains formidable. In addition, a new infrastructure may be required to service markets previously outside the supplier's sphere of activity which now fall within its global contract, meaning more new partners, languages and cultures to assimilate into the relationship.

1.3.4 The accelerating pace of change, particularly as new IT reshapes markets

It is already evident that many companies will have to make huge adjustments very quickly as customers adapt to electronic commerce.

Information technology, in particular electronic commerce, is forcing huge changes in the way companies work and how their markets operate. As always, there is a lag between the availability of the new technology which is possessed by the enlightened few and mass uptake with full-scale revision of the basic practices and processes. While it is not yet clear what the ultimate impact of IT development will be for business, it is already evident that many companies will have to make huge adjustments very quickly as customers adapt to electronic commerce and demand similar immediacy and intimacy from their existing suppliers.

1.3.5 The emphasis on strategic alliances

New needs may be satisfied on both sides of the relationship by the creation of a strategic alliance with another company, which has strength in a specific area rather than through the development of existing internal expertise and physical assets. Selling companies may find themselves supplying third-party associates of their customers instead of their customers directly. They may also be supplying customers alongside other suppliers who may have been selected by them or by the customer. As supply chain management reaches further up- and downstream, more complex relationships are being formed involving more participants. Communication is likewise complicated and, because strategic alliances are often forged as a fast and flexible response to market change, opportunities for misunderstanding and confusion abound.

Case study insight

Customer perspective

'We deal with our suppliers on product development, marketing and ordering, but our warehouse is managed for us by Tibbett & Britten, so suppliers deal with them on inbound logistics.'

With today's flattened management structures, cross-functional teams are encouraged to take part in the activities traditionally allocated to lower levels of responsibility, including direct customer contact and decision making. Key customer relationships put more people and more functions in direct contact with the customers or supplier than ever before.

While the internal interactions required to drive the machine which actually delivers the customer promise are discussed later in Chapters 3 and 4, it is already abundantly clear that relationships and, in particular, key account relationships are undoubtedly complicated by the increased quantity and variety of contact with the customer.

Summary

The external context in which buyer–seller relationships exist is becoming increasingly extensive and complex. Change drivers include the rapid pace of change, the refinement of processes, market maturity, heightened customer power and the globalization of business. At the same time, the internal, organizational context is also changing, removing traditional delineations of remit and responsibility. Conditions are more conducive to 'partnering' between suppliers and customers and, hence, the nature of marketing has altered. Marketers are moving away from a traditional transaction focus towards a customer focus. Thus, there is a pressing need for finding ways of describing relationships as a basis from which to understand them better and build them stronger – and this has led to the ascendancy of KAM.

2 Selecting and categorizing key customers

Choosing the customers that your company wants to treat as key accounts ought not to be too hard, certainly when compared with some of the difficult cultural and structural issues that arise from key account management. However, many companies approach the task in a rather casual fashion first time around, and only later realize how many onward decisions are driven by their selection of key customers, and how awkward it may be to unpick inappropriate choices.

The key customers you seek should be those that are aligned to your corporate strategy and will therefore make a major contribution to its achievement. If they do not, who will? So your portfolio of key accounts should contain these customers, and only these customers. If you dilute it with customers with dissimilar agendas, which will not respond particularly favourably to your strategies, you will be unable to demonstrate sufficiently positive results from the key account management programme, and you risk sinking the whole initiative. Undoubtedly, there will be pressures to include unsuitable accounts, but they must be resisted. Counter such pressures by adopting an objective criteria-based process, and applying it rigorously.

Whatever the size of the organization, there seems to be an almost universally appropriate number of key accounts, which is probably between 15 and 35, with 5 and 50 as the outer limits. Certainly, anything with three digits is too many. In fact, the process of selection and categorization starts with deciding, more or less, how many key accounts your company can handle.

The identity of the customer deserves careful attention. It not only determines how the customer will score against the criteria, and hence how much resource it should receive, but it also has implications about how it should be managed. Customers should be identified in their terms, not carved up according to the supplier's structure, unless it is well matched with the customer's.

Selection criteria should be chosen and their importance weighted by a senior management group, and then rolled out to be scored to people who know the customer. These criteria are applied to assess the customer's attractiveness to your company, and the data are then used on the vertical axis of the key account selection/categorization matrix to build a picture of your portfolio of customers.

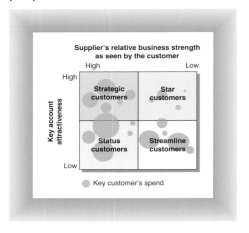

To complete the picture, you need the customer's view of you as a supplier, in their terms. Obviously, that will be different for each customer, and you must resist the urge to apply a standard set of criteria on the horizontal axis. If you did that, it would only be a reflection of what you think of yourselves, and would not represent their views and differences at all. You would also, in effect, be saying that these customers are all the same and all want the same things, which is contrary to the whole philosophy of key account management, apart from being patently untrue.

The matrix identifies four kinds of key customers, to which it is appropriate to offer four generic strategies that should guide the specific strategies that are developed for each customer individually:

1. Star key customers – investment for growth

2. Strategic key customers – strategic investment

3. Status key customers – proactive maintenance

4. Streamline key customers – management for cash.

The systematic assessment approach described in this chapter enables suppliers to build a portfolio view of their customers that drives many further insights, decisions and expectations about them, which is much more realistic and powerful than the key customer lists that many suppliers use. We will refer to it frequently in the rest of this book.

In this chapter

Introduction

The selection of key customers that a company makes has a crucial effect on the success of its key account programme and the perception of its success. Unless the key customer portfolio performs better than groups of customers not receiving the same level of investment, why would a company continue with it? Any customers who do not respond positively are diluting the results and endangering the whole programme.

The task of categorizing customers needs to be carried out methodically and thoroughly. It will probably take more effort than suppliers expect, but the importance of getting it right cannot be overestimated. All kinds of onward decisions depend on it, from what resource the customer receives, to who should be appointed to manage them, and what expectations may be set for them. Companies failing to tackle the task of selection and categorization properly should expect to fail at key account management.

This chapter gives clear guidelines on how to go about the process, to be applied carefully and systematically.

2.1 Why is choosing the right customers so important?

2.1.1 Fulfilling corporate strategy

> Key customers must be those that will make a substantial contribution to the fulfilment of your strategic vision.

Key customer selection is one of the most important decisions that suppliers face in key account management (KAM). Whether key customers currently represent 20 per cent or 80 per cent of your business, they should, by definition, be business leaders – leaders in your business, and/or leaders in their own sectors as well. The key customers to which you give special attention must be those that will make a substantial contribution to the fulfilment of your strategic vision, so making the right choices is critical.

If you fail to choose appropriately, your portfolio is likely to contain a mixed bag of big names, old friends and difficult/overdemanding customers, which is not going to take your business anywhere, never mind the vision of the future that you have mapped out. Your other customers are typically smaller and more often driven by their markets than leading in them, and it is very unlikely that they can fulfil both their own part in your strategy and make up for what the key accounts fail to deliver. So to achieve corporate objectives, you must select the right key customers.

> Choosing key customers is one of the most important decisions in KAM, and also one of the earliest.

Although choosing key customers is one of the most important decisions in KAM, and also one of the earliest, some companies believe that their key customer portfolio is a 'given', and appear to avoid making the decision at all. In essence, they are saying that their biggest customers now are also their best, and will always be so. This is a very dangerous assumption, and should be challenged and investigated objectively. Look for phrases like 'We don't need to do that – our key customers choose themselves' and 'It's obvious – we all know who they are anyway.' Check your selection process against the list below.

CHECKPOINT

Is your key account selection process:

1. Focused on current results rather than the longer term?

2. Selecting too many customers?

3. Based on poor and/or largely internal information?

4. Opaque, unaudited and easily manipulated?

5. Succumbing to internal political pressure to include unsuitable accounts?

6. Producing an unbalanced portfolio (see Section 2.3.1)?

7. Not differentiating enough between customers?

8. Not helping to assess potential new key accounts?

Given the importance of selecting the right key customers, it is something of a puzzle to work out why many suppliers make such a poor job of it. Although enlightened companies understand the need for rigour and care in making their choices, the selection process is still, in many companies, approached rather casually and intuitively. It is only further down the line, when some of the consequences begin to bite, that suppliers realize their mistake. Numerous companies have had to backtrack with some very large customers when they realized that they could not – or did not want to – deliver on their promises of special treatment.

Real key account management requires suppliers to deliver customized, innovative strategies to individual customers, and that capacity is seriously limited in any company, however large. Obviously, if there are not going to be many key accounts, then choosing all the right ones and none of the wrong ones is crucial to success.

> Choosing all the right ones and none of the wrong ones is crucial to success.

2.1.2 Selecting for superior returns

It quickly becomes clear that KAM and key customers will be a major pull on resources. If they are not, then it will be just a cosmetic programme, soon to be discredited by customers and your own organization alike. However, when your company is investing in customers, it will be expecting better performance from these customers than it receives from the rest of its customer base, whether in terms of growth, increased margins or some other contribution to profit.

The customers picked out for special treatment should be those who will give a superior yield in the future. Ultimately, that is how your Board will judge whether the approach is successful, and more worthy of their investment than, say, buying more equipment, more staff training or more advertising. Otherwise, why bother?

It follows that including any customers in your selection who do not respond to KAM could bring down the whole initiative, because the overall return on investment will be the poorer because of them (see Chapter 6 on key account profitability). In fact, while you are working hard with the 'right' accounts to increase shareholder value, the 'wrong' accounts can destroy shareholder value just as fast, by taking all they are given and doing exactly what they would have done anyway. BOC described these customers as the ones that 'want-it-all-but-don't-want-to-pay-for-it' (or can't).

> Including any customers in your selection who do not respond to KAM could bring down the whole initiative.

Even if you did a good job on selection at the outset, unless you have a process for deselecting key customers as well as choosing them, then your company will inevitably have accumulated some poor performers a few years into KAM. The portfolio should be reviewed with relegation and promotion in mind on an annual basis. Obviously, performance will be examined more frequently, but customers should not be selected, deselected and reselected on a quarterly basis. They do not appreciate this kind of fickle behaviour and are inclined to respond negatively.

> ## CHECKPOINT
> Make sure that the selection process is:
> - based on valid, forward-looking criteria
> - objectively applied
> - resistant to political pressures
> - dynamic.

Sensibly, underperforming customers should be identified at a regular, annual review, and then put 'on probation' for the next 12 months. Whether you decide to tell them in advance, or just observe what happens during the year, depends on your relationship with the account. Some companies are quite clear with their customers about what they have to do to become a key account, and therefore what they will have to do to stay as a key account. Others find this approach uncomfortable, and apply a mix of more subtle hints and negotiations.

Nevertheless, if no response is received, or you see that none is achievable, then restrictions should be placed on the resources accessible to the customer. Of course, you need to remember that these customers probably still give your company substantial business, so resource restriction needs to be accomplished with tact – but nevertheless, it must be done.

2.1.3 How many key accounts?

There is a ceiling to any supplier's capacity for intimacy.

Why would key customers spend their time with you if they did not expect significantly special treatment from their key relationships? Genuine KAM reaches deep inside a company to come up with the kind of breadth of offer and innovation that these customers seek. It requires a considerable change from traditional ways of working and, even if that is achieved, the capacity of a supplier to deliver this kind of treatment profitably is not infinitely expandable. There is a ceiling to any supplier's capacity for intimacy, which needs to be recognized. Hiring an extra bunch of key account managers to go out and be nice to customers does not shift the ceiling – but it may bring the house down!

Big companies with big customer databases often talk about their key customers as the 'top 100' or 'top 200', or even the 'top 300'. We can assume these have been badly chosen (usually just on past sales volume) and are inadequately served, certainly below the level expected by a key customer. As suppliers realize the limitations on their capacity to support key customers properly, they invariably tighten up on the numbers admitted to the portfolio.

Numbers of genuine key customers may range from about 12 to 50 (Figure 2.1). They may stretch from extremes of 5 to 75, but usually

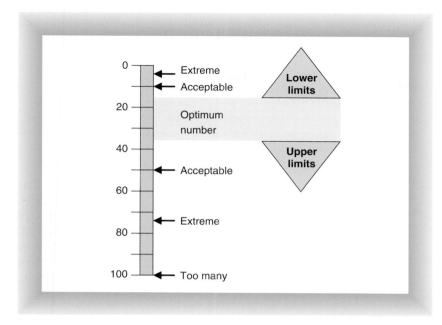

Figure 2.1
Key account numbers.

those at the upper end of this range are actively working to reduce the number. In fact, about 50 key customers seemed to be the ceiling for successful KAM in even the largest corporations. The optimum number of key customers, i.e. that are most commonly observed in companies running successful KAM programmes, is somewhere between 15 and 35.

> The optimum number of key customers is somewhere between 15 and 35.

Your company should balance the number of key customers it can handle with a number that represents enough business potential to make the initiative and the effort involved worthwhile. Adopt too many key customers and you risk falling down on internal and external commitments, with a strong chance that the KAM programme will die a messy death. Adopt too few and KAM will be seen as a marginal activity and not given enough attention and resources to be successful. Alternatively, if this few represents a major part of the business, then while you are reducing the risk by strengthening your relationships with these critical customers, you are also exacerbating the situation by growing your company's dependency on them. You should increase your portfolio by growing some other customers into key accounts and/or attracting segments of smaller customers to your business.

> Your company should balance the number of key customers it can handle with the number that represents enough business potential to make the initiative and the effort involved worthwhile.

Curiously, some companies do not seem to know exactly how many customers they count as key. In that situation, it is hard to believe that KAM is a real, living strategy in the organization. If you cannot even name and count your key customers, it is highly unlikely that you are genuinely managing them as key accounts, or that they will know and believe that they are key accounts.

Case study insight

Controlling numbers in the portfolio

A global company started with a portfolio of 18 key accounts, which crept up to 34 over time. Results were outstanding – growth was double that of the rest of the customer base at no loss of gross margin. As the programme had been so successful, a decision was taken to roll out the programme to the 'top 250'. Unfortunately, the company could not cope with individual treatment for this number of key customers. Not only were the expectations of the new key accounts disappointing, but delivery of value to the existing portfolio began to break down as well. The supplier had to back-track on the status of most of the new key customers (who were nonetheless big and valuable customers) and was eventually left with 72 on its list, still more than it could handle well. The episode left a legacy of cynical customers and staff that will take some time to overcome.

Nevertheless, it makes sense for novices to err on the side of caution until they have some experience to use as a benchmark. Somewhere between 15 and 35 is often about the right number, but it will finally depend on the particular company and the sector in which it operates.

2.2 Selection criteria

2.2.1 Identifying customers

Obviously, the potential of customers is fundamental in selecting them to be key accounts and, equally obviously, you cannot assess their potential until you have described the identity of the customer you are considering, which includes defining its boundaries. The identity of the customer is often simply assumed to be self-evident, but that can be dangerous.

Case study insight

Clarifying a key customer's identity

This discussion about the identity of a customer took place at the beginning of a customer selection workshop:

'So which key customer are we talking about here?'
'Nokia.'
'Is that all of Nokia?'
'Yes.'
'All of Nokia, including televisions, mobile phones, and any other divisions.'
'Oh no, not all that, it's the mobile phone division. Our sister companies deal with the rest.'

'So it's all of Nokia mobile phones, worldwide.'

'No, because we only deal with Western Europe. We have companies in Asia Pacific and the Americas which deal with those areas.'

'OK, so the customer as far as you are concerned is actually all the business units of Nokia mobile phones that buy in Western Europe?'

'Yes.'

In the Nokia case above, the real identity of the customer was quickly clarified, but often this simple question provokes a lot more debate, either because it has never been clearly defined, or because it challenges the status quo in terms of who 'owns' various parts of the customer. Quite often, suppliers cut up the 'carcass' of the customer and hand out a limb to everyone in the family, but each separate piece is never going to have as much potential as the whole and, besides, maybe the arms and legs work together! In summary, beware of making artificial divisions of the customer ahead of rating them as a potential key customer; you can do that later, if you must.

> Beware of making artificial divisions of the customer ahead of rating them as a potential key customer.

Consider the case above: if Nokia moved manufacturing from Finland to Malaysia, it would inevitably result in a decline in business for the Western European part of this supplier. So, if Nokia is identified as the Western European part only, and if such a move were expected, it is unlikely to be accorded key account status by its current 'owner'. But treating the segment leader accordingly would be most unwise for the global supplier as a whole. Figure 2.2 illustrates the need for clarity when defining the customer. It can have a major impact on the extent to which you see true key account potential.

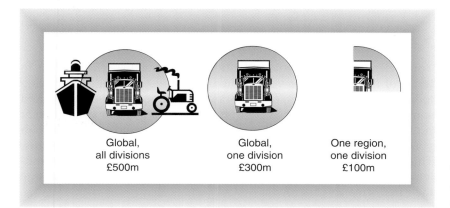

| Global,
all divisions
£500m | Global,
one division
£300m | One region,
one division
£100m |

Figure 2.2
The importance of defining the customer clearly.

In fact, defining a customer in such a way is a figment of the supplier's organization, and often does not reflect the customer in its own terms. Sometimes suppliers justify the arrangement in terms of the customer's supposed purchasing history: 'They only buy from their office in this region, so it fits well with our structure.' But is that true? Do they buy in this way because you made them? When did you last check?

So even identifying key customers can be a complex issue, and because it can have far-reaching implications, it should receive proper consideration at an early stage in a KAM programme. Failure to do so can, at worst, result in some very wrong and costly decisions and, even at best, it may mean that work done on evaluation and planning will have to be repeated when it is realized that the wrong customer identity and scope has been used.

Case study insight

Revealing a customer's true identity

One company saw limited potential in a customer who had been on their books for six/seven years, with fairly regular levels of business handled by a regional salesman. When he researched the customer properly he discovered:

- The customer was a global market leader in its field.

- It had 19 other sites in the UK which the company had not recognized.

- All of the other sites were buying from the supplier's competition.

This customer can be defined as one site with minimal growth potential (following on from the last six/seven years) or as 20 sites with huge potential, albeit with a strongly entrenched competitor. The former is not a key account; the latter may well be.

2.2.2 Choosing selection criteria

Your selection criteria should identify the customer's attractiveness in terms of its potential for your company, not just what it is delivering today. Best practice companies work with a three-year timeframe, and some with longer. If you overemphasize current size or even current profit, you will put too much resource into those whose lifecycle with you is maturing, and you will under-resource those who can grow. This is all too common, but under-resourcing growth is a serious problem when most companies (and their investors) quite rightly judge their performance on growth.

Try to involve a range of senior managers in arriving at your selection criteria, not key account managers themselves: these customers represent the future of your company, so you need a balanced, strategic and unbiased view. Indeed, the debate they will have is itself invaluable in uniting cross-functional views of what makes a 'good' key customer.

Your selection criteria should identify the customer's potential . . . not just what they are delivering today.

CHECKPOINT

Avoid overemphasizing current performance by:

- Thinking about cases where you have grown customers and look at what it was about those customers that enabled success – did they have anything in common?

- Focusing on the customer – their potential, their position in their marketplace, their strategy – more than on your company and its current yield from the customer.

- Looking for customer characteristics and strategies that are aligned with your strategy – you will be investing in strategies that support their needs, and your alignment should win customer preference.

Having collected a large number of sets of selection criteria, we observed that they fall into three main categories, as shown in Figure 2.3. These all relate to specific, individual accounts. However, there is also a fourth, rather different, category, which contains criteria that represent characteristics of customers that are deemed to be 'for the good of the company', such as 'reference point' or 'innovation partner'. Such criteria are valuable if they are applied with caution and restraint, but often they seem to be a proxy indicator or excuse for customers who are particularly unrewarding financially. Suppliers may need reference customers and innovation partners, but only a few and, even then, they should not have to lose money on them.

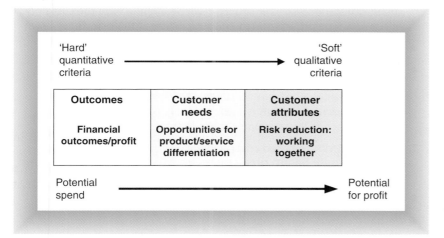

Figure 2.3
Three types of selection criteria.

Suppliers should aim to have a balanced spread of criteria which will reflect not only how much business the customer could offer (outcome-based criteria), but how much business the customer is likely to offer (needs-based criteria), which is another matter, and how profitable it could be (attribute-based criteria), which is another matter again, as illustrated in Table 2.1. For each criterion, from any category, two important questions remain.

- How important is each in the view of your company and how should it be weighted to represent its relative importance?

- How can you measure customers against your criteria: what metrics should be collected?

Table 2.1
Characteristics of three types of categorization criteria

1. Customer outcome-based criteria
These are the criteria that come to mind first. They are generally:

- 'Hard' or quantitative factors, i.e. they can be unambiguously defined and objectively measured

- Outcomes that represent the business which suppliers like you could do with the customer, like:
  - purchases
  - margin
  - contribution
  - profit

- Factors that reflect the customer, independent of your company:
  - customer size/turnover
  - growth in customer's markets
  - spend with any supplier on goods and services from the category into which they put your company

2. Customer needs-based criteria
Customer needs-based criteria suggest the likelihood that your company in particular will retain the business, and are therefore:

- Aligned to your company strategy specifically

- Representative of the chance of your company securing and retaining the business (because your strategy will be aligned with the customer and you will be differentiated and supportive of their strategy)

- Qualitative but should be quite specific and are still measurable

- Factors that reflect your strategy, and are therefore different for each supplier; examples are:
  - global presence
  - dedication to compatible platforms
  - importance of low customer churn in their business

3. Customer attribute-based criteria
Customer attribute-based criteria represent what the relationship might be like and are therefore:

- Indicators of whether the business will be successful and profitable

- Perhaps 'softer' than either of the other two categories, but can still be quantitatively assessed

- Factors about how the customer may behave in relationships (which is not necessarily the same as in the relationship you have with them currently), like:
  - central decision-making structure
  - right attitude to relationships
  - prepared to pay for value
  - prepared to invest in relationships

CHECKPOINT

Review your selection criteria:

- Do they differentiate between customers?

- Are they stated clearly and unambiguously and can they be consistently interpreted by others?

- Are they measurable?

- Do they include a mix of 'hard' factors and 'soft' factors?

- Are there between four and seven in number?

2.2.3 Applying selection criteria

Rating and scoring customers in this way allows suppliers to compare customers who may be quite different, through bringing each back to a numerical score that reflects their differences, but still enables valid comparisons to be made. One customer may score well on potential size, but its attractiveness is genuinely reduced by its attitude to relationships, which will have an impact on the business. Another customer may be smaller, but is better to work with, and its overall score may turn out similar to the larger customer. Indeed, the profit each delivers to the supplier in the end may well be similar, which is what the score should represent.

Figure 2.4 shows how selection criteria are applied. Suppliers should aim to have no more than seven, and preferably fewer, which are chosen, defined and weighted by senior management. These criteria are

Account attractiveness criteria	Relative importance weighting	Account A		Account B		Account C	
		Rating (0–10)	Score (weight × rating)	Rating (0–10)	Score (weight × rating)	Rating (0–10)	Score (weight × rating)
Total	100	Total		Total		Total	

Figure 2.4
Account attractiveness assessment for selection as a key customer.

then rolled out to other staff who will rate the customers against them. Potential key customers are rated against the criteria and their ratings multiplied by the weighting to arrive at a score on each criterion. The total of the scores is the customer's overall attractiveness score. At an early stage, run a reality check with a few likely candidate customers to see whether the relative scores turn out as expected. If they do not, do not necessarily make changes to the criteria or the weightings; establish whether, although the results are surprising, they also make good sense on closer examination.

In order to get as much consistency in rating as possible, the criteria will need to have measurements and scales attached to them. Ratings should be drawn up on a linear, 10-point scale:

- From the least acceptable for any key account, rating zero
- To the best that is anticipated, anywhere, in three years' time (or whatever time horizon is appropriate), rating 10 points.

Table 2.2 shows two examples, one of a quantitative criterion and one of a qualitative criterion rated against short scenarios. Each of your criteria needs to be supplied to the people scoring the customers with a definition and scale like these.

Table 2.2
How to scale and score selection criteria: examples

Example of quantitative criterion		*Example of qualitative criterion*	
'Potential relevant spend in three years' time'	*Rating*	*'Approach to risk and value sharing with suppliers'*	*Rating*
<£25 m	0	Takes win/lose approach	0
£25–49 m	1		
£50–74 m	2	Prepared to work outside contract	2
£75–99 m	3		
£100–124 m	4	Prepared to consider innovative solutions	4
£125–149 m	5		
£150–174 m	6	Partnering: risk equally shared	6
£175–199 m	7		
£200–224 m	8	Risk and reward equally shared	8
£225–249 m	9		
£250 m	10	Trust-based open-book partnerships	10

The process of key customer selection should be as objective and informed as possible – this is one of the main reasons for using a clear and criteria-based approach. So, while senior management should certainly be instrumental in determining the selection criteria, they should not rate and choose the customers. They rarely have a sufficiently close involvement to have the extensive, balanced and current knowledge required – but they might think they do!

Senior management should not choose the customers.

At the same time, although key account managers should not misrepresent their customers in order to squeeze them into the portfolio, the temptation is there and many fall into it. To combine customer knowledge and objectivity, roll out the task of rating customers against the criteria to several people in each case, not just the key account manager. Other functions that have customer contact, like customer service, logistics and accounts, should be included.

However, arriving at a set of relative attractiveness scores does not yet confirm the identity of your key customers: their views need to be taken into account as well. The next section describes how.

2.3 Categorizing key customers

2.3.1 The key account selection matrix

Listing the customers that your company finds most attractive is not the end of key account selection – it is more like the beginning. Whether the customer will respond to KAM depends on their view of your company, and it would be ridiculous to ignore it. It is also dangerous to assume you know what that view is, without even talking to the customer about it.

The matrix in Figure 2.5 effectively captures these two views: yours of the customer (on the vertical axis), and theirs of you (on the horizontal axis), expressed in terms of your relative business strength with them (see Section 2.3.2). The size of the shaded circles can be used to represent the volume of business – either the customer's potential spend on the category of goods or services you supply (in three years' time) or their current spend with your company. A simple software package, Key Account Selection Matrix (KASM), can produce this matrix view from your data.

The key account selection matrix is, in fact, a four-box adaptation of the matrix developed by GEC, which is normally applied to markets rather than individual customers. It suggests that different customers, at different stages of their lifecycle with the supplier, will therefore require and respond to different approaches. In managing these key accounts, it is useful to group them according to the way you intend to treat them and what you can expect from them, as well as understanding them as individual customers. The matrix identifies four groups, all of which are nevertheless key customers, and deserve complimentary titles.

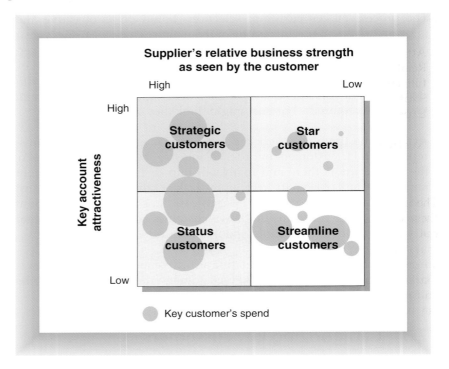

Figure 2.5
The key account selection matrix.

Star customers

Attractiveness:	high
Relative business strength now:	low
Lifecycle stage:	start-up/development
Strategic approach:	invest for growth
Expectation:	substantial growth in volume/sales
Net free cash outflow:	present neutral/negative

These are the strategic customers of the future. They probably do not do a lot of business with you at the moment, but analysis shows that they are the kind of customer that is aligned with your strategy and has good potential too. They do not rate your company highly, because: (a) they do not know what you have to offer, (b) they do know what you have to offer, but it does not actually suit their needs. If the reason is (a), you have a job of communication to do, but if it is (b), you have serious development and change work on your hands, and you will need to investigate the business case carefully before taking it on. In both cases, investment is required to change your position: probably more to change the offer than to execute the communication required.

Strategic customers

Attractiveness:	high
Relative business strength now:	high
Life cycle stage:	deep, close relationship
Strategic approach:	strategic investment
Expectation:	growth in volume/sales and profits
Net free cash flow:	positive, optimized rather than maximized

The most innovative and important projects should be developed with these customers. Your company has a large amount of their business, but you continue to find ways of developing it further together. You make money from the customer, but you should also be investing on an ongoing basis to bring new value to them, and even to expand the market through what you can offer together. Suppliers need a deep and multilevel relationship with such customers, requiring multiskilled key account managers to handle the relationship and the business.

Status customers

Attractiveness:	low
Relative business strength now:	high
Lifecycle stage:	maturing
Strategic approach:	proactive maintenance
Expectation:	stable profits
Net free cash flow:	very positive

These are very likely to be your strategic customers of the past: you have a great relationship, but you judge that their market or their business is not going to grow, so while they form a hugely important role in paying everyone's salaries and dividends today, they cannot deliver your strategic vision of the future. You need to treat them well, without lavishing your most innovative and exclusive ideas on them. At the same time, manage the cost base carefully to make sure profits are maximized, and that the excellent relationship you have does not allow them to draw down resources that they cannot repay.

Streamline customers

Attractiveness:	low
Relative business strength now:	low
Lifecycle stage:	mature
Strategic approach:	manage for cash
Expectation:	low price, low gross margin
Net free cash flow:	positive

These customers are the ones who constantly query the price, who negotiate on everything. Indeed, there may be less polite names you would like to call them. However, they are key customers because they give you a lot of business, and your company may feel that it needs the volume, or something else these customers can give you. Otherwise, why do it? There may come a time when you feel that you are prepared to resign the business, but until then suppliers should manage the costs very carefully, and make sure that the gross margin is positive, even if it is not large.

The position of the customer in the matrix suggests the outcome of some important decisions about them: on investment, management and pricing, for example. But as one key account manager commented on the exercise of constructing the matrix, 'It's an objective and transparent process. It should get better buy-in from everyone. There won't be any disputing that some customers aren't worth the effort.'

2.3.2 Relative business strength

Relative business strength represents the customer's view of your company as a supplier relative to the best competitor, whoever that may be in its view, and however it may view the merits of that competitor (rather than how you would see them). Since this evaluation is designed to capture the customer's point of view, it is important that the customer decides:

- the criteria
- the importance of the criteria
- how your company is viewed against the criteria
- how your best competitor is viewed against the criteria.

Second-guessing the customers' views is only the first step towards finding out what they really think.

In order to take a first cut of candidate key customers, however, you may decide to second-guess the customers' views, but this is only the first step towards finding out what they really think. However, it is legitimate to make a preliminary attempt at the customers' view based on the best analysis and evaluation you can do, in order to identify the customers whose attitudes should be explored further.

It is the essence of KAM that each customer is different, which includes understanding that each has different criteria for suppliers.

Try putting yourself in their position and considering what you, as this particular customer, would seek from a supplier for your kind of business. There will be some essential performance requirements, and there will be some 'softer' factors, which will probably be to do with the customer's strategy and how you might help them (or not); what your company is like to work with; and what added value you bring them. However, research (Woodburn and McDonald, 2001) has shown that suppliers frequently mistake what customers care about and the extent to which they care about it, so you should realize that nothing is better than asking them. That will take time and money; hence the reason for a preliminary assessment to identify which customers should be investigated in depth.

It follows, therefore, that each key customer will have a different set of criteria, even compared with others in the same sector. Indeed, it is the essence of KAM that each customer is different and is worthy of being addressed on an individual basis, which includes understanding that each has different criteria for suppliers, and dealing with these differences. While applying a uniform set of criteria is entirely appropriate on behalf of one company (e.g. as in your account attractiveness criteria), it is entirely inappropriate on behalf of any more than one company (e.g. as in the customers' relative business strength criteria for suppliers).

Yet suppliers do exactly that, rationalizing it as 'keeping things simple' or, in reality, 'making life easy for ourselves' (even at the expense of common sense and success). In spite of this, many suppliers impose criteria supposedly representing the customer's view, which usually represent their own ideas of what worthwhile performance looks like, and apply it to all key customers. At a stroke, they have eliminated the opportunity to understand the customer's unique set of requirements. There seems little excuse for this nonsense (especially when there is uncomplicated software to help). Figure 2.6 shows an example of one customer's supplier criteria, which will clearly differ from another customer's.

Headline criteria	Breakdown	Score 0–5
Assured supply	Product quality management Supply management	
Values/trust-based business relationship	Teamwork Openness, honesty, fair play	
Management excellence	Quality management Environmental management Management depth	
Low cost – best value	Competitive validation Process optimization Financial strength	
System player	Communication Best practices Customer satisfaction	
Technical competencies	Health & safety Product consistency	
Overall score		

Figure 2.6
One global customer's statement of its requirements of its suppliers.

To complete your preliminary assessment of key customer candidates:

● Identify the set of criteria that each customer would use, taking into account its pressures, its markets, its strategies, its performance requirements and its expectations of suppliers.

This table alone, completed for each customer, provides excellent guidelines on what to do to make progress with the customer.

● Give the criteria the weighting you think the customers would, bearing in mind that customers generally rate soft factors like 'easy to do business with' higher than suppliers rate them.

● Estimate their rating of your company against each criterion, based as far as possible on their current perceptions, not what you think they ought to be. You may think they misunderstand, or are ignorant or unfair, but the score should still reflect what they themselves would put down in real research.

● Estimate their rating of the best competitor on the same basis, and on any competitors who have distinctively different approaches. If you have no direct competitor in this customer, rate the best supplier of any goods or services that the customer is using.

Complete the table in Figure 2.7.

Customer:					
Suppliers' business strengths	Relative importance weighting	Your company		Best competitor:	
		Rating (0–10)	Score (weight × rating)	Rating (0–10)	Score (weight × rating)
Total	100	Total		Total	
		Difference:			

Figure 2.7 Relative business strength for comparative supplier evaluation.

This methodology brings customers' appraisals of your company to a series of scores that, while based on different criteria, can nevertheless be compared on a numerical basis. Obviously, a high score and a positive difference versus the best competitor says that as far as that customer is concerned, your company is excellent compared with the options available to it. A low score and a negative difference versus the best competitor indicate a poor perception from the customer, which has a better alternative supplier available. This table alone, completed for each customer, provides excellent guidelines on what to do to make progress with the customer.

The results of this exercise should be matched with the results of the customer attractiveness exercise and plotted in the matrix in Figure 2.5, which is then used as the basis for the provisional selection of key customers. However, before finalizing the key account portfolio, you must go and verify your assumptions with the customer, ideally through neutral third parties. In fact, best practice companies go and ask customers for their point of view even though what they hear may be uncomfortable at times, but poor companies just go on guessing.

2.3.3 Rebuffs and exits

Rebuffs

Only reciprocated relationships are real relationships. So you may want to put 'desire to have a relationship' with your company as an account attractiveness criterion. However, 'desire to have a relationship' is more like a killer 'make-or-break' clause than an account attractiveness criterion. Used as a criterion in account attractiveness assessment, the customer could score low on that count but still score high overall if it performed well on most other criteria. It could look like a company that must be in your key customer portfolio, being treated as a development or strategic account. That would be a nonsense, though, if it refused to have a relationship with your company. The best way to treat the issue is to rate the attractiveness of the customer independently of its 'desire to have a relationship' with your company, and then consider afterwards whether it wants the relationship, or could be persuaded to want it, as a final decision on how to deal with it.

> Only reciprocated relationships are real relationships.

Ultimately, however wonderful you think a customer is, if it does not want a relationship, and is most unlikely to change in the foreseeable future, there is no point in selecting it as a key customer. It may be that it is perfectly aware of what you have to offer, but is highly satisfied with a competitor which suits it very well, and has no intention or need to make any changes. Alternatively, it may be that its company philosophy keeps suppliers at arms' length. For whatever reason, if 'prepared to trade, no closer relationship allowed' is its settled view, including it in your key account group is futile.

The judgement would be different from that in which the customer does not have much relationship with you now, but would potentially be prepared to have a closer relationship if you positioned your company correctly. In the former case, it is assumed that you will get no opportunity to work towards that situation: in the latter, it is believed that it would respond, given the right approach.

Exits

In order to manage a customer portfolio, it must be possible to retire accounts as well as adopt them. Most suppliers find this difficult, and end up with unmanageable portfolios because inappropriate customers have never been cleaned out. But while these customers sit in the customer portfolio, they take up resources without making the level of response that justifies their staying.

> Most suppliers end up with unmanageable portfolios because inappropriate customers have never been cleaned out.

There are a number of reasons why customers may be inappropriately labelled as key:

- They are often very good customers who have been included because the supplier did not recognize its limitations in capacity for KAM and has simply selected too many (see examples in Figure 2.8).

- The supplier has overrated the customer's performance against selection criteria, and found out its mistake later.

- The customer overrepresented its ability or willingness to respond to KAM treatment, whether inadvertently or by design, and is not delivering value to the supplier now nor will do in the foreseeable future.

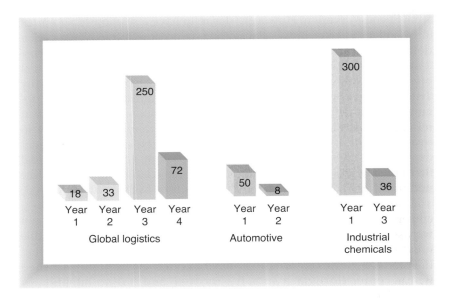

Figure 2.8
Reducing numbers of key customers.

However the situation has arisen, it cannot be left unaddressed. There are two options for customers who should leave the portfolio: exit to the next tier down, or complete exit and loss of the business to the supplier.

- **Exit to next tier down:** Some companies opt not to tell the customer about its change of status, but carefully and slowly withdraw resources. Others are clear about it, in order to give the customer the chance to respond if it wants to remain a key account. The choice probably depends on relative power positions.

- **Complete exit:** Most suppliers find it difficult to let go of a major customer, even when it is clearly making a loss for them, and even when there was no other good reason for continuing to do business with them that gave any alternative value to the supplier. Sometimes letting such customers go can make a significant improvement to the supplier's profitability, but it should be regarded as a last resort, if the profitability cannot be turned round.

Whether a step down or a total separation, careful management of exits is an essential part of customer portfolio management.

Whether a step down or a total separation, careful management of exits is an essential part of customer portfolio management.

Case study insight

When losing customers put a stop to losing money

Having had to make a major change in pricing strategy forced upon it by the marketplace, one supplier feared that it would lose some of its key customers. In fact, only a few of them walked away. The combination of the new pricing strategy and the disappearance of those few large, loss-making customers did wonders for the supplier's profitability, and over a fairly short space of time it moved up to the number two spot in the industry, from being number eight.

2.3.4 Categorization versus selection: portfolios versus lists

Treating your key customers as a list is a lot less appropriate than viewing them as a portfolio, as in the matrix shown in Figure 2.9. First, it is often assumed that once they are 'on the list', they have passed some kind of test and should now all receive the same approach and resource: an idea which this chapter hopes to have dismissed by now. Second, lists are generally seen as having a top and a bottom, so the notion creeps back in that there are customers at the top of the list who are the 'best', and almost inevitably, they are those with the biggest current turnover. Thus your carefully applied criteria-based process is bypassed and frustrated, and in so doing, your company loses a lot of good KAM practice aimed at optimizing the return on effort. Third, decisions about key customers on a list are commonly made on a case-by-case basis, often on individual contracts rather than via a proper view of the key customer group. As a result, there is a danger that the performance of the group will depend on a series of unconnected

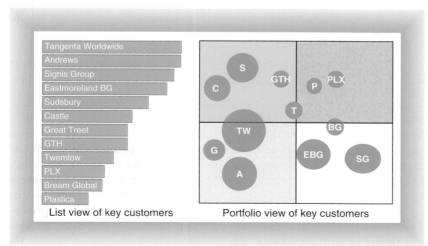

Figure 2.9
Unidimensional list versus multidimensional portfolio.

decisions and hence is likely to be suboptimal. In particular, the longer term is likely to be traded off against the short term, and the short term may be compromised as well.

> A supplier should be focused on the performance of its portfolio of key customer relationships, like a share portfolio.

Suppliers should focus on the performance of their portfolio of key customer relationships, like a share portfolio. When the customer is seen as a member of a portfolio, temporary shortfalls in some customers can be consciously balanced against returns from others. Managing key customers as a portfolio ensures that the supplier maintains a balance between those making a contribution through net cash outflow now and those who will in the future. When customers are managed as individuals only, there is more pressure to maximize returns from each of them at any given time, which may be inappropriate and even detrimental to their growth in the longer term.

CHECKPOINT

To have real portfolio management in place you need:

1. Customer categorization: a view of key customers as a group, subcategorized according to their potential.

2. Forecasting: an ability to forecast outcomes and model the responses to different levels of resource, given the customer's position in the portfolio.

3. Value-based prioritization: a process that compares the potential values of customers, and agrees customer priorities based on strategy and balance in the portfolio.

4. Resource allocation: a process of allocating resources in line with strategy and the optimization of the portfolio.

Some companies claim to manage their key customers as a portfolio but, digging deeper, they have none of the essential processes in place to achieve it. They have a view of the portfolio as a picture, but no more than that: they have not operationalized that view, so they cannot benefit from it.

2.3.5 Allocating scarce resources

In any sensibly managed company resources are made scarce, in order that those available should be used most economically. Key customers have the potential to eat up huge amounts of resource, so any resource within their reach needs to be managed very carefully indeed. In fact, their reach goes well beyond the key account manager, who is, effectively, the conduit through which the customer accesses the supplier's resources.

Even when customers have passed the first hurdle and been admitted to the portfolio of key accounts, their consumption of resources should not be standardized, but should be determined by their anticipated potential. Choices still have to be made about who does, and who does not, get resource-intensive solutions and tailoring. Failure to make clear distinctions between key customers according to where you expect to get the best return results in inappropriate allocations.

In our research (Woodburn *et al.*, 2004), we discovered that mis-allocation of resources occurred for several reasons, mainly:

- Lack of individual customer strategy: No customer policy guidelines existed to indicate whether there was, or was not, an accepted desire to develop with that particular customer, against which the merits of specific proposals could be decided.

- Lack of commitment to strategy: In spite of having clearly categorized the customer, its treatment in practice might be quite different from that identified as strategically appropriate. One supplier said, 'We throw more at our worst key account than we do at any of the others, in spite of the relationship.'

> 'We throw more at our worst key account than we do at any of the others, in spite of the relationship.'

- Poor implementation: No process existed to link together individual decisions into a consistent customer treatment. Resource allocation was a series of separate submissions decided on their individual merits.

We should add 'application of key account managers' powers of persuasion and influence' to that list. It is the responsibility of all employees in a supplier to use its resources as wisely as possible, but one key account manager's words, 'You have to fight for your customer, don't you?', represent a very common view. However, you should not be 'fighting for your customer'. If it has been objectively decided and agreed that investing in your customer is not the best use of your company's resources, then you should not be trying to gain more than allocated. You will be destroying shareholder value and might reasonably be accused of acting in your own best interests rather than those of your company.

So you should not expect applause for engaging in that kind of battle. If you won it, you would then have put yourself in the position of having effectively guaranteed a performance superior to that of selected customers – not just a good performance – and even then, you might not be congratulated for robbing your company's strategic customers of resource. So it may be tempting to massage the figures to get your customer into the programme, or to grab resources if it remains outside, but consider very carefully before you do so.

> It may be tempting to massage the figures to get your customer into the programme, but consider very carefully before you do so.

Some companies have good, objective, criteria-based processes for evaluating projects, contracts or requests for tender that they might attempt to win (although surprisingly many do not), but relatively few bring the customer dimension into the evaluation, even in the simple manner shown in Figure 2.10. As a result:

- Important information is not considered, which would be indicative of the chance of winning the bid and/or its success in terms of profitable fulfilment.

- Resources are tied up by less important customers and are not available to strategic customers when required.

Case study insight

Allocating resource selectively in hi-tech

A global hi-tech supplier was renowned for the quality of its R&D people. As creative, blue-sky thinkers, they liked to pursue exciting ideas wherever they appeared. However, the supplier discovered that a lot of its R&D time was being spent with start-up companies, which had bright ideas but were poorly positioned to exploit its innovations commercially. Meanwhile, key customers were being starved of R&D resources, so they were not getting the innovative products they needed to feed their well-developed markets. The supplier introduced a policy that major R&D projects would only be offered to key customers in the future.

Clearly, as Figure 2.10 suggests, good projects in good customers are ideal and, just as clearly, suppliers should avoid poor projects in poor customers. However, an apparently good project in a poor customer should be challenged because it may easily not turn out as well as expected with a difficult customer; equally, an apparently poor project in a good customer may be explored and improved within the kind of relationship that allows that to happen.

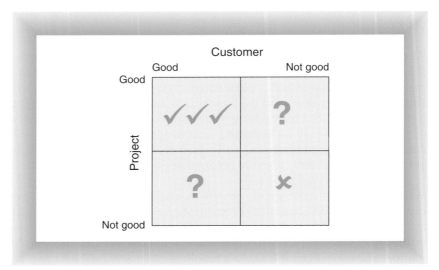

Figure 2.10
Adding the customer dimension to project approval.

Summary

In summary, selection and categorization of key customers largely exist in order to ensure that resources are correctly allocated to them in line with your company's strategies, and with theirs. So your categorization needs to be backed by a sound and effective process that applies the categorization through identifying resource requirements, approving their allocation to certain customers and withholding them from others, and ensuring that these intentions are followed through in practice. Unless your company makes its categorization mean something, there is little point in doing it at all.

Selection of key accounts is often a contentious issue, as it obviously involves the non-selection of some customers that give the company substantial amounts of business currently, and/or customers that are important to particular individuals. People will fight to have these customers included; sometimes using internal politics, sometimes warping the data input to the selection process, or applying other means. You will need to be rigorous, vigilant and firm. There are a variety of onward effects of allowing the wrong customers onto the programme, all of them unfortunate and likely to bring the KAM initiative into disrepute.

In any case, as time goes on, there will be customers to take out of the key account portfolio, even if their selection was right at the beginning: their circumstances may have changed, or they may have made promises to respond that you now see they are not going to fulfil. Make sure you and colleagues consider the implications and process of relegation at the outset, so that you all recognize the necessity of relegation and agree how to approach it, before a specific customer is involved.

3 | Relationship stages

Key account management (KAM) is very much concerned with managing the relationship with the customer, but remember that the relationship is a means to an end, that is, business development, and not an end in itself. Nevertheless, it is important to understand these relationships, which vary from simple, transactional forms to intimate and complex liaisons. There is a distinct hierarchy of relationship levels which describes the progression from the simple trading stage right up to a configuration that is only a short step away from a merger. Whatever level of relationship is reached, the requirements for efficient fulfilment of basic transactions remains, although a good relationship might allow a greater period of tolerance and assistance with poor performance than a simple, easy-to-exit relationship. Ultimately, however, a customer will have to buy from the supplier who gives them the offer they need, however good the relationship.

Both the key account manager and the supplier organization need to know what kind of relationship they have with each customer, and therefore what they can and cannot do with it. Suppliers generally have delusions of intimacy with the customer, and believe that they are one stage closer than the customer does. Since the essence of a relationship is reciprocation, then the supplier can only work with the level of relationship that both parties agree on.

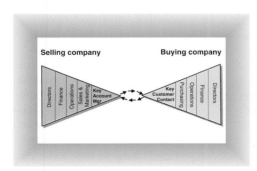

Exploratory relationships
Suppliers need to recognize potential key accounts from the outset and treat them as such. The bigger the customer, the longer it takes. Be prepared to be patient and manage internal expectations. Monitor the signals sent out rigorously.

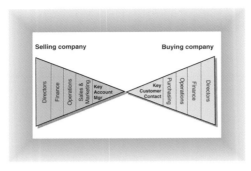

Basic relationships

This simple, transactional relationship has benefits of efficiency, clarity and resource control alongside its disadvantages of vulnerability to competition, fragility to change, potential for bias, limited understanding of each other and limited opportunity.

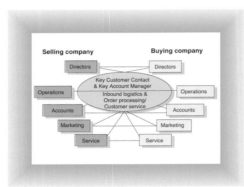

Cooperative relationships

To be regarded as a transitional stage, this stage is hard to control and likely to be losing money. It may be a necessary rite of passage, but not a stage to prolong. Key account managers are still 'out in the cold' and 'in the dark', and the supplier is not yet trusted, so the more positive feel has yet to be translated into real advantage.

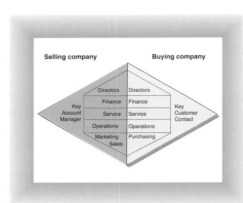

Interdependent relationships

This is the stage to which suppliers developing KAM normally aspire with the right kind of customer. These relationships involve trust, much more exchange of information, proactive strategies based on a much deeper understanding of the customer and opportunities for joint strategic planning leading to substantial business growth.

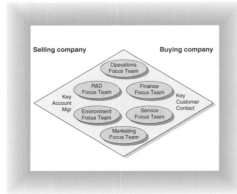

Integrated relationships

These relationships are just short of a merger. Boundaries between the two companies are dissolved, since a high degree of trust eliminates the need for protection. *Integrated* relationships are few in number because they take a lot of dedicated resource, are not easy to put together, and tend to repel other customers in the same marketplace.

Even close relationships do not necessarily last forever, although there are some that have worked for decades. Disintegration may be driven by changes in the ownership or market position of either company, or by the supplier's failure to develop the relationship. Ultimately, the supplier has to be able to offer the customer what it wants, so a relationship, however good, cannot compensate if the supplier's product or service fails to meet the customer's needs.

Introduction

Not surprisingly, relationships between complex suppliers and complex customers are likely to be complex too. They are made up from a web of people interacting with other people in the partner organization, which is not easy to manage. In addition, those relationships need to be supported by a web of internal relationships in order to respond to an ever-moving picture of the customer's needs, and to achieve effective and timely implementation.

Inevitably, these relationships will not be uniform, and quality and cooperation will vary with different people in different functions and different parts of the customer's organization at any given time. Nevertheless, it is possible to identify characteristic stages of relationship between two organizations that takes this variation into account. Several research groups have been able to describe levels of relationship, which the companies involved can also recognize.

Clearly, the way a relationship between two organizations works is different from the way a relationship between two people operates. A great deal has been written about interpersonal relationships elsewhere, so we have taken it as our job to discuss the relationship between two organizations. Parallels between person-to-person relationships and business-to-business relationships can certainly be drawn, but there are also major differences in how they should be managed and developed. This chapter describes the stages relationships can reach with key customers, while the next chapter discusses more specifically how they may be achieved.

3.1   Understanding key relationships

3.1.1   *Why do you need to know?*

In personal relationships, you behave differently towards different people according to how well you know them and what they mean in your life. If you treated your oldest friend with distant formality, he or she would be puzzled and upset: old friendships should be warm and relaxed, frank and open to new ideas. Similarly, if you treated an acquaintance like your postman or your child's teacher as an old friend, they would be equally puzzled and upset, or even offended and enraged by your familiarity. It is the same with intercompany relationships. If you have just started trading with a customer in a limited way, trying to involve the chief executive in a strategic planning workshop would be seen as unnecessary at best, and presumptuous at worst. Asking for inside information about the business may be greeted with suspicion, if yours is seen as a simple trading relationship, but it may be welcomed and even expected if you have a highly collaborative liaison with the customer.

You need to understand when you do not yet have the kind of relationship that entitles you to call on that amount of attention. Many customers have thousands of suppliers, so they have to prioritize their time very carefully (see Chapter 4). Your best plan is to:

- understand your current position in the relationship hierarchy,
- decide how far this relationship can go and how far you want it to go, and
- make a plan to move forward, matching your strategies to the stage you have reached.

Be aware of the fact that customers do not usually see the relationship in the same way as the supplier, particularly the key account manager (Figure 3.1). When we asked suppliers what level of relationship they

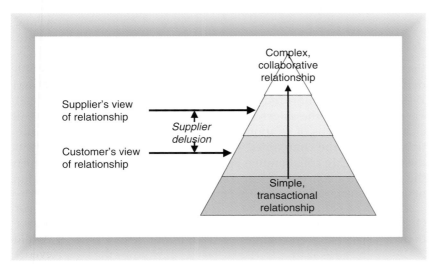

Figure 3.1
The relationship perception gap.

> Suppliers suffer from delusions of intimacy much more than customers.

> Only the reciprocated part of a relationship is effective. It follows that the rest is either an investment or a waste.

had with a key customer, and then asked their customers the same question, we found that the answers were almost always different. The supplier usually rated the relationship one level higher than the customer. But only the part of the relationship that is agreed by both sides can be real. If you think about it, you cannot be closer to me than I am to you. Of course, the reverse is true too, that your customer cannot be closer to you than you think you are to them but, in general, it is suppliers that suffer from delusions of intimacy much more than customers. In fact, only the reciprocated part of a relationship is effective. It follows that the rest is either an investment or a waste.

Investing resource

It may be right to behave as if the relationship were more advanced than it is currently, in order to develop it to that higher level, provided that:

- you have calculated that the customer can and will respond,
- you are intentionally investing in the customer,
- you monitor the development of the relationship and the return from it, and
- you take action if progress is not achieved.

Wasting resource

If you have somehow slipped into a stage of relationship which is one-sided and not moving forward, you should stage a cautious retreat:

- consider what you are doing that is not appreciated by the customer
- withdraw resources carefully to a more appropriate level.

The following sections describe the different stages of the relationship in some detail to help you identify at what level you cooperate with your customers currently, and what that indicates in terms of your behaviour and opportunities.

3.1.2 The hierarchy of key relationships

For some time now, researchers have been aware of a hierarchy or ladder of relationships between suppliers and key customers (Scott and Westbrook, 1991; Dunn and Thomas, 1994; Millman and Wilson, 1996). Each group gave the stages slightly different names, but they are all clear that the focus of relationships of the lowest order is on transactions between the companies, while at the high end the focus shifts towards a highly collaborative approach to the relationship, in which the companies concentrate on combining their strengths to develop new, joint business initiatives that challenge existing boundaries.

Of course, the development of key relationships is a continuum rather than a series of step-changes, but different levels with different

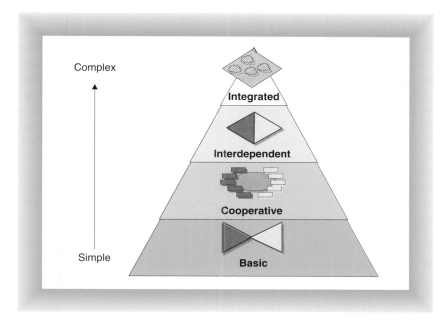

Figure 3.2
Hierarchy of key
relationships.

characteristics can usefully be identified. They can effectively be
described as a pyramid, as in Figure 3.2. This way of looking at
key account relationships suggests that each layer of the pyramid is
built on the one below. As the relationship develops to a higher, more
intimate and more complex level, it still depends on the sustained satisfaction of needs at the lower levels and does not ignore those elements. They continue to form the base of the pyramid and of the
relationship. A buying company, however closely involved with
its supplier at a strategic level, still expects that its transactions will
be carried out efficiently. Two characteristics define a watershed in
supplier/customer relationships. Try the litmus test below for a quick
check on where your relationships are.

CHECKPOINT

For each of your key customers

1. Trust
   - Do they and their company trust you and your
     company?
   - Do you and your company trust them?

2. Mutual importance
   - Do both sides consider that they need each other
     and are important to each other, and are prepared
     to state that explicitly?

Trust implies that both companies believe that the other would not indulge in opportunism. Opportunism means taking advantage of the other, for example maintaining or even increasing prices, assuming that the customer is ignorant of a cut in raw material costs which would actually enable a price cut. Trust, at least on the customer's side, does not really appear until the *interdependent* stage of the relationship, which is the most common aspirational level beyond the *basic* stage. In addition, at lower levels of the relationship the customer still sees that it can exit the relationship quite easily (although suppliers are rather shocked by this view and often do not share it), and only at the *interdependent* stage would it acknowledge its need for the supplier. These two questions therefore give you a quick idea of whether your relationships have reached the higher levels of collaboration or are still on the other side of the watershed, at a transactional or transitional stage.

Portrayal of key relationship stages as a pyramid is reminiscent of Maslow's hierarchy of human needs (Maslow, 1943). Stated very simply, Maslow suggested that the needs of an individual could be positioned in a hierarchy according to the order in which they must be satisfied. At the lowest level, the individual has fundamental physiological requirements, such as food, water and warmth, and unless these are adequately fulfilled, the individual will show no interest in fulfilling other, less urgent needs.

At a slightly higher level, people have a need for safety and freedom from threat. If they are preoccupied with protecting themselves, then they are unlikely to be motivated by more esoteric issues, such as self-image, for example. At a yet higher level, people have a need for relationships that give them love and esteem from their fellows, and if this requirement is satisfied, they can proceed to develop themselves to their fullest and most creative potential. In other words, the motivation of individuals towards achievement at the higher levels of their capabilities requires underpinning by the satisfaction of more basic needs.

The development of key account relationships seems comparable with Maslow's scheme (Figure 3.3). At the lowest level, which can be compared with the individual's physiological needs, the *basic* relationship requires the fulfilment of normal sustainable trading as a minimum, i.e. the efficient handling of transactions (orders, deliveries, payments and so on). If your company cannot manage ordinary transactions adequately it will, quite rightly, have little success in developing the business further.

At the *cooperative* stage, equivalent to Maslow's need for safety, relationships reach a point where the parties are, at least, no longer in constant fear of losing the relationship. Supplier and customer act in a cooperative way, rather than being constantly suspicious of or threatening towards each other. As the companies get to know each other better, they begin to understand each other's modus operandi and can predict the future, up to a point. It becomes possible to discuss forecasts of demand.

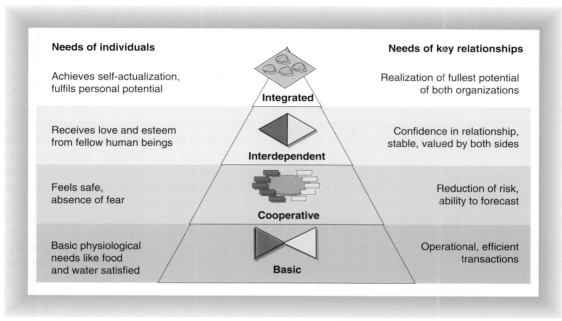

Figure 3.3   Needs of the individual compared with the needs of key relationships.

The *interdependent* stage is perhaps equivalent to Maslow's need for 'love and esteem'. Both companies recognize their ongoing relationship and this is reflected in their confidence and high regard for each other. Since neither company anticipates or considers termination of the relationship, both can adopt behaviour appropriate to longer-term business development.

> The *interdependent* stage reflects both companies' confidence and high regard for each other.

At the highest or *integrated* level, the relationship is so close that the two companies act as a single entity without internal barriers although, by definition, it stops short of being an actual, legal merger. The companies trust each other and do not feel the need to operate protective measures against opportunism. The relationship can now be at its most creative, using the potential of both partners to develop innovative, mould-breaking strategies.

> At the *integrated* level, the two companies act as a single entity without internal barriers.

Relationships may start at the bottom of the pyramid and work their way up, but not always. Some will begin at a higher level, although it is hard to imagine companies entering into an *integrated* relationship without prior experience of each other. However, a fairly close relationship may exist from the outset if the product/service is very complex or customized, or particularly important to either or both companies. In those cases, the relationship may well spend longer at the pre-trading, or *exploratory*, stage.

Even among the elite group of customers selected by companies as 'key' accounts, the number of relationships that can be maintained at each stage becomes fewer as the level of complexity and collaboration increases. Logically, there is a limit to the number of close relationships that any company can sustain (see Chapter 2). Such relationships require the adaptation of standard offers and services, and the investment of time, money and people, especially people with sufficient seniority – and the supply of all of these is constrained.

> An *integrated* relationship with one customer is likely to deter others from trading with the same supplier.

> Increasingly, companies linked together in integrated supply chains are appearing as the unit of competition.

Notably, *integrated* relationships are relatively rare, not just because of the resources they require. An *integrated* relationship with one customer in a marketplace, with all the commitment and joint activity that it implies, is likely to deter others from trading with the same supplier, as they, not unreasonably, fear that the best ideas, the latest developments and any exclusive offers will go to the customer with the *integrated* relationship. They suspect they will receive second best, added to the danger of their commercial secrets leaking to their competitor. Major players are therefore likely to look for alternative suppliers with whom they can develop a similar position. Increasingly, rather than individual companies competing independently with each other, companies linked together in integrated supply chains are appearing as the unit of competition (Christopher, 2005).

To what extent does this statement apply to the relationship? Score:

Strongly agree: 4   Agree: 3   Disagree: 2   Strongly disagree: 1

Statement	Score
Both companies would find ending our relationship difficult and complicated	
There is a real spirit of partnership and trust between our two companies	
Together we have produced long-term strategic plans for the development of our relationship	
Both companies have set up cross-functional teams of people dedicated to meeting the customers' needs	
People at all levels in the organization are in constant communication with each other	
Both companies acknowledge that the other is important to them	
Total	

Score   Relationship stage
 6–10   = Basic
11–16   = Cooperative
17–22   = Interdependent
23–24   = Integrated
NB: Remember, suppliers tend to overstate the relationship reached by one stage.

3.2   Stages in key relationships

3.2.1   *Exploratory relationships*

The *exploratory* stage is the earliest stage of relationship development, before trading begins, so it could be described as a stage of investigation and development of understanding. Where the potential importance of the relationship qualifies the customer as a future key account, it should be treated as such from the start, and distinguished from the handling of the general run of new leads and prospects.

Failure to recognize potential key accounts early enough is a sad waste of opportunities. Unfortunately, some companies do not adapt their response to the potential, so they burn up resource in a relentless tendering process that delivers a uniform standard of mediocre bids, which are unnecessarily rich for straightforward customers and nothing like good enough for potential key accounts.

Needless to say, current key accounts can be lost, so the recruitment of replacements is critical. As major openings are few and infrequent, it is essential to approach promising prospects in the right way from the first contact, so *exploratory* KAM should be operated with those customers selected as 'key', and only those. Selection methods are described as part of the categorization approaches in Chapter 2. Ideally the same criteria should be used for selection as for categorization, but sometimes suppliers analysing their customers include criteria which can only be satisfied where there is actual business.

To decide whether a prospect qualifies for an *exploratory* relationship, the supplier should concentrate on customers which will support the achievement of its corporate strategy. For example, if the supplier's aim is to enter a new market segment, then it may target a well-regarded participant in the sector. Failing that, it should target a company which operates in a sector with similar issues, in order to tap into their knowledge of tackling those issues. If the supplier is attracted by the opportunity to learn from leading-edge customers, they should build their desires into the criteria they use for evaluating prospects, as in the example shown in Table 3.1.

In an *exploratory* KAM relationship, the key account manager and the purchasing manager tend to keep the process of exploration very focused. They tightly control the amount of interaction with others in their organizations until a decision to work together has been reached. Typically, all communication will go through these two people so that they can monitor and control each exchange. They may interact on a regular basis, possibly over a long period of time, in order to bring the two organizations closer together. The *exploratory* relationship is represented diagrammatically in Figure 3.4.

At this stage, the companies have very little history of interaction or experience of each other, so they will be trying to form an opinion of each other, probably on both objective and subjective grounds. Like bats in the mating season, both seller and buyer are sending out signals and exchanging messages prior to the decision to get together. They will make judgements objectively based on the information they

Table 3.1
Criteria-based
qualification of a
potential key account

Key account selection criteria	Weight	Potential key account	
		Rating	*Score (weight × rating)*
Size: spend on products we offer	35	8	280
Strategic alignment: potential to use our planned product innovations	25	7	175
Rate of growth in their market(s)	20	5	100
One of top three suppliers in their marketplace	10	8	80
Has long-term relationships with suppliers	10	6	60
Total	100		695
Minimum score to qualify as key account = 650			

are given and, more subjectively, on 'signals' that may be generated directly by the other company, or indirectly by third parties. Reputations and signals are examined very carefully, and the impact of any event, communication or rumour can be magnified, sometimes disproportionately so.

> On both sides, managing the signals transmitted and their implications needs to be a deliberate, conscious process and one supported by the whole of the organization.

On both sides, managing the signals transmitted and their implications needs to be a deliberate, conscious process and one supported by the whole of the organization. If the key account manager claims that his or her organization is flexible and responsive, then the purchasing manager will look for signs to support the truth of that

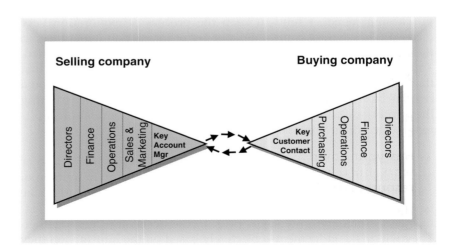

Figure 3.4
Exploratory KAM
relationship.

assertion. Naturally, the claim will be discounted if, for example, instead of the tailored version promised, a standard service specification arrives with just a few suggestions as to how it can and cannot be changed to meet the specification.

At this initial stage of the relationship, the selling company will be courting the customer in order to explore its particular needs and aspirations; determine the size and scope of the opportunity; identify how it might differentiate itself from the current supplier; and understand how the decision on supplier selection will be made. Selling skills will be important, but care should be taken that pushing for short-term sales results does not destroy a larger, longer-term relationship.

> Trust is a slow-growing and fragile seedling, which must be cultivated with care.

At the same time, the customer with an unfulfilled or underfulfilled need will be exploring the supplier's offer, capabilities and credentials, and quite possibly doing so with more than one supplier simultaneously. It is unlikely that either party will disclose truly confidential information at this stage, for trust is a slow-growing and fragile seedling, which must be cultivated with care.

The key account manager and the purchasing manager have to manage a difficult balancing act between investing enough to secure the business and using up too many resources speculatively. At this investigative stage, the major share of investment comes from the selling company, as the buyer asks for inspection visits, evidence of organizational capability, samples made to their specification, costings and other information which may not be readily available. All too often, the key account manager's requests for assistance in complying with these demands are seen by colleagues as an irritation and a secondary priority. Rather than being aligned supportively behind the key account manager, colleagues are busy pursuing other objectives.

> At this investigative stage, the major share of investment comes from the selling company.

CHECKPOINT

For *exploratory* relationships

- Does the customer potentially qualify as a key account?
- Have you identified what you need to explore?
- Are all the signals the customer receives properly managed? By whom?
- Have you planned how to promote and back up your company's reputation?
- Has your company agreed how long it may need to work on developing this relationship and allocated resources to it?
- Have appropriate progress-tracking milestones been set?

Case study insight

The consequences of misaligned views

The supplier's production manager saw his priority as hitting targets for a high volume of output and a low reject rate. He saw no good reason to compromise his targets by switching production equipment to developing samples for people who were not even customers yet. So production-quality samples promised to a prospective key customer were late: more than one deadline was missed and when the delivery eventually arrived, the supporting data were absent. By this time, the prospective customer had become sceptical about promises that real orders would be treated differently, and placed its business elsewhere.

Overcoming a lack of cooperation from other managers is one of KAM's greatest problems. The key account manager must have high-level status and/or top-level backing, and the implications of KAM must be made blatantly clear throughout the supplying organization. The stakes are too high to risk any unnecessary gaffes or avoidable mishaps that may prevent the relationship from ever getting beyond the *exploratory* stage.

3.2.2   Basic relationships

The *basic* KAM stage implies a relationship with a pronounced transactional emphasis.

Basic relationships are most like a traditional sales relationship, but they are still appropriate for a great many key customers. The *basic* stage implies a relationship with a pronounced transactional emphasis, in which the key account manager and purchasing manager are now in regular contact, although their organizations are still aligned behind them rather than alongside them. The standard trading management approach that both companies normally adopt will be applied, and no customized arrangements have been set up. The key account manager and the purchasing manager still expect all communication and exchanges to be channelled exclusively through them, so as yet no one else on either side has really developed a relationship with his or her opposite number. Figure 3.5 depicts a *basic* KAM relationship.

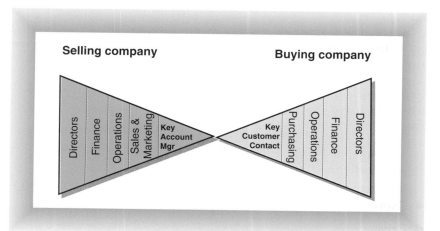

Figure 3.5
Basic KAM relationship.

The interest level on both sides is limited, so the relationship is managed as efficiently as possible and, indeed, channelling interaction through a single point of contact should be efficient, even if it has other downsides. Responsibilities are normally clear, and communication and control simple, so overhead costs should be contained because the constriction of interaction between the two companies naturally curbs the amount of management time that each party can take up. Key account managers handling such relationships can have about five of them in their portfolio, so they have enough to do just responding to ordinary customer requests, without raising the activity level further. With everything going through the key account manager as the single channel of communication, he or she does not have the time to use up a great deal of extra cost or develop resource-hungry projects for the customer.

Channelling interaction through a single point of contact should be efficient.

At the *basic* stage, neither party feels particularly committed to the relationship. The business is based on a stripped-down, simple exchange of money for goods and services that is not surrounded by extra systems and services valued by the customer which it would find awkward and inconvenient to surrender. The perception is that barriers to exit are low, especially on the buyer's side, and the key account manager is well aware of this. After all, the buyer is probably sourcing from a competitor simultaneously, so switching is not a big problem. The buying company may also use other suppliers of the same product/service in order to play one off against another.

At the basic stage, neither party feels particularly committed to the relationship.

In *basic* relationships the customer tends to be very focused on the price, which features heavily in discussions, negotiations and measurements of success. The key account manager is equally focused on his or her reward package, which is generally based on short-term volumes. With strong, short-term financial drivers in place on both sides, there is little room or appetite for relationship development and therefore for major growth. Supplier organizations do not seem to recognize the limiting effect of the incentives they commonly operate.

With strong, short-term financial drivers in place on both sides, there is little room or appetite for relationship development and therefore for major growth.

There is not a great deal of information shared in a *basic* relationship, partly because the emphasis on transactions limits the topics discussed, and partly because a foundation of trust between the two companies has not been established. If neither side is sufficiently well informed to be more proactive, then both parties will behave reactively, simply responding to situations as and when they arise. The level of exchanges is likely to be low generally, in terms of both quantity and quality. The volume of communication on operational subjects may be high, but this 'noise' level may be obscuring the fact that discussion on more important issues is not happening, and the supplier should not be misled into thinking this indicates a closer relationship than is really the case. The characteristics of a *basic* relationship are as follows:

● Transactional, emphasis on efficiency

● Driven by price, success measured by price

- Probably one of several suppliers

- Seen as easy to exit

- Single channel of communication

- Business relationship only

- Very little information sharing

- Reactive rather than proactive

- Driven by personal reward structures

- Standard organization.

The most pressing problem is the vulnerability created by having only a single point of contact.

A *basic* relationship has its advantages and disadvantages (Table 3.2). It may deliver goods and services efficiently, but it is not robust, nor is it likely, for example, to create new opportunities in the marketplace or find major cost savings through process re-engineering. However, the most pressing problem is the vulnerability created by having only a single point of contact that may easily be opened up by the competition. This is a fairly superficial business relationship, devoid of any deeper commitment that might persuade a buyer to be tolerant of a mistake or to warn of impending threats.

Table 3.2
Advantages and disadvantages of *basic* relationships

Advantages	Disadvantages
Efficient	Seen as easy to exit
Simple	Driven by price
Clear objectives	Very little information sharing
Easier to control: standard approach single channel of communication	Reactive rather than proactive
Easier to measure	Overdependent on the relationship between two people
Key account manager skills more readily available	Open to biased view: coloured by principal contacts
	Easy to break up
	Hard to grow

Turnover of key staff is often cited as the reason for relationship breakdown.

Even if there were some kind of personal chemistry between the key account manager and the purchasing manager, should either person leave his or her job, that bonding would be lost. The successor might not be able or willing to continue the relationship and, indeed, successors often make a point of changing 'old' suppliers and bringing in those with which they are familiar. Turnover of key staff is often cited as the reason for relationship breakdown.

A *basic* relationship is clearly not all bad, and in some circumstances it is the most appropriate. Because of its potential for efficiency, a *basic* relationship is indicated for large accounts that are aggressive price-fighters with no interest in added value, or no intention of paying for it. Some companies should always be treated in this way, because they adopt this stance in all their purchases. However, there are others who build closer relationships when purchasing their core inputs, but not when the product is not critical to them. Suppliers need to be able to recognize the difference, although it may be right to work within a *basic* relationship anyway.

However important the customer may be to the supplier, a genuinely closer relationship will not develop with a customer who is not pre-pared to reciprocate. In such circumstances, there is a ceiling to the level of relationship that can be attained, and any attempts to take it beyond this point are doomed to fail (see Chapter 4). Suppliers are wise to recognize this fact and avoid the fruitless investment of time, money and 'free gifts' in terms of extra services. Although the customer may happily accept an enhanced offer, it remains uncommitted, buying on price as usual. The supplier should only develop the relationship further if the customer meets strategic selection criteria, including a propensity to reciprocate.

A relationship can be very successful at the *basic* level, but it still may not be possible or advisable to develop it further, for a number of good reasons:

- The length of life of the relationship may be limited by changes pending in the environment in terms of legislation, technology, market, company ownership and so on.

- The buying company may be low-price focused and unresponsive to added value.

- The buying company may be known for supplier-switching behaviour.

In summary, a *basic* relationship is indicated when the overall lifetime value of the relationship is not expected to repay investment in terms of time, resources, customization and so forth. In order to decide whether and how the account should be developed and what objectives it should have, a deep understanding of the customer and the markets in which it competes will be needed.

If the relationship is at a *basic* stage just because it is new, then it may be effectively a trial time during which the selling company has to prove its ability to deliver its offer in an efficient manner. Buyers will obviously prefer to develop business with suppliers who have demonstrated that they can live up to minimum operational requirements. However, trial experience is not always possible, as in the case of major one-off contracts. As in the *exploratory* relationship, the supplier should be very aware of the signals it sends: even at this stage, it must always look like a supplier that has the potential to take on a greater role in the customer's business.

3.2.3 Cooperative relationships

The *cooperative* relationship becomes something akin to a network, albeit a fairly loose one. The key account manager and the purchasing manager work more closely together and now, in addition, the relationship involves a wider range of people and a wider range of interaction than before. Indeed, the people in the front line of transaction handling, that is to say, order processing and customer service, are generally in much more frequent contact with their counterparts than is the key account manager with the purchasing manager.

> The growing web of involvement means that the relationship is better protected against the departure of the key account manager or the purchasing manager.

More people have an understanding and appreciation of the business than in *basic* KAM, though their contact may not be regular or frequent. Nevertheless, the growing web of involvement means that the business is better protected against the departure of the key account manager or the purchasing manager, but the major thread of the relationship still runs between the original two key players. Although the relationship begins to draw in more people and harness more resource, it is not a highly organized state, so there are many things that can go wrong. The multifunction links of a *cooperative* relationship are represented in Figure 3.6, although they are shown in a much tidier way than they would be in reality.

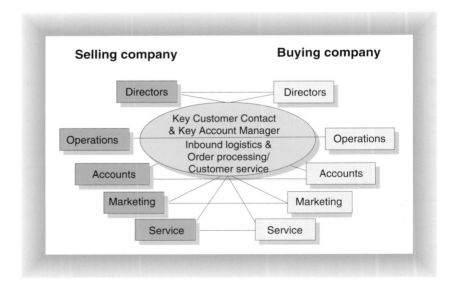

Figure 3.6
Cooperative KAM relationship.

> *Cooperative* relationships are messy and hard to manage.

Cooperative relationships are messy and hard to manage. Clear lines of communication, responsibility and authority have not been established in *cooperative* relationships, and activity is at least uncoordinated, or even out of control. For example, you may find that just as you have sealed a sensitive deal with some people in the customer organization, your accounts receivable department has put the customer on 'stop' because they have exceeded their credit limit. Perhaps you did not tell accounts that this customer had acquired a new status with the company and should be given a higher limit; or perhaps they do not know who is the key account manager, or even that one exists, and did not think of consulting you first.

At this stage, the supplier is looking for opportunities to add value for the customer, in order to develop the relationship, and the buyer adopts a positive and communicative attitude towards the supplier. The buyer may identify further opportunities to do business together or help you to solve operational problems that arise, rather than just passing them on. The underlying shape of the organization on either side does not change. The customer is still handled within the supplier's existing structure, and no significant organizational adaptations are normally made.

However, a social context begins to appear, often fostered by the selling company through organized events like golf days and trips to sports fixtures, or through smaller events like lunches and dinners. In the beginning, some of the most valuable gatherings are the more casual lunches or after-work get-togethers where people get to know each other in a more relaxed setting, having set work aside for a short period. This network brings new strength to the relationship. Participants become driven by a desire not to let personal contacts down, which is a far more effective motivation than formal statements of intent or customer charters. The key characteristics you might expect to see in a *cooperative* relationship are as follows:

- Selling the company adds value to relationship
- May be preferred supplier
- Exit not particularly difficult
- Multifunction contacts
- Relationship still mainly with buyer
- Organization mainly standard
- Limited visits to customer
- Limited information sharing
- Forecasting, not joint strategic planning
- Not really trusted by customer.

Suppliers have more access to their key customers than they do in *basic* relationships, and that gives them more information with which to work. You may still feel that the amount of contact you get is not quite as much as you want (see Figure 3.7), and you know that there are other suppliers (possibly, but not necessarily, competitors) who get a much greater share of the purchasing manager's time. Like a climber reaching

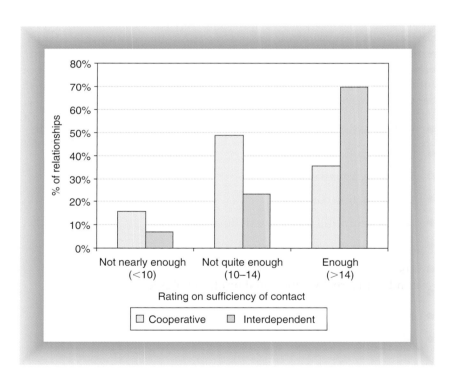

Figure 3.7
Contact between selling and buying companies.

the first peak of a mountain range, the realization dawns that there are further, higher peaks to climb which were simply not visible before.

Visits to the customer continue to be limited by the time the purchasing manager is willing and able to devote to the type of product and supplier concerned. While information is shared across a broader range of topics than before, it is still confined to material that is fairly readily available. The supplier is not trusted sufficiently for the buyer to volunteer highly confidential information, and the key account manager remains somewhat 'out in the cold' and 'in the dark'. Joint strategic planning is not really possible and does not develop much beyond simple forecasts of price and volume. However, even forecasting constitutes useful progress compared with *basic* KAM, which may not offer medium-term demand visibility, never mind demand security.

> The key account manager remains somewhat 'out in the cold' and 'in the dark'.

Even at this stage, exit is still not regarded as particularly difficult; inconvenient, possibly, but certainly not unthinkable. The selling company has not achieved sole supplier status, and the buyer continues actively to scan the competitive landscape to make sure it is getting best value for money. The business is still very vulnerable to competitors, and another supplier with the inside track might gain advance information, for example, on new customer sites or new strategic directions, which is denied to a selling company at only a *cooperative* stage of relationship development. A competing supplier who has inside knowledge can work out an interesting and innovative proposition, long before the latter gets the same information.

> Exit is still not regarded as particularly difficult: inconvenient, possibly, but certainly not unthinkable.

So although a *cooperative* relationship has a positive feel, and is less defensive and more open than a *basic* relationship, some reserve remains; doors are opened, but not flung wide. More useful information is made available, but this does not include sensitive material, because the supplier is not really trusted by the customer. It is often at the *cooperative* stage that the real potential to progress the relationship is grasped, or lost. It is still an uphill task to break out of the cycle of limited information and limited capability to make better and more exciting offers to the customer.

> It is still an uphill task to break out of the cycle of limited information and limited capability to make better and more exciting offers to the customer.

Cooperative KAM can be a difficult stage, having lost the efficiency and control of *basic* KAM, but not having gained the benefits of openness and joint activity of *interdependent* KAM. Indeed, we believe many of the relationships with key customers that lose money for suppliers are at the *cooperative* stage (see Figure 3.8). At this stage, the supplier is probably spending a lot on the relationship, as the number of contact points and activities grows, but the customer is not yet ready to respond with a really substantial uplift in volume.

> Many of the relationships with key customers that lose money for suppliers are at the *cooperative* stage.

While making a loss on these relationships is not inevitable, they should certainly be challenged and their profitability be properly investigated and monitored. This view strongly suggests that sticking at a *cooperative* stage is not a good idea, so you should work to move the relationship forward as quickly as possible, or carefully take it back to *basic*.

3.2.4 Interdependent relationships

In an *interdependent* relationship, the organizations collaborate across a range of functions. Interactions are orchestrated and managed by,

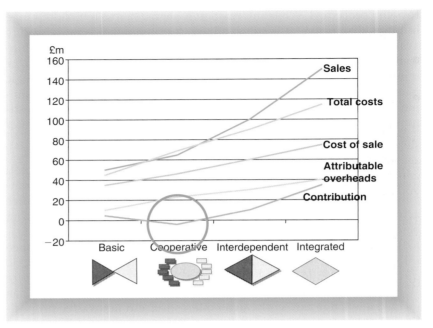

Figure 3.8
Customer profitability
and the relationship
trap.

rather than channelled through, the key account manager and the purchasing manager, whose role is now to oversee the interfaces and
ensure that nothing occurs which will discredit the partnership. The
companies are locked into each other, not inextricably, though if the
relationship were to end, retreat would be difficult and inconvenient.
They may have set up various initiatives together, such as common
working practices, shared product specifications and joint marketing
activity, which would take considerable time and effort to unravel.
Figure 3.9 shows how the two companies have become closely aligned,
with direct function-to-function communication at all levels.

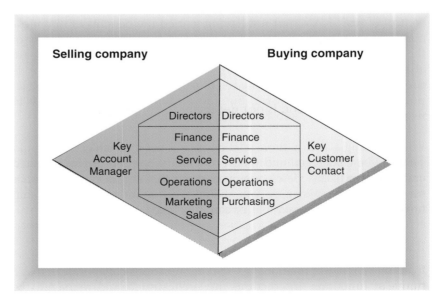

Figure 3.9
Interdependent KAM
relationship.

Remember, two characteristics of the relationship are critical in establishing the existence of an *interdependent* relationship:

- Buyer and seller both acknowledge the importance of each to the other.

- They trust each other.

Buyer and seller acknowledge the importance of each to the other.

If either of these is missing, then this is not an *interdependent* relationship. You need to bear in mind the optimism that generally leads key account managers to overestimate the relationship, because customers generally do not rate their commitment and trust at the same level as you do.

The management of this relationship is not at all like managing a *basic* or normal selling relationship. Instead of getting on and doing things him or herself, the key account manager needs to consider how to work through other people in the business, how to coordinate what they do, and how to gain an appropriate level of visibility of activity without drowning in communication and tasks. Often, this is unfamiliar and uncomfortable territory, but it is nevertheless what is required to do the job in these circumstances.

CHECKPOINT

Visualizing interdependent relationships

Draw models based on Figure 3.9 for each of your *interdependent* relationships. Put in the actual people and functions involved on both sides.

- Have you explicitly stated how this relationship will be operated and managed?

- Have you aligned your company's functions and the people in them with the customers' functions and people, so they all know their counterparts?

- Does everyone know their role in this relationship?

- Do they understand what decision-making remit they have, and when it is and is not necessary to contact you?

There is a lot going on in this kind of relationship that cannot be left to casual, ad hoc contacts. We would expect that the selling company has now become the sole or first option supplier, at least, and the customer now regards the supplier as a strategic external resource. The two will actively share sensitive information and engage in joint problem solving. There is also a tacit understanding that experience and skills will be shared. The expertise of either, or both, companies may be directed towards product improvement, quality control procedures or administrative systems that underpin commercial transactions. A current focus will be the deployment of new e-commerce systems to streamline processes. The characteristics of *interdependent* relationships are as follows:

- Both acknowledge importance to each other
- Principal or sole supplier
- Exit more difficult
- Larger number of multifunctional contacts
- Developing social relationships
- Deep understanding of customer
- High volume of dialogue
- Streamlined processes
- Exchange of sensitive information
- Proactive rather than reactive
- Both sides prepared to invest in relationship
- Wider range of joint and innovative activity
- Joint strategic planning, focus on the future
- Development of trust.

The volume, quality and scope of information exchange increases considerably in an *interdependent* relationship, as more people in the selling company are talking to more people in the buying company. Strategic and sensitive material will be added to the information previously shared, which would have been more transactional and tactical in a *cooperative* relationship, and just transactional in a *basic* relationship. This new level of communication and interaction is a key driver at this stage of the relationship. The two companies develop a better understanding of each other in a business and organizational sense, and individuals build closer social relationships with people in the other company.

The whole web of interaction and communication draws the two companies even closer together, like a positive gravitational pull. The two companies are reaching further into each other's internal environments and touching more points in the internal value chains. Team members from both companies often work together to lobby or gain senior management approval for a project. A selling company in an *interdependent* relationship is 'inside the magic circle', in contrast to the 'out in the cold' position those in *cooperative* relationships have to accept. Figure 3.10 shows the difference in information exchange between the two stages.

Such is the level of maturity and understanding of both parties that each allows the other to profit from the relationship. Consequently,

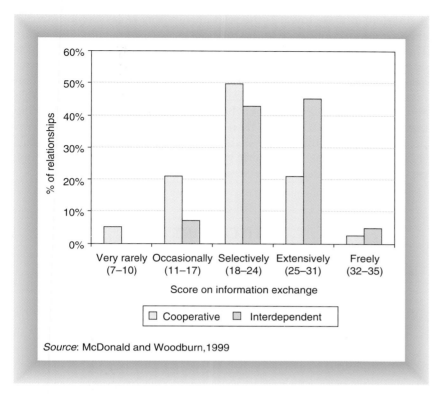

Figure 3.10
Extent of information exchange between selling and buying companies.

pricing should be long term and stable, perhaps even fixed, or varied to a formula that allows both sides to plan and removes the need for constant haggling/negotiating. Setting the expectations of both sides clearly and realistically at the outset is key to the building of successful relationships.

It is at this stage that what is arguably the most important benefit of excellent relationships with key accounts emerges: the opportunity for mutual cost reductions. At previous stages of relationship development the major opportunity for the selling company has been business development, but now, in addition, genuine cost savings also become available to both sides. In an *interdependent* relationship the companies are sufficiently well informed and familiar with each other to be able to work together closely to achieve those savings. Hence the emphasis on seriously nurturing a relationship that has reached the *interdependent* stage.

Companies in an *interdependent* relationship can focus on the medium- and longer-term future, rather than just the present and short term, and can adopt a more proactive than reactive approach to business development. Jointly conducted strategic planning begins to appear, though not in all cases. Where strategic planning is not collaborative, it is often due to the fact that the individual companies are still rather poor at strategic planning anyway.

The level of maturity and understanding of both parties allows the other to profit from the relationship.

Arguably the most important benefit of excellent relationships with key accounts emerges: the opportunity for mutual cost reductions.

A different attitude towards the relationship now exists. Senior managers have more confidence in the relationship's sustainability and value. They look more favourably on requests for investment into the development of the business, and are prepared to wait longer for the payback. Normally, financial managers demand a quick return on investment into customer accounts. They are much less comfortable about investing in a situation where they have little control over the use of funds (i.e. a customer) than they are with investing in their own people, plant or equipment. However, investing in a stable relationship should begin to look comparable with some of these other investments, especially if presented in appropriate terms, like a business case.

CHECKPOINT

Talking to finance

- Do you know how to put together a business case for customers and customer projects?

- Did you put your last customer proposal to finance in terms of a discounted cash flow/net present value?

Trust must be nurtured at all times; it is hard won and easily lost.

Mutual trust begins to develop, provided that, of course, each company has proved itself trustworthy. The key account manager and the purchasing manager must be vigilant and watch out for any opportunistic behaviour on the part of anyone in their own companies that might breach that trust. Trust must be nurtured at all times; it is hard won and easily lost.

Case study insight

Making the business case for finance in a global services company

One company reckoned it took a year to assemble and agree a proposal for investment with a customer. It took another year to deploy the money, making it at least two years before any return could possibly appear. In the initial stages of the KAM programme it was hard work to gain approval for such investment and little was granted. Then one key account manager worked closely with an accountant to put his proposals in sound financial terms and, with some reluctance, the proposal was accepted. After several projects with key customers, prepared in appropriate financial terms, the company was more comfortable with such projects and the key account managers were more comfortable with making them in the language of finance.

For example, if the selling company gains a raw material cost reduction, the production manager or product manager may decide to maintain prices to improve the profitability of the line, at least until the competition appears to be reducing their prices. That may be fine for the bulk of customers, but if key customers in an *interdependent* relationship are not informed of the cost reduction, they would see exclusion from sharing in the cost savings as opportunism on the part of the selling company, and react adversely.

Care must be taken to avoid breaches of trust inadvertently as well as deliberately, and to ensure that everyone is aware what constitutes a breach of trust in the customer's eyes. It is critical that all those involved with the relationship, in any respect, are aware of the way in which the particular customer should be treated in order to ensure that any action or decision will build, and not undermine, the position of trust achieved. *Interdependent* relationships are too precious to break accidentally.

3.2.5 *Integrated relationships*

In a few cases, it may be possible for the seller/buyer relationship to advance beyond a separated, albeit interdependent, partnership. In an *integrated* relationship the two parties come together to operate as a single entity, while maintaining their separate identities, to create value over and above what either could achieve individually. External boundaries as well as internal boundaries now fall away as the two companies realize that together they can accomplish feats previously unimaginable to either.

> The two parties come together to operate as a single entity to create value over and above what either could achieve individually.

Integrated KAM involves working together in cross-boundary functional or project teams, as depicted in Figure 3.11. By this means the

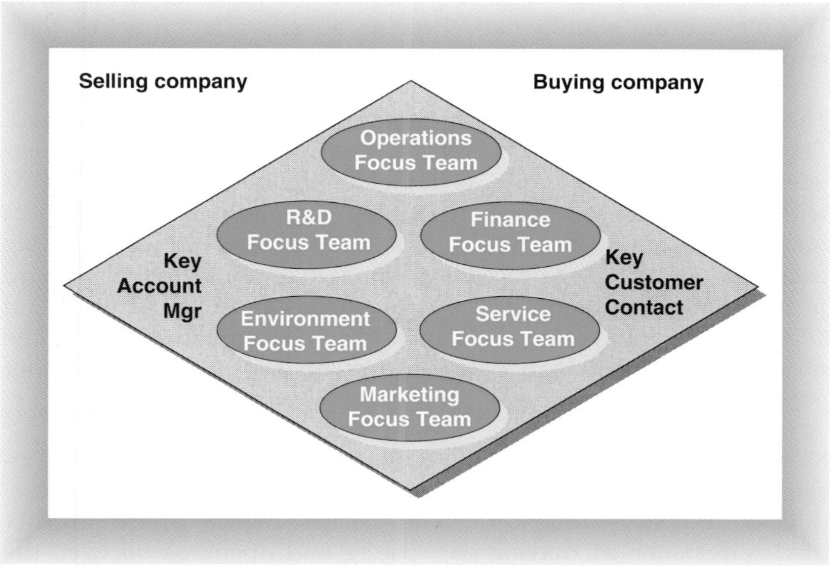

Figure 3.11
Integrated KAM relationship.

organizations become so intertwined that individuals may feel more affinity with their focus team than with their official employer. The borders between buyer and seller have become blurred. The teams, rather than either organization, run the business, making decisions about their interactions with other teams according to the strategy they are implementing. Staff may even be based at the partner's premises, though not necessarily. If it came, exit would be traumatic at both personal and organizational levels.

Case study insight

Outsourcing a vital function

Fashion is a fast-moving and fickle industry that lives or dies by its latest collection. In order to concentrate on designing and producing new clothes, a leading fashion brand decided to focus its own people and resources on the supply side and to outsource the management of its warehouse and delivery logistics to a specialist company. This company employs the logistics director, although he is treated as if he were head of one of the manufacturer's own functions. He sits on the Board and has the same access to information as any other director. The two companies keep very few secrets from each other, and the service is run on a completely open-book basis.

The roles of the key account manager and the purchasing manager have fundamentally changed. The appearance of competent teams to handle day-to-day processes and develop specified projects enables these two people to assume a more strategic role, ensuring that the whole business is moving in a profitable and sustainable direction. Troubleshooting should have become a very minor part of their activity.

The focus teams may be functional, issue based or project based. They will meet regularly, or have their own communications networks if meeting is difficult, as in global relationships. Data systems will be integrated, information flow streamlined and barriers removed. A single business plan can now be produced, linking back into the planning processes of the two organizations. *Integrated* relationships are characterized by openness and transparency that allow everyone to get on with the job of creating new value for the relationship, rather than defending themselves against the other party.

More of the benefits that start to flow from an *interdependent* relationship can be realized now. There is greater confidence in the trustworthiness and commitment of both parties, which allows further disclosures such as transparent costing and openness on even the most sensitive subjects. The feeling shared by both companies that 'we are in this together' transcends normal defensive business behaviour. The characteristics of an interdependent relationship are as follows:

- Real partnership: complementary, mutually dependent
- Few in number
- Sole supplier, possibly handling secondary suppliers
- High exit barriers, exit is traumatic
- Individual organizations subsidiary to team socially
- Dedicated, cross-boundary functional/project teams
- Open information sharing on sensitive subjects
- Transparent costing systems
- Assumption of mutual trustworthiness, at all levels
- Abstention from opportunistic behaviour
- Lowered protection against opportunism
- Joint long-term strategic planning
- Better profits for both.

Each *integrated* relationship requires the dedication of considerable resource from both sides, and the number of customers with whom a company can have this kind of relationship must therefore be very few. In fact, the number of companies who have even one *integrated* relationship appears to be small.

> The number of companies who have even one *integrated* relationship appears to be small.

It would be difficult, in most cases, to operate two such relationships in parallel within the same market area. In fast-moving consumer goods especially, advertising agencies work closely with their major clients, often for a very long time, but they can only work with one such client in each sector. Top clients are unwilling to trust an agency that is working with a competitor, however much it claims to operate sealed cells inside its business.

> It would be difficult to operate two such relationships in parallel within the same market area.

Since both parties work so closely together in an *integrated* relationship, any opportunistic behaviour would be spotted very quickly. In fact, as the relationship will have established itself within both companies and its value will be generally accepted, the chances of anyone taking inappropriate decisions should be much less than at the lower level of relationship development.

Mutually transparent costing in this kind of relationship should not be mistaken for the approach used in some sectors, such as retail and car manufacturing, where powerful buyers have demanded open-book accounting from suppliers in a weak position, in return for continuing to do business at all. A liaison between unequals, in which certain aspects of a relationship are dictated by the more powerful partner, should not be confused with a genuinely open and collaborative relationship with a key account.

Overall, an *integrated* relationship offers the best chance of maximizing opportunities to cut costs, develop a broader business base, enhance expertise, make creative and innovative approaches to the market, and secure a long-term future. As relationships at the *integrated* stage cannot be numerous, they should be especially well chosen and very well managed.

3.2.6   Disintegrating relationships

At any time and at any stage, the relationship can fall apart. Breakdown may occur for one or more of a number of reasons (Table 3.3), for example a takeover of either company, which changes its position in the marketplace and means that it now competes with the other company in some way. Changes of key people, especially the principals engaged in the relationship; changes in structure, so that production is moved to another country; changes in culture, from added-value to lean; and, indeed, many other changes, are potentially dangerous.

> Price or product is rarely the reason for relationship breakdown.

Table 3.3
Causes of *disintegrating* relationships

Change	Relationship	Performance
Key personnel Market positions New culture, organization ownership	Key account manager's approach or lack of skills Failure to forge multilevel links Breach of trust Complacency	Prolonged poor performance against agreed programme

Price or product is not that often the reason for relationship breakdown. Ultimately, however, a customer will have to buy from the supplier who gives them what they need, however good the relationship, so suppliers cannot afford to be complacent about their core offer. Relationships facilitate business: they are not an end in themselves, and you should remember that they are not what the customer is buying.

Poor performance is much less often the cause of disintegration than might be supposed, at least, not from an *interdependent* relationship. In fact, if a supplier has built up a good relationship, then it may get a surprising amount of tolerance for poor performance, provided that the customer understands what the supplier is planning to do to remedy the situation, and sees that it is making every effort to implement the remedy.

More commonly, disintegration is caused by failure at the heart of the relationship, which depends very much on the key account manager.

Some customers are quite clear with their supplier if they do not like their key account manager, and get a replacement, but others would rather give up on the relationship without explaining why. Customers are frequently frustrated by the inability of the key account manager or supplier organization, or both, to appreciate the vision of what they are trying to achieve and to be prepared to play a part in it, rather than just sell goods or services. In some cases this is a limitation of the key account manager, but in other cases it is the fault of a 'deaf' and complacent supplier.

So a failure to forge multilevel links with the customer may be the key account manager's fault, but it may equally be the fault of the supplier, which does not have and is not prepared to develop an interesting proposition for the customer that would warrant the attention of anyone other than the buyer.

Disintegration can be sudden and followed by exit, or it may be prolonged through a return to a lower level of relationship where the companies continue to do business together, but on different terms. In any case, *disintegrating* KAM is a purely transitional stage, not a stable state, as any of the other stages can be. Given the complexity of some relationships and the variety of links involved, disengagement may take some time, so *disintegrating* KAM may last for quite a long while.

> The business developer who was ideal at the growth stage is unlikely to be the right person to manage a *disintegrating* relationship.

The key account manager's role may change to one of damage limitation. The business developer who was ideal at the growth stage is unlikely to be the right person to manage a *disintegrating* relationship.

Summary

Understanding the nature of key relationships, and the behaviour of companies involved in them, is crucial to the profitable management of the business they represent. Without it, companies can easily attempt inappropriate strategies, which are unlikely to succeed. Failure may be expensive, both in terms of actual expenditure and lost opportunity.

Five stages of key supplier/customer relationships have been identified. To characterize the nature of the relationship from the point of view of either party, they are described as *exploratory* (precedes actual trading), *basic, cooperative, interdependent* and *integrated*. Relationships may develop progressively through each stage in turn, or they may not. They can also start at a fairly mature stage in certain circumstances where multi-sourcing is inappropriate, for example, or they can remain at any given level indefinitely.

Disintegration may occur at any stage, for a large number of reasons. More distant, less sophisticated relationships (*basic, cooperative*) are more vulnerable than closer relationships (*interdependent, integrated*), which is why suppliers, in particular, are often keen to develop them further. However, companies have a limited capacity for intimacy, partly because of the potentially heavy costs associated with key relationships, and they should choose very carefully the partners with whom they wish to develop close ties.

Suppliers at a lower stage of relationship development have to work hard to overcome the self-perpetuating cycle of being kept 'in the dark' and 'out in the cold'. Recognition of their current relationship position should at least help them to identify what action to take in order to break the pattern.

The key features of the five types of relationship are summarized in Table 3.4.

Table 3.4 Summary of development stage characteristics

Relationship feature	Exploratory	Basic	Cooperative	Interdependent	Integrated
Relationship emphasis	Research, reputation	Transactional and price	Mainly transactional but positive	Mutual and developmental	Open and strategically focused
Supplier status	One of several/many	May be one of several	Preferred	Principal or sole, possibly managing secondary suppliers	Sole, possibly primary
Ease of exit	Easy: not started trading	Easy	Not difficult, slight inconvenience	Difficult	High exit barriers, separation traumatic
Information sharing	Careful, as necessary	Very little, based around transactions	Limited	High volume, some sensitive	Open, even on sensitive subjects
Contact	Channelled through individual key account manager	Channelled through key account manager and Buyer	Close: key account manager and Buyer, Logistics and Order Processing. Occasional: others	Close: all functions as necessary	Intimate: focus groups and teams
Access to customer	Customer request only	Limited	More, but not quite enough	Much more, enough	Constant, both sides
Adaptation of organization and processes	Standard	Standard	Mainly standard	Streamlining of processes, some organizational adaptation	Joint processes, new organization
Relationship costs	May be small or large. Speculative investment	Limited	Increasing for selling company, few savings if any	Major running costs and investment, offset by savings and more business	As for interdependent: probably larger sums but easier to identify
Level of trust	Exploring reputation and 'signals'	Neither trusted nor mistrusted	Not wholly trusted	Real trust developing, protective barriers lowered	Trustworthiness assumed at all levels
Planning	Variable	Little or none, probably only short-term forecasts if any	Forecasting rather than planning	Joint strategic planning, though not all cases	Joint strategic, long-term planning
Relationship potential	Important, to qualify as key account	Limited	Could be good, but not easy to win from here	Very good	Very good/excellent in revenue and profits

4 Developing key relationships

Most companies embarking on key account management (KAM) are hoping to develop their customer relationships. We hope you will do so having first decided, very carefully, which ones are suitable for development – because some are not.

But what does deciding to develop a relationship mean? How do you know where to start? Charm has very limited leverage in corporate purchasing today and, indeed, the procurement department will make sure that it does not count for much. If you want to be a key supplier, much more tangible value is expected.

In fact, the way to a customer's heart is through its business – not your business. As a minimum, the customer expects its key suppliers to understand:

- Its marketplace
- Its strategies
- What its customers want
- How it adds value in its business
- Where it makes its money.

There are no shortcuts that are likely to last, so Chapters 7 and 8 give you a systematic process to gain the deep customer understanding you need, plus a process to help you come up with strategies that add value to the customer's business. Added value (for the customer, not necessarily for you) is what gains commitment. Your company is expected to bring an ongoing stream of value propositions to the customer, and you cannot possibly do that without a real understanding of what adds value and why, where and when.

Customers classify suppliers according to the potential they have to bring value to their business, in terms of the supply-side market risk and their purchasing power. If what you have to offer is, in the customer's eyes, a commodity product delivered in a commoditized way, you are wasting your time trying to build a relationship. What would they gain? Customers, like suppliers, have a limited capacity for intimacy, and they will use what capacity they have where it gives them most advantage.

Given a strong foundation of customer understanding, relationship development can be accelerated through doing a good job of mapping the people inside the customer who matter to you, and deciding with whom you want to have your relationships. You should also decide who, in your organization, will be the 'owner' of that relationship – no key account manager can or should 'own' them all. Rather, it is the key account manager's job to encourage and build a balanced set of relationships from top to bottom of both organizations, supporting the supplier's staff in working out strategies to help their counterparts in the customer organization. Rather than responding to purely personal needs, ideally, they will be adding value to the contact's working life and area of the business, which is a more robust way to build a relationship anyway.

Many people seem to believe that relationships 'just grow', but if you have good business development strategies and adopt a process of applying them through good relationship development strategies, you should really be a winner with your customers. Try picking the features of an *interdependent* relationship and working on those alongside your business development strategies. The synergistic effect of the two together should give the relationship and its outcomes some real acceleration. Having achieved the relationship your company wants, there are a few traps to be avoided. They may seem obvious when simply stated but, sadly, they appear quite frequently:

- complacency
- lapses in integrity
- leaking profitability.

Relationships with key customers can and should be developed with purpose and with process (see Chapter 9). These relationships are too valuable and too risky to leave to any less focused approach.

Introduction

Suppliers are keen to push their key account managers out of the office to develop relationships with customers, frequently overlooking the obvious fact that customers have a strong point of view of their own on whether it is worth spending time with your company or not. Not surprisingly, customers do not care whether the conversation would add value to your business. They are as short of resources as any other company, and they cannot afford to waste them in conversations that add no tangible value to their business.

So when key account managers do get in front of a customer, they need to have something interesting to say, which means they need a real and deep understanding of the customer's business, just as a beginning. This chapter describes what customers now expect from their key suppliers, while Chapter 7 explains how to analyse a customer to gain the level of understanding required. Chapter 8 goes on to show how to create worthwhile strategies that keep the customer interested.

Running alongside the development of those business strategies, however, there should also be relationship development strategies. While not enough on their own, suppliers can apply some useful tools and techniques to develop their relationships more quickly and more successfully.

4.1 The customer's point of view

4.1.1 What do customers want?

The kind of customer that is attractive to your company is probably seen as equally attractive to your competitors. They are likely to be the market leaders, the innovative companies who succeed and go on succeeding, year in and year out. Either they already have a very substantial business which is still growing, or they have great potential and are on a steep upward path. Such companies have plenty of choice in suppliers, and if your company is not giving them what they want, they will be welcomed with open arms by your competition. Having said that, most customers do not want the upheaval and cost of changing suppliers unless they have good reason to change.

Obviously, if customers are getting what they want from a relationship, then they will stay with it. However, suppliers often fail to recognize all the potential benefits of the relationship to the customer, so they overestimate the value of a few elements of support they offer, and oversupply them too, while underestimating the importance of some of the other things they can do.

Some worthwhile initiatives might appear from seeing a broader list of benefits, such as that below, which was collated from the advantages cited by customers in our research:

- Trust – always behaving appropriately
- Leverage – something unique, and not always price
- Unique competitive advantage/customization – or else why bother?
- Cost reduction – without sacrificing value targets
- Simplicity – reducing their complexity
- Continuity – being around in the future as well as the present
- Supply chain integration – smoother, cheaper
- Global consistency – the same offer, anywhere
- Consultancy – calling on the supplier's expertise
- Strategic concentration of resources and investment – where worthwhile.

Above all, customers want suppliers they can trust and with whom they can build open, trusting relationships. Trust may be defined as: 'The expectation that a company will behave in a predictable and mutually acceptable way.' That works up to a point, but a customer expects more from a supplier with which it has substantial business and a close relationship than it does from one from which it buys a modest amount of commodity products. Indeed, the customer looks for different minimum levels of trustworthiness at different stages in the relationship, as Figure 4.1 shows.

Essential in:		Customer expects supplier to:
All relationships	**Contractual Trust**	• Keep promises (written and oral) • Abide by accepted rules of business practice and behaviour
All, except possibly *basic* relationships	**Competence Trust**	• Perform competently (technical, managerial etc.) • Operate in accordance with professional standards
Interdependent and *integrated* relationships	**Goodwill Trust**	• Show 'open' commitment, willing to do more than formally required • Potentially accede to partner requests or to any observed performance-improving opportunity • Refrain from opportunistic behaviour

Figure 4.1
Customer expectations of minimum levels of trust and relationship.

Most customers have thousands of suppliers, and if the bulk of them fulfil the terms of their contracts, that will be seen as quite adequate in transaction-focused relationships and is, indeed, the least that is expected in any trading relationship. Relationships would not reach a *cooperative* stage unless the customer believed in the supplier's competence, but even that is not enough for a key supplier at an *interdependent* stage of relationship. Key customers interpret trustworthiness differently at this level, and they look for a flexible response within the spirit of the relationship which is known as 'goodwill trust', when the customer expects that, however circumstances change, the supplier will endeavour to deliver what is best to meet new needs.

> Key customers expect a flexible response within the spirit of the relationship, not the letter of the contract.

Trust may be the first thing that customers want from a key supplier, but it is not the last thing, by any means. As David Heede, Director of Purchasing at Coors Brewers, said, 'We want a key supplier who shares our vision and is a competitive weapon for us! We expect tangible, measurable, substantive evidence of (suppliers') short-term contribution toward our long term vision.'

> 'We want a key supplier who shares our vision and is a competitive weapon for us!'

In common with many other key customers, Heede looked for suppliers who anticipated his company's needs. He wanted proactive suppliers who would spot supply chain weaknesses, point them out and help come up with solutions. Some suppliers still say, 'We'll do anything the customer asks us to do', without realizing that the customer sees innovation in the supplier's offer as the supplier's job, not theirs. After all, the customer is not an expert in your business, so how can you expect them to know what to ask for? However, if you are an expert in their business, and also understand your own, then you should be able to suggest some new and relevant ideas to them.

> The customer sees innovation in the supplier's offer as the supplier's job, not theirs.

In the past, suppliers could just explain their products, negotiate price and fulfil the deal, but clearly that is nothing like enough now. Some are still trying to take the short cut to the sale but, without a far deeper understanding of the customer's business, they will not build the relationships they seek.

4.1.2 A deep understanding of the customer

Customers are aware that salespeople's expressions of interest in their business are mostly only skin deep. The perception is that they will collect just enough facts to sprinkle through their selling arguments, but that they do not make the effort to understand the customer's marketplace or its position and strategies in its marketplace. Whether that is because the salesperson does not have the time or the inclination or the intellectual capacity is immaterial: the customer perceives that the supplier is only interested in what it can extract from the relationship, without trying to add value to it, and responds accordingly.

Case study insight

A retailer's reaction to superficial approaches

A major retailer clearly recognized the surface-deep approach of most of its suppliers. The purchasing director said, 'Last January they came in here in their droves, with their PowerPoint presentations and their flipcharts – I think they'd all been on the same course – but it was just the same as usual. They called it "strategic planning" but it was all about how much more we were going to buy from them. They didn't bother with what we wanted, so we just ignored it all.'

Best practice suppliers realize the importance of understanding the customer and put real resource behind it. EDS, for example, has sector specialists that form part of the team that works with individual key customers. Other companies put resource into hiring market analysts who collect, interpret and distribute the information required by their key account managers. The understanding of the customer's world and the customer's business cannot be outsourced by the key account manager, but it can be made more accessible and easier to acquire.

As one purchasing director said, 'We want our key suppliers to help us realize our objectives. To do that, they have to understand our business, understand our marketplace and understand how we accumulate value: how we add value to our customers, and how we make money in our business.' This is a long way from 'Seven Steps to Closing the Sale', but it is the way forward in developing relationships with key customers.

> Key account managers' 'value-added strategies' add a lot more value to the supplier than to the customer. Not surprisingly, they often fail.

We have heard a lot of talk about key account managers' 'value-added strategies', but even a cursory examination shows that these strategies add a lot more value to the supplier than to the customer. Not surprisingly, they often fail, because the 'what's in it for me?' is missing for the customer – so why should they disturb what they already have in place? But if you understand how your customer adds value to their customers, you will see many more ways of really adding value to your customer than you did before.

IBM was one of the earliest adopters of key account management (KAM) and among the first to appreciate what best practice should look like. Every year, it tasked its global account managers with building on their in-depth understanding of their customers to identify or create at least one strategy for each customer that did *not* involve selling more IT equipment or services – as a purely added-value contribution to the customer. Not only did it demonstrate how well they knew their customers, it also showed that IBM would support them without expecting any direct return. Figure 4.2 illustrates the layers of understanding that suppliers need to consider when analysing a customer and its market.

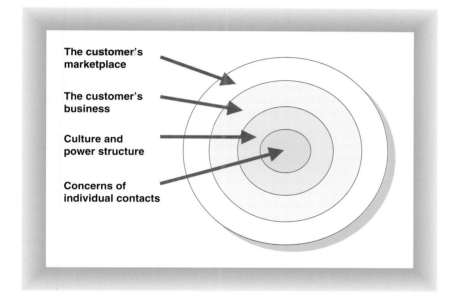

The customer's marketplace

The customer's business

Culture and power structure

Concerns of individual contacts

Figure 4.2
Layers of understanding of the customer.

To gain a deep understanding of the customer's business:

● collect and analyse all the information you have and all the information you can get about the customer and its marketplace,

● work out what that means in terms of its likely issues and strategies,

● sit down with the customer and see what is correct, what needs to be amended, and confirm what the analysis means in terms of its strategies,

● clarify what the customer expects of your company.

At Cranfield School of Management, we have shown a large number of key account managers how to approach this exercise, starting with

It is astonishing that something as obvious as analysing the customer's marketplace is still so neglected.

the customer's defining reality – its marketplace – the importance of which is often overlooked. We have had many reports that such engagement in understanding the customer's business, even on its own, has helped immensely in developing their relationships, and developing them into territory they had never reached before. It is astonishing that something as obvious as analysing the customer's marketplace is still so neglected.

Case study insight

IMI Cornelius: developing a relationship through aligning strategy

IMI Cornelius specializes in drinks dispense systems. When it first started working with Bass (later bought by Coors Brewers) it focused on providing excellently engineered equipment. As the company began to understand the customer and the beer business better, it realized that its equipment represented the brand at the point of sale and played a very important role in the consumer experience. The key account manager studied the beer market and consumer behaviour, and changed IMI Cornelius's mission for the customer from maximizing its own sales to supporting the customer in developing beer consumption. Together the two companies came up with some excellent ideas, including Arc – beer frozen at the point of pouring. The relationship survived and indeed thrived after the takeover by Coors, and the business grew substantially over five years.

If your relationship with your customer is already close and *interdependent*, then you should have much of the information that you need, and you can go on to work to develop strategies for building the business you have together. If your relationship with your customer is at a more transactional stage, at a *basic* or *cooperative* level, then try 'putting yourself in the customer's shoes' and carry out a strategic analysis of the customer as if you were yourself in the customer's position. You will be able to understand not only the pressures that its people face, but also how they are likely to respond (see Chapter 7 on how to analyse a customer).

Customers generally do not explicitly tell suppliers which generic supplier management strategy has been selected for them, but that does not make it any less real.

In addition, suppliers should understand the customer's supplier management strategies (see Section 5.2), in order to understand how the customer sees them and whether they will want to develop a relationship. It should come as no surprise to learn that buyers operate strategies for working with suppliers that run parallel to those that selling companies use. That view governs the attention they get and the treatment they receive. Customers generally do not explicitly tell suppliers which generic supplier management strategy has been selected for them, but that does not make it any less real. Buyers are more inclined to 'let them work it out for themselves'. The problem is that many suppliers have clearly failed to work it out for themselves, maybe because they do not want to face up to that task and its implications.

Customers may apply different strategies to different products, and they may apply different strategies to the same products at different times. For example, their strategy may depend on the stage in the product's lifecycle, which will affect the choice of suppliers. The relationship with you as a company will largely be managed by the prevailing strategy for your products, with some variation if they are buying a range of items from you.

KAM will not compensate for an inadequate marketing strategy and undifferentiated, commoditized offers, and applying it against all the indications that the customer is 'agog with indifference' will only result in misdirected, wasted resources. You will need to understand your customer's buying strategies as well as their business strategies.

> KAM will not compensate for an inadequate marketing strategy and undifferentiated, commoditized offers

4.2   Developing relationships

4.2.1   Choosing the right relationship stage

Before you start to develop a relationship, you should first decide what stage of relationship you want to reach and believe is achievable with the customer. That choice will govern how you approach the relationship, even in the early stages, and how much your company invests in it. The *cooperative* stage should not be seen as an ultimate choice, but as a transition stage not to be prolonged unnecessarily.

The relationship you want to have with the customer should depend on the category into which the customer falls (see Section 2.3.1). What would be the point in aiming for an *interdependent* relationship with a customer you intend to manage for cash because of their relentless pressure on prices? Similarly, it would be impossible to apply strategic investment to a customer with whom the relationship was still at the *basic* level: the initiative would be hampered by the lack of contacts, limited understanding of the customer, and limited interest from the customer's side.

The matrix that categorizes customers by strategy, together with a version that overlays the portfolio with appropriate levels of relationship, is shown in Figure 4.3.

> What would be the point in aiming for an *interdependent* relationship with a customer you intend to manage for cash because of their relentless pressure on prices?

Many people make the mistake of thinking that KAM means the development of close relationships with all selected customers. We would say that all of the customers in the portfolio are key accounts defined by the supplier's categorization criteria, but that they should be recognized as being different in nature and hence different in their treatment. That includes choosing the 'right' level of relationship to have, which will often *not* be *interdependent* or *integrated*. The matrix

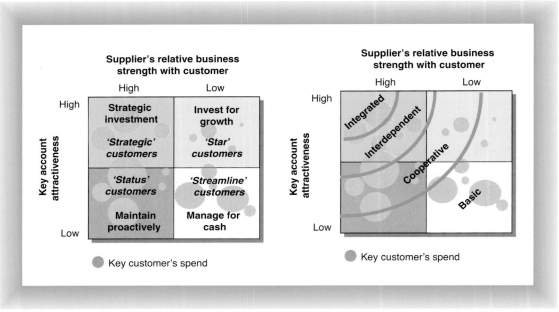

Figure 4.3   Matching relationship level with key customer strategies.

should drive the relationship stages targeted, although they do not fall exactly into the four boxes. However, it indicates that:

- *Basic* relationships are for:
  - 'streamline' customers (see Section 2.3.1) offered a 'manage for cash' treatment
  - declining 'status' customers
  - 'star' customers with whom not much progress has yet been made.

- *Cooperative* relationships are for:
  - growing 'star' customers
  - 'status' customers where the relationship is being scaled down from *interdependent*.

- *Interdependent* relationships are for:
  - the majority of 'strategic' customers.
- *Integrated* relationships are for:
  - a few, exceptional, 'strategic' customers.

Taking into account the limited number of *interdependent* and *integrated* relationships that any supplier can handle (see Section 2.1.3), it is clearly important to consider very carefully how many of this kind of relationship can be sustained, and which companies will be targeted. It is not at all a good idea to give key account managers free rein to develop any of their customers as they see fit, because the company will be unable to support all of them. Indeed, the relationship level targeted should be included in the strategic account plan and formally approved.

> It is not at all a good idea to give key account managers free rein to develop any of their customers as they see fit.

4.2.2   Contact mapping

Of course, you need to understand the people in your customer's company and their positions in it, particularly those who affect your business. As early as you can in developing the relationship, build up a structured picture of them in a way that allows you to add more information as you find it. At the least, you will need a chart of the customer's formal organization so that you can see who reports to whom.

You can improve on this kind of chart in a number of ways. For example, consider building up a picture of the informal information-sharing networks that operate within the customer, so you can best decide how to spread the messages that you want transmitted inside the company. This will take some time, investigation and experience. Meanwhile, you can make better use of the organization chart by superimposing onto it two critical pieces of information for each person/position; first, how important are they to your business with the customer, and second, what is the status of your relationship with them currently? Figure 4.4

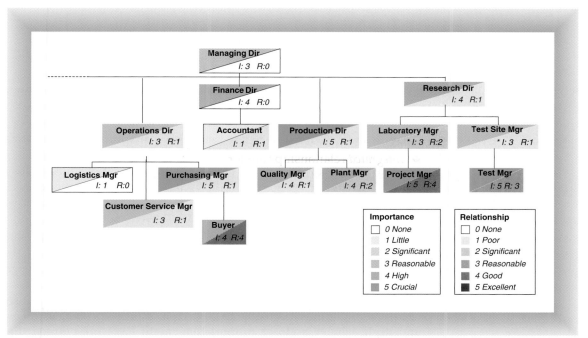

Figure 4.4   Customer organization chart overlaid with contact importance and relationship.

shows how this would look, together with scales for these two pieces of information, importance and relationship.

'Importance' here means relevance and influence in your business with the customer, not the individual's seniority within their own company. You can assign importance on a simple, intuitive scale of 0–5, or it may be more objectively evaluated by using criteria; like the extent of the position's involvement in activities relating to your area of interest, or the position's role in innovation, or the power of the position in making decisions on choosing between suppliers, etc.

Similarly, 'relationship' may be judged directly, or through drawing up a scale of thumbnail sketches of the relationship against each score. Avoid assessing the relationship in terms of how they feel about you personally: you should be assessing their relationship with your company, rather than you as an individual.

CHECKPOINT

Customer contacts

- Do you have an up-to-date copy of your customer's organization chart?
- Do you understand the relevance and importance of each person/position to your business?
- Do you know how each feels about your company?
- Have you looked at the overall picture and identified relationship gaps that need to be addressed?

Case study insight

The right relationships in the wrong places

One company reported that it had excellent, level 4 and 5 relationships in one of its key customers. However, when it added importance and relationship to the customer's organization chart, it became apparent that these relationships were mostly with people they worked with day to day, but that relationships with key decision makers were few and weak. At about the same time, they received the news that a director of their main competitor had been appointed as a non-executive director on the customer's Board. Their best relationships were in the wrong places, not with people who really mattered.

If this company had seen the gaps in its relationship sooner and more clearly, it might have been able to target senior people in the customer and itself achieve a closer rapport that might have pre-empted the competition winning a seat on the Board. It was now faced with accepting a position as an 'also-ran', or a very tough task to regain parity.

CHECKPOINT

Are your relationships with the right people?

- Are your strong relationships with people who are really important, or are they with nice, friendly, but less important people?

- Do you have any poor or weak relationships with people who are important?

- Are your relationships balanced across relevant areas of the company, or are there gaps in certain functions?

- Do you cover all levels in the customer or are you over-concentrated in one level? Are you missing certain levels like the Board, or the user level?

Visual representations of the situation are invaluable in making diagnoses and decisions, but you are likely to need software to help you coordinate and keep information up to date on all customer contacts as well. Make sure that you keep within the Data Protection Act if you are operating in the UK or in another country with similar legislation, and be careful if you are sharing information with subsidiaries in other countries that may not operate under the same restrictions. Very broadly, you should have no problems if you save information which relates to the post but not to the individual who holds it. Consider whether you would be comfortable if the customer demanded to see the information, and check your company's policy.

In large organizations there is constant change of personnel, as people enter and leave the company and, in many cases, people move on to new jobs internally every two years as well. Add to that the regular restructurings which seem to be a feature of corporate life and you will see that updating your contact map needs to be a regular and frequent exercise.

Updating your contact map needs to be a regular and frequent exercise.

In *interdependent* and *integrated* relationships, and also in *cooperative* relationships which are being managed towards *interdependence*, the links with customer contacts need to be shared out to the key account team and beyond, to ensure that each receives the attention he or she deserves. In order to manage the intercompany relationship, the key account manager needs a structured view of these interactions, such as that shown in Figure 4.5. This table is a simple way of capturing who (in your company) has links with whom (in the customer), and how good those relationships are. A similar scale can be used here as well as for the organization chart at the beginning of this section, reflecting the relationship between the individual in the customer and

Supplier	Customer					
Staff	R Downly	W Brady	S Potter	V Bingley	D Plowright	T Trevor
N Marrer	2 > **4**		4 > **5**		1 > **2**	
O Lilley		3 > **5**				2 > **4**
G Frome		1 > **2**		1 > **3**		
H Dennis				2 > **3**	3 > **4**	

Relationship strength on scale of 0 to 5 (bold = target level)
Relationship 'owner' or principal contact denoted by ☐

Figure 4.5
Mapping team-based relationships.

the supplier as a company. It also allows targets to be set for the individuals in your company to develop that relationship to a higher level, not just on a personal basis, but on behalf of the company.

Furthermore, the 'owner' of the relationship, or principal contact, can be identified by simply highlighting the relationship (e.g. with a blue box, as in the example in Figure 4.5). It should tell anyone who wishes to talk to a contact in the customer that it will be a good idea to have a word with the relationship 'owner' first, to understand how his or her approach might fit in with other activity and communication.

Just giving people a target does not necessarily help them understand how to develop a relationship, so most fall back on dinner and golf, which are not the only ways of doing it, nor even welcome in many cases today. Alternative strategies and ideas are needed, and discussed in the next section.

4.2.3 Relationship-building strategies

If building relationships is at the core of the key account manager's job, should it be left to the individual's intuition and luck?

Asked about how his company's key account managers went about building relationships, one sales director said, 'I can't tell you. We just assume they know how to do it.' Well, often they don't. His attitude is common enough, if rather curious. How often in other parts of the company are people appointed to do a very specific job and then left to do it without training, guidance or even observation? If building relationships is at the core of the key account manager's job, should it be left to the individual's intuition and luck? Or would their efforts stand a better – and earlier – chance of success if they were supported with structured approaches and visible processes?

Relationships between complex companies are about much more than the chemistry between two people. The range and nature of the links is

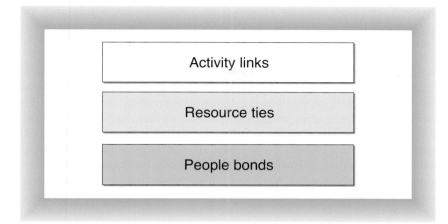

Figure 4.6
Intercompany
relationship layers.

potentially large and varied. However, many key account managers still believe in the overriding importance of 'people bonds' to the exclusion of many other levers that they could and should operate, if they want to build robust relationships with customers. Professor Ivan Snehota (Håkansson and Snehota, 1995) identified three layers in inter-company relationships (see Figure 4.6). While people bonds are impor-tant, they are not an end in themselves, just as customer satisfaction is not an end in itself: it is an intermediary objective in delivering a sus-tainable stream of business. Your objective should be to develop such links with the people who can help put into place the other perhaps more robust and valuable elements of the relationship, which might involve better coordination through activity links, or investing in change through resource ties. This is likely to mean approaching people outside your normal sphere of operations who are therefore outside your 'comfort zone', but it is the route to lasting relationships.

> While people bonds are important, they are not an end in themselves.

The three layers identified by Snehota are:

- **Activity links:** Broadly, these are based around activities your company and your customer do together – like joint training, joint marketing campaigns, joint planning – which are often aimed at coordination of effort.

- **Resource ties:** These may be considered as investments – such as R&D projects, a jointly owned warehouse, or a new IT system used by both – which indicate and require a commitment between the two parties.

- **People bonds:** Only through interacting with people do any of the above get agreed and implemented, so people are the facilitators of all these other links, hence their importance.

It is easy to lose your way in relationship development. Everyone finds it more congenial to be welcomed by a friendly face in the buying com-pany than to push forward to meet new people who speak unfamiliar languages, like finance and IT, who are not convinced that they want to meet suppliers anyway. However, you should focus firmly on your purpose, which is, after all, the development of the intercompany relationship, not comfortable socializing.

Some key account managers believe that getting close to their contacts means meals and entertainment. This kind of approach has its place in developing relationships but it is often overemphasized. It is not the only way of developing relationships and, increasingly, not the most appropriate. Many customer staff, for example, those in the public sector and quite a few big companies, are not allowed to accept hospitality, and others simply do not have the time or inclination for it. They may work long days and have to fight to preserve their private space, so they do not really want it taken up by suppliers. Certainly, key account managers need to understand the customer's attitude to hospitality before offering it. Acceptance of hospitality from suppliers is often a cultural issue, which may stem from the national culture, the industry or sector, or the culture of that particular organization.

However, remember that the customer's staff are always representing the company that employs them. Very often, delivering a benefit to their area of the business is a better way of satisfying their objectives. In fact, delivering a business benefit might satisfy more than one individual's agenda, as well as having a more visible and enduring effect than any dinner or sporting event. Consider how you might add value in their business life: if you can save them hassle or make them business heroes, you will be building a strong relationship.

Of course, the intercompany relationship will necessarily be achieved through relationships with individuals. As Figure 4.7 suggests, both types of relationship have to be considered in determining strategies: the organizational level determines the overall nature, depth and opportunities of the relationship, but understanding and working at the individual level is crucial in facilitating it.

Suppliers talk a lot about 'added-value' strategies. However, the customer's view of what it perceives as adding value is somewhat different. They expect product support, training for their people about your products, providing accessible information about your products and services, etc. as part of the package, and do not regard them as 'value-adding' services, even though they cost your company money to deliver. From the customer's point of view, these are all things that promote or support the sales of your product, which they see as adding value to your business at least as much as, or more than, to theirs. Such services may be useful, but they often see them as something they pay for in the price of the product. Consider the definition of value expressed in the following equation:

$$\text{Value} = \text{Perceived benefit} - \text{Perceived sacrifice (price/cost)}$$

The value calculated by this equation must be greater than 0 in order to gain a perception of added value in the customer's eyes. So, to build

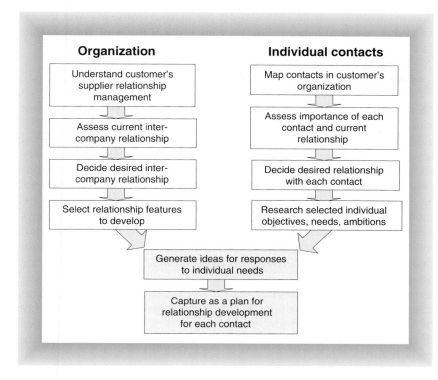

Figure 4.7
Combining organization and individual levels in relationship-building strategies.

the relationship through adding value, you need to increase the customer's perception of the benefit received without increasing their price/cost.

> ## CHECKPOINT
>
> ### Do you add value to your customer?
>
> Which of the following or similar initiatives have you put into practice for your key customer in the last year?
>
> ● Help with solving glitches in their processes?
>
> ● Saving cost for their department?
>
> ● Providing useful information from your organization that is not readily available to them: market research data, for example?
>
> ● Lending them an expert to advise on something which is new to them?
>
> ● Supporting training for their staff to develop their skills (not training on your products)?

Added-value strategies are excellent relationship developers, which work really well when fitted to the needs of the company and the needs of the individual at work as well. In particular, those activities that involve interaction between people in your company and theirs, and have practical benefits, are very effective at building bridges that can come into play on other occasions as well.

4.2.4   Building an interdependent relationship

Most commonly, the aspirational level of relationship in key account management is *interdependent*, since *basic* relationships are not hard to achieve, and the *cooperative* stage is best regarded as a transitional level. *Interdependent* relationships generally demonstrate the features shown in Figure 4.8. If you want to develop an *interdependent* relationship, try working on developing these features specifically. However, as Figure 4.8 suggests, there is, to some extent, an order of development: for example, you should map the people in the customer's organization and understand their positions before you spend too much time developing relationships. You may be using your time on people who are ultimately irrelevant. Similarly, you should facilitate an exchange of information that allows you to understand the customer very well before you embark on a joint strategic planning exercise, when you want to make a contribution through your knowledge of the customer's business, rather than exposing your ignorance of it. Table 4.1 contains some ideas on how to go about developing these features.

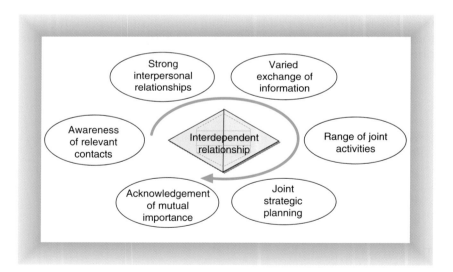

Figure 4.8
Features of
interdependent
relationships.

More companies are adopting joint strategic planning as a regular part of the way they do business with their key accounts.

Ideally, strategic planning should be carried out jointly. Our original research showed that joint strategic planning (longer term than straightforward action planning) was found in only about a third of even the most important relationships (based on the top two or three in each case), so it was even more rare with key customers as a whole. However, best practice is spreading and more companies are adopting joint strategic planning as a regular part of the way they do business with their key accounts.

Table 4.1 Building relationships through developing specific features

Relationship feature	Aim	Hints
Awareness of relevant contacts	All relevant contacts in the customer organization identified, mapped and researched	Increase quantity of contacts (number of people) Increase quality of contact (contacts' importance to your company) (see Section 4.2.2)
Strong interpersonal relationship	Strong relationships with relevant contacts developed	Pair contact with designated member of staff (see Section 4.2.2) Develop specific relationship strategies for each (see Section 4.2.3)
Varied exchange of information	Two-way sharing of a range range of information, sometimes confidential	Assess existing inventory of knowledge and gaps Create a need to know and address requests to information holders
Range of joint activities	Joint participation in activities outside simple buying and selling, possibly joint marketing, IT projects, R&D projects, training, etc.	Develop list of value-adding options (see Section 4.2.3) Propose those with most benefit for both parties
Joint strategic planning	Joint analysis of the market situation and formulation of a joint strategy for business development, annually at least	Identify worthwhile outcome of investment of time for senior people on both sides Clarify process and schedule well in advance Create some kind of innovation (see Chapter 7)
Acknowledgement of mutual importance	Explicit recognition by both sides of their importance to each other	Develop and manage individual and organizational trustworthiness Encourage public expressions of relationship, at the right time

The relationship is the all-important medium that facilitates business growth, and deserves its own development strategies. Key account strategic plans should contain not only business strategies, but also statements of how the relationship itself will be developed.

A healthy medium is needed to support the interactions that will translate the agreed strategic intent into customized value propositions, and the interactions that will facilitate their delivery as part of regular operations. Everything will move forward faster and better when facilitated by a good intercompany relationship while if, on the other hand, the relationship is poor, the process will be slow, difficult, expensive, fraught with misunderstanding, and likely to have a disappointing outcome.

4.3   Managing relationships

4.3.1   Multilevel relationships

Healthy, close relationships with customers should function at all levels in the supplier. Each participant should have a role assigned, even the most senior, and the operation of those roles should be coordinated by the key account manager. Indeed, that is what a large part of the job becomes at an *interdependent* level. Different levels have different roles to play:

- **Senior management** may only meet each other occasionally, but the links are there to confirm strategy, iron out any difficult issues, especially cross-boundary problems, and act as the last resort point of recourse.

- **Middle management** does the work of keeping the relationship moving forwards and bringing in a flow of new developments that make adding value changes for the customer.

- **Operations/transactions** keeps the wheels turning and ensures that delivery is as promised and hassle-free.

Furthermore, the key account manager is the person to monitor and adjust the balance in the relationship.

Mapping the links between people on the two sides of the relationship at different levels in both organizations can be very illuminating (Figure 4.9). Internal relationships can be added as well, if the resulting picture does not become too confusing. Figure 4.9 shows a network of relationships involving all levels and a variety of functions on both

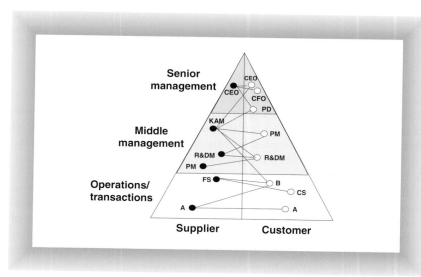

Figure 4.9
Mapping relationship links with the customer at different levels of management.

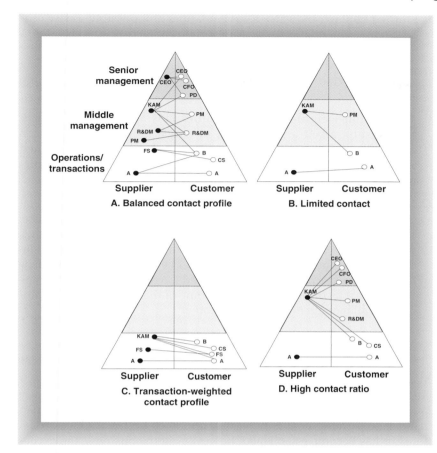

Figure 4.10
Mapping relationship links at different levels of management.

sides (the example shows abbreviated functions, but individual positions can be used instead). Provided that the key account manager has the internal relationships that allow him or her to gain and manage a full view of these interactions, then the picture should indicate a healthy, well-balanced relationship at the *interdependent* stage.

Try charting the links between staff in your company and your customer, and compare that picture with those shown in Figure 4.9. It will help you to understand the contact map you currently have, and how you might change it to what you want. Is the relationship balanced as in the figure above or, if not, in what way is it skewed? Figure 4.10 shows four variants, but there may be others too.

A. **Balanced contact profile:** Indicates an *interdependent* relationship, if the key account manager is managing, briefing and coordinating the internal relationships as well. If not, it could indicate a *cooperative* relationship with insufficient coordination and control. There could be many more contacts than shown, but this kind of number is probably the least necessary for an *interdependent* relationship. Good coordination and management required.

B. **Limited contact:** Indicates a *basic* relationship, possibly a new one. To develop the relationship, appropriate contacts need to be identified on both sides and at all levels. People need to understand how the key account manager will run the relationship, what it is trying to achieve, what their role in it is, and what others will be doing as well.

C. **Transaction-weighted contact profile:** This also indicates a *basic* relationship, albeit an older one, in which more links have been established. However, links are all focused on people concerned with short term transactions. To develop this relationship, efforts need to be made to form links higher up the organization.

D. **High contact ratio:** The ratio of customer staff involved in the relationship to supplier staff involved is a good diagnostic measure. Here the key account manager is holding on to almost all the links, although there are a substantial number of them. Nevertheless, relationship and business development will be hampered in this situation, and the key account manager needs to delegate and encourage others to act as principal contact in some of these links, while retaining overall management of the customer.

4.3.2   Avoiding relationship traps

Maintaining a relationship is a different job from developing it. New customers seem more interesting than the customer you already know, and driving towards an achievable goal is a natural human instinct, so development is not so hard to keep on track. Once a relationship has become established, however big the business, the excitement may go out of it, and it is easy to take the customer for granted. However, these customers have plenty of other suppliers for comparison, and they are still the most important, so they are unlikely to settle for second best. Suppliers need to guard against three dangers in particular:

- Complacency

- Lapses in integrity

- Leaking profitability.

Complacency

Warning against complacency seems so obvious that it should not even be necessary to say it, like announcements such as 'Please take your baggage with you when leaving the plane'. Of course, you have no intention of being complacent. Nevertheless, companies often do take some of their oldest and best customers for granted and give them a poorer treatment than newer or more difficult and demanding customers. There is a danger that the individual key account manager will become casual in his or her dealings with the customer, but there is also a danger of institutional complacency which requires even more vigilance.

Lapses in integrity

Over a long period of time, one or other party in a relationship may want to change the original commitments and understanding on which the relationship was built. Indeed, as people move in and out of jobs, the original understanding may just get 'forgotten'. However, changing the parameters of a relationship without the full knowledge *and* consent of the other party will generally be seen as a lapse in integrity. Even if it is with the knowledge of the customer, then 'moving the goalposts' will be seen, not unreasonably, as a lack of integrity and result in a loss of trust if the customer is too enmeshed in the relationship to withdraw without great difficulty.

> The fact that the supplier has stayed within the letter of the contract is immaterial if it has reneged on the spirit of the relationship.

Case study insight

Taking a customer for granted

One supplier had a long-term close relationship and steady business with one of its key customers. During a restructuring/cost-cutting exercise the decision was taken to reduce its resource from a full-time key account manager to just 10 per cent of her time. The supplier wrongly assumed that the business was 'theirs' in spite of the reduction in support. In fact, the relationship deteriorated to the point where the business was close to being lost.

To reclaim the business, the supplier had to reinstate the key account manager, reallocate her other customers, and dedicate a taskforce to retrieve the position. The relationship began to improve although the customer was not likely to forget the episode. In the end, the supplier had spent just as much on the relationship as it would have done anyway, if not more, had lost the trust of the customer and caused long-lasting damage to the relationship.

We have seen this pattern repeated many times over. Suppliers sometimes have to make tough decisions for the business, and *in extremis* they may have little choice. However, too often the decision to change the way customers are managed seems to be a more individual and personal choice, or one driven by non-customer-facing functions like finance or operations, which has been taken without a real understanding of the long-term damage that is wrought by such U-turns. The fact that the supplier has stayed within the letter of the contract is immaterial if it has reneged on the spirit of the relationship.

Opportunism is also seen by the customer as a breach of integrity. For example, customers in collaborative relationships expect that if a supplier receives an unexpected windfall that cuts its costs, like a fall in raw material prices, then the customer will be informed and some or all of the benefit will be passed on. Both research and experience show that failure to share the benefit of a cost saving is seen by the customer as a breach of trust. Presumably, suppliers' finance directors who refuse to realign prices do not share this view, or perhaps they do not

> Failure to share the benefit of a cost saving is seen by the customer as a breach of trust.

realize that, in making such a decision, they are not acting with the integrity expected by the customer. Key account managers must take conscious and special care to manage their company's integrity as well as their own.

Case study insight

'Once bitten, twice shy'

Strongly sponsored by its sales director, a hi-tech company had developed a good key account programme and excellent relationships with clients. However, the sales director left the company and was replaced with a new sales director with a 'back to basics' philosophy. Service and support levels were reduced and a number of joint customer projects were dropped. When, later on, the supplier wanted to reinstate KAM, customers were sceptical and unresponsive. They felt the support was part of the deal and that the supplier had gone back on its promise.

Leaking profitability

In theory, profitability improves through the 'learning curve' effect as you work with a customer and get to understand the best way of dealing with their business. However, it can also decline over a period of time, through successive rounds of negotiations in which the customer squeezes down prices and wins new and incremental service concessions with significant costs attached (see Chapter 5). In fact, suppliers as well as customers are responsible for leaking the profits.

> Suppliers make a lot of assumptions about customer profitability that have never been even tested in some companies, let alone properly monitored.

Suppliers make a lot of assumptions about customer profitability that have never been even tested in some companies, let alone properly monitored. One key account director investigated one of his company's top three accounts to test his assumptions, and found the result was 100 per cent different from his expectation. Where there is substantial business the stakes are too high to leave profitability to guesswork, so the first task must be to get genuine profitability measurement in place.

CHECKPOINT

Preventing profitability leakage

- Do you know what the real profitability of each key customer is, not just sales revenue or gross margin?

- Have you carried out a wide-ranging price and service review with the customer?

- Do you identify and clear out obsolete costs and anomalous prices from time to time?

Summary

Too many companies think developing relationships alone will make a difference to the business. In fact, a good relationship is just the beginning, not an end in itself: some real benefit needs to materialize for the customer as well as the supplier. The relationship should be seen as the facilitator that allows the supplier to reach the people it needs to talk to and work with to deliver the business strategies and added value the customer seeks.

Conversely, some suppliers think that just doing business will develop relationships automatically. This is also a fallacy: there are many examples where companies have nothing going on between them that can be called anything other than straightforward trading although they have been trading for years, and they still have a very limited understanding or appreciation of each other.

Really, business and relationship development should go hand in hand, and a supplier that wants to achieve a closer relationship should consciously work on both simultaneously to reach the stage it desires more quickly and more certainly. In this chapter we have identified some of the major influences in relationship development, and discussed some practical approaches to managing and developing the relationship. In particular, we have highlighted the customer's view of relationships with suppliers, particularly the importance of the supplier's integrity and trustworthiness, to which suppliers could usefully give more explicit care and consideration.

5 The buyer perspective

As buying companies seek new routes to competitive advantage and value for their customers, they now look to key suppliers to help them. Naturally, customers are far more likely to act according to their own perceptions and aspirations than to any view or objective that selling companies might wish to impose on them. A buying company has its own set of strategic decision support tools to help it select the suppliers who are important to the fulfilment of its aspirations.

First, a selling company needs to understand whether it has the opportunity of being a key supplier. The chances are small if it is one of many competitors, or it is in a weak position relative to the customer, or it supplies a product or service which does not contribute to the customer's critical path. If analysis reveals that this is the selling company's situation with this customer, the supplier should look elsewhere for its own key relationships or possibly reposition itself through developing its offer. It should not waste money and effort on trying to develop a relationship that is unlikely to succeed and bear fruit.

At the same time, the supplier should decide what this customer can contribute to its own strategic objectives, using the methods described in the following chapters. These methods require an in-depth understanding of the customer's situation, needs and strategies and, indeed, successful key account managers are those who really know how their customers operate and why.

Generally speaking, only if buyer and seller strategies are complementary in terms of products, their approach to business and to the relationship between them will it be possible to develop the relationship beyond a fairly simple level towards an interdependent or integrated stage. However, if all these elements are in place and closer involvement is achieved, the flow of benefits to both parties can be very exciting.

At less-developed stages of the relationship the cost of nurturing the relationship can easily outweigh the benefits. The range and extent of cost savings increase on both sides as trust between the two parties grows and barriers are reduced. In some situations, reducing risk by working with a known partner can allow costs to be cut, for example by eliminating duplication of processes. In other situations, reduction of costs may increase risk, for example by moving to just-in-time supply and eliminating buffer stocks. Clearly, reduction of costs and reduction of risks are closely linked and need to be managed jointly from a foundation of a thorough understanding of the partner and its concerns.

Trust is a mediator through which most interactions pass and activities will be interpreted. Care should be taken to manage the partner's perceptions, as reserves of trust may be crucial in carrying a supplier through any difficult patches in performance or in the relationship. In the end, powerful customers still call the shots.

In this chapter

Introduction

Books on selling and account management, and suppliers as well, often make the mistake of assuming that the customer is bound to fall in with a well-developed, well-presented plan. This is, of course, quite untrue. Customers have their own agendas, their own strategies and their own priorities. If, and only if, the selling company's plans fit the customer's plan, are they likely to succeed.

It follows that understanding the customer is fundamental to the selling company in adopting the right strategy and making acceptable offers. Yet suppliers generally devote remarkably little time and effort to gaining this crucial knowledge about their customers. In order to understand the customer's perspective fully, this chapter considers the buyer's standpoint and looks at the world and the supplier through the buyer's eyes, rather than viewing the customer from the buyer's standpoint.

We will look at the circumstances which provide fertile ground for close, cooperative relationships and at the circumstances which suggest that attempts at greater intimacy will fall on stony ground. However, even if intimacy is not an option, being very good at what you do still is.

5.1 The purchasing context

The companies in a modern supply chain are more closely connected together than ever before. The market environment of one becomes a factor in the market environment of the next. Pressures felt by one are passed on to the next. To understand its own business, each company needs to understand the business of the others to a far greater extent than it has in the past.

Within companies too, the aim is now cross-functional integration. Traditionally, buyers were quite remote from their own company's customer strategy and therefore operated to a different agenda. Suppliers responded to that agenda and sold on specification and price. Now that buyers are generally much more in tune with the concerns of their whole company, the key account manager can make more creative offers and business propositions to them. That kind of applied creativity can only come from a deeper and more extensive knowledge of the customer's business.

Even when a supplier is working with a deep understanding of the customer, this is still only one side of the equation: the receptiveness of the customer is also critical in achieving relationship success. Key account relationships do not generally exist at the higher levels discussed in Chapter 3 unless they are reciprocated. Selling companies are liable to delude themselves about the favourability of their position with the customer. In fact, close business relationships are constructed from two-way linkages wrought by frequent operational interactions, dedicated resources, shared assets, joint planning and other business-based bonds between buying and selling companies. Such linkages will not exist unless the buying company as well as the selling company chooses to participate actively in the relationship (McDonald and Woodburn, 1999).

There is a tendency for selling companies to view their relationships with buying companies in isolation as if buyers do not have relationships with other suppliers or with other kinds of organization. This is obviously not the case, and understanding the network of relationships within which the buying company operates can be very illuminating as a way of identifying what drives buyers to behave one way and not another.

Figure 5.1 illustrates the different types of organization with which any company might have a relationship. As the buyer and supplier and, indeed, every other body represented in Figure 5.1 will each belong to a similar network, the business reality is exceedingly complex.

For suppliers competing in increasingly challenging business environments, understanding the purchasing context can provide valuable insight into buyer behaviour. Knowing, for example, what are the buyer's resources, motivations, pressures and sources of information can provide a supplier with a lucrative competitive edge. An intelligent supplier realizes that the best route to the achievement of its own

An intelligent supplier achieves its objectives by helping the customer achieve theirs.

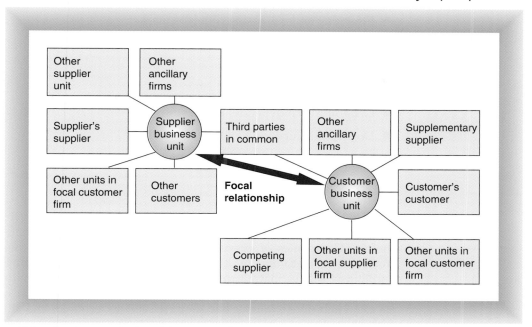

Figure 5.1 Business relationship network.

objectives is by helping customers to achieve their objectives. In summary, it is a simple three-step process:

1. Acquire an in-depth understanding of the customer environment and the customer drivers.

2. Discover or deduce the customer's objectives and strategic response in relation to suppliers.

3. Develop solutions to match the customer's strategy and needs.

Let us next examine the common customer drivers and the strategies customers adopt in relation to their suppliers. The actual processes by which companies deliver solutions are described later in Chapters 7 and 8.

5.1.1 Customer drivers

Often, the information held by a supplier about a buyer is either rudimentary and confined to contact details, purchase history with the company and sometimes wider purchasing activity, or it is more extensive but diffused around the company. However, the data do not attempt to identify the forces which are really driving the customer's business. These underlying influences are a combination of factors exclusive to the buying company, its business, its relationship network, and its environment. Some of the major forces that affect customers and, therefore, influence customer purchasing behaviour are as follows:

● Speed of change and flexibility

● Fast innovation and shorter product lifecycles

- Emerging and collapsing routes to market
- Supply chain integration and customization
- Globalization
- Longer reach competition
- Geography – independent prices
- Downsizing, upsizing, merging
- Cost reduction
- Risk reduction.

Arguably, the business world is changing faster now than it ever has before: certainly it is more interconnected across the globe than ever before. Companies of every kind are fighting to deal with the new forces in order to manage this new speed of change. Managing and exploiting this escalating rate of change requires new creativity and competencies. Businesses need additional flexibility in order to respond in the timeframes available and they are seeking resources and allies to help them. Speed is of the essence in maximizing opportunities. Nimble competitors catch up very quickly, so 'windows' of profit-taking and competitive advantage are getting smaller all the time.

Nowadays, buying companies are less confident of the shape of the future, and so they prefer to secure their needs through supplier partners, rather than through wholly owned assets.

In the past, buying companies were reasonably confident about anticipating the future and were prepared to commit to assets which could be expected to provide a good return in the longer term. Nowadays, however, buying companies are less confident of the shape of the future, and so they prefer to secure their needs through supplier partners, rather than through wholly owned assets. Buyers are willing to trade off some of the margin they might have made themselves in order to maintain their flexibility and speed of response.

One of the most important components of the rapid pace of change is faster innovation, which leads to faster product obsolescence and, hence, shorter product lifecycles. As a result, companies which have developed a product or service innovation must capitalize on their lead very quickly before it is overtaken by the next development. This means that they need to get to market quickly, achieve wide penetration quickly and amortise the costs quickly. Traditional trial, production and launch processes do not work well enough at high speed, so companies are trying out all kinds of new formulas, such as concurrent engineering, modular design, electronic commerce and strategic alliances for every stage of the value chain. Suppliers who do not keep up with their customers will very soon be left behind.

Turmoil at the product end is now amplified by upheaval in the marketing and distribution channel.

This turmoil at the product end is now amplified by upheaval in the marketing and distribution channel. Not very long ago, companies could concentrate on the development of new products and concepts and then simply release them through the value chain via well-understood processes. Today, with the arrival of electronic commerce, new routes to market are emerging while traditional routes are collapsing. Companies are no longer able to make standard assumptions about the most effective way of reaching their markets. They will be trialling new routes to market at the same time as they launch new products. Until electronic commerce has ceased to be a revolutionary force and a different pattern of doing business has established itself, and this will take some time, businesses will be multiplying their risk because they are venturing into the relatively unknown on two fronts simultaneously.

Some customers are making a late start on supply chain integration. Others are well advanced and have achieved smooth-running, robust processes, while others are only now discovering the pitfalls along with the benefits. Selling companies need to engage with the integration process and to work with the buying company in order to achieve the goals of the supply chain as a whole. Those who simply supply what they are asked for are likely to find themselves divorced from their original customer and managed by a primary supplier. However, closer collaboration is bound to demand customization rather than the provision of standardized offers, and suppliers need to be geared up to respond appropriately.

> Selling companies need to engage with the integration process and work with the buying company in order to achieve the goals of the supply chain as a whole.

Many blue-chip companies, and some smaller ones as well, now operate as global suppliers and/or in global markets. Nevertheless, almost all suppliers struggle to match the needs of customers who are involved in global markets. In fact, globalization is probably not as ubiquitous as we suggested in Chapter 1. It is a dominant factor in some markets, such as computer software and high-technology business-to-business products, which are driven by short product lifecycles and a need to maximize sales in the least possible time. In other markets, particularly where services are consumed as they are produced, it is generally not so important.

Advances in information technology and telecommunications, which have culminated in the arrival of electronic commerce technology, have enabled customers to extend their reach to encompass the globe. Equally, competitors are lengthening their reach and are moving into yet more markets. Competitors who were previously confined to serving home markets by the costs of attracting customers overseas are joining the global arena, now that they can market from their base country and no longer need an expensive marketing infrastructure. This lowering of entry barriers opens the field to smaller companies as well, so that customers are not only facing an incursion of good competitors from elsewhere in the world, they are also facing an explosion in the range, size and quality of competitors. As long as these new competitors can deliver, or hold out a reasonable expectation of delivery, prices will inevitably come under pressure.

In some markets the Internet acts as a 360-degree periscope on pricing. Buyers can surf the Web looking for best prices. Although they then return to the supplier they know, it will be with new targets for price decreases. Where the products they seek are made by well-known brands with global guarantees, the premium they will pay for using a familiar distributor will be minimal. Now that internal constraints have been removed, many selling companies inside the European Community are fighting a rearguard action on geography-independent pricing and may not succeed in maintaining differentials. Thus, suppliers and customers operating in high-cost areas such as Western Europe will have to work much better in order to maintain margins. The pressure will be felt all the way up the supply chain. Buying companies will seek to work with suppliers whose objective is to maintain margins on an equitable basis, while suppliers who are focused on maintaining their prices are likely to be abandoned.

> Suppliers who are focused on maintaining their prices are likely to be abandoned.

Inevitably, the current turbulence will affect organizational structure. The rate of downsizing, upsizing and merging taking place has reached new highs as companies jostle to reposition themselves in growth markets and to escape from mature and declining markets. Second-tier companies are generally no longer viable and many have been subsumed into larger or more resourceful companies. The big and the bold are getting bigger and bolder still. The turbulence contains a mix of dangers and opportunities. Companies operating in the expectation of a takeover or acquisition are obviously limited in the commitments they can make and this presents difficulties for buyers as well as suppliers. A buyer in such a transitional situation needs a 'safe pair of hands', flexibility and understanding from its suppliers as it undergoes radical change. In the meantime, a supplier will want to protect the robustness of its buyer contact base in case some of its key contacts become casualties. Threats may appear from competitors who supply the other company in a takeover, while outsourcing opportunities may emerge from downsized companies. In short, uncertainty is increasing.

> Underlying all these customer drivers are the two most enduring ones: cost reduction and risk reduction.

Underlying all these customer drivers are the two most enduring ones: cost reduction and risk reduction. As the pressure to reduce costs features so strongly in customer purchasing behaviour, it is imperative that suppliers appreciate why customers pursue cost savings and what cost savings are potentially available. Suppliers also need to understand how customers perceive the risk in their relationship and how it might best be managed.

Case study insight

Understanding customers' needs

A public sector organization was merging several buying functions from very different parts of the organization. The buyers would have to move locations, deal with cultural issues, understand their new role and develop strategies to match. Meanwhile, if services to current users were not maintained, they would get off to a bad start with their customers. The supplier could have stood back until the situation became more settled. Instead, it aimed to increase support during the transition to gain commitment from the newly integrated buying function when it emerged from this period.

5.1.2   Cost reduction

While suppliers concentrate on customer value and profitability, the priority for buying companies is often cost reduction. Figure 5.2 shows the dramatic impact of cost savings on a customer's net profits. The authors were presenting to over 50 buying directors from some of the world's biggest multinational companies and most confirmed that cost reduction is indeed their number one priority. Indeed, in *Time* magazine, 1 August 2005, it was reported that most European corporations are doing spectacularly well, their profit growth being driven by cost-cutting.

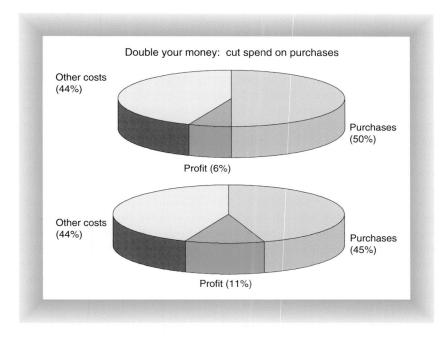

Figure 5.2
Impact of cost savings on net profits.

This section examines the financial aspects of key account relationship management in terms of cost savings, which are not necessarily limited to the buying company. Some of the cost savings that are potentially available to companies when two links in the supply chain work closely together are as follows:

● Better information and reduced uncertainty

● Reduction of protective measures

● Elimination of duplicated processes

● Better flow of supplies

- Routinized transactions

- Tighter quality control

- Improved supply chain efficiency

- Reduced production costs

- Better, more cost-effective design of new products

- Cost sharing on research and development

- Lower sourcing/business development costs.

Undoubtedly, this list is not complete, nor will all of these savings be available in a single trading relationship. How much cost saving is available will clearly depend on the nature of the product or service and the environment in which it is used. It will also depend on how well the two parties know and trust each other. In a *basic* relationship (see Chapter 3) the parties may well enjoy a degree of familiarity, but very little trust and, therefore, standard processes should be employed wherever possible. Efficiency is characteristic of a *basic* relationship.

The level and nature of cost savings in *cooperative* relationships will vary. If the relationship has been singled out by the selling company as appropriate for development, then the selling company should be expecting to invest in it. The two companies will decide together how that investment can be used to deliver mutual cost savings and enhanced customer value. If, on the other hand, the selling company's strategy is only to maintain its business and competitive position (see Chapter 8), then the opportunities for reducing or saving costs will be limited, which will place constraints on enabling investment and underlying trust.

In an *interdependent* relationship, however, much more becomes possible. Buyer and seller will identify the cost elements most important to them and both parties will have the commitment and confidence in each other to make major changes in order to achieve savings in those costs. Where a high proportion of the cost savings listed above are achieved, this may signal arrival at the *integrated* stage of relationship development.

On both sides of the relationship, an openness and willingness to share information is important, both in itself and as an indicator of the closeness of the relationship.

Better information and reduced uncertainty can save costs for buyers and sellers alike in all kinds of ways. Whether or not this is achieved through a better understanding of the market through making commitments, accurate demand forecasting can save substantial costs. Finance, staffing, use of plant and premises and marketing resources can all be optimized if requirements can accurately be predicted. Inputs can be bought at good rates rather than high, emergency prices. Strategies can be more useful, more effective and more likely to succeed. Shareholder expectations and share prices can be managed better. On both sides of the relationship, an openness and willingness to share information is important, both in itself and as an indicator of the closeness of the relationship.

When companies do not trust each other, they will install protective measures in order to prevent their trading partners from damaging their business. Vertical integration is one example of how buying companies protect themselves against unreliable or opportunistic suppliers. Upstream integration is designed to ensure continuity of supplies of a key input to core processes (Ellram, 1991). For example, oil and chemical companies own mining operations which feed their refineries and plants. In fact, they may not always be the most efficient producers and they may be able to buy in at lower prices than the cost of their own production. However, since the companies must run their plant continuously in order to achieve competitive costs, they could not surrender their own sources of raw materials unless they had cast-iron and entirely credible guarantees from their suppliers that deliveries will be made on time.

Although vertical integration is clearly appropriate in certain sets of circumstances (Williamson, 1985), companies are now more inclined to question whether their funds are invested in strategically valuable assets or outmoded supply formats. There are many other examples of expensive protective measures for buying companies, including large buffer stockholdings, advance payments for shipments, legal fees and contract policing, quality checks on goods inwards, constant competitor monitoring and 'mystery shopping'. While buying companies may not be prepared to dismantle all barriers, substantial savings can be made even through partial reductions in protective measures.

> Substantial savings can be made even through partial reductions in protective measures.

The elimination of duplicated processes is an obvious candidate for cost savings. For example, the selling company counts goods out as they leave the factory and the supplier counts them in to confirm delivery in full. Quality is also checked by the producer and again by the receiver. Accounts departments in both companies are engaged endlessly in the reconciliation of purchase orders, delivery notes and invoice payments. These procedures cost money and cause delays, so many companies have gone part of the way to reducing the costs incurred in checking everything by operating spot checks. Some companies have gone one step further and reconfigured the whole process on the assumption that a check conducted by either party will be acceptable to the other.

This case is a good example of how the better flow of supplies and routinized transactions can affect efficiency and cost savings. Here, users receive their supplies the following day, whereas previously, availability varied from immediate delivery for a select few items to two to three days for most items. A transaction procedure was established, specifically tailored to the buying company's specification. It operated to a very regular and efficient routine because it was slimmed down exactly to the services required and omitted any 'frills'. Cutting out superfluous handling is one way of improving the flow of supplies. Other ways of streamlining processes include combined process engineering, joint forecasting and improved management gained from a better understanding of requirements, which is achieved through greater information sharing.

Case study insight
Reducing procurement costs

The buying function of a major international company now only involves itself and its warehouses in purchases where it can add value to the process. Office supplies have been taken out of the goods received–store–internal requisition order sequence. Users manage their own budgets and orders directly, and their materials are delivered to their desks. The buying function sets up the supplier contract, receives a single monthly report which is automatically generated, and pays one monthly invoice for everything received. Substantial time and effort are saved by the buying company, while the supplier's costs balance out and prices remain competitive.

Case study insight
Valued-added pricing

A multinational components company has developed a systematic approach to price negotiations with customers. Discussions focus on a matrix based around Porter's (1985) value chain, which identifies sources of cost. Together, the parties concerned identify which elements are valuable to the customer and which are not, and derive an appropriate price from this resulting menu of tailored and standard elements.

Waste of material as reject product and waste of time in services are both regularly targeted sources of cost. However, reject product is a relatively minor part of the real cost of poor quality and, hence, the constant attention to tighter quality control is driven by the wider implications. For example, substantial amounts of time and money can be absorbed in handling and remedying complaints if a customer receives poor service or a defective product. Further, losing customers to the competition as a result of poor quality can result in substantial loss of earnings, with further repercussions if disappointed customers spread their disenchantment by word of mouth.

Today, after more than a decade of concentration on quality and the adoption of Japanese methods, quality standards have reached new highs: some companies are even committed to zero-defect production. However, quality is not cheap for suppliers. In addition, buying companies are always seeking to achieve tighter quality control at lower cost. In order to concentrate on the quality of their own processes, buyers want to be able to assume the quality of inputs. Suppliers who can meet buyers' stringent standards are saving costs for the buying companies, but they must equally control the costs for themselves.

These last three elements are major contributors to the improvement in supply chain efficiency overall, where the aim is the creation of a lean, mean, low-cost supply machine. Efficiency has been defined as 'doing things right' and effectiveness as 'doing the right things'. In fact, by working closely with a supplier, a buyer can significantly improve supply chain effectiveness as well as efficiency. Improvement of effectiveness in supply chain terms will mean identifying the critical pathways on both sides and ensuring that these processes in particular are seamless and robust.

Traditionally, suppliers would encourage customers to buy as much as possible from them and, if customers were using more of the product than was really necessary, so much the better. However, this kind of opportunistic behaviour generally meets with disapproval from buyers. Buyers expect trusted suppliers to point out overspecified products, unnecessary wastage or inefficient usage and to reduce production costs, even if it means lower revenue for the supplier. High production costs will make the buying company uncompetitive in the marketplace and, ultimately, the supplier will lose out as well. Suppliers (not necessarily the key account manager) should therefore have a high degree of technical understanding of their own products and be able to offer their expertise in order to support the customer's production function in various ways, including reducing the consumption of other inputs. To make gains beyond the normal levels, the buying company may have to give the supplier access to closely guarded production secrets, in the confidence that such critical information will not reach competitors.

> Buyers expect trusted suppliers to point out overspecified products, unnecessary wastage or inefficient usage.

However, information from the European Institute of Purchasing and Supply shows that, in many cases, as much as 90 per cent of the final unit cost of a product is determined before it reaches full production, most of which is committed in the design stage (Figure 5.3).

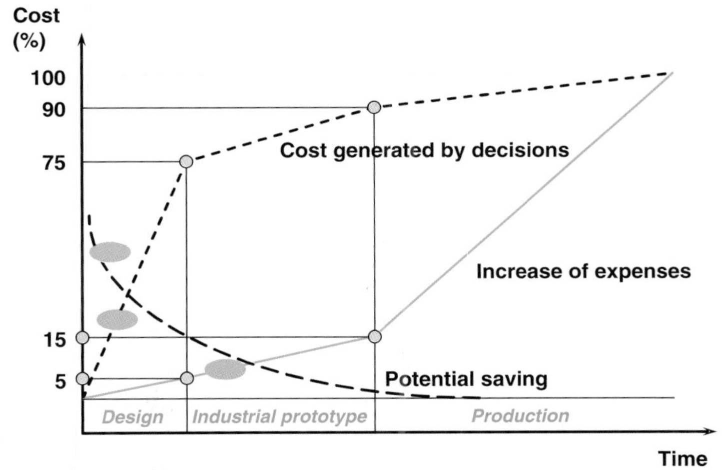

Source: Bernard Gracia, European Institute of Purchasing, 2001.

Figure 5.3
Progress of product development compared with commitment of final unit cost.

The major opportunity for achieving low unit costs for the manufacturer lies in the design stage.

Thus, the major opportunity of achieving low unit costs for the manufacturer lies in the design stage. Research at Cranfield has shown a large difference between *cooperative* relationships and *interdependent* relationships on this point (Figure 5.4): a substantial proportion of suppliers in *interdependent* relationships are admitted to the buying company's development process and can therefore contribute to better, more cost-effective design of new products, while suppliers in cooperative relationships are largely excluded from product development activity.

If the buying company trusts the selling company and involves it in new product development activities, this can potentially lead to the creation of a new role for the supplier in the buyer's long-term research and development (R&D) effort. Participation may mean contributing expertise and/or project funding. Much mutual benefit can be gained from such collaboration, including cost sharing on R&D, particularly where programmes are long-running and expensive. Further, pooling resources in order to secure the input of experts who may be scarce and costly can help to avoid the pitfalls of entering into projects with insufficient vision and directional guidance. Figure 5.4 also depicts the degree of information exchange on product development compared with other subjects.

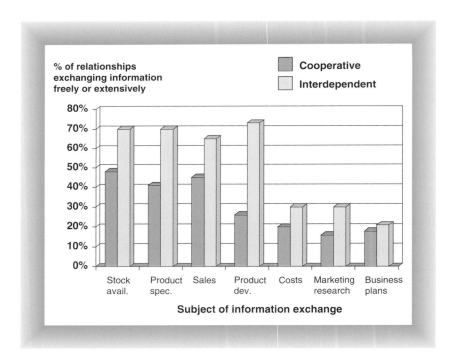

Figure 5.4
Topics for information exchange in KAM relationships.

Buyers can also achieve lower sourcing costs and suppliers will benefit from lower business development costs through involving trusted trading partners in development activity. They can work together in helping develop specifications and sourcing criteria and, if the supplier can then fulfil the need, the buying company may decide to look no further. If the buyer believes that the selling company is a good source for the product required and will not make opportunistic profits, then the working processes and widespread familiarity which already exist represent a real bonus: the buyer can avoid the effort, delays and costs involved in evaluating alternatives.

The public sector seems reluctant to take this pragmatic approach and generally insists on compulsory competitive tendering, which not only incurs huge bid costs for suppliers, but also means that buyers ultimately carry the costs of implementing the process through higher prices. In the private sector the supplier's unique expertise and competence may prove so invaluable to the buyer that, even where the selling company itself may not represent an attractive source for the product or service required, the partnership may grow to the point where the supplier takes on the sourcing and ongoing management of the supply as a primary contractor managing smaller, secondary contractors. This arrangement is increasingly common as buying companies seek to reduce their supplier base.

Clearly, close relationships between buying and selling companies have the potential for saving a substantial amount of cost for both sides. However, both sides will have to invest significantly in order to secure these cost savings, in relationship building, communication and committing time to joint projects, and also in new facilities, equipment, staff or whatever is needed for implementation. Expenditure on the less tangible activities, such as relationship building, is as real as expenditure on tangibles, though often the systems applied to accounting for it are very poor or non-existent.

> Both sides will have to invest significantly in order to secure these cost savings.

It is important for business success that expectations are set correctly and that the timescales used for evaluation are of a suitable length. In *basic* or *cooperative* relationships, both sides realize that exit is quite easy and either company will look for a quick return on any investment it makes because it cannot be sure that the relationship will last. Obviously, many cost-saving opportunities are barred if only those with rapid payback are acceptable. Therefore, the value of cost savings which can be made at these relationship stages is limited and may not even exceed the costs of running the relationship. In contrast, in *interdependent* or *integrated* relationships there is an expectation of durability and trustworthiness which lowers the perceived risk and allows longer-term investments to be considered.

> Many cost-saving opportunities are barred if only those with rapid payback are acceptable.

In effect, reducing risks leads to lower costs and, indeed, risks and costs are closely linked. Sensible companies and, in particular, companies in their buying capacity are extremely concerned about risk. Risk reduction is therefore worthy of a separate discussion and this follows in the next section.

> ## CHECKPOINT
> ### Cost-saving opportunities
> Can you identify any strategies that could achieve cost savings benefiting both a key customer and your own organization?

5.1.3   Risk reduction

Reduction of risk is one of the major drivers that cause companies to seek closer relationships and encompasses the following:

- A reduction of uncertainty generally
- Protection against pressures from the business environment
- Protection against opportunism by powerful trading partners
- Protection against losing the business altogether.

If buyers or sellers were to articulate the main reason why they strive so hard to make closer relationships work, it would be because they seek the security of retaining trading partners who will be critical to their long-term business future.

The value of risk reduction to both parties can easily be overlooked in the day-to-day management of the relationship. It is therefore a worthwhile exercise for companies to understand what risks their partner perceives and to deconstruct them to see how they might be diminished and/or be seen to be diminished. The model developed by the International Marketing and Purchasing (IMP) Group (see Figure 5.5) provides a useful framework from which to view sources of risk.

Business risks derive from two dimensions: external to the relationship (environment in the IMP model) and internal to the relationship (atmosphere of relationship in the IMP model). External risks originate in the marketplace or the wider environment, but have an impact on the market, for example government legislation. A wide range of external factors potentially have implications for both parties, such as new technology (for example, substituting for current products), economic recession (downturn in demand), competitor activity (downturn in demand and pressure on prices) and many more.

Buyers perceive plenty of internal risks as well. The buying company's first concern is always opportunism on the part of selling companies (Williamson, 1985). Will suppliers pass on any lower costs to the buyer? Will they hold the buyer to ransom for higher prices if they have the advantage? Will they respect confidential information? Will they provide continuity of supply? Buying companies can and do protect themselves against such behaviour in all sorts of ways, such as

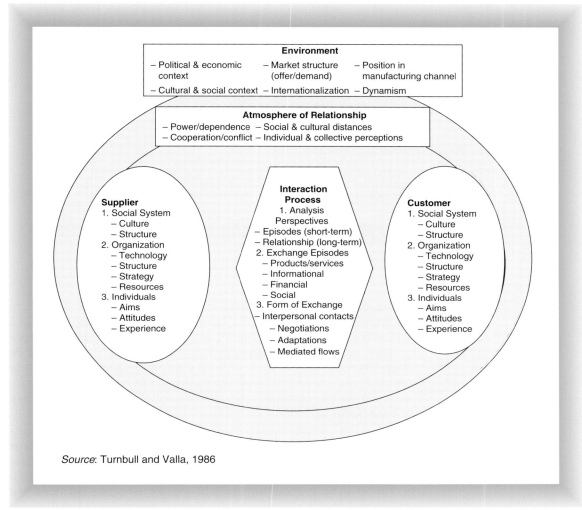

Figure 5.5 The IMP model.

broadening their supplier base, playing one supplier off against another and insisting on contracts being fully specified to every last detail. However, these 'protective' measures cost buyers money and flexibility, and tend to reduce their leverage with suppliers. Nor do buying companies which carry such 'sandbags' stand up well today against leaner competitors who have taken calculated risks in order to work with suppliers and who have opted for speed and adaptability rather than security and safety.

'Protective' measures cost buyers money and flexibility.

Assuming the supplier is indeed ethical, honest, committed and currently competent, the buyer's second concern is the long-term orientation and capability of the selling company. Does the supplier represent the best available partner? After all, an honest fool is not necessarily more valuable as an ally than a talented knave. The buying company is likely to be looking for a partner who is at the

The buyer's second concern is the long-term orientation and capability of the selling company.

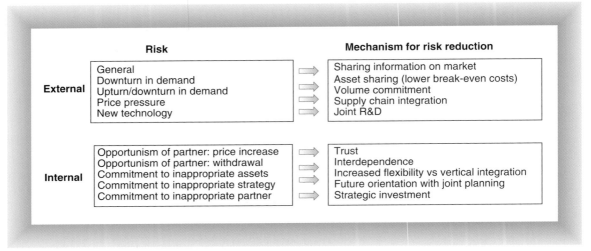

Figure 5.6 Risks and risk reduction mechanisms.

leading edge of current products and practice and looks certain to stay there. If they have to make investments in assets dedicated to a particular supplier's products or systems, buyers want to be sure that they are making prudent purchases. They do not want to be obliged to write off the costs of such equipment and systems in the event that they need to change their supplier in order to stay ahead. Figure 5.6 shows some examples of risks and the ways in which they can be tackled.

There will be people inside the buying company, particularly those who are not normally in contact with the selling company, who are uncomfortable about lowering their protective barriers against suppliers. Unfortunately, they may well be people who can maintain the barriers and effectively prevent the desired development of the relationship. The structure in Figure 5.6 can be used to expose the kinds of risks that are of real concern from their point of view. The mechanisms that could address those specific areas can then be identified. An audit of the relationship's current exchanges and structure will show whether new action is required in order to reduce the risk itself or whether the need is really for internal communication in order to show more clearly how risk is already being managed.

Key account managers need to 'get inside the skin' of their customers in order to piece together the concerns that kindle further commitment to the relationship, as well as the underlying strategies that together determine the buying company's behaviour. In fact, many selling companies list 'a desire to partner' (with acceptance of the risks involved) and 'strategic fit' as two of the most important criteria in selecting key accounts and developing close relationships with them. They believe that compatibility of strategies is necessary to the fulfilment of their own corporate objectives and, indeed, to the development of an intimate relationship.

Selling companies believe that compatibility of strategies is necessary to the fulfilment of their own corporate objectives and, indeed, to the development of an intimate relationship.

5.2   Buying company strategies

5.2.1   *Strategy independence*

It should come as no surprise to learn that buyers operate strategies for working with suppliers which run parallel to those that selling companies use. The most successful buying companies, and particularly those focused on achieving drastic reductions in their supplier base, develop specific strategies for their key suppliers individually. However, many buying companies take a more generic approach and work to simple strategies such as 'cut supplier numbers', 'reduce prices by 10 per cent all round' or 'use ISO 9000 suppliers only'. Even if these generic strategies are not entirely and explicitly exposed to suppliers, they are very real and suppliers need to understand them.

Selling companies are rarely good at acknowledging and responding to the customer's strategy. At one level, selling companies know that their customers have some kind of strategy and yet, at another, they are capable of ignoring it completely and developing their own strategy to be applied to the key account, quite independently of the customer's strategy. Not surprisingly, customer buy-in is poor and the exercise tends to be swept to one side.

> Selling companies are rarely good at acknowledging and responding to the customer's strategy.

When selling companies do not understand what causes their customers to respond to them in the way that they do, they have little chance of developing an appropriate strategy, in other words one that is likely to succeed. Ideally, strategic planning should be carried out jointly, but research has shown that this is still not the norm (McDonald and Woodburn, 1999). Joint strategic planning was found in only approximately one-third of even the most important relationships (the top two or three in each case) and it is presumably even rarer at the next level down.

> An appropriate strategy is one which is likely to succeed.

5.2.2   *Strategy direction matrix*

If the selling company's relationship with the customer is not close enough for joint planning, then the next best approach is to carry out a strategic analysis from the customer's point of view and to deduce an appropriate strategy on the basis of the findings. To do this, selling companies may find it helpful to employ the strategy direction tool commonly used by buyers to determine how they should manage their suppliers (Figure 5.7). This is the equivalent of the selling company strategic direction matrix shown earlier in Figure 2.5.

The horizontal axis 'Supplier preference' is self-explanatory. The quantity purchased will obviously be the most important factor, but others may also be taken into account, such as stability of demand, product quality and competitive position in the marketplace. The vertical axis 'Attractiveness' is a proxy for market risk and refers to the supply position. Market risk will include factors such as the number and quality of suppliers, capacity to cope with demand, market turbulence and price stability. Stability and plenty of choice for the buying company will give a low market risk assessment. Unpredictable fluctuations and few

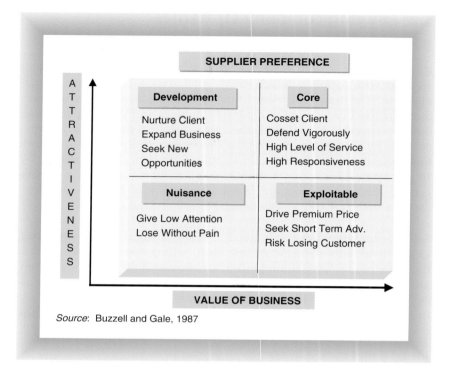

Figure 5.7
Buying company's strategy direction matrix.

suppliers to choose from will result in a high market risk assessment. Each buying company will define the criteria by which it wants to measure its purchasing power and the market risk for itself, largely depending on the sector in which it operates.

If the buying company has low purchasing power in a low-risk market situation (bottom left box), then it will simply seek efficiency and a transactional relationship. The purchase will not be deemed sufficiently important to warrant further engagement with the supplier and the buyer will not be in a strong bargaining position anyway.

If, on the other hand, the product market is high risk, then there is a chance that supplies could be interrupted (top left box). The buying company is not in a strong enough position to apply leverage and protect itself. Buyers in this situation may react by increasing buffer stocks, seeking a substitute product or finding a more reliable source.

In situations of high purchasing power and a low-risk market (bottom right box), the buying company can use its muscle to play one competitor off against another in order to secure a better price or some kind of additional value. However, in a high-risk market, where buyers purchase large quantities and, thus, have high purchasing power (top right box) and where the product is important to them, they may seek a strategic relationship with their supplier in order to reduce risk and uncertainty. Here the buying company is more likely to look at the value or the total cost of acquisition rather than just the price.

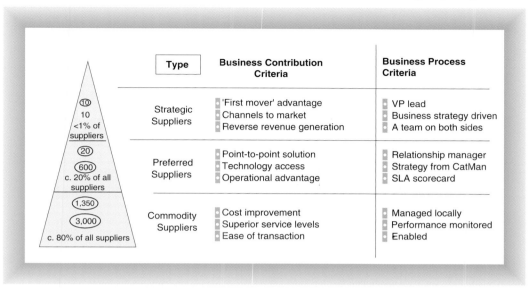

Figure 5.8   Supplier relationships as a source of business advantage.

The authors have spent many years working with the buying directors of some of the world's biggest companies. On many occasions, buying directors have admitted that many of their suppliers think that they are 'strategic' suppliers, when the reality is that they are in the low-price, commodity, exploitable, leverage-price category. Consequently, they play their suppliers along and, when it comes to the crunch, they drive prices down relentlessly.

Indeed, looking at Figure 5.8 (provided by a global buying director), it can be seen that it is highly unlikely that more than a handful of suppliers will be considered to be strategic suppliers. Also, for those suppliers who really want to be considered as strategic suppliers, the same global buying director provided the set of criteria shown in Figure 5.9.

Of the four options in Figure 5.7, only in the top right box is a high-involvement relationship with the supplier likely to take root. Buying companies, like selling companies, have a limited capacity for intimacy and they cannot squander it on situations and suppliers that are not important. It therefore follows that, if the supplier's product/service falls into one of the other boxes of the matrix, however important that customer is to the supplier, the selling company is unlikely to succeed in developing a close relationship.

Buying companies, like selling companies, have a limited capacity for intimacy.

This conclusion suggests that the selling company should not waste its resources on such a relationship. Investment would be better employed in becoming super-efficient in order to operate effectively in either of the two boxes on the bottom than in developing a different offer which is designed to fall into the top right box of the matrix. If the matrix indicates a need for strategic product development, it should not be mistaken for a need for relationship development. Key account

A need for strategic product development should not be mistaken for a need for relationship development.

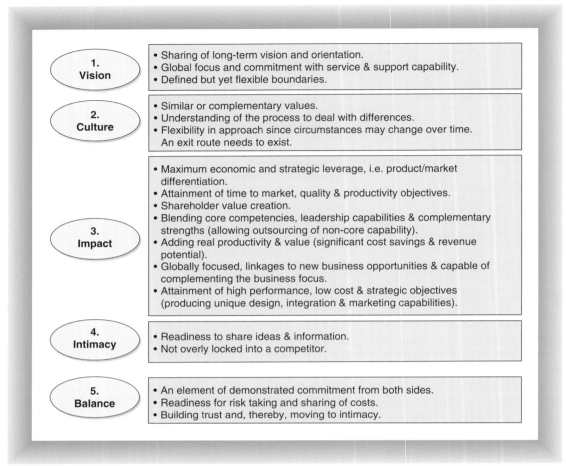

Figure 5.9 Strategic supplier criteria.

management (KAM) will not compensate for an inadequate offer and misapplication will only result in misdirected, wasted resources.

5.2.3 Supply chain integration

Determination of strategy should be a collective process.

Supply chain management and integration strategies, which are often accompanied by supplier base reduction, have had a major impact on many selling companies in recent years. New electronic commerce capabilities will drive this trend forward and few companies are likely to be unaffected. Figure 5.10 shows the development of supply chain management from the baseline of traditional management to current advanced practice in which companies are operating cross-boundary integration.

Figure 5.10 charts the change from a traditional manufacturing approach, which keeps the supplier on the doorstep, to one in which the supplier has become part of an extended enterprise. The boundary between one company and the next in the chain is breached and may even be dissolved. Processes and strategies must be integrated. As the organizations are so closely linked, they cannot operate to different strategies

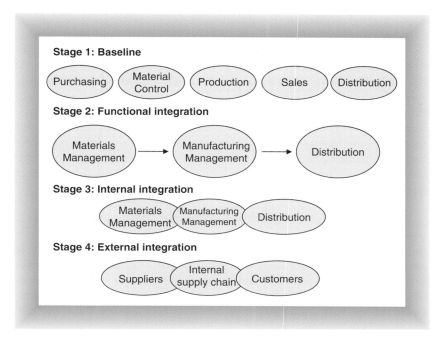

Figure 5.10
Development of
supply chain
management.

successfully and, therefore, determination of strategy should be a collective process, not a process owned by an individual member of the chain.

The roles played by the supplier, its customer and other members of the extended enterprise are clearly different from the role played in the other configurations. Some companies are very uncomfortable with the loss of distinction between 'us' and 'them'. Other companies, such as Amazon, the Internet bookseller, can operate the model with equanimity. It is undoubtedly easier to start a company in a new mode than convert an existing one, which will have innumerable functions and processes orientated in a different way. However, the arrival of electronic business in force, which we are now witnessing, will oblige many companies to adapt to cross-boundary activity. The contrast between single-company, boundary-confined thinking and extended-enterprise, cross-boundary thinking is shown in Table 5.1.

> The arrival of electronic business in force will oblige many companies to adapt to cross-boundary activity

Single company thinking	Extended enterprise thinking
Focus on the customer	Focus on the ultimate consumer
Increase own profits	Increase profits for all
Consider own costs only	Consider total costs
Spread the business around	Team with the best
Guard ideas, information and resources	Share ideas, information and resources
Improve internal process efficiency	Improve joint process efficiency

Table 5.1
Single company
thinking versus
extended enterprise
thinking

The external context in which buyer–seller relationships exist is becoming increasingly extensive and complex. Change drivers include the rapid pace of change, the refinement of processes, market maturity, heightened customer power and the globalization of business. At the same time, the internal, organizational context is also changing, removing traditional delineations of remit and responsibility. Conditions are more conducive to 'partnering' between suppliers and customers and, hence, the nature of marketing has altered. Marketers are moving away from a traditional transaction focus towards a customer focus. Thus, there is a pressing need to find ways to describe relationships as a basis from which to understand them better and build them stronger – and this has led to the ascendancy of KAM.

> A selling company which is not selected as a dependable ally in a newly integrated core supply chain is likely to end up as a secondary supplier.

Supply chain integration is probably the strategic development that is most critical for suppliers. A selling company that is not selected as a dependable ally in a newly integrated core supply chain is likely to end up as a secondary supplier, dealing with the original customer through an intermediary. Being separated from the customer limits the supplier's access to information and restricts its ability to demonstrate added value. The supplier becomes much more vulnerable to the agenda of the intermediary.

Most opportunities for cost reduction and value enhancement are currently seen to lie at the interface between members of the supply chain. Much has therefore been written about this subject and it cannot be adequately covered here. Clearly though, understanding the position and strategy of neighbouring members in its supply chain is fundamental to the buying company's strategy and the management of the relationship between itself and its upstream suppliers and its own downstream customers.

5.2.4 Matching strategies

> In many cases suppliers have found the new partnering philosophy to be little more than skin deep.

The climate and culture of purchasing has changed in recent years and supply chain partnerships have become more acceptable and, indeed, popular. Even so, in many cases suppliers have found the new partnering philosophy to be little more than skin deep. Customers have promised a partnership approach with a focus on added value and mutual benefit and then have forced prices to the floor anyway, resulting in the sorry state of customer profitability described in Chapter 6.

Of course, buying companies are not absolutely bound by the strategic direction indicators discussed here: they can choose to adopt different approaches and behaviour. However, buyers will readily revert to type if that strategy is not founded on sound logic and sense, so selling companies should beware of a customer promising a strategy which is out of line with that indicated by analysis.

Companies naturally seek to work with other companies whose strategies and goals match theirs. If the selling company has adopted a strategy of developing high-involvement partnerships with key customers, then it will look for buying companies whose strategies mirror its own and who will reciprocate. The customer's propensity to partner must be a criterion for admission to a supplier's KAM programme. Some companies have managed to be fairly ruthless in wielding that criterion and have excluded any customer who, however huge, operates a price fighter strategy and plays competitors off against one another. Key account managers are often horrified at the thought of excluding this type of customer but, of course, there is no obligation to tell the customer of the decision.

KAM programmes restricted to customers who offer genuine opportunities for mutual and committed relationships have shown excellent growth in revenues and margins, even astronomical in some cases. Pressure from key account managers and buyers to include other types of large customer is often considerable, but the temptation should be resisted. As emphasized elsewhere in this book, a company's capacity for close business relationships is limited and expansion of the customer base will inevitably detract from the focus on the most important customers. Inclusion of other, less-suitable customers will add plenty of cost and probably not much growth. Of course, these customers are still very important to the selling company. They probably represent a large part of its current cash income, but they should be managed in a different way, with a focus on efficient transactions.

> *The customer's propensity to partner must be a criterion for admission to a supplier's KAM programme.*

Case study insight

Managing intimacy (Hewlett Packard)

Hewlett Packard started their global account programme in 1993 with 26 global key accounts. By 1996 it had grown 10-fold to 250. The following year, Hewlett Packard cut the number back to 95.

5.2.5 Supplier delusions

A relationship is intrinsically reciprocal: you cannot be married to someone unless they are married to you. Only the reciprocated elements of a relationship are relevant and real. If there is a mismatch of perceptions, the relationship is defined only by the elements that are matched. Figure 5.11 illustrates this point: the genuine extent of the relationship is represented by a square, which defines an equal and shared perception. Anything outside the square is delusion.

> *Only the reciprocated elements of a relationship are relevant and real.*

Determining what stage of development a relationship has reached depends on the views of both of the parties involved. Research has shown, perhaps not surprisingly, that key account managers tend to overestimate the stage relationship by approximately one development stage (McDonald and Woodburn, 1999). From the buyer's perspective, the two parties are not as close as the supplier probably imagines. Selling companies need to be aware of this phenomenon if they are to avoid engaging in inappropriate behaviour and embarking on premature strategies.

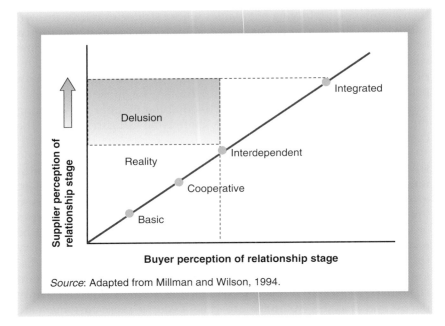

Figure 5.11
Buyer and supplier perceptions of relationships.

5.2.6 Trust

| Trust plays a major role in buyer behaviour.

Trust, or confidence in a partner's reliability and integrity, is one of the most important elements in high-involvement relationships. A significant body of research supports the notion that trust plays a major role in buyer behaviour. Buying companies rated 'integrity/honesty' as one of the two most important attributes of a good key account manager (equal with 'product knowledge') (McDonald *et al.*, 1996). Interestingly, when selling companies were similarly questioned, they selected completely different attributes and scarcely rated integrity at all. This difference in opinion suggests that selling companies might be wise to re-evaluate their priorities if they want to align themselves more closely with their customers.

Trust can be regarded as a mediator through which many of the interactions between buyer and seller pass. Interactions potentially increase the level of trust but, as in a game of snakes and ladders, they also have the potential to damage it. Suppliers would do well to manage interactions with a view to how the buyer might perceive them and whether they build or destroy trust. Activities such as improving performance, sharing more information, improving communications and even admitting mistakes should all help to build trust if they are handled sensitively. In addition, trust will, according to the degree to which it pre-exists, either add to or detract from the perceived value of these activities.

Achieving a high degree of trust has numerous positive outcomes. There will be more readily offered cooperation between the two sides, less uncertainty when sensitive information is shared, more commitment to the relationship and a lower probability that one or other will exit. Trust can also bridge a patch in the relationship where something is going wrong. However, if the problem persists for too long, then it will eat away at the 'reserves' of trust and, eventually, relationship breakdown will occur. In effect, a dynamic balance exists in the relationship between past experience of performance and behaviour and current perception of performance and behaviour, which is buffered by trust.

Trust is certainly more than an abstract concept in buyer–seller relationships. Lack of trust has significant cost implications for buying and selling companies at both the strategic and tactical levels. At the strategic level, there are many initiatives that a customer could undertake jointly with a supplier to their mutual benefit. However, if the supplier is not trusted sufficiently, the customer may pursue the opportunity alone or with a more appropriate and trusted partner.

At a tactical level, the existence of trust can open up a range of processes for the examination of cost-cutting opportunities. For example, a selling company undertakes an internal environmental audit. Meanwhile, a buying company looking to do business with the selling company requires assurance that the supplier complies with certain environmental standards and proceeds to conduct its own audit of the supplier. Obviously this duplicate auditing adds extra cost. Much of the cost could be avoided if the buying company trusted the selling company to carry out the audit objectively and if the selling company trusted the buying company to respond sensibly to the audit's results.

A retailer formalizes the degree of trust it places in its numerous suppliers. On the arrival of deliveries, the retailer may quality check 100 per cent, 10 per cent or 1 per cent of the goods. Suppliers are effectively penalized for being 'untrustworthy' by being charged for the cost of checking deliveries at the level deemed appropriate. In a very few cases of trusted suppliers, 0 per cent of the goods are checked (saves handling costs) and the retailer invoices itself (saves 'paperwork').

It is not by accident, or course, that these costs are widely incurred. Naturally, many companies feel a need to guard themselves against the opportunism of other companies. Indeed, in innumerable cases companies have been shown to be right in dealing cautiously with other profit-seeking entities. So, although there has been a cultural shift over the last five years towards closer relationships with trading partners, the shift has not been universal. Many companies have not bought into the idea and, even where they have in theory, they may not have done so in practice.

In contrast, where trust exists between two companies, a considerable range of cost savings become available, as shown in Section 5.1.2. As a further incentive, greater profits may be achieved through tackling opportunities together.

Companies should therefore adopt a policy of scepticism, but stop short of cynicism. Treating all-comers with universal suspicion is,

Companies should therefore adopt a policy of scepticism, but stop short of cynicism.

ultimately, rather limiting. Trustworthy partners do exist, either because they have enshrined ethical principles or because they see it as being in their long-term interest to behave in a trustworthy manner. It is important that companies first choose their strategic trading partners carefully and then work concertedly to develop a productive, mutually beneficial relationship with them. They can continue to work with other companies more cautiously.

Case study insight

Defining 'trust'

Customer managers in a commercial banking organization were asked to predict whether their key customer relationships would survive another two years at least. The results were analysed against a number of relationship parameters. The research concluded that holding a favourable 'balance of power' or the previous 'duration of the relationship' did not affect expectations of the continuation of relations, whereas 'trust' was strongly linked to expected relationship life (Perrien *et al.*, 1999).

5.3 Balance of power

It is abundantly clear to practitioners of KAM that, although the balance of power between a supplier and a customer might not affect the duration of a relationship, it certainly makes a huge difference to its nature. However, to date, little academic attention has been given to studying the role of control and influence in trading relationships, perhaps because it is not an easy subject to research.

Power is linked to the perceived degree of dependency on the partner.

Power is obviously linked to the perceived degree of dependency on the partner. In fact, the one is the reverse of the other. Dependency increases as the size of the business with the trading partner increases and as its share of the company's turnover grows. Dependency also increases if loss of the business would damage either company's reputation and trigger the defection of other partners, or if finding a substitute would be difficult. For a selling company with high fixed costs, the consequences of losing a major customer can be devastating, but where most costs are variable the effects are more manageable.

Table 5.2 outlines the sources of power in a buyer–seller relationship as identified by a group of practitioners from blue-chip companies. Whether the company is buying or selling, most of the sources of power are potentially mirror images of each other. What differs is the list of them possessed by each organization in a given relationship at a given point in time. For example, the balance of power may favour a selling company over a small buying company in need of its advanced technological support.

Table 5.2 Sources of power

Nature of source	Buyers' sources of power	Sellers' sources of power
Size/importance	Big Consolidation: bigger Globalization: even bigger Share of total supplier business	Criticality to buyer Capacity to meet demand Share of purchases

Competitor options	Supply excess
	Commodity markets
	Globalization: cherry-pick suppliers
	Globalization: pick currency and
	  prices
		Supply shortage
		Key differentiation
		Access to innovation
		Patents and monopolies
		Brand/demand pull
		Erect barriers to new
		  competitors

Buying/selling skills	Access to information Leverage market knowledge Higher expectations Competent buyers	Access to information Leverage market knowledge Easy to work with Competent key account managers
New strategies	Supply chain management Supplier rationalization Globalization E-commerce	Recognized relevant expertise Track record and reputation Global competence Flexible
Threat of exit	Low cost of switching for customer High cost of switching for supplier Effect of loss on supplier cost base	High cost of switching for customer Low cost of switching for supplier Limited availability of alternatives
Leverage of contacts	Within supplier Within markets/ability to damage reputation Within regulatory bodies	Within customer Within markets Within regulatory bodies

Suppliers can be just as powerful as buyers, although that is not the everyday perception of their key account managers, who usually feel that buyers have the upper hand.

Power may be thought of in terms of the overall 'quantity' of power, as well as the balance of it in a relationship. The framework shown in Table 5.2 can be used to audit the power position in a particular relationship. First, identify the actual sources of power for each side using Table 5.2 as a preliminary checklist. Then give each source of power a score that represents its relevance and strength in the relationship and total scores afterwards. This exercise will help to clarify the nature of the power that may be leveraged. It will also indicate the direction and degree of any imbalance in an objective way.

Regardless of the relative power positions, companies with the balance of power in their favour can still choose how they exercise their advantage. Power can be used constructively or destructively. For example, a buying company in a very powerful position could demand very low prices and stand a good chance of obtaining them. However, the selling company's profits may be depressed to the point where it cannot invest in innovation which would ultimately benefit its customer, or it might go out of business. Alternatively, the customer could decide that its long-term interests lie more in imposing specific strategies or higher standards of practice on the supplier because it would make the supplier a better trading partner, to the benefit of both companies.

So, while the balance of power is clearly important in determining the nature of a relationship, it does not provide sufficient explanation on its own. Linking the balance of power with the concepts of common interest/mutual benefit does, however, offer further insight into relationships (Krapfel *et al.*, 1991). Common interest may be defined as the compatibility between the goals of the companies that are trading together. Companies that approach the business between them in the same manner and share the same aims and objectives are said to have a high degree of common interest. A good example is to be found where both supplier and buyer are dedicated to the same industry sector and have evolved similar responses to the environmental forces at work in that sector. Figure 5.12 plots the balance of power against the degree of common interest and summarizes the different situations to be found in each of the six sets of circumstances shown.

The research behind the development of this matrix showed that, in situations of a low degree of common interest (bottom three boxes), the

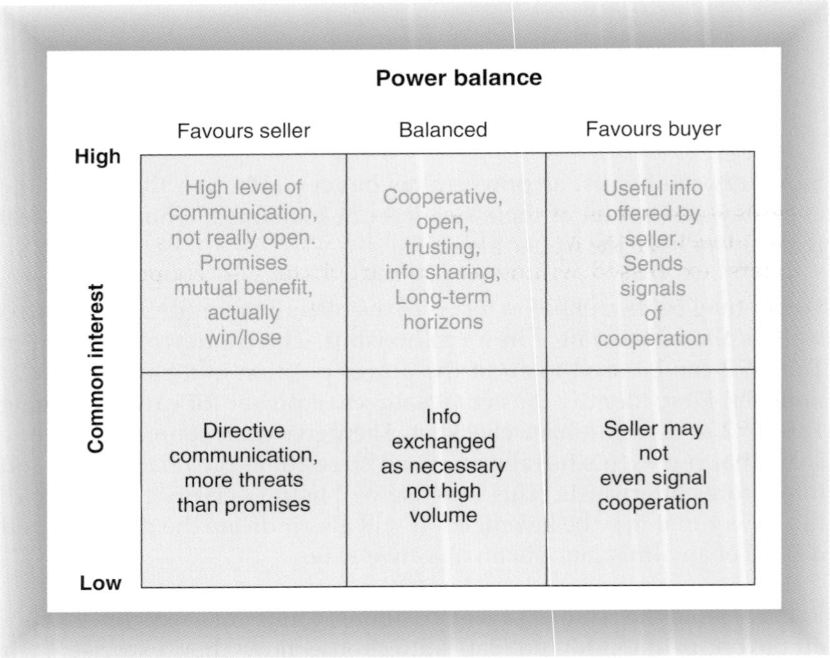

Power balance		
Favours seller	Balanced	Favours buyer
High level of communication, not really open. Promises mutual benefit, actually win/lose	Cooperative, open, trusting, info sharing, Long-term horizons	Useful info offered by seller. Sends signals of cooperation
Directive communication, more threats than promises	Info exchanged as necessary not high volume	Seller may not even signal cooperation

Common interest — **High** (top) to **Low** (bottom)

Figure 5.12
Balance of power versus common interest.

volume of communication is generally not high, and information is only exchanged as necessary. The volume of communication is much higher where a high degree of common interest exists. However, this volume does not necessarily indicate information sharing: a large part of it may be directive, more like a one-way 'lecture' than a two-way 'conversation'. Chapter 3 highlighted the important roles that communication and information exchange play in key account relationships. Clearly, the quality and nature of each as well as the quantity need to be taken into consideration in understanding the relationship.

The matrix suggests that the only situation in which a collaborative, cooperative relationship will exist is where the two parties have the same amount of power and a high degree of common interest. In fact, even where the balance of power lies in favour of one of them, a collaborative relationship could exist if the company with the upper hand chooses to behave in a cooperative manner. Nevertheless, the weaker side should always be wary of the possibility that a policy of cooperation which is not backed up by necessity is liable to change. For example, a selling company might agree to investment in equipment dedicated to a powerful customer, on the understanding that the price of the product will yield a margin sufficient to give a return on the investment in, say, two years. In a relationship based on balanced power and mutual necessity, the agreement might safely be quite flexible and relatively informal. In a relationship based on the benevolence or enlightenment of a powerful partner, a sound contract might be wise protection against the chance of a change in the partner's policy.

> The only situation in which a collaborative, cooperative relationship will exist is where the two parties have the same amount of power and a high degree of common interest.

Case study insight

Identifying the balance of power (NHS Supplies)

NHS Supplies divided its contracts into eight major product groups. The organization held meetings with its most important suppliers in each group in order to promote dialogue with them. The organization noticed that, although the meetings had the same agenda and were held in the same kind of environment, each meeting had a very different atmosphere in terms of the suppliers' expressed willingness to participate and cooperate with NHS Supplies. The turnout at some meetings was almost 100 per cent while for others it was relatively low. Afterwards, the organization mapped the balance of power between itself and each group against the evident degree of common interest. The predictions matched the actual responsiveness of the suppliers and the degree of cooperation offered.

Summary

The most important point to be made in this chapter is that suppliers need to understand where they currently sit in the buying company's classification matrix of its suppliers. Some suppliers will be seen by the customer as truly strategic and will want an inter-dependent or integrated relationship with them by dint of their crucial importance to their organization's success. Such suppliers, however, are few in number and if a supplier is merely one of many who can offer similar products or services, success is likely to accrue to the supplier with the lowest prices. In such cases, the supplier should either seek to get its own costs down, or strive to develop a business model that adds value to its selected customer's operation.

6 Key account profitability

Marketing as a discipline has failed during the past 60 years by concentrating on promotion rather than on developing world-class marketing strategies. The result is that in most companies, marketing has been relegated to running promotional campaigns and designing T-shirts and does not deserve a place at the high table, that is, the board of directors (McDonald, 2009).

The result of this sad lack of marketing leadership is the demise of many of our erstwhile famous organizations. Most of the highest earning return on investment plcs during the decade up to 1990 have gone into liquidation or were acquired in desperate circumstances, while many of the leading companies in different sectors up to 2000 also got into financial difficulties or were acquired.

At the time of writing, it is too early to complete a comparable analysis of performances of top companies for the first decade of the twenty-first century, but even a cursory glance at what happened in many of the world's top financial institutions such as Lloyds Banking Group, Lehman, Merrill Lynch, AIG, Freddie Mac *et al.*, is sufficient to indicate that things have not improved.

All of this happened against a background of three major challenges that industry was facing during this period and still faces – market maturity, globalization and customer power.

The most dramatic challenge has been the massive shift of power to customers away from suppliers. Today, customers are destroying old make/sell business models, while technology has empowered customers to have more information about their suppliers than they have about them. Meanwhile, a new wave of business metrics and new pressures from institutional shareholders to report meaningful facts about corporate performance, combined with demands from other stakeholders for exemplary corporate behaviour, have resulted in a need for strategies other than downsizing and cost-cutting as a route to increased profitability.

Never before has the need for real marketing professionalism in relation to key account management been greater.

This raises the question of what marketing is. It is a function, just like finance, with its own professional institute and body of knowledge. The challenge is to understand the needs of customers, then to formulate strategies for meeting these needs in a way that enables the company to create long-term net free cash flows which, having taken account of the associated risks, represent a financial return over and above the cost of capital, thus creating shareholder value. This strategic imperative is quantitatively measurable using the body of existing marketing knowledge and CEOs must demand of their chief marketing officers that their strategic forecasts for their key account performances are subjected to the same rigorous due diligence as other initiatives, such as acquisitions.

Some key accounts will inevitably reduce shareholder value, but providing these are managed to increase net free cash flows and to reduce risk, this is acceptable. Overall, as long as the aggregate of the net forecast value from all key accounts is positive, having taken account of the risks and the cost of capital tied up in servicing them, then it is possible to prove to the Board and to shareholders that the key account performance is creating shareholder value continuously.

Introduction

Marketing accountability has become one of the burning issues facing boards of directors today. Given the increasing power of a small number of major customers in many sectors, key account profitability has risen to the top of the agenda as part of this movement towards marketing due diligence, which is why a whole chapter has been devoted to this topic.

This chapter puts key account profitability within the context of marketing accountability and goes on to explain a state-of-the-art method for proving to the Board that the key account programme as a whole is creating shareholder value added.

6.1   Profitability in the context of key accounts

There are so many definitions and interpretations of the word 'profit', that it would take a whole chapter to cover them. But today, in capital markets, companies are judged solely on whether or not they deliver shareholder value added. So this is the principal method we look at in the context of key account management, as this is most likely to have resonance in boardrooms.

6.1.1   Sustainable competitive advantage and key accounts

Marketing has a central role in creating sustainable competitive advantage. In fact, the overall purpose of strategic marketing is the creation of sustainable competitive advantage.

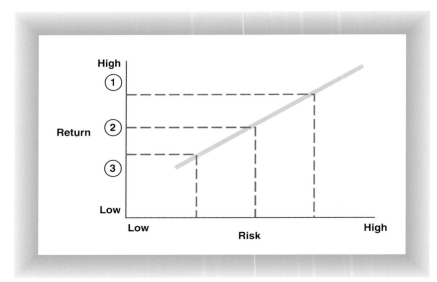

Figure 6.1
Financial risk and
return.

Typically, stock exchanges scatter the shares of companies in a graph according to return and according to their own estimates of risk. The diagonal line (the line of best fit) is known as the beta. Figure 6.1 shows a typical array from any stock exchange of the relationship between risk and return. Any firm on the line will normally be making industry-average returns for its shareholders – in other words, making returns equal to the weighted average cost of capital (WACC). Firms making consistent returns greater than the WACC are creating shareholder wealth, known generally as shareholder value added, economic value added, positive net present value, super profits, sustainable competitive advantage and so on.

Figure 6.2 shows diagrammatically how sustainable competitive advantage can be achieved. This shows that, when an organization

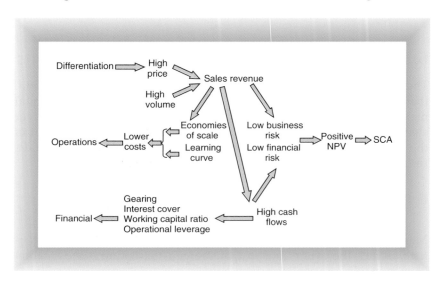

Figure 6.2
The route to
sustainable
competitive advantage
(SCA).

has state-of-the-art operations, has its cash flows firmly under control and, more importantly, when its offers are sufficiently differentiated by being matched to the specific needs of market segments, these all combine to create positive net free cash flows (positive net present value, having taken account of the risks inherent in future strategies, the true value of money and the cost of capital) or shareholder value added.

Modern finance is based on four principles:

1. Cash flow (the basis of value)

2. The true value of money

3. The opportunity cost of capital (other investments of a similar risk)

4. The concept of net present value (the sum of the net cash flows discounted by the opportunity cost of capital).

Also, it is well known that, while accountants do not measure intangible assets, the discrepancy between market and book values shows that investors do. Hence, expenditures to develop marketing assets make sense if the sum of the discounted cash flow they generate is positive.

A little thought will indicate that every single corporate activity, whether it be R&D, IT, purchasing or logistics, is ultimately reflected in the relative value put on a firm's offer by its customers. The marketing function is central to this, as every one of the four (or five, six or seven Ps) can only be improved by the whole organization focusing its attention on its customers.

The crux of the matter is failure to align marketing with the fundamental shareholder value objective. Marketing objective setting is, in practice, murky or, at worst, downright wrong. Increasing sales volume, the most widely cited marketing objective, can easily be achieved by sacrificing profitability, for instance. Increasing profit, another commonly cited marketing objective can be also attained in the short term by relinquishing investments for future growth.

Perhaps more worrying than comments about lack of alignment between marketing strategies and corporate objectives are charges of poor marketing professionalism. There is widespread evidence from research that very few marketing professionals actually understand or know how to use the widely available strategic analysis tools that would help them to dovetail their plans with what is going on in the wider marketplace, and elsewhere in their organizations.

There are numerous tried and tested tools that can be of immediate value in improving marketing's contribution to the main board agenda. For example:

● Financial rigour in appraising marketing objectives would be a useful start. Financial managers have used tools such as shareholder value added for at least 10 years now to support investment appraisal and resource allocation. However, these methods are mainly applied to capital projects and mergers and acquisitions. Although discounted cash flow is occasionally used to calculate brand valuations, it is not widely used to support marketing decision making. Now frequently referred to as NPV (net present value), it is still in widespread use by accountants for capital projects.

● Marketing planning methods should be more strategic. Unfortunately, the annual budget cycle has a stranglehold over marketing objective setting. Studies of the marketing planning processes reveal that less than 20 per cent of marketing professionals use strategic objective-setting methods. Objectives are predominantly short term and have little connection with wider corporate plans for growing shareholder value.

● Resource allocation to support customer projects needs to be aligned with business growth. Yet there is a widespread disconnect between customer-related objectives, and corporate cost-cutting objectives. Symptoms of this disconnect can be observed in the exceedingly poor service provided by the majority of call centres, and the inadequate customer response from many Internet business ventures, which are very often set up as corporate cost-cutting ventures. Again the treatment is conceptually easy. Surprisingly few marketing plans adequately assess their resource implications (especially not cross-functionally).

● Customer profitability is also known to be a key driver of shareholder value, according to academic studies. Again the state of marketing practice is poor. Remarkably few organizations use this vital tool.

● Customer retention analysis and root-cause customer defection analysis are widely written about, yet our research at Cranfield shows that few companies bother to measure them (Figure 6.3).

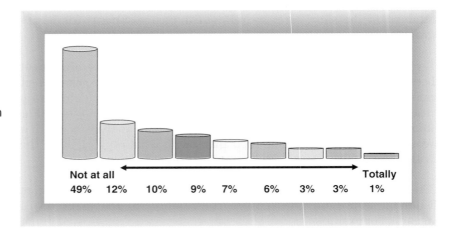

Figure 6.3
Customer retention by segment (answers to a Cranfield questionnaire using an audience response system to guarantee anonymity. The question was 'We measure customer retention by segment').

Not at all ←——————————————→ Totally
49%   12%   10%   9%   7%   6%   3%   3%   1%

The low value that marketing places on measurement is brought home by looking at what marketing spends today on market research – about 700 million euros annually in each of the major Western European economies. Compare this with the amount *one* oil company recently spent on a new financial information system – 700 million euros – the same figure that each Western European market spends on marketing information.

It is in response to the challenges outlined above that the authors have developed a process for auditing the main elements of marketing investments and for linking these investments to shareholder wealth. We have named this process 'marketing due diligence' in order to indicate that marketing should be treated in exactly the same way as, for example, an organization's financial audit, with the Board, through their marketers, held accountable for the investments made in building shareholder value. This process has been developed in this book to cover investments made in key accounts and will be described in detail later in this chapter.

First, however, an explanation is necessary of what marketing due diligence is.

The purpose of a financial audit, which is a legal requirement, is to ensure financial due diligence and, while the Enron scandal demonstrated that it does not always work as it should, in the main, the financial audit process has served the business community well. A more recent example is the failure of the Lloyds Banking Group to carry out rigorous financial due diligence before their acquisition of HBOS. Nonetheless, it works in the main and it is clear that the time has come for a similar process of due diligence to be initiated for marketing processes and this includes key account management (KAM).

> The time has come for a due diligence process to cover marketing.

As we have already indicated, in capital markets success is measured in terms of shareholder value added, having taken account of the risks associated with the proposed strategies, the time value of money and the cost of capital. This is totally different from what is commonly referred to as 'profit'. The problem with this approach is that it is backward looking. Later in this chapter we will show how to calculate shareholder added value for the future.

The following simple calculation shows the principle of shareholder value added:

Operating profit after tax	£2000
Capital employed	£15 000
Cost of capital	10%
Operating profit after tax	£2000
Less cost of capital	£1500 (15 000 × 10%)
Economic profit	£500

Figures 6.4(a) and (b) illustrate how intangible assets have become the major proportion of an organization's assets. The first illustrates that in the USA, for example, in 2004, 87% of all assets were intangible. The second illutrates how this changed substantially during the recession, as tangible assets tended to retain their value. By 2010, however, the value of intangibles went back almost to their pre-recession levels. Brand Finance estimates that for the FTSE top 350 and the Fortune 300 companies, about 75 per cent of their value is in intangibles. Indeed, the recent takeover of Gillette by Procter and Gamble showed that

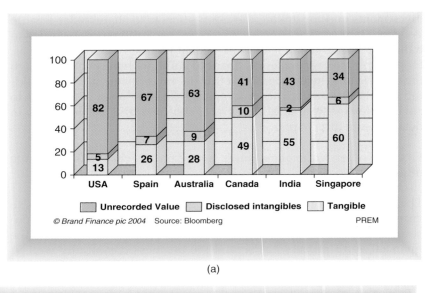

(a)

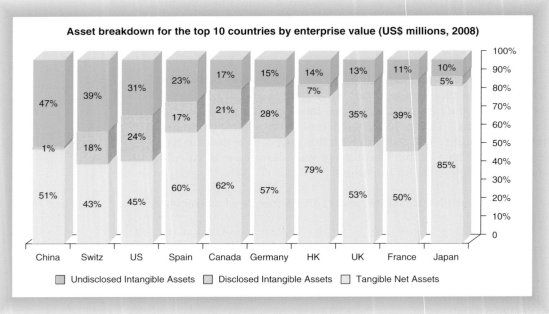

(b)

Figure 6.4 Intangibles are the key driver of shareholder value.

Gillette brand	£4.0 billion
Duracell brand	£2.5 billion
Oral B	£2.0 billion
Braun	£1.5 billion
Retail and supplier network	£10.0 billion
Gillette innovative capability	£7.0 billion
Total	**£27.0 billion**
Source: Haigh (2005)	

Table 6.1
Intangible assets acquired by Procter and Gamble when they bought Gillette for a total price of £31 billion

they bought £27 billion of intangible assets out of the total price of £31 billion. Thus, £4 billion of their purchase was for tangible assets (Table 6.1).

There are four main types of marketing asset:

1. **Marketing knowledge** (skills, systems and information)

2. **Brands** (strong brands often earn premium prices and can be enduring case generators)

3. **Customer loyalty** (loyal customers buy more, are cheaper to serve, are less price sensitive and refer new customers)

4. **Strategic relationships** (channel partners provide access to new products and markets).

It will be seen from this that customers are a significant part of these intangible assets and it is to this aspect of value that the remainder of this chapter is devoted, because just as certain markets can either create or destroy shareholder value, so can major customers. Later in this chapter, we will give a step-by-step process for valuing key accounts.

First, however, let us briefly look at another vital aspect of profitability – customer retention.

6.1.2 Customer retention and profitability

It has been suggested by international consultants Bain and Company that it costs up to five times as much to win a new customer as it does to retain an existing customer. Despite this finding, many organizations have traditionally focused their marketing activity on acquiring new customers rather than retaining existing customers. The costs of capturing market share are not always easy to gauge, but there are many companies who now regret earlier strategies based upon the blind pursuit of sales volume. While strong evidence exists to suggest a link between market share and profitability there is equally strong evidence to show that it is the quality of the market share that counts. In other words, does our customer base comprise, in the main, long-established, loyal customers or is there a high degree of customer turnover or 'churn'? If the latter is the case, then the chances are that we are not as profitable as we might be.

> It has been suggested that it costs up to five times as much to win a new customer as it does to retain an existing customer.

Bain and Company have suggested that even a relatively small improvement in the customer retention rate (measured as a percentage of retained business from one defined period to another) can have a marked impact upon profitability. They have found that, on average, an improvement of five percentage points in customer retention can lead to profit improvements of between 25 and 85 per cent in the NPV of the future flow of earnings.

Case study insight

Customer retention in the car industry

A study of the North American car industry found that a satisfied customer is likely to stay with the same supplier for a further 12 years after the first satisfactory purchase and during that period will buy four more cars of the same make. It is estimated that, to a car manufacturer, this level of customer retention is worth $400 million in new car sales annually.

So why should a retained customer be more profitable than a new one? According to Reichheld and Sasser (1990), there are several reasons. First, the costs of acquiring new business may be significant and, thus, it may take time, even years, to turn a new customer into a profitable customer. Second, the more satisfied customers are with the relationship, the more likely they are to place a larger proportion of their total purchase with us, even to the extent of single sourcing. Third, as the relationship develops, there is greater mutual understanding and collaboration which serves to reduce costs. Retained customers become easier to sell to and economies of scale produce lower operating costs. These customers are also more willing to integrate their IT systems (for example, their planning, scheduling and ordering systems) with ours, leading to further cost reductions. Fourth, satisfied customers are more likely to refer others to us, which promotes profit generation as the cost of acquiring these new customers is dramatically reduced. Finally, loyal customers are often less price sensitive and less inclined to switch suppliers because of price rises.

These factors collectively suggest that retained customers generate considerably more profit than new ones. Figure 6.5 summarizes this connection between customer retention and profitability.

There is a direct linkage between the customer retention rate and the average customer lifetime, meaning the lifetime of a customer relationship. For example, if the customer retention rate is 90 per cent per annum (meaning that we lose 10 per cent of our existing customer base each year), then the average customer lifetime will be 10 years. If, on the other hand, we manage to improve the retention rate to 95 per cent per annum (meaning that we lose 5 per cent of our customers each year), then the average customer lifetime will be 20 years. In other

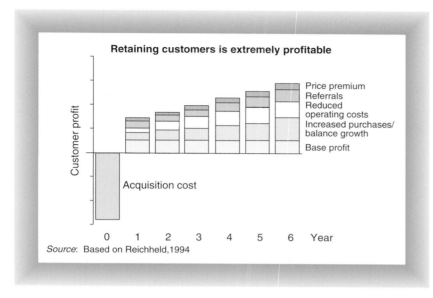

Retaining customers is extremely profitable

Customer profit

Price premium
Referrals
Reduced
operating costs
Increased purchases/
balance growth
Base profit

Acquisition cost

0 1 2 3 4 5 6 Year

Source: Based on Reichheld,1994

Figure 6.5
Customer profit
contribution over
time.

words, a doubling of the average customer lifetime is achieved for a relatively small improvement in the retention rate. Figure 6.6 illustrates the relationship between the retention rate and customer lifetime.

An important statistic that is not always measured is the lifetime value of a customer. Put very simply this is a measure of the financial worth to the organization of a retained customer. If customers are loyal and continue to spend money with us into the future, then clearly their lifetime value is greater than that of a customer who buys only once or twice from us and then switches to another brand or supplier.

Measuring the lifetime value of a customer requires an estimation of the likely cash flow to be provided by that customer if he or she achieves an average loyalty level. In other words, if a typical account lasts for 10 years, then we need to calculate the NPV of the profits that would flow from that customer over 10 years. We are now in a position to calculate the impact that increasing the retention rate of customers will have upon profitability and also what the effect of extending the customer lifetime by a given amount will be. This information provides a sound basis for marketing investment decision making, indicating how much it is worth spending for either improving the retention rate or extending the life of a customer relationship. The key question is who to retain and who to invest in.

Let us revisit the hierarchy of key relationships model (Figure 6.7). The development of profitable key accounts begins with the development of the key account relationship. Having qualified 'prospective' key accounts and selected certain accounts for investment strategies, the next step is to implement the plan.

If customers are loyal and continue to spend money with us into the future, then clearly their lifetime value is greater than that of a customer who buys only once or twice from us and then switches to another brand or supplier.

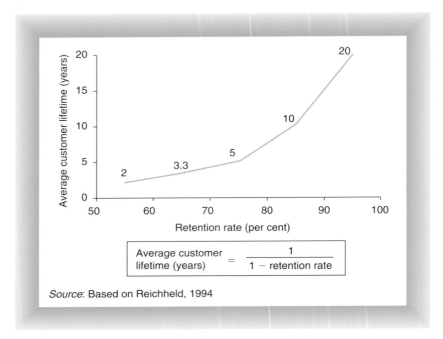

Figure 6.6
Impact of customer retention rate on customer lifetime.

Once a sale has been made, then we have a *basic* customer. For many companies, the closing of a sale is regarded as the culmination of the marketing process. However, smart marketers realize that this is only the beginning of a process of building customer loyalty leading to potentially lucrative, long-lasting customer relationships.

> For many companies, the closing of a sale is regarded as the culmination of the marketing process.

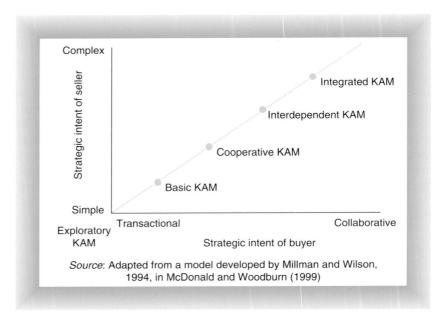

Figure 6.7
The relationship development model.

To convert the customer into a *cooperative* client requires that we establish a pattern of repeat buying by making it easy for the customers to do business with us. However, being a *cooperative* client does not necessarily signal commitment. For example, banks have regular customers who might be termed *cooperative* clients. However, many of those customers may express high levels of dissatisfaction with the service they receive and, if it were possible to move accounts easily, would defect to another bank. What is required is for us to develop such an effective customer-oriented approach that these *cooperative* customers become *interdependent* customers, meaning they are pleased with the service they receive. In fact, if they are really impressed with the quality of the relationship, they may become *integrated* customers who are moved to tell others about their satisfaction with our offer. Given the power of word of mouth, this type of advocacy can be worth more than any amount of advertising.

The *integrated* customer relationship reaches the ultimate rung on the ladder of customer loyalty. It marks the achievement of a mutually rewarding relationship where neither party intends to leave the other. Increasingly, the idea of 'partnership' is being accepted as a desirable goal of business relationships. This is particularly the case in industrial marketing and business-to-business marketing.

> The *integrated* customer relationship reaches the ultimate rung on the ladder of customer loyalty.

The relationship development model, while a simple idea, can provide a practical framework around which to build specific customer-retention strategies. The first of these strategies concerns financial risk and business risk, as represented in Figure 6.8. The top left quadrant in the matrix denotes high financial risk combined with high business risk, an often lethal combination. Experience and logic dictate that where the business risk is high, financial risk should be low and vice versa.

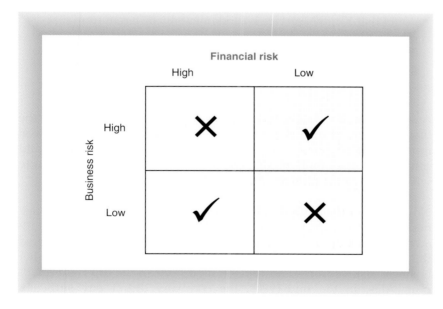

Figure 6.8
Financial risk versus business risk.

Case study insight

High risk in the banking sector

The 2008 recession was in the main caused by banks who placed far too much emphasis on the sub-prime market, where high financial risk, combined with high business risk, brought down many longstanding institutions

High risk in the airline market

Although the next two examples are 30 years old, we include them along with the example above as evidence that there is such a disease as corporate amnesia and that the risks of investing in combinations of high financial risk and high business risk are too serious not to be taken seriously

Consider the late Sir Freddie Laker's Sky Train venture in the 1980s. With a very high financial gearing, given the high cost of entering the airline business, he entered the most competitive market in the world – the London–North Atlantic route. Furthermore, his strategy against the mighty global airlines was one of low price, which, given Laker's high breakeven point, became unsustainable in the long run against special price promotions mounted by the top airlines to counteract the impact of Sky Train.

Low risk in the airline market

Turning now to the top right quadrant (low financial risk/high business risk), compare this situation with Richard Branson's market debut with Virgin Airlines. He entered the market with very few planes and low financial gearing, initially leasing his aircraft. Like Sir Freddie Laker, he also entered the lucrative North Atlantic route, but his strategy was one of differentiation, something he has very successfully sustained ever since. There is no doubt that Virgin's service is fundamentally different from that of other airlines, particularly Virgin Upper Class, which the younger travellers find particularly appealing. Virgin Airlines continues to go from strength to strength.

A similar impact was experienced in the UK housing market in the first few years of the twenty-first century. As homeowners borrowed more and more money against the hope that property values would continue to rise, millions of people were left with negative equity when house prices plunged dramatically.

Now consider the bottom right quadrant (low financial risk/low business risk). Any organization in this delightful position would be ill-advised to hoard the cash! For many years, Marks & Spencer adopted this type of strategy until the company cleverly invested in higher business risk ventures and repositioned itself in the top right quadrant. Alas, in the mid-1990s, the company didn't pay sufficient attention to the needs of its customers and today is only a shadow of the once great Marks & Spencer.

On the other hand, in situations of low business risk, it seems sensible to opt if necessary for a higher financial risk (bottom left). A low business risk, high financial risk position would describe organizations in the buy-to-let market before the 2008 crash.

Having briefly examined the concept of business and financial risk, we can now begin to appreciate why some businesses do better than others over extended periods of time. The world's stock exchanges as represented by the line of best fit shown in Figure 6.1 earlier in this chapter show financial return plotted against financial risk. Successful organizations produce either the same return for a lower perceived risk or a higher return for the same risk or both. Being north-west of the line of best fit year after year is the mark of organizations whose shares continuously outperform the sectors to which they belong. Taking the cost of capital and using this as a discount rate against future earnings to produce a positive NPV is indicative of super profits or sustainable competitive advantage.

This is not to be mistaken for producing super profits in one single year, which can be achieved relatively easily by cutting costs, limiting capital expenditure or even by selling off some of the company's assets. The trouble with short-term strategies such as these is that financial markets today are much too sophisticated to be taken in by this, so it is a common phenomenon to see the capital value of the shares fall after an increase in a single year's profits and an increased dividend.

The following two examples illustrate the tenuous nature of the future profitability of many organizations. Table 6.2 shows the performance of a fictitious company which appears to be excelling on virtually every business dimension. Table 6.3, however, shows the same company's performance compared with the market as a whole. Here the performance figures reveal severe underperformance, indicating that the company is heading for disaster when market growth slows down.

Table 6.4 is taken from Hugh Davidson's book, *Even More Offensive Marketing*, and is reproduced here with his kind permission. The table shows two companies making the same return on sales on the same turnover, but even a cursory glance at the two sets of figures clearly shows that Dissembler plc is heading for disaster. Financial investment institutions around the world are rarely fooled by so-called 'successful' annual results.

The Cranfield/*Financial Times* research report into KAM (McDonald and Woodburn, 1999) concluded that there is much supplier delusion about the stage of development that customer relationships have reached and that much of the profitability of key accounts is leaked

Table 6.2
Example of market growth performance: InterTech's five-year performance

Performance (£ million)	Base year	1	2	3	4	5
Sales revenue	£254	£293	£318	£387	£431	£454
Cost of goods sold	£135	£152	£167	£201	£224	£236
Gross contribution	£119	£141	£151	£186	£207	£218
Manufacturing overhead	£48	£58	£63	£82	£90	£95
Marketing and sales	£18	£23	£24	£26	£27	£28
Research and development	£22	£23	£23	£25	£24	£24
Net profit	£16	£22	£26	£37	£50	£55
Return on sales (%)	6.3%	7.5%	8.2%	9.6%	11.6%	12.2%
Assets	£141	£162	£167	£194	£205	£206
Assets (% of sales)	56%	55%	53%	50%	48%	45%
Return on assets (%)	11.3%	13.5%	15.6%	19.1%	24.4%	26.7%

Table 6.3
Example of market-based performance: InterTech's five-year market-based performance

Performance (£ million)	Base year (%)	1 (%)	2 (%)	3 (%)	4 (%)	5 (%)
Market growth	8.3	23.4	17.6	34.4	24.0	17.9
InterTech sales growth	12.8	17.4	11.2	27.1	16.5	10.9
Market share	20.3	19.1	18.4	17.1	16.3	14.9
Customer retention	88.2	87.1	85.0	82.2	80.9	80.0
New customers	11.7	12.9	14.9	24.1	22.5	29.2
Dissatisfied customers	13.6	14.3	16.1	17.3	18.9	19.6
Relative product quality	+10.0	+8.0	+5.0	+3.0	+1.0	+0.0
Relative service quality	+0.0	+0.0	−20.0	−3.0	−5.0	−8.0
Relative new product sales	+8.0	+8.0	+7.0	+5.0	+1.0	−4.0

away through the provision of levels of service which are not justified by the revenue.

This is perfectly in order if it is done deliberately as an investment strategy in key accounts selected as having the best potential over, say, a three-year planning horizon. However, where there is no such proactive strategy, money is being lost without justification.

Table 6.4 Quality of profits

%	Virtuous plc (%)	Dissembler plc (%)
Sales revenue	100	100
Cost of goods sold	43	61
Profit margin	57	39
Advertising	11	3
R&D	5	–
Capital investment	7	2
Investment ratio	23	5
Operating expenses	20	20
Operating profit	14	4
Key trends	Past five year revenue growth 10% pa Heavy advertising investment in new/improved products Premium priced products, new plant, so low cost of goods sold	Flat revenue, declining volume No recent product innovation, little advertising Discounted pricing, so high cost of goods sold
The make-up of 14% operating profits		
Factor		
Profit on existing products over three years old	21	15
Losses on products recently launched or in development	(7)	(1)
Total operating profits	14	14

Note: This table is similar to a profit and loss with one important exception – depreciation, a standard item in any profit and loss has been replaced by capital investment, which does not appear in profit and loss statements. In the long term, capital investment levels determine depreciation costs. Capital investment as a percentage of sales is an investment ratio often ignored by marketers, and it has been included in this table to emphasize its importance (Reichheld and Sasser, 1990).

Source: Davidson (1998)

Let us examine Figure 6.9. The line of best fit indicates a perfect match between the strategic intent of both the supplying and buying companies. In Figures 6.10 and 6.11, however, we see an obvious mismatch and it is likely that both companies are losing money unnecessarily. This judgement of the situation of course presupposes that supplying organizations have systems that can measure *attributable* costs, that is to say those costs which are directly related to a particular account. Alas, our database at Cranfield shows that a very substantial majority of Western European companies do not measure attributable costs. Figure 6.12 – from a Cranfield database of over 500 leading European

Supplier delusion about relationships leads to profitability leaking away through unjustified levels of customer service.

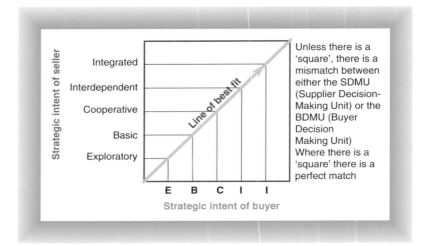

Figure 6.9
A match between
buyers and sellers.

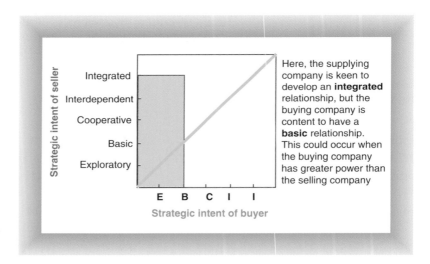

Figure 6.10
Mismatch between
buyer (*basic*) and seller
(*integrated*).

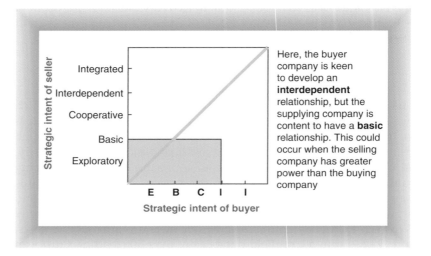

Figure 6.11
Mismatch
between buyer
(*interdependent*)
and seller (*basic*).

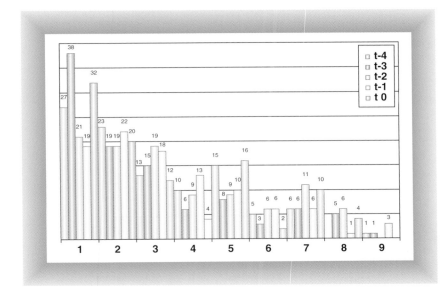

Figure 6.12
Cranfield survey on key account profitability.

companies over a five-year period – illustrates this point. The figure shows the spread of answers to the question: 'How well do you know the real profitability of your top 10 accounts, having taken into account attributable costs' (1 = not at all, 9 = totally).

Yet suppliers still persist in using operating systems that spread the overheads across the customer base according to turnover, in effect penalizing customers who are easy to serve and rewarding customers who are difficult and costly to serve.

Figure 6.13 shows the current profitability of the top 10 per cent of customers of a major European print company as compared with 15 years ago. This comparative example is taken from Charles Wilson's excellent book, *Profitable Customers: How to Identify, Develop and Keep Them* (Wilson, 1998), and confirms the Cranfield research finding highlighted in Figure 6.12 that most companies today fail to keep a prudent check on key account profitability. This disturbing trend must be of particular concern to chief executives and also to financial directors. To understand and measure key account profitability is to direct/ define the destiny of your customer relationships and, thus, your business future!

CHECKPOINT

Partner level relationships

- Are you able to measure the real profitability of your key accounts?

- How has the level of profitability changed over the past three years?

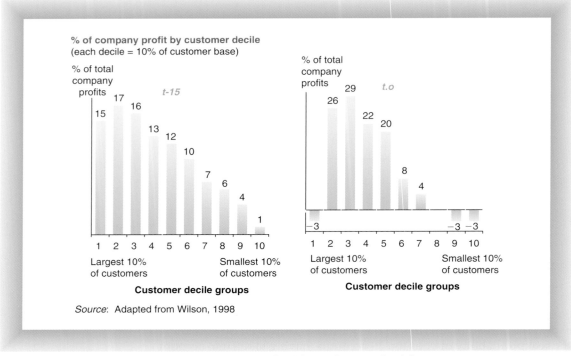

% of company profit by customer decile
(each decile = 10% of customer base)

Source: Adapted from Wilson, 1998

Figure 6.13 The widening rift between profitable and unprofitable customers.

6.1.3 The impact on business of this lack of customer focus

On top of all the pressures referred to earlier, a new wave of business metrics such as shareholder added value and balanced scorecards, together with pressure from institutional shareholders to report meaningful facts about corporate performance rather than the traditional, high-level financial reporting that appears every year in corporate accounts, are forcing business leaders to re-examine tired corporate behaviours such as cost-cutting, mergers and downsizing as a route to profitability.

Finally, business leaders are under intense pressure to deliver against stakeholder expectations; customers are demanding greater levels of customization, access, service and value; shareholders are expecting to see continuous growth in earnings per share and in the capital value of shares; and pressure groups are demanding exemplary corporate citizenship.

> At long last the world has genuinely moved from *caveat emptor* to *caveat vendor*.

The result is that, at long last, the world has genuinely moved from *caveat emptor* to *caveat vendor*. No longer can we continue to hammer into the soggy brains of erstwhile supine customers the messages that *we* want them to receive. No, the world has changed forever and 'marketing' (in the sense that it contains the word 'market') must now be taken seriously.

Some evidence of the results of a lack of a robust strategy towards markets follows.

Table 6.5 Performance of selected companies 1979–1989

Year	Company[a]	Market value (£m)	Return on investment[b]	Subsequent performance
1979	MFI	57	50	Collapsed
1980	Lasmo	134	97	Still profitable
1981	Bejam	79	34	Acquired
1982	Racal	940	36	Still profitable
1983	Polly Peck	128	79	Collapsed
1984	Atlantic Computers	151	36	Collapsed
1985	BSR	197	32	Still profitable
1986	Jaguar	819	60	Acquired
1987	Amstrad	987	89	Still profitable
1988	Body Shop	225	89	Still profitable
1989	Blue Arrow	653	135	Collapsed

[a] Where a company has been top for more than one year, the next best company has been chosen in the subsequent year, e.g. Polly Peck was related top 1983, 1984 and 1985.
[b] Pre-tax profit as a percentage of investment capital.
Source: Professor Peter Doyle, Warwick University

What better place to start than with *In Search of Excellence: Lessons from America's Best-Run Companies* (Peters and Waterman, 1982)? According to Richard Pascale, of Tom Peters' original 43 excellent companies, 14 were still excellent five years later and only six were still excellent eight years later! (Pascale, 1990).

Table 6.5 shows clearly that many of Britain's best-performing companies during the decade up to 1990 subsequently collapsed and Table 6.6 shows a selection of leading companies in different sectors during the decade up to 2000 and what happened to them.

Table 6.7 shows the retention rate of a real company by segment. Other unpublished research from the Cranfield University School of Management research club that looks at marketing measurement shows that, almost 16 years after the famous Reicheld and Sasser (1990) article, very few companies have learned the lesson about retaining profitable customers.

As we have already indicated, at the time of writing it is too early to complete a comparable analysis for the first decade of the twenty-first century. Nonetheless, even a cursory glance at some of the world's major financial institutions will indicate that short-term success is no indicator of sustainable success.

To summarize this section, we conclude that short-termism – in the sense of maximizing profits in a single fiscal period to the detriment of

Table 6.6   Performance of sector leaders 1990–2000

Year	Company[a]	Market value (£m)[b]	Return on investment (%)[c]	Subsequent performance
1990	Maxwell Communications plc	1.0	5	Collapsed
1991	Imperial Chemical Industries plc	8.6	13	Collapsed
1992	Wellcome plc	8.3	40	Acquired
1993	ASDA Group	1.6	7	Acquired
1994	TSB Group plc	3.7	20	Acquired
1995	British Telecommunications plc	22.2	17	Not profitable
1996	British Steel plc	3.3	19	Collapsed
1997	British Airways plc	6.1	7	Not profitable
1998	National Westminster Bank plc	19.6	14	Acquired
1999	Marconi plc	29.8	22	Acquired
2000	Marks & Spencer plc	5.3	7	Not profitable

[a] Each company was a FTSE100 when selected.
[b] Market values as of 31 December of each year.
[c] Pre-tax profit as a percentage of equity and long-term debt.

long-term profitability – is a 'disease' of management rather than of the financial investment community, who fully understand that the two are not mutually exclusive. Indeed, it has always been those companies such as Procter and Gamble, 3M, General Electric and Tesco which grow their short-term profits annually, while investing in a long-term profitable future, that have been continuously successful financially for many years.

Table 6.7   Retention of customers by segment

	Total market	Segment					
		1	2	3	4	5	6
Percentage of market represented by segment	100.0	14.8	9.5	27.1	18.8	18.8	11.0
Percentage of all profits in total market produced by segment	100.0	7.1	4.9	14.7	21.8	28.5	23.0
Ratio of profit produced by segment to weight of segment in total population	1.00	0.48	0.52	0.54	1.16	1.52	2.09
Defection rate	23%	20%	17%	**15%**	28%	30%	**35%**

6.2   Valuing key accounts

It will be clear to discerning readers that everything we have said above about sustainable competitive advantage, customer retention and risk applies equally to key accounts and we now turn our attention to this specific topic

6.2.1   Risk, return and shareholder value in key accounts

First, it is necessary to understand the concept of net free cash flow in relation to key accounts. This is the total sales revenue generated from a customer, less all the costs that are incurred in servicing that account. As already stated, overhead costs include a proportion of overhead costs in relation to their use in servicing the account. Activity-based costing (ABC) can be used to determine how much this should be.

Knowing key account profitability in terms of net free cash flow:

- assists in deciding whether to keep the customer and on what terms,
- helps in strategic decisions about the allocation of scarce company resources, and
- enables informed decisions to be taken in negotiations and in pricing.

A basic profitability model is shown in Figure 6.14

Related to these calculations, the following kinds of questions need to be discussed:

- How much does the customer buy in a year?
- What is the direct cost of those goods?
- Are the products standard or bespoke?
- Is it steady work, or seasonal peaks?
- How many orders do they place in a year? By what mechanism? How many of these are 'emergency' orders? Are they small quantities or large?
- How many times do sales people have to visit them?
- Do you have to maintain stock for them, or do you make to order?
- How many delivery sites are there? Where? What delivery terms?
- How many invoices do you raise to them? How many credit notes?
- Do they pay promptly? What are your credit control costs? How much does it cost you to finance their debts?
- How much after-sales service do they need?
- What is likely to change in the future?

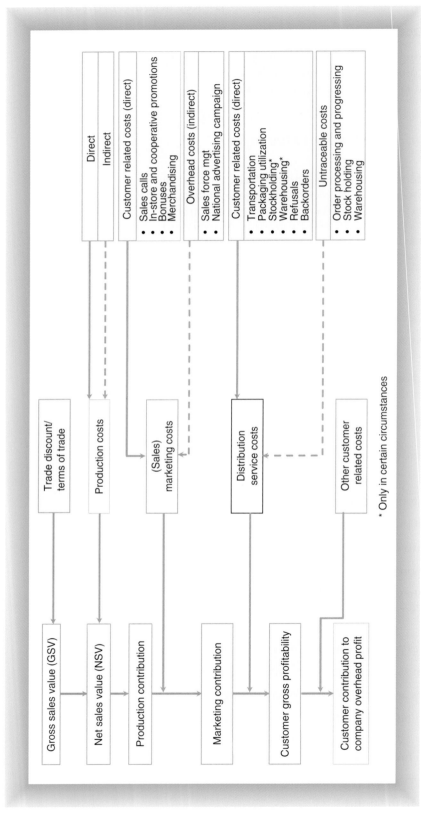

Figure 6.14 A basic profitability model.

It is worth remembering that in the early stages of dealing with a major customer, cash flows may be negative while a position of strength is established, so it is important to calculate cash flows over a planning period of at least three years.

However, these cash flows need to be reduced using a probability assessment based on the risks associated with particular accounts, such as the risk of:

● Defection or migration

● Volatile purchasing patterns

● Negative word of mouth

● Default, fraud or litigation

● Slow payment.

Professor Lynette Ryals of Cranfield University School of Management established a method for such a probabilistic quantification of risks during a five-year doctoral study into key account profitability (Ryals, 2002). The factors considered and shown in the methodology that follows in Section 6.5 can be easily amended to suit a company's particular circumstances.

First, however, Figure 6.15 shows that key accounts can be positioned on a risk/return graph in the same way that companies or markets can. Those below the line are destroying shareholder value; those above are creating shareholder value. The reality, of course, is that there will always be some key accounts that are not creating shareholder value, but as long as these are managed appropriately (i.e.

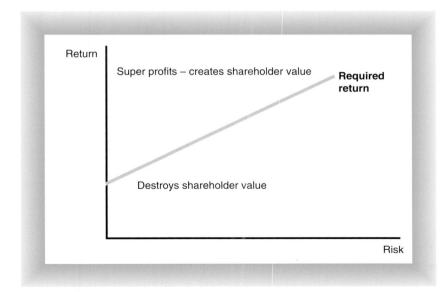

Figure 6.15
How organizations build value from key accounts.

trying to increase revenue and reduce costs) and as long as the aggregate of key accounts is creating shareholder value over the strategic planning period, this is acceptable.

6.2.2 Implementing the methodology

In this section we provide a step-by-step method for calculating whether key accounts create or destroy shareholder value.

Background/facts

● Risk and return are positively correlated, that is, as risk increases, investors expect a higher return.

● Risk is measured by the volatility in returns, that is, the likelihood of making a very good return or losing money. This can be described as the quality of returns.

● All assets are defined as having future value to the organization. Hence assets to be valued include not only tangible assets like plant and machinery, but intangible assets, such as key accounts.

● The present value of future cash flows is one of the most acceptable methods to value assets including key accounts.

● The present value is increased by:
    - increasing the future cash flows,
    - making the future cash flows 'happen' earlier, and
    - reducing the risk in these cash flows, that is, improving the certainty of these cash flows, and, hence, reducing the required rate of return.

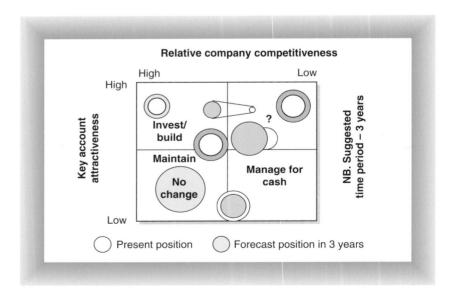

Figure 6.16
Portfolio analysis –
directional policy
matrix.

Suggested approach

● Identify your key accounts. It is helpful if they can be classified on a vertical axis (a kind of thermometer) according to their attractiveness to your company. 'Attractiveness' usually means the potential of each for growth in your profits over a period of between three and five years (Figure 6.16).

- Based on your current experience and a planning horizon that you are confident with, make a projection of future net free cash in-flows from your key customers. It is normal to select a period such as three or five years.

- These calculations will consist of three parts:
  - revenue forecasts for each year,
  - cost forecasts for each year, and
  - net free cash flow for each key customer for each year.

- Identify the key factors that are likely to either increase or decrease these future cash flows. These factors are risks.

- These risks are likely to be assessed according to the factors shown on the relationship risk scorecard shown in Table 6.8 (used here with the kind permission of Professor Lynette Ryals of Cranfield University School of Management).

Table 6.8   Relationship risk factors

Relationship risk factors	Minimum value	Maximum value	Assigned probability
Overall relationship with the company			
1. Number of relationships with other business units	0	3	0 = 40%, 1 = 60%, 2 = 80%, >2 = 90%
2. Number of business lines within this business unit	3	10	1 = 40%, 2 = 50%, 3 = 60%, 4 = 70%, 5–10 = 80%, >10 = 90%
3. Longevity of relationship (years)	0.5	16	≤3 = 40%, 3 = 60%, 4 = 70%, 5 = 80%, >5 = 90%
Account relationship			
4. Company's relationship with broker[a]	1	5	1 = 40%, 2 = 60%, 3 = 70%, 5 = 80%, 5 = 90%
5. Quality and warmth of company/client relationship[a]	1	5	1 = 40%, 2 = 60%, 3 = 70%, 4 = 80%, 5 = 90%
6. Number of relationship contacts company has at client	2	8	1 = 50%, 2 = 60%, 3 = 80%, >3 = 90%
7. Number of relationship contacts client has at company	3	10	1 = 50%, 2 = 60%, 3 = 80%, >3 = 90%
Understanding of client			
8. How good was our understanding of their company[a]	1	5	1 = 40%, 2 = 60%, 3 = 70%, 4 = 80%, 5 = 90%
9. How good was our understanding of their industry[a]	1	5	1 = 40%, 2 = 60%, 3 = 70%, 4 = 80%, 5 = 90%

[a] 1 = very poor, 2 = poor, 3 = fair, 4 = good, 5 = excellent.
Source: Ryals (2002). Reproduced with her kind permission.

- Now recalculate the revenues, costs and net free cash flows for each year, having adjusted the figures using the risks (probabilities) from the above.

- Ask your accountant to provide you with the overall strategic business unit (SBU) cost of capital and capital used in the SBU. This will not consist only of tangible assets.

- Deduct the proportional cost of capital from the free cash flow for each key customer for each year.

- An aggregate positive NPV indicates that you are creating shareholder value – that is, achieving overall returns greater than the weighted average cost of capital, having taken into account the risk associated with future cash flows.

CHECKPOINT

Partner level relationships

- Are you able to measure the real profitability of your key accounts?

- How has the level of profitability changed over the past three years?

Summary

Marketing accountability is one of the biggest challenges facing all organizations today and a major component of this is key account profitability. Major customers are assets, just like buildings and cash. This chapter has positioned key account profitability firmly within the context of marketing accountability and has spelled out a state-of-the-art methodology for calculating whether the key account programme creates or destroys shareholder value.

7 Key account analysis

Correct market definition and market segmentation are essential prerequisites of successful key account management. A market is the aggregation of all goods and services that can satisfy a particular need or set of needs. Drawing a map of how goods and services flow through the value chain helps a key account manager understand the customer's business, as well as revealing ways in which you may be able to add value as a supplier.

Market segmentation is the process of breaking a market down into smaller groups of customers who share the same or similar needs. It is important at two distinct levels. First, key accounts in one segment may have different needs from those in another segment. Second, understanding how your customer's market is segmented provides much potential for helping them to succeed.

The total process of preplanning prior to producing a strategic plan for your customer is shown in the following diagram.

Steps 1, 2 and 3 should, ideally, be completed centrally to avoid duplication of effort by key account managers. Step 3 is about understanding in depth the forces that are being brought to bear on competitors in an industry. These are: customers, supplies, substitutes, potential entrants and, of course, industry competitors. A PEST analysis (political, economic, sociological, technological) is also an extremely useful way of understanding more about the customer's trading environment.

Each key account manager can now use this information to delve further into each customer's specific business processes. This includes understanding the customer's objectives and strategies, their financial ratios, how their business processes work, their buying processes, their sales history and their dealings with competitors.

One extremely useful vehicle for summarizing much of this is the traditional SWOT analysis (strengths, weaknesses, opportunities and threats), completed as if it were the customers themselves completing it.

All the CSFs (critical success factors) for the customer can now be sorted into those categories that merely help them to avoid disadvantage and, crucially, those that can create advantage for them, for clearly it is this latter group that will encourage a key customer to prefer dealing with you rather than with one of your competitors. You now have everything you need to approach the customer with your proposals for how you can help them increase sales, reduce costs, avoid costs or add value in other ways. They are usually so impressed that they are prepared to give you additional confidential information. You are now ready to prepare a strategic plan for the customers.

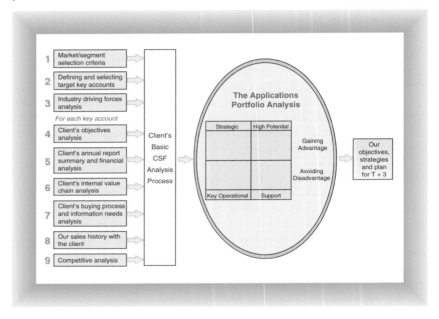

In this chapter

Introduction

One of the objectives of this chapter is to place key account management (KAM) in the context of market segmentation, for it is creative market segmentation which is universally recognized as the key to sustainable competitive advantage. Another is to spell out how to understand in depth the environment in which key accounts operate. Finally, it explains in detail how to understand how key accounts run their business as a route to revealing ways in which you can help them to increase sales, avoid costs, reduce costs or add value.

7.1 Market segmentation and key account management

7.1.1 Understanding markets

Most organizations' different market segments will contain a number of key accounts. Before proceeding to analyse the needs of key accounts and set objectives and strategies for them, it is necessary to ensure that you have the clearest understanding of how your own market works, what the key segments are and where you can exert the most influence on decisions about what is bought and from whom. It is equally important to understand your customers' segmentation and how their market works. This is essential knowledge, for it will provide the backcloth against which plans for key accounts are evaluated and eventually controlled. Indeed, it would be fair to say that an appreciation of market segmentation is an essential criterion for effective KAM. Before explaining a little more about market segmentation, however, here are some introductory comments by way of background.

'The good thing about being mediocre is you are always at your best.' Someone once said this about corporate life. Imagine getting your salesforce up at five every morning to go out and kill for 'We are really mediocre!' Everyone has heard of Alexander the Great. Had he been mediocre, he certainly would not be in our history books. So what makes any of us think that making mediocre offers to our customers is ever going to have anything but mediocre results?

Taking this theme a stage further, we can ask ourselves what sort of company would make a commodity out of bread, fertilizer, glass, chlorine, potatoes, mobile phones, etc.? By way of an answer, ask whether anyone can 'taste' the difference between Castrol GTX or any other manufacturer's oil, or between Alfa Laval Steel, SKF Bearings, Intel Microprocessors and so on. Yet these great companies, dealing with low differentiation products in mainly mature markets, are perennially successful. So, what is the secret of success?

A review of the work of a number of gurus, such as Sir Michael Perry, ex-chairman of Unilever, Tom Peters and Phillip Kotler, reveals a striking similarity between what they consider to be the key elements of world-class marketing.

1. A profound understanding of the market

2. Market segmentation and selection

3. Powerful differentiation, positioning and branding

4. Effective marketing planning processes

5. Long-term integrated marketing strategies.

> It is intensely irritating when the questioners know so little about their markets.

While this is not the complete list, it is interesting to note the order of the elements listed here. We find it remarkable that, even in the new millennium, so many companies are changing their brand strategies without really understanding their market and how it is segmented or their competitive position. Indeed, 'What shall we do with our brand?' is one of the most recurrent questions and, while it is easy to understand why it is asked, branding being the glamorous part of marketing, it is intensely irritating when the questioners know so little about their markets.

Let us explain what we mean. We frequently run workshops for the Boards of strategic business units. Before we start the workshop, we ask the directors to write a list, in order of priority, of their key target markets. Often they write down their products, such as pensions or mainframe computers. Rarely is there any sensible grasp of the meaning of the word 'market'. So, they fail the first test. The second part of the exercise is to write down their sources of differential advantages against each key target market listed. When these senior people fail such an elementary test, it is clear that their organization is either in or heading towards trouble.

We recently came across one insurance company which prided itself on its market segmentation. On questioning, however, its segments turned out to be sectors, which explained why it had little or no differentiation and was competing mainly on price. Indeed, this is one of the most commonly observed misconceptions about market segmentation. Everyone knows that a segment is a group of customers with the same or similar needs and that there are many different purchase combinations within and across sectors, yet companies still persist in confusing sectors with segments.

> A segment is a group of customers with the same or similar needs. Companies still persist in confusing sectors with segments.

Perhaps the most frequent mistake, however, is *a priori* segmentation, which is largely the result of the vast amount of prescriptive literature on the subject of segmentation. All books state that there are several bases for segmentation, such as demographics, socioeconomics, geography, usage, psychographics, geo-demographics, lifestyle and so on, and the literature is replete with proponents of one or more of these. However, this is to miss the point completely, for in any market there is only one correct segmentation. One hundred per cent of goods and services are 'made', distributed, influenced and used and the purchase combinations that result are a fact not a figment of someone's imagination. The task is to understand the market structure, how it works and what the actual segments are at different junctions in the market.

This brings us to the starting point in market segmentation – market definition and market structure. Correct market definition is crucial for measuring market share and market growth, identifying relevant competitors and, of course, the formulating of marketing strategies in order to deliver differential advantage.

The general rule for defining a 'market' is that it should be described in terms of a customer need in a way that covers the aggregation of all the alternative products or services which customers regard as being capable of satisfying that same need. For example, we would regard the in-company caterer as only one option when it comes to satisfying lunchtime hunger. That need could also be satisfied at external restaurants, public houses, fast food outlets and sandwich bars. The emphasis in the definition is therefore clearly on the word 'need'.

Figure 7.1 is an example of a complete 'market map', showing how goods move from originators through to final users, with volumes, values and market shares all adding up in a manner not unlike a balance sheet. However, few companies give sufficient intellectual thought to market definition – witness Gestetner, who thought it was in the duplicator market, and IBM, who thought it was in the mainframe market. Hence few can draw anything approaching an accurate market map and have little chance of doing any kind of sensible segmentation at the key influence points of junctions along the market map.

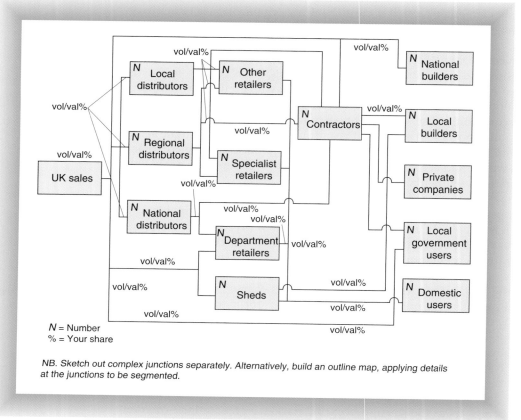

Figure 7.1 Example of a market map including the number of each customer type.

7.1.2 Market segmentation

At each of these key junctions, segmentation is not only possible, but necessary. It is here that the process becomes quite complicated, for the trick is to make an exhaustive list of all the different purchase combinations that take place at each junction. This entails listing what is bought (to include applications, features, where, when and how products or services are bought), together with the associated descriptors (who buys what). This will often produce somewhere between 30 and 50 different purchase combinations, or what we term micro segments. A micro segment is one of a large number of different purchase combinations that take place in a market. However, the reality is that these micro segments do indeed represent what actually happens in the market.

The next step is to specify the benefits that each of these micro segments seek by buying what they buy in the way they do. This is crucial. It is often here that external market research is necessary.

It is now simply a question of using one of the many software packages available to cluster micro segments with similar requirements; clusters are given a dimension of size by adding the volumes or values

Cooking appliances
Is it a single market or several separate markets?

Volume	(units)
Value	
Domestic/commercial	
Fuels	(gas, electricity, coal, oil, etc.)
Cooking methods	(heat, radiation, convection)
Cooking function	(surface heating, baking, roasting, charcoal, etc.)
Design	(free standing, built-in, combination)
Prices	
Product features	
OEM/replacement	
Geography	
Channels	(direct, shops, wholesalers, mail order)
Why bought	
Others	(promotional response, lifestyle, demographics)
Usage	

Figure 7.2
Determining the presence of market segments.

represented by each micro segment. It is our experience that most markets can be broken down into 10 or fewer segments. The only remaining task is to ensure that our offers meet the requirements of each segment and that we, as suppliers, are organized to sell, deliver and support the appropriate value propositions.

Faced with a plethora of options for segmentation, as illustrated in Figure 7.2, it is not difficult to understand why most organizations take an overly simplistic approach to segmentation and end up with little or no differential advantage.

One thing is abundantly clear from our detailed segmentation work: price is rarely the prime motivator in the way people buy. The following case history will illustrate the point.

> Price is rarely the prime motivator in the way people buy.

Case study insight

How ICI used market segmentation to its advantage

ICI Fertilizers went through a severe loss-making period during the late 1980s as the market matured and foreign competitors entered the market with cheap imports. Prices and margins fell to disastrous levels. However, the company had the perspicacity to go through the segmentation process described here and discovered seven relatively distinct segments of farmers, only one of which was price sensitive. This segment represented only 10 per cent of the market, not 100 per cent, as had been previously

> thought. One segment was highly technological in its approach, while another was more influenced by the appearance of crops. Yet another was loyal to merchants. Yet another was loyal to brands. Each segment was given a name and the needs of each were researched in depth. Products were developed and offers made to match the precise needs of the individual segments, while the company and its processes were reorganized in order to ensure that the appropriate value could be delivered. ICI Fertilizers became an extremely profitable company in an industry whose own governing body had officially designated fertilizer as a commodity!

Hopefully, this heartening story of creative segmentation leading to sustained profitability in a mature and generally unprofitable industry will encourage readers to rethink their approach to segmentation. The market segmentation process described here is summarized in Figure 7.3.

7.1.3 Why market segmentation is vital in key account planning

In today's highly competitive world, few companies can afford to compete only on price, for the product has not yet been sold that someone cannot sell cheaper – apart from which, in many markets it is rarely the cheapest product that succeeds anyway. What this means is that we have to find some way of differentiating ourselves from the competition, and the answer lies in market segmentation.

The truth is that very few companies can afford to be 'all things to all people'. The main aim of market segmentation as part of the marketing planning process is to enable a business concern to target its effort at the most promising opportunities. However, what is an opportunity for firm A is not necessarily an opportunity for firm B. So a firm needs to develop a typology of the customers or segment it prefers, for this can be an instrument of great productivity in the marketplace.

The whole point of market segmentation is that a firm must either:

- define its markets broadly enough to ensure that its costs for key activities are competitive or
- define its markets in such a way that it can develop specialized skills in serving them to overcome a relative cost disadvantage.

Both strategies have to be related to a firm's distinctive competence and to that of its competitors.

To summarize, the objectives of market segmentation are as follows:

- To help determine marketing direction through the analysis and understanding of trends and buyer behaviour.

The product has not yet been sold that someone, somewhere, cannot sell cheaper.

Few companies can afford to be 'all things to all people'.

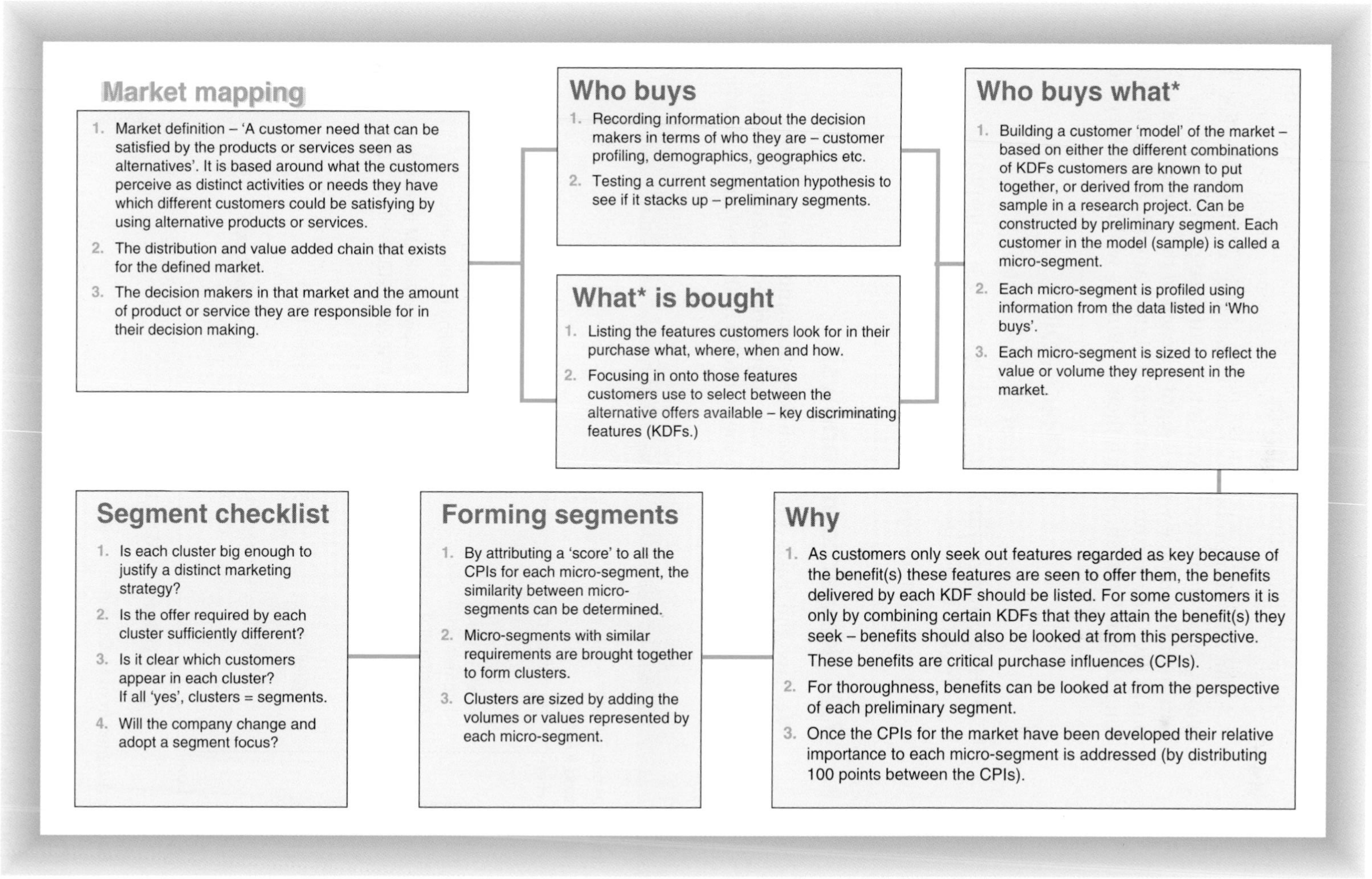

Market mapping

1. Market definition – 'A customer need that can be satisfied by the products or services seen as alternatives'. It is based around what the customers perceive as distinct activities or needs they have which different customers could be satisfying by using alternative products or services.
2. The distribution and value added chain that exists for the defined market.
3. The decision makers in that market and the amount of product or service they are responsible for in their decision making.

Who buys

1. Recording information about the decision makers in terms of who they are – customer profiling, demographics, geographics etc.
2. Testing a current segmentation hypothesis to see if it stacks up – preliminary segments.

What* is bought

1. Listing the features customers look for in their purchase what, where, when and how.
2. Focusing in onto those features customers use to select between the alternative offers available – key discriminating features (KDFs.)

Who buys what*

1. Building a customer 'model' of the market – based on either the different combinations of KDFs customers are known to put together, or derived from the random sample in a research project. Can be constructed by preliminary segment. Each customer in the model (sample) is called a micro-segment.
2. Each micro-segment is profiled using information from the data listed in 'Who buys'.
3. Each micro-segment is sized to reflect the value or volume they represent in the market.

Why

1. As customers only seek out features regarded as key because of the benefit(s) these features are seen to offer them, the benefits delivered by each KDF should be listed. For some customers it is only by combining certain KDFs that they attain the benefit(s) they seek – benefits should also be looked at from this perspective. These benefits are critical purchase influences (CPIs).
2. For thoroughness, benefits can be looked at from the perspective of each preliminary segment.
3. Once the CPIs for the market have been developed their relative importance to each micro-segment is addressed (by distributing 100 points between the CPIs).

Forming segments

1. By attributing a 'score' to all the CPIs for each micro-segment, the similarity between micro-segments can be determined.
2. Micro-segments with similar requirements are brought together to form clusters.
3. Clusters are sized by adding the volumes or values represented by each micro-segment.

Segment checklist

1. Is each cluster big enough to justify a distinct marketing strategy?
2. Is the offer required by each cluster sufficiently different?
3. Is it clear which customers appear in each cluster? If all 'yes', clusters = segments.
4. Will the company change and adopt a segment focus?

Figure 7.3 Market segmentation process.

- To help determine realistic and obtainable marketing and sales objectives.

- To help improve decision making by forcing managers to consider the available options in depth.

A clear and comprehensive understanding of their market, how it works, how it breaks down into natural segments and the specific nature of the unique value sought by each of these segments will obviously give key account managers a significant advantage in building long-term relationships with their customers within these segments.

CHECKPOINT

Market segmentation

- Has your organization developed a segmentation that meets the criteria described in this section?

- How many segments are there in your market?

7.2 Key account analysis

We saw the basis on which key accounts should be defined and selected in Chapter 2. This was summarized diagrammatically in Figure 2.4. Another version of the portfolio is shown here in Figure 7.4.

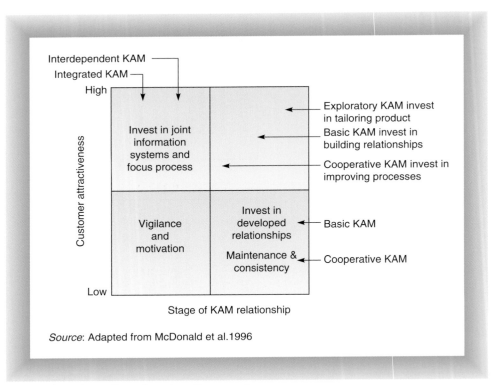

Source: Adapted from McDonald et al. 1996

Figure 7.4   A four-box directional policy matrix.

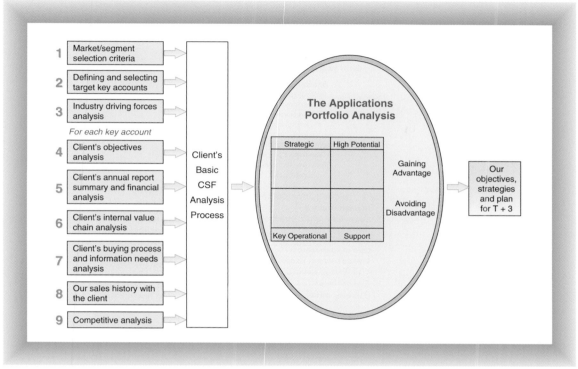

Figure 7.5 Business partnership process.

We now provide a set of specific and detailed procedures for key account analysis prior to producing a strategic marketing plan for each key account selected as being worthy of focused attention by the key account team. An overview of the total process, which we have called the business partnership process, is given in Figure 7.5.

Step 1 in Figure 7.5 has just been described and step 2 was dealt with in Chapter 2.

7.2.1 Industry driving forces and PEST analysis (step 3)

Step 3 is known as Porter's industry five-forces analysis. It is taken from Porter's book *Competitive Strategy* (Porter, 1980) and has been of enormous value to generations of managers since its first publication. It is shown in summary form as Figure 7.6.

Put simply, any industry has a number of competitors (located in the centre of the figure) and the relative performance of these competitors is determined by recognizable forces:

- Potential entrants
- Customers
- Potential substitute products and services
- The power of suppliers.

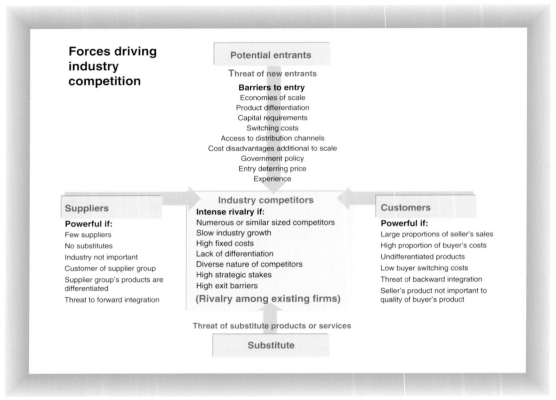

Figure 7.6 Forces driving industry competition.

The words in Figure 7.6 aptly describe the implications of each of the four outside forces on the competitors and it is clear that all competitors in a sector or industry will be affected by these driving forces.

It is worth repeating that this analysis is obviously best done by someone in central support services, perhaps marketing, as there is little point in a number of key account managers in the same industry all spending their time conducting the same analysis. If this is not practicable, then the job will indeed have to be done by individual key account managers for their own sectors.

It must be stressed, however, that such an analysis is a prerequisite to the individual account analysis described later in this chapter, as it provides key account managers with a deep analysis of their customers' industry and how it works and affects their performance.

In Tables 7.1 and 7.2 there are checklists of areas that should be investigated as part of the process of understanding your customers' business environment. This is analysed in greater detail in Table 7.3. The first section is about the business and economic environment in which your customer operates (PEST). The second part is about understanding your customer's market. The third part is about understanding your customer's internal operations (Table 7.4). The second and third parts (the

customer's market and their operations) should be carried out by each
key account manager for specific customers.

The next section of this chapter expands on how the information and
data should be used. It is fully appreciated that this long list is an ideal
and you will be unable to find some of it. Nevertheless, by knowing
what you need to know you can continuously search for answers.

Operations and resources

- **Marketing objectives:** Are the marketing objectives clearly stated
  and consistent with marketing and corporate objectives?

- **Marketing strategy:** What is the strategy for achieving the stated
  objectives? Are sufficient resources available to achieve these objectives? Are the available resources sufficient and optimally allocated
  across elements of the marketing mix?

Table 7.1   External audit

Business and economic environment	*Competition*
● Economic	● Major competitors
● Political/fiscal/legal	● Size
● Social/cultural	● Market shares/coverage
● Technological	● Market standing/reputation
● Intracompany	● Production capabilities
	● Distribution policies
	● Marketing methods
The market	● Extent of diversification
● Total market, size, growth and trends (value/volume)	● Personnel issues
	● International links
● Market characteristics, development and trends	● Profitability
● Products	● Key strengths and weaknesses
● Prices	
● Physical distribution	
● Channels	
● Customer/consumers	
● Communication	
● Industry practices	

Table 7.2   Internal audit

Marketing operational variables	*Marketing mix variables*
● Own company	● Product management
● Sales (total, by geographical location, industrial type, by customer, by product)	● Price
	● Distribution
	● Promotion
● Market shares	
● Profit margins/costs	
● Marketing procedures	
● Marketing organization	
● Marketing information/research	

Table 7.3 PEST analysis and market factors – external (opportunities and threats)

Business and economic environment		
Economic	Inflation, unemployment, energy, price, volatility, materials availability, etc.	As they affect the customer business
Political/fiscal/ legal	Nationalization, union legislation, human rights legislation, taxation, duty increases, regulatory constraints (e.g. labelling, product quality, packaging, trade practices, advertising, pricing, etc.)	As they affect the customer business
Social/cultural	Education, immigration, emigration, religion, environment, population distribution and dynamics (e.g. age distribution, regional distribution, etc.), changes in consumer lifestyle, etc.	As they affect the customer business
Technological	Aspects of product and/or production technology which could profoundly affect the economics of the industry (e.g. new technology, the Internet, cost savings, materials components, equipment, machinery, methods and systems, availability of substitutes, etc.)	As they affect the customer business
Intracompany	Capital investment, closures, strikes, etc.	As they affect the customer business
The market		
Total market	Size, growth and trends (value, volume). *Customers/consumers:* changing demographics, psychographics and purchasing behaviour	
Market characteristics developments and trends	*Products:* principal products bought; end-use of products; product, characteristics (weights, measures, sizes, physical characteristics packaging, accessories, associated products, etc.)	
	Prices: price levels and range; terms and conditions of sale; normal trade practices; official regulations; etc.	
	Physical distribution: principal method of physical distribution	
	Channels: principal channels: purchasing patterns (e.g. types of product bought; prices paid, etc.); purchasing ability; geographical location; stocks; turnover; profits; needs; tastes; attitudes; decision makers, bases of purchasing decision; etc.	
	Communication: principal methods of communication, e.g. the Internet, sales force, advertising, direct response, exhibitions, public relations, etc.	
	Industry practices: e.g. trade associations, government bodies, historical attitudes, interim comparisons, etc.	
Competition	*Industry structure:* make-up of companies in the industry, major market standing/ reputation; extent of excess capacity; production capability; distribution capability; marketing methods; competitive arrangements; extent of diversification into other areas by major companies in the industry; new entrants; mergers; acquisitions; bankruptcies; significant aspects; international links; key strengths and weaknesses	
	Industry profitability: financial and non-financial barriers to entry; industry profitability and the relative performance of individual companies; structure of operating costs; investment; effect on return on investment of changes in price; volume; cost of investment; source of industry profits, etc.	

Sales (total, by geographical location, by industrial type, by customer by product)	
Market shares Profit margins Marketing procedures: ● Market research ● Product development ● Product range ● Product quality ● Unit of sale ● Stock levels ● Distribution ● Dealer support ● Pricing, discounts, credit ● Packaging	Marketing organization Sales/marketing control data Marketing mix variables: ● Samples ● Exhibitions ● Selling ● Sales aids ● Point of sale ● Advertising ● Sales promotion ● Public relations ● After-sales service ● Training

Table 7.4
Internal factors
(strengths and
weaknesses)

● **Structure:** Are the marketing responsibilities and authorities clearly structured along functional, product, end-user and territorial lines?

● **Information system:** Is the marketing intelligence system producing accurate, sufficient and timely information about developments in the marketplace? Is information gathered being used effectively in making marketing decisions?

● **Planning system:** Is the marketing planning system well conceived and effective?

● **Control system:** Do control mechanisms and procedures exist within the group to ensure planned objectives are achieved (e.g. meeting overall objectives, etc.)?

● **Functional efficiency:** Are internal communications within the group effective?

● **Interfunctional efficiency:** Are there any problems between marketing and other corporate functions? Is the question of centralized versus decentralized marketing an issue in the company?

● **Profitability analysis:** Is the profitability performance monitored by product, served markets, etc. to assess where the best profits and biggest costs of the operations are located?

● **Cost-effectiveness analysis:** Do any current marketing activities seem to have excess costs? Are these valid or could they be reduced?

It should also be stressed here that steps 4–9 in Figure 7.5 are all concerned with the analysis/diagnosis stage, which must be completed by each key account manager before preparing a strategic plan for each key account.

The remainder of this chapter explains how the data and information collected by the key account manager should be used.

7.2.2 Key account analysis preplanning

Before it is possible to plan for key accounts, a detailed analysis of each key account must be undertaken by each individual key account manager and their team, somewhat in the manner of conducting a marketing audit. First, however, steps 1, 2 and 3 in Figure 7.5 should be completed. The reason steps 1 to 3 are separate from the next six steps is that it is recommended that if you have a marketing department, these first three steps should be carried out by them, otherwise individual key account managers may consume their valuable time by repeating analysis already completed elsewhere.

Step 4 (Figure 7.5): Client's objectives analysis

The exercise given in Figure 7.7 should be completed for each key account being targeted. It can be seen that the intention is to take the industry driving forces analysis and apply it specifically to any individual account in order to understand better what advantages and disadvantages it has. The main reason for doing this is to help you to understand ways in which your products or services may enable the customer to exploit advantages and minimize disadvantages.

It is not the intention to complete this document as if it were a proforma. Each heading is intended merely to act as a trigger for some

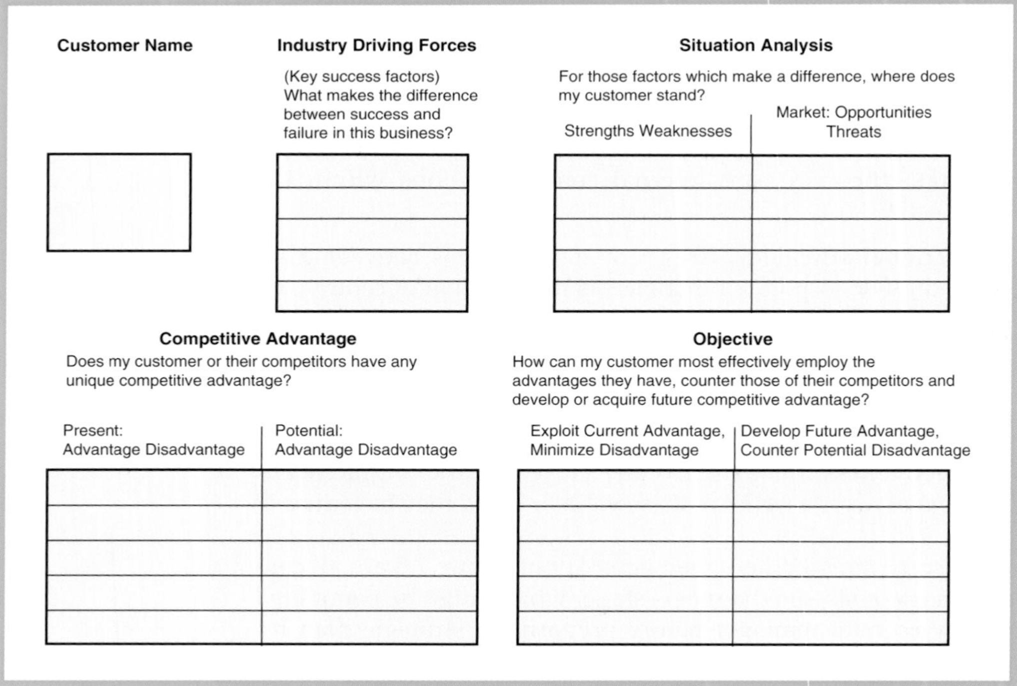

Figure 7.7 Objectives analysis exercise (industry driving forces).

powerful conclusions about your customer's competitive situation. This information will be used along with the further information to be gathered in steps 5–9.

Step 5 (Figure 7.5): Client's annual report summary and financial analysis

Figure 7.8 enables a summary to be made of the analysis referred to in the previous section and of a careful reading and analysis of a customer's published annual report. Even if there is not a formal report published for the shareholders (say, for example, if your customer is a subsidiary or division of a larger company), the directors do nonetheless tend to produce internal reports and newsletters that can be used instead.

Such documents can be a major source of information on what your customer believes to be the major issues facing them, their achievements and their objectives and strategies – in other words, their hopes for the future.

It is always possible to extract valuable information which can be used in helping you understand how your organization might be of assistance. This information can now be put alongside the information gleaned from the previous objectives analysis summary.

Figure 7.9 focuses on the financial affairs of your customer and concerns information which can also be obtained from annual reports and other published sources. At first sight, this might appear to be some way removed from the reality of selling goods and services to a major account. However, a little thought will reveal that most organizations today are acutely aware of their financial performance indicators:

Most organizations today are acutely aware of their financial performance indicators.

- Current ratios
- Net profit margins
- Return on assets
- Debtor control
- Asset turnover.

1. Major achievements	
2. Major problems/issues	
3. Objectives	
4. Strategies	
5. Conclusions/opportunities	

Figure 7.8
Annual report summary.

Financial ratio indicator	Formula	Source				Company standing	Industry standing	Does it appear as though improvement is needed?		
		Annual report						Yes	No	
Current ratio	Current assets / Current liabilities									
Net profit margin	Net profit / Net sales									
Return on assets	Net profit / Total assets									
Collection period	Debtors less bad debt / Average day's sales									
Stock turnover	Cost of goods sold / Stock									

Description of indicators	Current ratio	Measures the liquidity of a company – does it have enough money to pay the bills?
	Net profit margin	Measures the overall profitability of a company by showing the percentage of sales retained as profit after taxes have been paid. If this ratio is acceptable, there probably is no need to calculate the gross profit or operating profit margins
	Return on assets	Evaluates how effectively a company is managed by comparing the profitability of a company and its investments
	Collection period	Measures the activity of debtors. A prolonged collection period means that a company's funds are financing customers and not contributing to the cash flow of the company
	Stock turnover	Evaluates how fast funds are flowing through cost of goods sold to produce profit. If stock turns over faster, it is not in the plant as long before it is saleable as a product.

Figure 7.9   Financial analysis.

The purpose of the analysis contained in Figure 7.9 is to help you focus on the financial issues faced by your customer and to encourage you to explore whether any of your products and services could improve any of these ratios.

It will be obvious that any supplier who has taken the trouble to work out what impact its products and services have on the customer's bottom line will be preferred to a potential supplier who focuses only on product features.

Step 6 (Figure 7.5): Client's internal value chain analysis

Figure 7.10 illustrates an organization's internal value chain as popularized by Professor Michael Porter in his book *Competitive Strategies* (Porter, 1980). It is assumed that readers are familiar with this concept. The value chain is introduced here as an invaluable tool in understanding how a major account actually functions. The bottom level shows bought-in goods or services entering the organization, passing through operations and then moving out to their markets through distribution, marketing and sales and service. Sitting above these core processes are organizational support activities such as human resource management, procurement and so on.

Figure 7.11 is a very simple illustration of some of these issues and how they could be improved, thus representing sources of differentiation in the value chain. All information emanating from this analysis can be usefully summarized using a format similar to that shown in Figure 7.12. From this, it will be seen that there are four general headings of customer benefits:

- Possibilities for increased revenue for the customer
- Possibilities for cost displacement
- Possibilities for cost avoidance
- Intangible benefits.

Another way of looking at this is to identify the methods of gaining competitive edge through value in use:

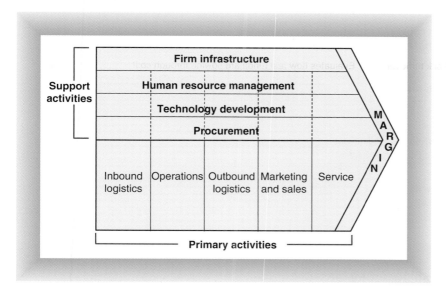

Figure 7.10
The value chain.

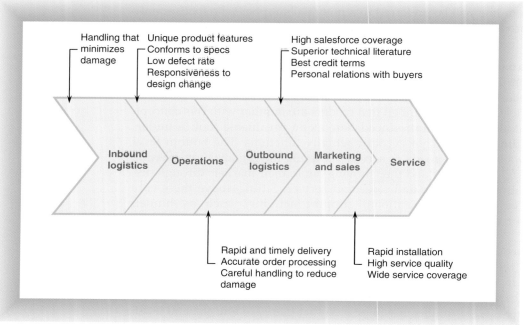

Figure 7.11 Sources of differentiation in the value chain.

Tangible benefits	Product solution	Analysis and comment
Increased revenue		
Increased sales volume		
Enhanced product line		
Cost displacement		
Reduced labour costs		
Reduced equipment costs		
Reduced maintenance costs		
Lowered stock costs		
Reduced energy costs		
Cost avoidance		
Reduced new personnel requirement		
Eliminate planned new equipment		
Intangible benefits		
Customer goodwill		
Improved decision making		

Figure 7.12 Value chain analysis summary.

- **Reduce the lifecycle/Alter the cost mix:** Customers are often willing to pay a considerable higher initial price for a product with significantly lower post-purchase costs.

- **Expand value through functional redesign:** For example, a product which increases the user's production capacity or throughput, a product which enables the user to improve the quality or reliability of his or her end-product, a product which enhances end-use flexibility or a product which adds functions or permits added applications.

- **Expand incremental value by developing associated intangibles:** For example, service, financing and 'prestige'.

Case study insight

Value chain analysis for a packaging company

An international chemical company undertook this investigation process using a novel method. They organized a two-day event for eight very senior people from different functions in a large packaging company. These executives included marketing people, a health and safety executive, an environmental specialist, a logistics manager, a manufacturing manager and a couple of directors! These executives were matched by equivalent managers and directors from the supplying company. An independent consultant was asked to chair the two-day event.

The purpose of the event, which was held in a neutral location, was to investigate ways in which the several goods and services of the supplying company were received, used and perceived by the customer. This inquiry was obviously only possible because of the good relationships already enjoyed by the supplier.

While it took a few hours for the independent moderator to break down the natural barriers to honest and open communication, the event had a major impact on the processes and attitudes of the supplier. For example, at one stage the customers were asked to go into a syndicate room and write down all the things they did not like or found inadequate in the supplying company. The sheer size of the list and the contents so shocked the supplier that it immediately agreed to set up a number of functional and cross-functional working groups comprising executives from both sides in order to study how cost-effective improvements could be made.

All issues were investigated openly and honestly, ranging from the strategic issues faced by the customer in its industry, to very tactical issues concerned with processes. The end-result was a dramatically improved relationship, which led to substantial benefits to both sides.

It is not suggested that this is the only way to discover the kind of detailed information outlined in Figure 7.12. In many cases, much patience is required over considerable periods of time and the effectiveness and efficiency with which this investigative task can be carried out will be a function of how good and deep the existing relationships are. Nonetheless, it is difficult to see how improvements can be made without a thorough understanding of the customer's systems and processes.

The list of possibilities for improvement for the supplier is now growing quite considerably. However, there are still more aspects of the business which need to be analysed.

Step 7 (Figure 7.5): The customer's buying process

Figure 7.13 outlines the buying process for goods and services. In the remainder of this section it will be assumed that you are selling a product, although the same process applies equally well to services.

Selling to an organization can be a complex process because it is possible for a number of different people to become involved at the customer end. Although theoretically only one of these is the buyer, in practice he or she might not be allowed to make a decision to purchase until others with technical expertise or hierarchical responsibility have given their approval.

The personal authority of the buyer will to a large extent be governed by the following factors:

- **The cost of the product:** The higher the cost, the higher up in the organization will the purchasing decision be made (Table 7.5). (Please note that, although the level of expenditure figures will have increased substantially during the past 27 years, this table is included because it is indicative of a hierarchy of purchasing authority.)

- **The 'newness' of the product:** The relative novelty of the product will pose an element of commercial risk for an organization. A new and untried proposition will require support at a senior management level, whereas a routine, non-risky service can be handled at a lower level.

- **The complexity of the product:** The more complex the product offered, the more technical the implications which have to be understood within the client company. Several specialist managers might be required to give their approval before the transaction can be completed.

All those involved in the buying decision are known as the decision-making unit (DMU).

All those involved in the buying decision are known as the decision-making unit (DMU) and it is important for the key account manager to identify the DMU in all current and prospective customer companies. Table 7.6 provides some research findings which demonstrate how rarely salespeople reach all component members of the DMU.

Customer Analysis Form

Customer _____
Salesperson _____ Address _____
Products _____

Telephone number _____

Buy class   new buy _____   straight rebuy _____   modified rebuy _____

Date of analysis _____
Date of reviews _____

Member of Decision-Making Unit (DMU)	Production	Sales & Marketing	Research & Development	Finance & Accounts	Purchasing	Data Processing	Other
Buy Phase — Name							
1 Recognizes need or problem and works out general solution	___	___	___	___	___	___	___
2 Works out characteristics and quantity of what is needed	___	___	___	___	___	___	___
3 Prepares detailed specification	___	___	___	___	___	___	___
4 Searches for and locates potential sources of supply	___	___	___	___	___	___	___
5 Analyses and evaluates tenders, plans, products	___	___	___	___	___	___	___
6 Selects supplier	___	___	___	___	___	___	___
7 Places order	___	___	___	___	___	___	___
8 Checks and tests products	___	___	___	___	___	___	___

Factors for consideration
1 price
2 performance
3 availability
4 back-up service
5 reliability of supplier
6 other users' experience
7 guarantees and warranties
8 payment terms, credit or discount
9 other, e.g. past purchases, prestige, image, etc.

Adapted from Robinson et al., 1967.

Figure 7.13 Buying process for goods and services.

Table 7.5
Responsibility for
financial expenditure

Level of expenditure	Level at which decision is taken			
	Board (collective)	Individual director	Departmental manager	Lower management or clerical
Over £50 000	88%	11%	2%	–
Up to £50 000	70%	25%	4%	Less than 0.5%
Up to £5000	29%	55%	14%	2%
Up to £2500	18%	54%	24%	4%
Up to £500	4%	31%	52%	14%

Source: 'How British Industry Buys', a survey conducted by Cranfield School of Management for the *Financial Times*, January 1984.

Table 7.6
Buying influences by
company size

Number of employees	Average number of buying influences (DMU)	Average number of contacts made by salesperson
0–200	3.42	1.72
201–400	4.85	1.75
401–1000	5.81	1.90
41 000 plus	6.50	1.65

A useful way of working out who would be involved in the decision-making processes in a company is to consider the sales transaction from the buyer's point of view. It has been recognized that the process can be split into a number of distinct steps known as 'buy phases'. These buy phases will be followed in most cases, particularly for major purchases. It will be obvious that at stages beyond the *cooperative* KAM stage, the incumbent supplier will have an inside track and, hence, an advantage, throughout the process. In many cases, customers do not even bother to put their proposed purchase requirements out to tender, preferring to deal with their current trusted partner.

Buy phases relate to the stages through which organizations go when making major purchases. The phases can be listed as follows: (This section of the text owes much to the original research conducted by the Marketing Science Institute in the USA under the guidance of Patrick J. Robinson.)

1. **Problem identification:** A problem is identified or anticipated and a general solution worked out. For example, the marketing department finds that it has inadequate information about sales records and costs. It needs better information made available on the computer.

2. **Problem definition:** The problem is examined in more detail in order to grasp the dimensions and, hence, the nature of the ultimate choice of solution. Taking our earlier example of the international chemical company further, investigation shows that the supplier's original software system was not devised with the customer's current marketing planning requirements in mind. A new system is required which can also provide the option for the inclusion of other new data.

3. **Solution specification:** The various technical requirements are listed and a sum of money is allocated to cover the cost of investing in new software.

4. **Search:** A search is made for potential suppliers, in this case those with the capability of devising a 'tailor-made' system to meet the above requirements.

5. **Assessment:** Proposals from interested suppliers are assessed and evaluated.

6. **Selection:** A supplier is selected and final details are probably negotiated prior to the next step.

7. **Agreement:** A contract/agreement is signed.

8. **Monitoring:** The service is monitored in terms of meeting installation deadlines and performance claims.

If we happened to be running a computer programming service to industry, we could deduce from the buying process that the DMU at this company might well contain the following people: a marketing planner, a sales director, a sales office manager, the company computer specialist, the company accountant, the company secretary and perhaps even the managing director, depending on the nature of the contract and the buyer. Sometimes the buyer might be one of those already listed and not exist as a separate role.

We could also speculate with some certainty that each of these people would need to be satisfied about different aspects of the efficiency of our service and we would need to plan accordingly. For now, it is enough to recognize that, when selling to an organization, the person with the title of buyer is often unable to make important decisions on their own. Although he or she can be a useful cog in the company's purchasing machine, he or she is often not a free agent.

> The person with the title of buyer is often unable to make important decisions on their own.

There are also many pressures on the buyer. We know from our own experience – when we purchase something for the home, for example – how difficult it can sometimes be. Even if we are only buying a carpet, we have to agree whether or not it should be plain or patterned, what colour, what price, what quality and so on. Even seemingly straightforward considerations like these are clouded by issues such as whether the neighbours or relatives will think we are copying them or whether we are being too chic or too outrageous. The buying decision makers in a typical company are faced with a greater multitude of pressures coming from two directions: from outside the company and from inside the company.

External pressures can be many and various and may involve important issues such as the following:

- **The economic situation:** What will be the cost of borrowing? Are interest rates likely to rise or fall? Is it a good time to invest in a new service now? Is the market decline really over or should we wait for more signals of recovery?

- **Political considerations:** How will government fiscal policy affect our business or that of our customers? Will proposed legislation have an impact on either us or our markets?

- **Technology:** How are we as a company keeping up with technological developments? How does this new proposal rate on a technological scale? Is it too near the frontiers of existing knowledge? How long will it be before a whole new phase of technology supersedes this investment?

- **Environmental considerations:** Will this new service be advantageous to us in terms of energy conservation or pollution control? Does it present any increase in hazards to our workforce? Will we need more room to expand? Is such room available?

- **The business climate:** How do our profit levels compare with those of companies in general and those in our type of business in particular? Are there material cost increases in the pipeline which could reduce our profits? Is the cost of labour increasing?

Any one of these external issues could put pressure on the buying decision maker – and this is only half the picture. There are also many internal pressures on the buyer:

- **Confused information:** It is often difficult to obtain the correct information to support a buying decision. Either the information does not exist or it has not been communicated accurately from the specialist department. Sometimes it is not presented in a convenient form and leads to confusion and misunderstanding.

- **Internal politics:** The relative status of individuals or departments can sometimes hinder the buying process. Personal rivalries or vested interests can create difficulties about priorities or standards. The 'politics' might entail non-essential people being involved in the decision-making process, thereby elongating the communication chain and slowing down decision making.

- **Organizational:** How the company is organized can affect the efficiency of its buying process. It is essential for everyone within the company to be aware of their role and level of authority if they are to perform effectively.

Finally, there are a number of personal pressures on the buyer. Buyers can be pressurized by a number of personal matters, some real, others imagined. They might be unsure about their role and how their colleagues accept their judgement. They might lack experience in the buying role and be unsure of how to conduct themselves. They might prefer a quiet life and therefore be against change, preferring to continue transactions with tried and tested suppliers – even if it can be clearly demonstrated that there are advantages in changing them. They might be naturally shy and not enjoy first meetings. They might find it difficult to learn new information about technical developments or the special features of your particular service.

All of these pressures, both external and internal, have a profound bearing on the behaviour of the buyer and, if the account manager is to relate to the buyer, he or she must try to understand them.

By way of summarizing this section on business-to-business selling, it can be demonstrated that the successful account manager needs to be aware of all these things when approaching a buyer acting on behalf of an organization. All of the following elements need to be known and understood:

- The relative influence of the buyer in the context of the particular product or service being offered.
- What constitutes the DMU in the buying company.
- How the buying process works.
- The pressures on the buying decision maker.

With this information, the account manager is in a better position to plan his or her work and to adopt appropriate conduct when face to face with the buying decision maker(s). Exactly how this information should be used will be covered later in the chapter.

CHECKPOINT

Buying pressures

Can you compile a list of pressures that are particular to the procurement function in one of your key accounts?

Some explanation is needed of the 'buy classes' shown in Figure 7.13. Whether the account manager is selling to an individual or to an organization, the decision-making processes of the prospects can be divided into what are termed 'buy classes'. There are three types of buy class:

There are three types of buy class: new buy, straight rebuy and modified rebuy.

1. **New buy:** In effect, all the foregoing discussion has focused on the new buy category. It is here that those people who make up the DMU are fully exercised as the buy phases unfold. In the new buy class, the needs of all decision makers must be met and influenced by the key account manager. Not surprisingly, this takes time and

so it is not unusual for a lengthy period to elapse between the initial discussion and contract closure.

2. **Straight rebuy:** Once the key account manager has had the opportunity to demonstrate how the service can help the customer, further purchases of the service do not generally require such a rigorous examination of all of the buy phases. In fact, should the customer merely want a repeat purchase of the same service, then their only questions are likely to be: Has the price been held to the same level as before? Will the standard of the service be unchanged? Can it be provided at a specific time? Such issues can generally be resolved by negotiation with the buyer.

3. **Modified rebuy:** Sometimes a modification of the product or service might be necessary. It might be that the supplier wants to update the product or service and provide better performance by using different methods or equipment. Alternatively, it could be the customer who calls for some form of modification from the original purchase. Whatever the origin, all or some of the buy phases will have to be re-examined and again the key account manager will have to meet with and persuade and satisfy the relevant members of the DMU.

There are often advantages for an account manager in trying to change a straight rebuy into a modified rebuy. They are twofold:

> There are often advantages for an account manager in trying to change a straight rebuy into a modified rebuy.

1. A modified rebuy reactivates and strengthens the relationship with the various members of the customer's DMU.

2. The more closely a supplier can match its service to the customer's needs (and remember this matching only comes about as a result of a mutual learning, as communication and trust develop between the supplier and the customer), the more committed the customer becomes to the product or service.

> The higher the commitment the customer has to the particular product for service and the supplier, the more difficult it becomes for competitors to break in.

The higher the commitment the customer has to the particular product or service and the supplier, the more difficult it becomes for competitors to break in.

Finally, the 'decision maker' in Figure 7.13 needs to be identified. Recognizing that there is a DMU is an important first step for the account manager but, having done this, it is essential to identify who actually has the power to authorize the purchase. No matter how persuasive the arguments for buying your products, if you are not reaching the key decision maker, then all your efforts could well be in vain. Identifying this person is too important to be left to chance and yet many account managers fail to meet with them. Sometimes they just have not done enough research about the company to obtain an accurate picture of its character and key concerns. It is important that the account manager research the company sufficiently in order to obtain a thorough understanding of its operations, personnel and priorities.

> If you are not reaching the key decision maker then all your efforts could well be in vain.

Alternatively, many account managers prefer to continue liaising with their original contacts in the client company, the ones with whom they feel comfortable and have come to regard as friends, rather than to extend their network to include more influential client representatives. Because many purchase decision makers will hold senior positions, the thought of meeting them somehow seems a daunting prospect, particularly to complacent or ill-prepared account managers.

Yet many of these fears are groundless. There is no evidence that senior executives set out to be deliberately obstructive or use meetings to expose the account manager's possible inadequacies. In fact, quite the opposite appears to be true.

Certainly, the decision makers will be busy people and so will want discussion to be to the point and relevant. At the same time, they will be trying to get the best deal for the company and it is only natural that they should.

Step 8 (Figure 7.5): Your sales history with the client

Figure 7.14 is a very simple analysis of your sales over a designated period of time working with the customer. The purpose is merely

Your sales history with the client					
Products		T-2	T-1	T-0	Trend
Customer volume (Total)					
YOUR volume					
YOUR share volume					
YOUR share value					
Sales analysis					
Products		T-2	T-1	T-0	Trend
	Val				
	Vol				
	%				
	Val				
	Vol				
	%				
	Val				
	Vol				
	%				
	Val				
	Vol				
	%				
	Val				
	Vol				
	%				
Comments					

Figure 7.14   Sales analysis and history.

to summarize your business history, share and prospects with this customer.

Step 9 (Figure 7.5): Competitive comparison and competitor strategy

Figure 7.15 shows one of a number of possible ways of establishing how well you are meeting the customer's needs in comparison with your competitors. It is obviously better if this is done using evidence obtained from independent market research, but providing the analysis suggested in this chapter is carried out thoroughly and with diligence, it should be possible to complete this part of the analysis internally with sufficient accuracy.

Competitive comparison				
	Importance rating	You	Competitor 1 2 3	Implications
Product quality				
Product range				
Availability				
Delivery				
Price/discounts				
Terms				
Sales support				
Promotion support				
Other				

Importance rating
(by customer)
A – very important (essential)
B – important (desirable)
C – low importance

Rating
(customer view)
1 – consistently/fully meets needs
2 – meets needs inconsistently
3 – fails to meet needs

Competitors' strategy	
Competitor	Strategy
1.	
2.	
3.	

Figure 7.15 Competitive comparison and competitor strategy.

Some people prefer to carry out this analysis using a more traditional SWOT (strengths, weaknesses, opportunities and threats) format as given in Figure 7.16. The main point, of course, is that any organization hoping to get and keep business with a major account needs to provide superior customer value and this can only be achieved by comparisons with the best that competitors have to offer.

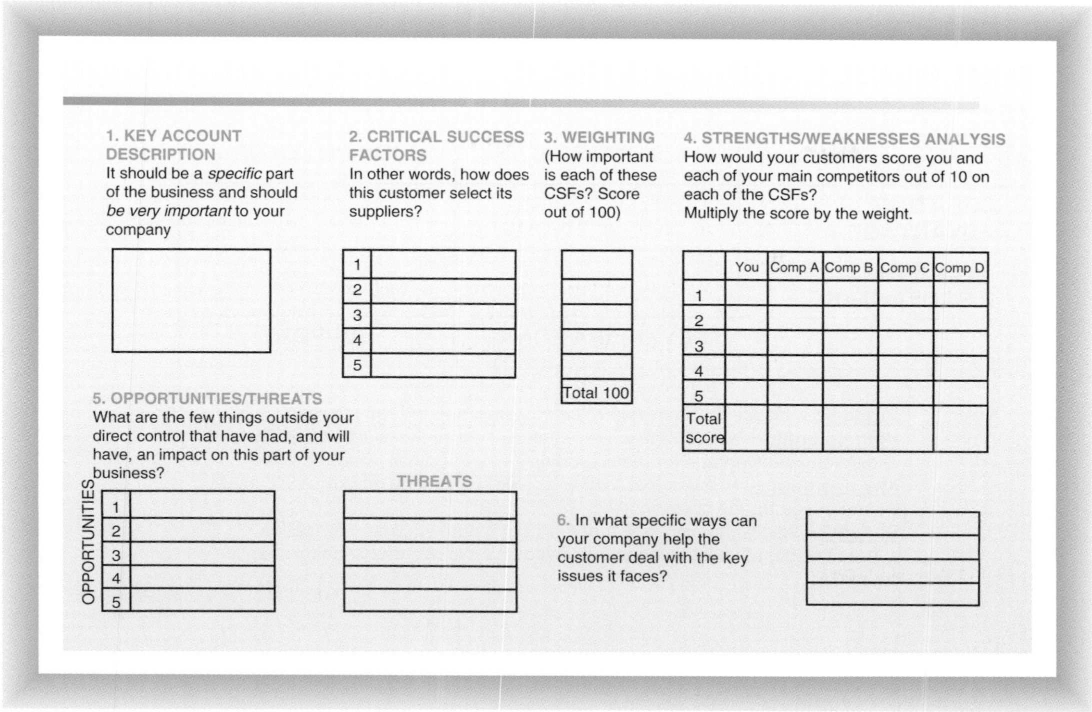

Figure 7.16 Strategic marketing planning exercise – SWOT analysis.

Case study insight

Gaining advantage

A classic example of a high potential application was Thompson's computer systems in the leisure/holiday market where the company was able to place its own holidays at the head of all travel agents' list.

7.3   Next steps

The painstaking key account analysis is now complete and a number of customer critical success factors will have been accumulated, together with specific ways in which your products or services and processes can help.

Figure 7.17 shows an applications portfolio, which is a useful way of categorizing your business solutions and approaches to your client prior to producing a strategic marketing plan for your customer, which will be explained in the next chapter.

The applications portfolio comprises four quadrants. The quadrants at the bottom left and right are labelled 'avoiding disadvantage'. While the meaning of this label might be self-evident, it is nonetheless worth

	STRATEGIC	HIGH POTENTIAL
CREATING ADVANTAGE		
AVOIDING DISADVANTAGE		
	KEY OPERATIONAL	SUPPORT

Key: **Strategic** = Issues that will ensure the customer's long-term success.
High potential = Issues that, while not crucial currently, could potentially lead to differential advantage for the customer.
Key operational = Issues that, unless solved reasonably quickly, could lead to disadvantage for the customer.
Support = Issues that, while of a non-urgent nature such as information availability, nonetheless need to be solved to avoid disadvantage for the customer.

Cranfield
UNIVERSITY
School of Management

Figure 7.17   The applications portfolio.

providing an example of this category. Take, for instance, a bank considering buying automatic teller machines (ATMs) for use by customers outside bank opening hours. Not having ATMs would clearly place the bank at a disadvantage. However, having them does not give the bank any advantage either. The majority of commercial transactions fall into this category.

The bottom left quadrant represents key operational activities, such as basic accounting, manufacturing and distribution systems. The bottom right quadrant might include activities such as producing overhead slides for internal presentations. In contrast, the top two quadrants represent a real opportunity for differentiating your organization's offering by creating advantage for the customer. The top right quadrant might be beta testing a product, service or process prior to making a major investment in launching it for the customer.

The reality of commercial life is that most of what any organization does falls into the 'avoiding disadvantage' category. However, leading companies adopt a proactive business approach. They work hard at developing products, services and processes designed to deliver advantage for their major accounts, for it is clear that creative, customer-focused suppliers will always be preferred over those who merely offer 'me too' products and trade only on price.

The KAM Best Practice Research Club at Cranfield has strong evidence to suggest that, once such an audit on a key account has been completed, if it is presented formally to senior managers in the account, the response is extremely favourable and, further, that additional confidential information is likely to be provided by the customer to enable the supplier to prepare a strategic marketing plan. This is the main topic addressed in Chapter 8.

Summary

Research at Cranfield (McDonald and Woodburn, 1999) has shown that organizations that invest resources in detailed analysis of the needs and processes of their key accounts fare much better in building long-term profitable relationships. We have termed this stage preplanning. Armed with a detailed knowledge of your customer's business, it is more likely that you can discover ways of helping them create advantages in their marketplace.

8 Planning for key accounts

Marketing planning is a logical sequence of events leading to the setting of marketing objectives and the formulation of plans for achieving them. The sequence is:

1. Mission statement
2. Set corporate objectives
3. Conduct marketing object
4. Conduct SWOT (strengths, weaknesses, opportunities and threats) analyses
5. Make assumptions
6. Set marketing objectives and strategies
7. Estimate expected results
8. Identify alternative plans and mixes
9. Set the budget
10. Establish first-year implementation programmes.

The plan itself contains:

1. Mission statement
2. Financial summary
3. Market overview
4. SWOT analyses
5. Portfolio summary
6. Assumptions
7. Marketing objectives and strategies
8. Forecasts and budgets.

All companies need to have a longer-term (strategic) marketing view as well as a short-term (tactical) marketing operation. Often

the most potent short-term tactic is the use of the salesforce. These can combine as shown in the matrix alongside.

From this it can be seen that being good at implementation of the wrong strategy can lead to a very quick death!

Exactly the same philosophy must be applied to planning for key accounts, as sophisticated customers will only build integrated relationships with suppliers who understand this business and can help them to increase sales, reduce costs, avoid costs and create value for them on a continuous basis. As this involves committing resources to such suppliers, they insist on well-researched strategic plans which are agreed jointly.

Even in cases where suppliers do not enjoy integrated relationships, it is still essential to prepare strategic plans designed to capture the inherent value planned for customers.

In this chapter a template is provided for preparing a strategic plan for a key account. Finally, a format used by customers for preparing strategies for their key suppliers is provided.

Introduction

The purpose of this chapter is threefold: to explain the key elements of marketing planning; to position key account planning within this context; and to provide a step-by-step approach to putting together a strategic plan for a key account. These themes are set out in three sections. The first section describes the nature of marketing planning and outlines the main steps involved in the marketing planning process. The second section locates key account planning within this process and explains its fundamental characteristics. The third section provides a step-by-step process for completing a strategic plan for a key account.

It is vital that key account managers understand marketing planning, because their major customers will engage in this process themselves and key account managers must understand what their customers are seeking to achieve if they are to help them as a supplier.

No matter where a key account is positioned in the relationship development model (RDM) (Figure 8.1), if a supplier has aspirations for building a relationship with a customer over time, then some kind of plan setting out a strategy for how this is to be achieved will be necessary. The problem with this is that most organizations are not very good at or even very knowledgeable about planning. Thus, this chapter will also explain how to prepare a strategic plan for a key account. However, key account planning must be placed firmly in the context of strategic marketing planning, otherwise it will not be effective.

> The problem with this is that most organizations are not very good at planning.

> Key account planning must be placed firmly in the context of strategic marketing planning, otherwise it will not be effective.

8.1 Strategic marketing planning

Marketing planning contributes to business success both by providing a detailed analysis of opportunities for meeting customer needs and by promoting a professional approach to making available those

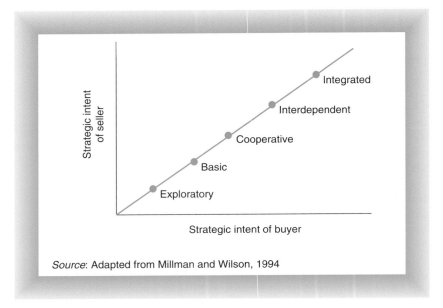

Figure 8.1
The relationship
development model.

Source: Adapted from Millman and Wilson, 1994

products or services that deliver the benefits customers are seeking to well-defined market segments.

Marketing planning should not be confused with budgets and forecasts. Marketing planning is specifically concerned with identifying what and to whom sales need be made in the longer term to give revenue budgets any chance of succeeding.

> There is no such thing as a 'market' – only people with needs and money.

There is no such thing as a 'market' – only people with needs and money. An organization must offer something to prospective customers that will make them want to buy from it rather than from any other supplier. Nowadays, markets are generally oversupplied and customers have a wide choice. So, if an organization is to persuade people to part with their money, it has to understand their needs in depth and to develop specific 'offers' with a differential advantage over competitors' offers. These offers are not just physical products or services, they are to do with the totality of the relationship between supplier and customer and include the organization's reputation, brand name, accessibility, service levels and so on.

In the less complex environments of the 1960s and 1970s, which were characterized by growth and the easy marketability of products and services, a 'production' orientation was possible, largely because demand seemed limitless. During the late 1980s, when demand was less buoyant, financial husbandry began its ascendancy. Indeed, it seemed to work for a while: profits continued to rise as costs and productivity increased. Alas, the ratio-driven, cost-cutting, margin-management mentality persisted. Every product had to make a prescribed margin over what it cost to produce it, otherwise prices were raised or it was taken off the market. Too little attention was paid to the number of times products were turned over, so low margin products were sacrificed. However, overheads either remained or were rationalized as organizations drove themselves towards fewer, more profitable products. Eventually 'anorexia industrialosa' (an excessive desire to be leaner and fitter, leading to emaciation and death) set in.

Companies went bankrupt at an unprecedented rate and even the innovative approaches developed in the 1990s (total quality management, balanced scorecards, business process re-engineering, relationship marketing, knowledge management, customer relationship management and so on) were unable to halt the rot that had set in.

Indeed, as described in Chapter 6, over a 20-year period up to 2000, most of Britain's highest return on investment public limited companies disappeared, downsized or got into severe financial difficulties. Nor was the contagion confined to Britain. According to Richard Pascale, author of *Managing on the Edge: How Successful Companies Use Conflict to Stay Ahead* (Pascale, 1990), only six of the 43 excellent companies named in Tom Peters and Robert Waterman's *In Search of Excellence: Lessons from America's Best-Run Companies* (Peters and Waterman, 1982) would have been considered excellent a mere eight years later.

It became increasingly clear that, sooner or later, corporations were going to have to turn their attention to addressing their markets and their customers instead of tinkering with their own internal processes, and this is where strategic marketing planning comes into its own.

There is now a substantial body of evidence to show that requisite marketing planning not only results in greater profitability and stability over time, but it also helps to reduce the friction and operational difficulties which arise within organizations.

Marketing planning is a logical sequence of activities leading to the setting of marketing objectives and the formulating of plans for achieving them. It is a management process which is conceptually very simple. As a planning system, it is a way of identifying options, of making them explicit, of formulating marketing objectives which are consistent with the organization's overall objectives and of scheduling and costing out the activities most likely to achieve the objectives.

> Marketing planning is a logical sequence of activities leading to the setting of marketing objectives and the formulating of plans for achieving them.

Marketing planning is a managerial process, from which there are two outputs:

- The **strategic marketing plan**, which covers a period of between three and five years.

- The **tactical marketing plan**, which is the scheduling and costing out of the specific actions necessary to achieve the first year's objectives in the strategic marketing plan.

The process itself and the output of the process are shown Figure 8.2.

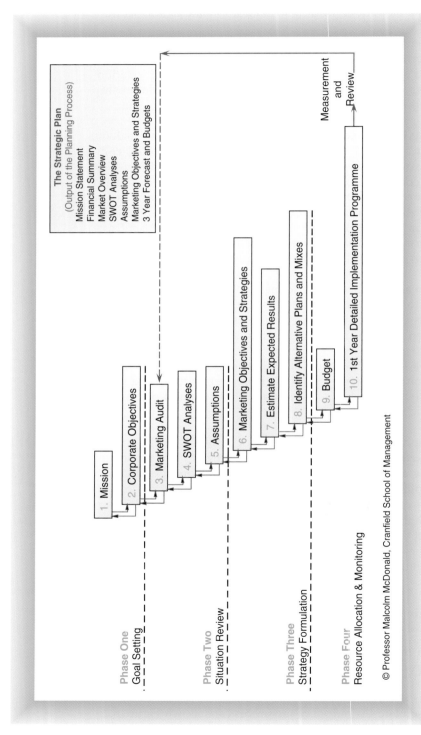

The Strategic Plan
(Output of the Planning Process)
Mission Statement
Financial Summary
Market Overview
SWOT Analyses
Assumptions
Marketing Objectives and Strategies
3 Year Forecast and Budgets

1. Mission
2. Corporate Objectives
3. Marketing Audit
4. SWOT Analyses
5. Assumptions
6. Marketing Objectives and Strategies
7. Estimate Expected Results
8. Identify Alternative Plans and Mixes
9. Budget
10. 1st Year Detailed Implementation Programme

Measurement and Review

Phase One
Goal Setting

Phase Two
Situation Review

Phase Three
Strategy Formulation

Phase Four
Resource Allocation & Monitoring

© Professor Malcolm McDonald, Cranfield School of Management

Figure 8.2 The 10 steps in the strategic marketing planning process.

The marketing planning process begins with an identification of the organization's mission and financial objectives, which serves to confirm the organization's purpose and outline its aspirations. The next phase embodies a comprehensive situation review or marketing audit in order to establish inherent problems and potential. This involves summaries in the form of SWOT (strengths, weaknesses, opportunities and threats) analyses for main products/markets, leading to the making of assumptions and the setting of draft marketing objectives and strategies for a three- to five-year period. At this stage, other functional managers get involved in order to ensure that the organization is capable of resourcing marketing's requirements.

Alternative plans and budgets are then finalized and, eventually, tactical marketing plans prepared. Company headquarters will often consolidate both the strategic plans and the tactical plans into business or corporate plans. At the start of the organization's fiscal year, the tactical marketing plan is implemented and monitored via the management information system, until the whole process begins again in the next fiscal cycle.

This strategic and operational planning system can be represented as a circle (Figure 8.3), which obviates the question about whether the process is top-down or bottom-up for, clearly, it is continuous.

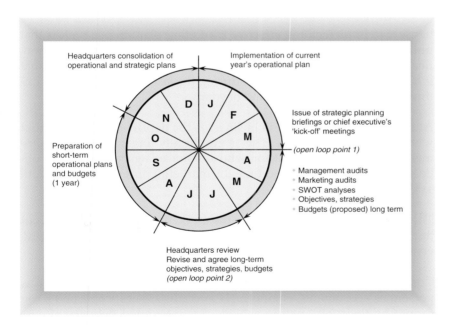

Figure 8.3
Strategic and operational planning.

The contents of a strategic marketing plan are listed in Table 8.1. The plan can be made as formal or informal as necessary according to the particular circumstances. The main point is that it should combine thoroughness with creativity.

Over 20 scholarly research studies have identified hostile corporate cultures and financially driven systems and procedures as the main

Table 8.1
Contents of a strategic
marketing plan

1. A mission or purpose statement

2. A financial summary

3. A market overview
   - What the market is
   - How it works
   - What the key segments are

4. A SWOT on each segment
   - What value does each require?
   - What value can we create to persuade customers to buy from us?

5. A portfolio summary of the SWOT
   - This classifies segments according to our relative strengths and the potential of each for growth in profits over the next three years

6. Assumptions

7. Marketing objectives and strategies
   - Prioritized in accordance with the portfolio summary

8. A budget
   - For three years

barriers to implementing effective marketing planning. It is clear that until organizations learn to grasp the nettle of customer orientation, financial husbandry will dominate corporate life, despite the fact that it has caused so many casualties during the last 30 years and will continue to do so well into 2007 and beyond.

Another endemic problem in business is the depth of ignorance about what marketing actually is. This is graphically illustrated by the comment of one managing director, who announced aggressively at a public seminar that 'There is no time for marketing in my company until sales improve!'

The simple truth is that, while it is the marketing people who work out the value required by customers, it is the whole company which delivers this value.

Companies that persist in organizing themselves around tribes such as personnel, accountants, engineers, IT specialists, salespeople and so on cannot by their very nature achieve this integrated delivery of customer value.

How can any
organization
achieve customer
focus while it
continues to
organize itself
around what it
makes rather than
around its customers
or its markets?

Such groups will never subjugate their own tribal goals to the broader aims of customer satisfaction and retention. In addition, how can any organization achieve customer focus while it continues to organize itself around what it makes rather than around its customers or its markets? Many corporate cultures are, in the main, hostile to the marketing ethic. Directors who got their job as a result of professional behaviour considered appropriate in the 1960s, 1970s, 1980s and 1990s do not know how to respond to increased competition and static or declining markets. Their natural reaction is to resort to traditional measures, one of which is to cut costs without addressing the fundamental issue of growth. However, crucially, growth requires customers who want to buy things from us rather than from our competitors.

It also takes intellect, confidence and courage to take a strategic rather than a purely tactical approach. Unsuccessful organizations do not bother with strategic marketing planning at all; instead, they rely on sales forecasts and associated budgets. It is a bit like steering from the wake – all right in calm, clear waters, but not so sensible in busy and choppy waters!

The problem with this route is that many salespeople sell the products they find easiest to sell (usually at a maximum discount) to those customers who treat them nicest. Thus, by developing short-term budgets first and then extrapolating them, companies only succeed in extrapolating their own inadequacies.

Preoccupation with short-term forecasts is typical of those companies that confuse this approach with strategic marketing planning. Such companies are being left behind by companies led by directors with a pioneering spirit anchored in practical expertise. These business frontiers men and women lead the effort in understanding their markets and customers, for they know that it is only by creating superior customer value that their companies will be able to survive and thrive.

Transforming 'vision' into reality is where strategic marketing planning comes in, enabling a number of plans or models to be developed which spell out quantitatively and qualitatively the value that each employee must create in order to achieve collective prosperity.

The authors' research has shown that in peering into the murky depths of organizational behaviour in relation to marketing planning, confusion reigns supreme, and nowhere more so than over the terminology of marketing.

This brings us to one of the most fundamental points in this chapter – an understanding of the difference between strategy and tactics and the association with the relevant adjectives 'effective' and 'efficient'. This point is illustrated by the matrix in Figure 8.4, in which the horizontal axis represents strategy as a continuum from ineffective to effective and the vertical axis represents tactics on a continuum from inefficient to efficient. Those firms with an effective strategy (top right) continue to thrive. Those with an effective strategy but inefficient tactics (bottom right) have merely survived. Those firms to the left of the matrix are destined to die, as too much emphasis is placed on tactics, so avoiding the underlying strategic issues surrounding changing market needs. Any organization doing the wrong things more efficiently (top left) is destined to die more quickly than their less efficient counterparts. It is a bit like making a

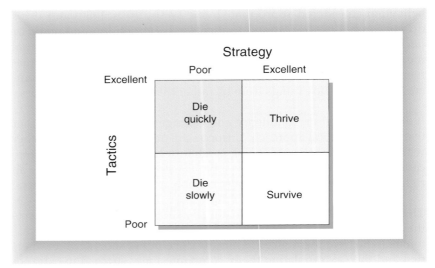

Figure 8.4
The impact of effectiveness and efficiency on success.

stupid manager work harder, thus doubling the chaos and probably offending twice as many customers!

As we have already said, companies led by chief executives with a proactive orientation that stretches beyond the end of the current fiscal year have begun to show results visibly better than the old reactive companies with only a short-term vision.

Case study insight

Preventing a potential case of anorexia industrialosa

One Scandinavian capital goods manufacturer was devoting its energies to stock control, headcount reduction, cash flow and the like. The problem, however, was of falling demand. Had it not been pointed out to the Board that this underlying marketing issue had to be addressed, it is easy to imagine how anorexia industrialosa could have resulted (an excessive desire to be leaner and fitter, leading to emaciation and, eventually, death).

Figure 8.5 shows the old style of company in which very little attention is paid to strategy by any level of management. It will be seen that lower levels of management do not get involved at all, while the directors spend most of their time on operational/tactical issues. Figure 8.6, on the other hand, is a representation of those companies that recognize the importance of strategy and who manage to involve all levels of management in strategy formulation.

The rule, then, is simple:

● Develop the strategic plan first. This entails greater emphasis on scanning the external environment, the early identification of forces

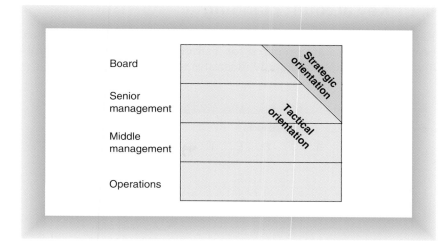

Figure 8.5
Tactical orientation.

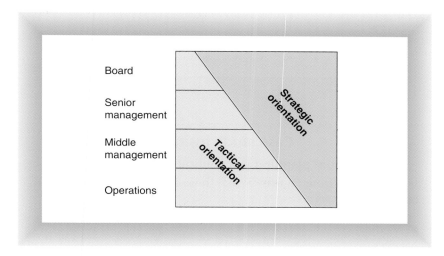

Figure 8.6
Strategic orientation.

emanating from it, and developing appropriate strategic responses, involving all levels of management in the process.

● A strategic plan should cover a period of between three and five years, and only when this has been developed and agreed should the one-year operational marketing plan be developed. Never write the one-year plan first and extrapolate it.

The emphasis throughout this chapter is on the preparation of a strategic key account plan. The format for an operational or tactical plan is exactly the same, except for the amount of detail.

CHECKPOINT

Strategic focus

Do you think that your company places sufficient emphasis on strategy?

8.2   Key account planning

Key account planning must take place at the same time as or even before draft plans are prepared for a strategic business unit. The following health sector case study illustrates why this is necessary.

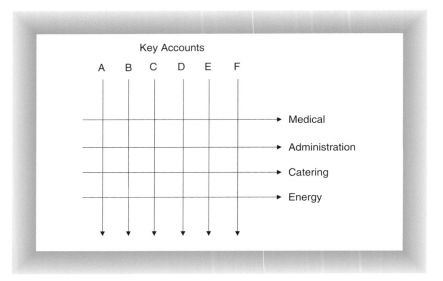

Figure 8.7
Hospital groups and key account managers.

Case study insight

Key account planning in a medical supplies company

It will be seen from Figure 8.7 that there are four 'markets' within hospitals to be served:

- Medical
- Administration
- Catering
- Energy.

The supplies company will service a number of hospital groups or key accounts, referred to here as A, B, C, D, etc. Each of these hospital groups may well have its own key account manager who has to plan for the group. Thus, for example, the key account manager for hospital A has to prepare a draft plan across all four markets and this would clearly be a key input to the planning process shown in Figure 8.2.

8.2.1   The position of key account planning in strategic marketing planning

All planning should start with the market where the customers are. Indeed, in anything other than small organizations it is clearly absurd to think that any kind of meaningful planning can take place without the committed inputs of those who operate most directly with customers.

Figure 8.8 shows a hierarchy of planning with key account planning at the base. Every principle outlined in this chapter applies right down to the individual key account. Thus, the planning process shown in Figure 8.2 would be first applied to key accounts.

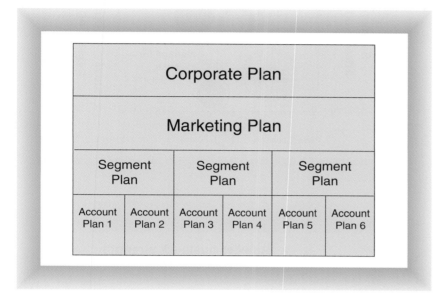

Figure 8.8
The planning hierarchy.

From this point onwards in this chapter the discussion of strategic and tactical planning will focus on key accounts.

8.2.2 Guidelines for setting key account objectives and strategies

The first point to be made is that all key accounts are not the same. This adage applies at two levels. First, it is obvious that all organizations will have preferred markets and preferred segments within these markets. Figure 8.9 shows the current and projected revenues from different segments within a single market.

Clearly, any organization without a distinct policy towards each of these market segments is unlikely to be able to make a success of key account management (KAM). On the understanding that your organization has a clear and well-communicated policy for each of its target markets, we can now turn our attention to setting objectives and strategies for key accounts within each segment.

Let us take another look at the key account portfolio matrix shown in Figure 8.10. Taking each quadrant in turn, it is possible to work out sensible objectives and strategies for each key account. Accounts meeting the profile of the bottom left quadrant are likely to continue to deliver

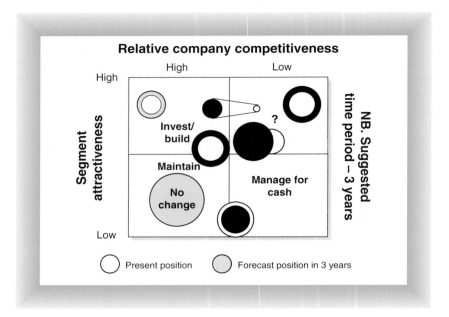

Figure 8.9
Prioritizing and selecting segments.

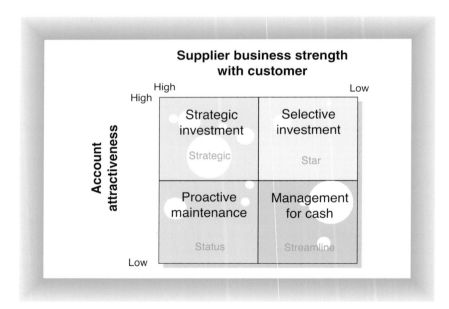

Figure 8.10
Portfolio analysis matrix.

excellent revenues for some considerable time, even though they may be in static or declining markets. Good relationships are already enjoyed and should be preserved. Retention strategies are therefore advisable, incorporating prudence, vigilance and motivation. More importantly, as the supplying company will be seeking a good return on previous investment, any further financial input here should be of the maintenance kind. In this way, it should be possible to free up cash and resources for investing in key accounts with greater growth potential.

The quadrant to the top left (high potential/high strengths) represents accounts with the highest potential for growth in sales and profits. These warrant a quite aggressive investment approach, providing it is justified by returns. Net present value (NPV) calculations may be used as a basis for evaluating these returns, having taken account of the additional risks involved. Any investment here will probably be directed towards developing joint information systems and collaborative relationships.

Accounts situated in the quadrant to the top right (high potential/low strength) pose a problem, for few organizations have sufficient resources for investing in building better relationships with all of them. To determine which ones justify investment, net revenue streams should be forecast for each account for, say, three years and discounted to take account of the high risks involved. Having made these calculations and having selected the promising accounts, under no circumstances should financial accounting measures such as NPV be used to control them within the budget year. To do so would be a bit like pulling up a new plant every few weeks to see if it had grown! The achievement of objectives should instead be monitored using measures such as sales volume, value, 'share of wallet' and the quality of the relationship, enabling selected accounts to be moved gradually towards partnerships and, in some cases, towards integrated relationships. Only then will it become more appropriate to measure profitability as a control procedure.

> To do so would be a bit like pulling up a new plant every few weeks to see whether it had grown!

Case study insight

Unipart Technology Logistics and Sky: Powerful account strategies

Unipart Technology Logistics' (UTL) mission to position itself at the core of its key customer's supply chain, and the strategies it develops to achieve such a partnership, set it apart from other logistics companies that that confine themselves to efficient 'fetching and carrying' services. Equipment repair in the mobile phone arena was a UTL proficiency and, while working with Sky, the company was in a position to observe opportunities not apparently visible to the existing supplier. Unipart felt it could improve the service Sky customers received, save cost for Sky, and contribute to Sky's 'green' agenda, which is very dear to its heart.

Unipart's strategy offered an integrated end-to-end repair solution, saving cost for Sky through intelligent forecasting, which enabled reduction in the stockholding of spare parts while actually improving availability and increasing the reliability of repair completion times. Unipart – counter-intuitively for most suppliers – committed itself to reducing, not growing, the business through reducing the amount of repairs, by introducing higher standards and remote diagnostics. Furthermore, the programme took 610 tonnes of carbon dioxide out of the atmosphere, implemented zero landfill recycling of set top boxes and recycled 98% of all engineer returns from the field. The 'green' strategy has turned a recycling and waste cost of £5 per set top box into a new revenue stream. This is very appealing to Sky and, in addition, UTL demonstrates that it holds the same values as its key customer, for which environmental sustainability and responsibility are major strategies.

Unipart expanded its business and importance to Sky substantially when it first won the repair business against existing and established repair contractors. Now, Sky sees the service as 'in-house', and discussions are about how to gain greater benefit from it, reducing costs further and increasing other revenues, and certainly not about tendering for alternative providers. Unipart and Sky have a real partnership, achieved through Unipart's strategy to challenge itself to meet Sky's ambitions.

Accounts which the company cannot afford to invest in should be managed in a similar way to those residing in the bottom right quadrant. Accounts found in this quadrant (low potential/low strength) should not occupy too much of a company's time. Some of these accounts can be handed over to distributors, while others can be handled by an organization's sales personnel, providing all transactions are profitable and deliver net free cash flow.

First, consider the problem of aiming for OTIF (on time in full) delivery. It is well known that, as shown in Figure 8.11, as delivery service levels increase, so the cost of holding inventory grows exponentially.

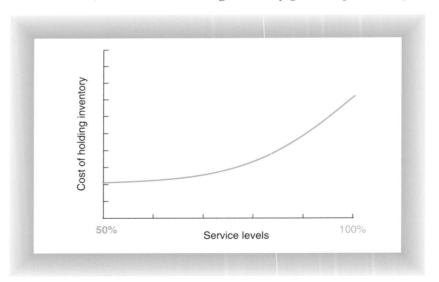

Figure 8.11
Delivery service levels versus cost of holding inventory.

It is worth expanding on this point, because so many suppliers have ridiculous mission statements that include a desire 'to delight customers'. Let us explain why such statements are ridiculous and are guaranteed to lose your company lots of money. It is easy to understand if you consider Figure 8.12. Let us assume that a research survey had shown that, in a given period, orders ranged from 500 to 10 000, with an average of 3000. Holding 3000 in stock would only provide a 50 per cent level of availability – clearly unacceptable. If one standard deviation was 100, putting 3100 into stock would provide an 85 per cent level of service (approximately). Two standard deviations would

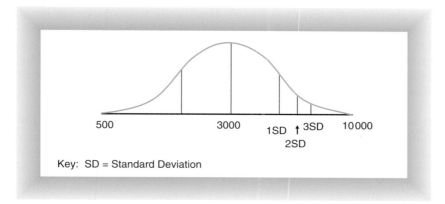

Key: SD = Standard Deviation

Figure 8.12
Results of a survey of orders over a defined period.

provide a service level of well over 90 per cent. Three standard deviations would provide a service level well into the high 90s, which would clearly be very acceptable. The only problem with this is that, for each small increase in service levels, large amounts of additional inventory have to be held, hence the big increase in the cost of inventory for high levels of service shown in Figure 8.11.

The answer, of course, is to select those segments that deserve very high levels of service. The same applies to key accounts.

The authors were involved recently in running a sales conference for a global company in the roller bearing business. The managing director announced at the beginning of the conference that in the forthcoming year, debtor days had to be reduced from 65 to 45. This objective depressed the salesforce considerably because there was a recession at the time and customers were taking extra credit. We solved the problem by asking the salesforce to categorize their customers according to sales potential for the forthcoming year – the vertical axis in Figure 8.13 – and according to whether their customers loved them or hated them – the horizontal axis (the lines in the matrix represent customers).

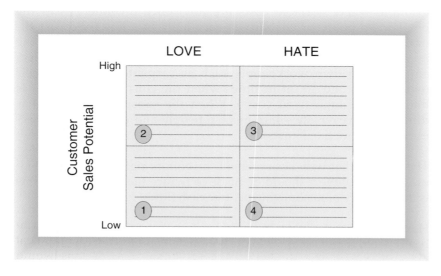

Figure 8.13
Short-term (one-year) customer classification.

We then advised them to offer 35 days' credit to customers in box 1 (being nice to them, as well, of course), to offer 45 days' credit to customers in box 2 (being even nicer to them, of course) and to offer 65 days' credit to those in box 3 (being mega nice to them as well). Finally, for customers in box 4, we advised them to ask for cash on acceptance of their order and to insist that they collected their orders personally!

It is clear that this story is a very exaggerated version of what actually happened. Nonetheless, it gives more than a clue that not all customers are created equal and throws into sharp relief the stupidity of those companies that set out 'to delight' their customers. The reality, of course, is that some kind of customer classification system is essential before setting objectives and strategies for them.

It is now appropriate to return to the issue of what kind of objectives and strategies to set for key accounts that fall into the bottom right hand quadrant of Figure 8.10. Sometimes, there are very big key accounts in this box – customers who do little other than drive suppliers' prices down and who do not want to build close relationships with any supplier. Nonetheless, their size ensures that they have to be in the key account programme.

For such companies, net free cash flow must be the prime objective. It makes sense to try to secure such accounts, by lowest prices if necessary in order to secure the high volume of sales, preferably via a two- or three-year contract. Thereafter, service should be kept to the minimum, orders should, if possible, be made via the Internet or a call centre and personal calls should be kept to a minimum in order to save costs. If such a customer insists on lots of free services, this pressure should be refused, remembering that the objective is to maximize net free cash flow.

Figures 8.14 and 8.15 indicate the implications of high fixed costs/ low variable costs versus low fixed costs/high variant costs. Even local traders, such as builders, instinctively understand this bit of traditional accounting theory. In a high fixed cost situation, for example where variable costs are low, once revenue passes the breakdown point, profitability is very high. In a low fixed cost situation where variable costs are high, once revenue passes the breakdown point, profitability is much lower. This is why builders employ their own workpeople such as carpenters and buy their own diggers and so on in times when the construction market is buoyant (i.e. high fixed costs). When the construction market is difficult, however, they hire in workpeople and equipment as necessary (i.e. low fixed costs).

The point is that with customers in the bottom right quadrant of Figure 8.10 every effort should be made to reduce the fixed costs, as this is the best way of maximizing net free cash flows.

Having explained all this, it should be clear that strategic plans should be prepared for all accounts in the bottom left and top left quadrants of

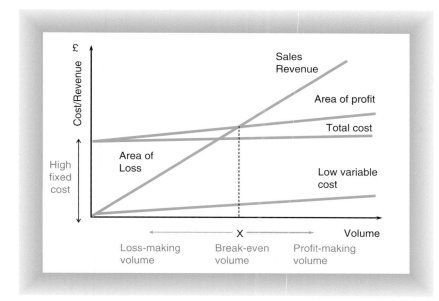

Figure 8.14
Breakdown chart with high fixed costs.

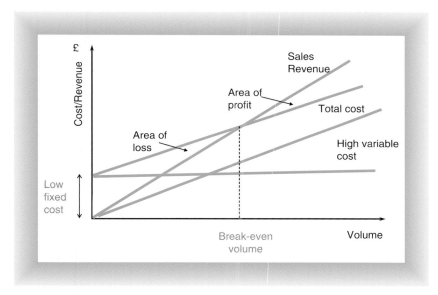

Figure 8.15
Breakdown chart with low fixed costs.

Figure 8.10, selectively for those in the top right quadrant, and not at all for customers in the bottom right quadrant, when short-term forecasts, budgets and action plans will suffice.

All other company functions and activities should be consistent with the goals set for key accounts according to the general categorization given in Figure 8.10. This rule includes the appointment of key account managers to key accounts. For example, some key account managers will be extremely good at managing accounts in the *exploratory*, *basic* and *cooperative* KAM stages where their excellent selling and negotiating skills are essential, whereas others will be better suited to the more complex business and

Table 8.2 KAM plan evaluation guidelines

Plan element	Reference sections	Level 1	Level 2	Level 3	Level 4	Level 5
Overall Business issues Presentation	Executive summary	Excellent understanding of KAM Complete, coherent Addresses key issues Appropriate emphasis Focused and clear Creative	Good understanding of KAM Mostly complete, some visible coherence. Addresses key issues Clear	Acceptable understanding of KAM Essential components No significant contradictions or omissions	Weak understanding of KAM Significantly incomplete or incoherent	Little or no understanding of KAM Incomplete and/or includes major contradictions
Analyses, esp. market map	Section A, outline Section B, customer Appendices	Comprehensive and effective use of tools Valid conclusions drawn Deep understanding of customer	Significant and effective use of tools Illustrates main points of customer situation	Some use of tools Elucidates key issues facing customer	Little use of tools Does not draw valid conclusions	Little or no use of tools No collusions, poor customer understandings
Objectives	Section C, your plans	Realistic Joined up with customer situation, customer and supplier strategies	Realistic Connects current situation and supplier strategies	Statement building from current situation	Unclear or not well connected to situation	Not stated, or just sales targets
Strategy	Section C, your plans	Clearly stated Targeted Added value for customer Feasible, clear resource requirement Consistent with objectives	Clearly stated Targeted Added value for customer Feasible, clear resource requirement Consistent with objectives	Clearly stated Targeted Added value for customer	Strategy simply stated	Strategy not stated, and/or stated strategies are outcomes or actions
Action	Section C, your plans	12 month development 3 year major action Matched with strategy Thorough measurement framework	12 month development 3 year major action Matched with strategy Focused measurement framework	12 month development Limited measurement framework	Short-term action Measurement is just sales targets	Short-term action No control mechanism

managerial issues surrounding *interdependent* and *integrated* relationships. The implications for key account managers are examined in Chapter 10.

8.3 Developing a strategic marketing plan for key accounts

We repeat here what we said in Chapter 1 about the need for a strategic plan as well as a tactical, short-term plan. We said that the good thing about not having a strategy is that failure comes as a complete surprise and is not preceded by a long period of worry and depression.

It is worth mentioning that preparing a strategic plan for a key account is an intellectually demanding task that cannot be accomplished merely by completing proformas. The authors have worked with many major organizations and the plans that emanate from them are rarely of the high quality that they need to be for the plans to have any chance of becoming reality. Accordingly, the authors have developed the criteria listed in Table 8.2 for evaluating the quality of strategic plans for key accounts. We should like to stress that only plans that fall close to the left hand side of the chart have any chance of achieving their objectives.

Earlier in the chapter, we outlined the contents of a strategic marketing plan in Table 8.1. We now provide an annotated set of proformas for completing a strategic plan for a key account.

Summary

Strategic plans for key accounts are essential, but these must be positioned clearly within the organization's strategic marketing planning process. Where possible, key account strategic plans need to be agreed and signed off with the functional managers within the organization who will be delivering the promises to the customer. Ideally, they should also be agreed with the customer.

Key Account Plan

Customer:

Customer relationship manager:

Dates: – completed/submitted:

    – approved:

    – last modified:

Notes

With notes

Please note that this is not a standalone document: it should be used following an aligned KAM development programme to explain and practise the approaches captured in this plan.

Index

Executive summary

Main elements	Potential for profit	
Account attractiveness score To be scored against CO criteria (see Worksheet 13)		
	Last year	**This year +3**
CO relative business strength Score against customer's criteria v best competitor: see Section C.1/Worksheet 7		
CO generic strategy for customer Manage for cash, proactive maintenance, selective investment/development, strategic investment: see Appendix 1.1		
Equivalent customer strategy for CO Efficiency, leverage, security, strategic: see Appendix 1.2		
Inter-company relationship Basic, co-operative, interdependent, integrated: see Appendix 1.3		
Forecast business State whether forecast given in terms of volume, GM, contribution: see Section C.5		

A.   Current position

Key points from Section A

B.   The customer's business

Key points from Section B

C. CO objectives and strategies

Business with customer	LY	TY	TY + 1	TY + 2	TY + 3
Total revenue					
Rev change v previous year					
Gross margin					
GM%					
Customer wallet					
Share of customer wallet					

Key points from Section C

D. Action and review

Key points from Section D

A. Current position

A.1 CO account team

Name	Title/Function	Role
		Examples:
		Overall account manager
		Customer operations
		Market analysis
		Quality issues

A.2 Principal customer contacts/relationships

Customer organogram/contact map

Name	Title/Function	Role in decisions, relationship with CO	Level of relationship with CO	Level of importance to CO
		Examples: Final contract, technical spec. Principal contact, Buyer	0–5, see Appendix 1.4	0–5, see Appendix 1.4
Stage of inter-company relationship overall			See Appendix 1.3	

Comments, e.g. on power structure and importance of contacts

A.3 Customer history with CO

Sales history

Sales by product/ product group	LY-2				LY-1				LY			
	CO sales	Sales inc/dec	CO GM		CO sales	Sales inc/dec	CO GM		CO sales	Sales inc/dec	CO GM	
	€m	%	€m	%	€m	%	€m	%	€m	%	€m	%
CO total												
Size of customer wallet												
Share of customer wallet	CO÷ total											
Definition of wallet	Scope of wallet: content and limits (what is included, what is excluded)											

*Customer's spend on the category of goods/services currently/potentially supplied by CO

Background to trading history

Customer attractiveness score	See Worksheet 13
Customer's supplier management strategy	See Appendix 1.2
Competitors currently trading with customer	See Worksheet 5c

Explain events influencing these results, especially pricing, contract renewals, competition.

A.4 Current issues

Recent sales history: to (month) . . . .

Sales by product/ product group	LYTD				TYTD			
	CO sales	Sales inc/ dec	CO GM		CO sales	Sales inc/ dec	CO GM	
	€m	%	€m	%	€m	%	€m	%
CO total								

Date when this section was last revised
Note significant current issues and activity

B. The customer's business

B.1 Market position

Outline of the customer's business: definition and scope

What do they do and where? What markets are they in?

B.2 Role/participation in marketplaces
Refer to the customer's market map as Worksheet 2

Summarize the type of companies with whom they trade/compete and draw conclusions from the market map

B.3 Market/business environment
STEEP and Porter analysis — See Worksheets 3 and 4a

Summarize important points from these analyses

B.4 Key opportunities and threats for customer

See Worksheet 4b for key external issues, i.e. opportunities and threats
Note key opportunities and threats for the customer

B.5 Competitive position: strengths and weaknesses

See Worksheets 5a, 5b and 5c for strengths and weaknesses relative to competitors
Draw conclusions on position relative to competition and value to the customer:

B.6 Customer objectives
Customer's mission statement and goals

Where your customer wants to take their business (beware website verbiage).
Examples: aspirations, status, image and range of activity.
Either: as stated by the customer itself, or as far as you know it (but state which).

Customer's quantified objectives

Your customer's specific corporate objectives, quantified and time-bound: i.e. WHAT exactly do they want to achieve in the foreseeable future? If you cannot obtain quantified information, give your understanding qualitatively.

B.7 Customer strategies

See Worksheet 6 for the customer's SWOT analysis and strategies
List the major strategies they are pursuing/intend to pursue: i.e. HOW exactly do they intend to achieve the above objectives? Which of these strategies do you know they are adopting/will adopt, and which have you deduced?

C. CO objectives and strategies

C.1 Customer critical success factors

See Worksheet 7

Critical success factor	Importance weighting	CO rating	CO score	Best competitor rating*	Best competitor score
				Identify best competitor	
Total	100				

C.2 CO's environment in this customer

See Worksheet 8a for Porter analysis
Summarize important points

C.3 Key for opportunities and threats for CO

See Worksheet 8b for key external issues opportunities and threats
Note key opportunities and threats for CO with the customer

C.4 Competitive position: CO strengths and weaknesses

See Worksheets 9a and 9b for strengths and weaknesses.

C.5 CO objectives

See Worksheet 10 for SWOT, objectives and strategies

Business/financial

Purchases by product/ product group	LY	TY				TY + 1				TY + 2				TY + 3			
	CO sales	CO sales	Sales inc/ dec	CO GM	CO GM	CO sales	Sales inc/ dec	CO GM	CO GM	CO sales	Sales inc/ dec	CO GM	CO GM	CO sales	Sales inc/ dec	CO GM	CO GM
	€ m	€m	%	€m	%	€m	%	€m	%	€m	%	€m	%	€m	%	€m	%
Existing business																	
Total existing																	
New business						Business not received as at date of completing plan											
Total new																	
Overall total																	
Customer wallet																	
Share of customer wallet																	

Do not complete green boxes

Other objectives e.g. relationships, image, product range, range of activity

Objective	Measurement	LY	TY	TY + 1	TY + 2	TY + 3
Inter-company relationship	Target stage: see Appendix 1.3					
Another						
Another						

C.6 CO business strategies
Planned and prioritized business strategies

See Worksheets 11 and 12

CO's customer management strategy overall					See Appendix 1.1							
CO strategy	TY + 1				TY + 2				TY + 3			
	Sales	GM	Reso-urce	Net	Sales	GM	Reso-urce	Net	Sales	GM	Reso-urce	Net

Comment on issues, barriers, alliances, feasibility

C.7 CO relationship strategies
Additional to business strategies

Relationship development strategy	Target contact name(s) and role(s)

Targeted relationship levels (by date) _ _ _ _ _ _ _ _ _

See Appendix 1.4

CO staff	Customer staff						
	Name 1	Name 2	Name 3	Name 4			
Name A	2 > 4			1 > 3			
Name B			1 > 2				
Name C							
Name D							

C.8 Risks, dependencies and barriers

What could go wrong? What external events could prevent your strategy being fulfilled (risks)? On what internal events (or lack of them) does your strategy depend for its fulfilment (dependencies)? What potential barriers, in your company or in the customers, will need to be overcome?

Issues	Chance of occurrence	Nature of impact	Potential difference from objectives		
			TY + 1	TY + 2	TY + 3
Strategy A:					
Risk					
Dependency					
Barriers					
Strategy B:					
Risk					
Dependency					
Barriers					
Strategy C:					
Risk					
Dependency					
Barriers					

D. Action and review

D.1 Key action plan

Key actions	CO owner of action	Other depart-ments involved	Resource demand	Progress measure	Metric target	Due date	Date completed
Identify CO strategy here							
Action to fulfil specific strategy							
Identify CO strategy here							
Identify CO strategy here							
Identify CO strategy here							

D.2 Review

Make copies of this page for the other review periods.

People involved	
Review due date	
Actual date completed	

Element	Progress measure		Corrective action	'Owner' of corrective action	Date for further review
	Target metric	Actual metric			
Objectives					
Strategy / **Key action**					
Risks/dependencies					

Background information and analysis: index

Appendices		Page no
1	Key to approaches used in the plan	
2	Additional information about the customer	
Worksheets		
1	Organization chart/contact map	
2	Customer's market map	
3	STEEP analysis of customer's environment	
4a	Customer's Porter analysis	
4b	Customer's opportunities and threats statement	
5a	Customer's value chain-based strengths, including finance	
5b	Customer's value chain-based weaknesses, including finance	
5c	Customer's competitors' strengths and weaknesses	
6	Customer's SWOT and strategies	
7	Customer's critical success factors for CO	
8a	CO's Porter analysis	
8b	CO's opportunities and threats statement	
9a	CO's value chain-based strengths, including finance	
9b	CO's value chain-based weaknesses, including finance	
9c	CO's competitors' strengths and weaknesses	
10	CO's SWOT and strategies	
11	Business strategy valuation	
12	CO's strategy priorities for customer	
13	Customer attractiveness assessment	

Add extra relevant information behind most appropriate worksheet, but keep numbering as is, to allow consolidation for management overview.

Appendix 1: Key to approaches used in the plan

1.1 Suppliers' customer management strategy matrix

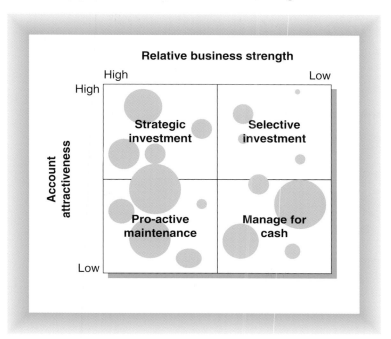

1.2 Customers' supplier management strategy matrix

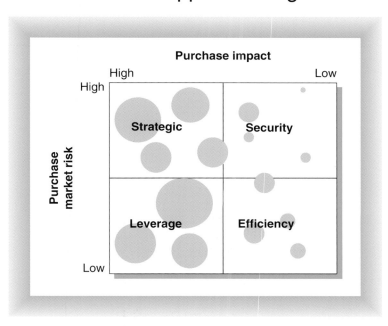

1.3 Relationship stages

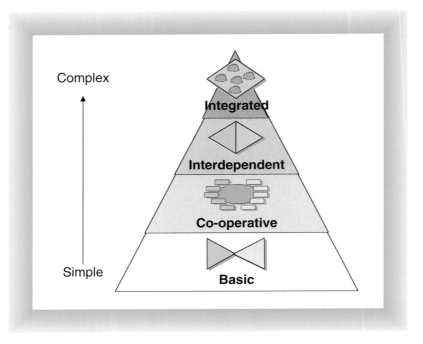

1.4 Scales for assessing relationship and importance levels in Section A.2

Relationship levels:		Importance levels:	
The relationship reflected here is that between CO as a company and the individual in the customer. Individuals within CO may have good or bad personal relationships with each person, but that is not what this table captures. Record the **customer's** view, even if it includes legacy opinions which **you** may regard as no longer valid.		The level of importance recorded here should reflect the level of importance of this person in the development of the relationship with CO	
Level	You/others in your company have:	Level	In developing supplier relationships this person:
0	never met this person, and they would know very little about us.	0	is irrelevant
1	just an acquaintance with this person OR this person has a very poor opinion of us and/or vice versa.	1	has no influence or control
2	some dealings with each other, but not consistently, and we do not have anything more than a basic relationship OR this person has opinions about us which inhibit our relationship with them.	2	has influence/control over their own personal relationship with providers
3	a reasonable understanding and a satisfactory working relationship with this person, but it does not extend to the exchange of confidences or special assistance.	3	has influence/control over a defined group within the organization
4	a good relationship, and work very well together. We are well disposed towards each other and reflect that to our own companies.	4	has a strong influence in the overall direction of the organization
5	an excellent working relationship; we trust each other and have a high opinion of each other. We are good friends and go out of our way to help each other.	5.	the most/one of the most important/influential person (s) in the organization

Worksheets

1. Customer's organization chart

Refer to Appendix 1.4 for further explanation of relationship scales in this diagram
Tip: can be constructed in PowerPoint and pasted in as a picture or scanned from customer's document.

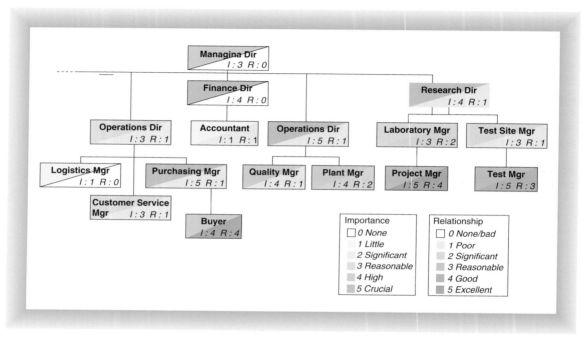

2. Customer's market map

This is an important first step in understanding the customer's business, and should not be omitted. Other analysis tools build on it. It is key to demonstrating your understanding of the customer's environment. Refer to Section 7.1 and Figure 7.1 for further explanation.
Tip: can be constructed in PowerPoint and pasted in as a picture.

3. STEEP analysis of customer's environment		
STEEP factor	**Change/development**	**Which means that?**
Social		
Technological		
Economic		
Ecological		
Political/legal		

4a. Customer's Porter analysis

Market participants	Segments Who are they?	Micro-environment factors What's happening with these people/companies?	Importance High/ Medium/ Low	Opportunity or threat O/T
Customer's customers				
Customer's competitors (current, new, potential)				
Suppliers to customer				

4b. Customer's opportunities and threats statement

Opportunities	Importance High/ Medium/ Low
Threats	

5a. Customer's value chain-based strengths, including finance

Value chain	Customer strengths	Which means that?	Different from competitors	Important to customers
Inbound				
Operations				
Outbound				
Marketing and sales				
Customer service				
Procurement and finance				
Technology development				
HR management				
Management and firm infrastructure				
Culture				

5b. Customer's value chain-based weaknesses, including finance

Value chain	Customer weaknesses	Which means that?	Different from competitors	Important to customers
Inbound				
Operations				
Outbound				
Marketing and sales				
Customer service				
Procurement and finance				
Technology development				
HR management				
Management and firm infrastructure				
Culture				

5c: Customer's view of competitors' strengths and weaknesses

Competitor	Competitor's strengths	Competitor's weaknesses	Overall assessment

6. Customer's SWOT and strategies

Objectives	Key strengths	Key weaknesses
Revenue	S1	W1
Profit	S2	W2
Market share	S3	W3
Key opportunities		
O1		
O2		
O3		
Key threats		
T1		
T2		
T3		

7. Customer's critical success factors for CO					
Critical success factor	**(A) Relative importance weighting**	**(B1) Your company's rating 0–10**	**(C1) Your company's score A × B1**	**(B2) Best competitor rating 0–10**	**(C2) Best competitor score A × B2**
					*
	100	Total =		Total =	

*Name the 'best competitor'.

8a. CO's Porter analysis

Market participants	Who are they?	Micro-environment factors What's happening with these people/companies?	Importance High/ Medium/ Low	Opportunity or threat O/T
The key customer				
CO's competitors (current, new, potential)				
CO's suppliers				

8b. CO's opportunities and threats statement

Opportunities	Importance High/ Medium/Low
Threats	

9a. CO's value chain-based strengths, including finance

Value chain	CO strengths	Which means that?	Different from competitors	Important to customers
?				
?				
?				
Marketing and sales				
Customer service				
Finance				
Procurement				
Technology development				
HR management				
Management and firm infrastructure				

9b. CO's value chain-based weaknesses, including finance

Value chain	CO weaknesses	Which means that?	Different from competitors	Important to customers
?				
?				
?				
Marketing and sales				
Customer service				
Finance				
Procurement				
Technology development				
HR management				
Management and firm infrastructure				

10. CO's SWOT and strategies

Objectives	Key strengths	Key weaknesses
Revenue	S1	W1
Profit	S2	W2
Market share	S3	W3
Key opportunities		
O1		
O2		
O3		
Key threats		
T1		
T2		
T3		

11: Strategy valuation

Statement of strategy

Strategy A	
Strategy B	
Strategy C	
Strategy D	
Strategy E	

Strategy	TY + 1				TY + 2				TY + 3				3 year net total
	Sales €	GM €	Resource €	Net €	Sales €	GM €	Resource €	Net €	Sales €	GM €	Resource €	Net €	
Strategy A													
Strategy B													
Strategy C													
Strategy D													
Strategy E													

12. CO's strategy priorities for customer*

Strategy prioritization criteria	A. Relative importance weighting	Strategy		Strategy		Strategy	
		B1. Rating 0–10	C1. Score A × B1	B2. Rating 0–10	C2. Score A × B2	B3. Rating 0–10	C3. Score A × B3
	100	Total =		Total =		Total =	

*Repeat table to evaluate more than three strategies

13. Customer attractiveness assessment

Account attractiveness criteria	(A) Relative importance weighting	(B) Account rating 0–10	(C) Account score A × B
	100	Total =	

9 Processes – making key account management work

Today, the delivery of superior customer value is as much about a company's business processes as it is about the core product or service, and yet implementation gets nothing like as much attention as it needs. If something has to be done more than once, and almost everything does recur, then there should be a process for doing it. A process can even be mapped for relationship development and, indeed, relationships might develop a lot faster if such a process were followed.

A process may be defined as 'A continuous and systematic series of actions performed in a definite manner directed to some end'. It should represent the most effective and efficient route to converting inputs into outputs. Suppliers' processes are generally designed to deliver to many customers in a standardized, replicable manner, which is good for costs but often not good for key accounts. Start by 'auditing' your processes to see which perform well for key accounts and which, from their point of view, are too slow, inflexible, unreliable, opaque, uninformative, uncosted and unsuitable for integration with the customer's processes.

While, at first sight, you may think that there are only a limited number of processes which impact on key customers, on closer examination you will see that there are far more. They can be divided into:

- **strategic** processes that involve senior management, to which key account managers contribute,

- **strategy realization** processes that add value to the supplier and customer through realizing the agreed strategy, with which the key account manager spends most of his or her time, and

- **operational/transactional** processes concerned with the delivery of what has been promised.

The key account manager plays a different role in each and has different levels of 'ownership' of the process. For example, key account managers need to understand operational processes and be alerted to deviations from expectations, but should not be part of the daily machinery or they will never do anything else.

Each process should be broken down into its component steps, and the role of the key account manager and others identified at each stage. This exercise demonstrates how the process works, and also builds up a picture of what their job should be.

Senior management is responsible for a number of processes in successful key account management, and if they are not aware of that at the outset, the requirement and the means to fulfil them should be identified for them at an early stage. The key account manager's role is mostly provision of information to these processes, so he or she needs to be aware of them, how they work, and what should be contributed. The strategic processes include:

- Selecting attractiveness criteria and key customers
- Managing the customer portfolio
- Considering implications of customer strategies
- Incorporating account plans in business planning
- Allocating/prioritizing resources
- Assessing and managing risk to the company
- Sponsoring key customers
- Coordinating across boundaries
- Enabling organizational learning.

Key account managers have another set of processes with which to work. 'Developing' occurs frequently in this list, because their job is to add value to both organizations by managing change:

- Analysing key accounts, developing strategy and planning
- Developing relationships with customers
- Developing business, capturing opportunities
- Selling and negotiating
- Pricing
- Developing new products
- Customizing products and service
- Managing the product mix
- Developing marketing programmes
- Developing the supply chain
- Developing transaction handling
- Providing customer training
- Developing internal relationships
- Providing information.

Below is a simplified list of operational processes, which run day in, day out. Key account managers, whether they like it or not, are held responsible by the customer for the delivery of what they have promised, so they need a process of two-way communication with operations by which they can brief operations with information they get from the customer, and operations can brief them as appropriate, about good and poor performance.

- Selling
- Processing orders
- Manufacturing/operations
- Servicing customers
- Delivering to customers
- Collecting payment.

A good deal of sales activity belongs at this operational/transactional level, and may be carried out by the field salesforce or telesales, rather than the key account manager.

Introduction

Today, the delivery of superior customer value is as much about a company's business processes as it is about the core product or service. Because many markets and products are mature and opportunities for differentiation are few, suppliers have to look further for means of differentiating themselves. Indeed, great implementation offers real competitive advantage, while good implementation is a minimum requirement at key account level.

> Implementation, rather than structure and strategy, is most often at the root of organizations' problems.
>
> (Bonoma, 1985)

It may be the least 'sexy' part of key account management, but it is arguably the most important. Key customers overwhelmingly prefer suppliers that are 'easy to do business with', and that means the ongoing management of the business at least as much as, if not more than, the deal-making process. Implementation gets nothing like as much attention as it needs.

Key account managers need to realize that they cannot do the whole job on their own, or even just with the team. Once that is admitted, it becomes clear that they must work with and through other parts of the company, and then their job becomes one of finding out how to get their plans implemented. This chapter focuses particularly on the idea that engaging a process is the best way to get things done, and that if key account managers embrace the processes in their organizations and work with them rather than against them, then the chances of success with customers, and repeated success, are much greater.

9.1 The role of processes in implementing key account management

9.1.1 The importance of processes

Over the last few years, the fields of supply chain management and procurement have upgraded their whole approach to their role in the organization. They have taken on new tools and techniques, developed new processes, and educated people to use them and do a really professional job. These disciplines have now made companies billions of pounds, and they have rightly taken a seat at the boardroom table on the back of those achievements.

Customer management is due, if not overdue, for the same kind of makeover. Indeed, it is essential if it is to have any chance of standing up to the fully analysed, carefully prepared and operationalized demands of the customer's procurement and supply chain management. It will involve learning much more about how the supplier operates and what its capabilities are, learning more techniques like process mapping, project management, activity-based costing, bid development, etc. to work with customers in a far less superficial way than in the past. Instead of being on the outside of the company's processes, key account managers need to get to grips with them and understand:

- How the process works
- How it interfaces with other processes
- What costs money to change or has negative onward effects
- How to go about getting modifications and who to talk to.

Without this understanding, key account managers cannot represent the customer's needs in the supplier's process design and specification; and if they do not, who will? When customer input is missing, companies can make decisions that make sense in their own terms of reference, but are potentially very damaging to customers.

However good the relationship with a customer, ultimately a supplier is judged by what it delivers, and quite rightly too. Key account managers cannot abdicate responsibility for current operations, even though they are not directly responsible. Customers are clear that, if the key account manager effectively makes a promise to them, as part of whatever deal is struck, then it is the key account manager who is responsible for its fulfilment. In that case, you would want to be sure that your promise can be delivered and that a robust way of doing it exists, or will exist within the timeframe agreed. Some companies

Key account managers cannot abdicate responsibility for current operations.

and key account managers have tried to separate the two, but unsuccessfully, as far as customers are concerned.

Chapter 12 discusses ways of organizing key account management and trying to minimize the 'silos' or independently operating divisions in a company that prevent a joined-up delivery to the customer. With all the goodwill in the world, companies will still operate in silos and, more than sometimes, goodwill is not enough to cross the boundaries. Far better is a defined and robust process.

Case study insight

The customer's take on responsibility for operational issues

'We realize now that the previous key account manager must have done a lot of fixing for us. The new one doesn't see that as his role, so now we're seeing all the warts. We have said we aren't happy, but he just doesn't seem to take it in. *He* wants to talk about new services, and *we* want to know when they're going to sort out what they've already got' (supply chain director, multinational company).

As companies get more complex on both sides, the need for transparent and trackable processes becomes more important, not less.

As companies get more complex on both sides, the need for transparent and trackable processes becomes more important, not less. You should be considering not only how you persuade and motivate people to support the key customer, but also how you can develop or modify a process that can deliver what is required with greater certainty, and over a longer period.

9.1.2   The nature of processes

We are really concerned with processes that relate to key accounts. However, these might turn out, on closer examination, to be quite a large proportion of the company's processes. Manufacturing processes, for example, might seem quite remote from key accounts, but they can block the creation of customized products, so they are highly relevant. In making the kind of commitments that will drive business with key customers forward, you are likely to encounter more processes than you ever thought existed in your company. They need to work well and in a way that satisfies key customers, and you need to engage with them. Understanding them is the first step.

A process (is) 'A continuous and systematic series of actions performed in a definite manner directed to some end.'

A process may be defined as 'a continuous and systematic series of actions performed in a definite manner directed to some end'. Processes may be seen as a way of converting inputs into outputs, where the inputs and outputs can be of many kinds, from very tangible physical materials to intangibles that may or may not even be captured in a physical form. 'Process' therefore contains the ideas of:

- Purpose
- Definition

- Inputs
- Linked steps
- Action
- Outputs
- Performance.

Whether you are trying to follow a process or develop a new one, you can use this as a checklist to systematically collect the information you need to understand how it works or should work. Figure 9.1 represents a process as a joined-up series of steps with inputs to and outputs from each. Process mapping is a well-developed technique, with commercially available software to support it, but you can get a long way by just drawing a series of boxes and linking them up. (Practical tip: use one large self-stick note for each step, and then you can move them as you learn more about the sequence, without having to start again!)

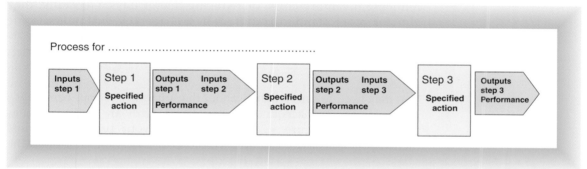

Figure 9.1   A process as a series of steps.

In some cases, a process might not currently exist and might need to be created, such as a process for relationship development. If an activity is genuinely one-off and will not be repeated, then developing and specifying a process may not be worthwhile but, in fact, many activities described as unique are not. Other people in the organization may be doing the same thing as another 'one-off', and could achieve their objectives faster, with less pain and more success, through following a specified process that someone else has trialled and tested.

Key customers have high expectations. From our research, we have identified what is required of a supplier's processes to meet their expectations and to meet the supplier's needs. Processes need to be:

- **Flexible:** Responsive to the customer's needs and open to customization.
- **Fast:** Performance to agreed timing is generally what is required but, when speed is important, the process needs to be able to shift up a gear to meet that need.

● **'Integratable':** Aligned and able to integrate with customers' processes, based on the same or a complementary framework to ensure a smooth 'handshake'.

● **Robust:** Reliable delivery to expectation every time, not fragile or likely to collapse under pressure or change.

● **Transparent:** Able to answer questions like 'What is happening now? What progress has been made?'

● **Informative:** To yield accurate, accessible, manageable performance measurement.

● **Costed:** Suppliers (possibly customers too) should have an understanding of where the costs are so the cost/saving impact of changes can be discussed.

For key customers, some kind of differentiation is obligatory.

You may feel that your company's processes do not perform well for key customers and, indeed, often they do not. They have been set up with different objectives in mind, for example handling a large number of smaller customers as efficiently as possible, or reducing inventory costs, or reducing debtor days. Generally, they aim for more standardization, whereas for key customers, some kind of differentiation is obligatory, and that differentiation may lie in how effectively the supplier operates its processes in delivering to the customer.

You may need to start a debate about the suitability of your company's processes for key accounts. If you begin with an 'audit' such as that shown in Figure 9.2, which assesses your processes against their expectations, you can quickly gather the views from around the

Process attribute	Process						Average score by attribute
	A ………	B ………	C ………	D ………	E ………	F ………	
Flexible							
Fast							
Integratable							
Robust							
Transparent							
Informative							
Costed							
Average score by process							

Figure 9.2 Audit framework for supplier processes.

company. Start by identifying the relevant processes (see Section 9.2) and then score each against the process attributes on a scale of 0–10. It could be interesting to see intuitive assessments gained by completing the grey boxes in the table first, and then comparing them with views gained more systematically.

Completing such an audit will help suppliers to:

- discuss where views are different and why, which should reveal misunderstandings and gaps in understanding

- identify which processes seem satisfactory and which are not, and start to address those most in need of attention

- identify in what way poorly performing processes are failing key customers, in order to clarify change objectives.

An audit of company processes clearly must start with identifying the processes concerned. The model of an organization in terms of layers of activity, as in Figure 9.3, provides a useful framework, since processes (and people) will be largely attached to each layer. Look for processes relevant to key account management in each of these layers.

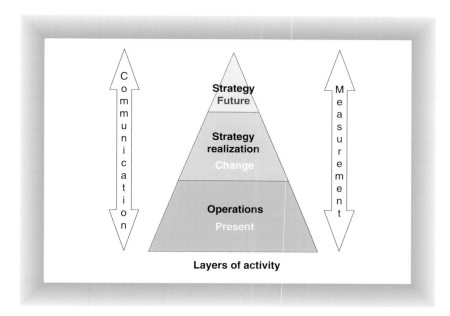

Figure 9.3
Layers of activity and processes.

At the top level, the Board's activities focus on strategy and managing the future. As key account management has a major impact on strategy, there are processes that the Board will need to implement to ensure that key account managers can do their jobs (see Section 9.2). The next layer, which includes key account managers, consists of value-adding activities to realize or fulfil the strategy, involving change. The operational level is very much to do with current delivery, and is generally the responsibility of people other than the key account manager, although he or she has an essential degree of involvement here too. Two processes, communication and measurement, stand out because they are important from top to bottom of the organization (see Sections 9.2 and 11.1).

CHECKPOINT

Are your company's processes friendly to key customers? Has your company:

- Mapped the processes that most concern key customers?

- Audited their performance against key customer's expectations and your company's needs in managing them?

9.1.3   The key account manager's role in processes

There is a grave danger of becoming sucked into being integral to the daily activity and fire-fighting, and only having time left to fulfil a minor part of the role.

Key account managers play different roles in the processes that belong to each of these levels. Most of their time will be taken up with activities in the value-adding layer, working to change current situations, but they also have major contributions to make to strategic layer processes and to operational activities as well. Indeed, it is very important that they have a sound understanding of how the operational processes work in order to clarify for themselves and for everyone else what they do and do not do at this level. Otherwise, there is a grave danger of becoming sucked into being integral to the daily activity and fire-fighting, and only having time left to fulfil a minor part of the role.

While the strategic processes 'belong' to senior managers, key account managers make important contributions to them, particularly in providing information. Consider carefully how you play this part, since that will have a major influence on the outcomes. For example, if your strategic account plan is late and incomplete, you cannot be surprised if you do not get backing for it. If you do not brief your executive sponsor clearly, he or she may not understand the issues fully and may say something inappropriate to the customer. You need to engage with the higher level processes as well as your own.

To identify how the key account manager should be involved with each process, start with breaking it down into its component steps and mapping the sequence, as in Figure 9.4. It is important to identify who is responsible for each step. For some steps it will be the key account manager, in others it will be someone else. Even when the main responsibility lies elsewhere, the key account manager may have a role to play that should be specified and accepted by all.

This exercise can expose serious gaps and misunderstandings, which can then be addressed. Figure 9.5 converts this diagram into a form that collects additional useful information. Where the picture shows

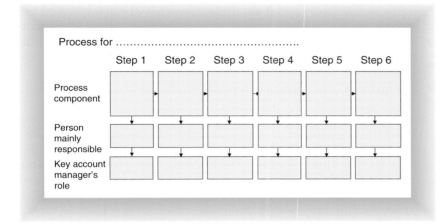

Figure 9.4
The key account manager's role by process component.

Specification	Step 1	Step 2	Step 3	Step 4	Step 5	Step 6
Process component						
Person mainly responsible						
Key account manager's role						
Other's role: who and what						
Inputs to process component						
Outputs from process component						
Flexibility						
Linkages with other processes						
Performance metrics						
Cost						

Figure 9.5   Process data capture proforma.

frequent interactions with particular people or functions, it suggests that these people should be part of the account team (see Section 10.2). Through completing a series of these maps, key account managers will build up for themselves and their colleagues a very clear view of their job, and how they interact with others in the company.

Companies that have carried out this exercise have been impressed by:

- The scope and variety of the key account manager's job
- The competencies required to carry out the responsibilities
- The quantity of activity that depends on the key account manager.

Indeed, the exercise provides valuable input to a discussion on whether the key account manager can carry out the substantial workload which normally appears in this investigation. Check your results against Dr Sue Holt's findings (Holt, 2003), that good key account managers typically spend their time as follows:

- 30 per cent interacting with the customer
- 60 per cent internal activity
- 10 per cent account planning.

The following sections describe the individual processes with which key account managers are normally concerned, but there will undoubtedly be more than can be mentioned here.

CHECKPOINT

Do you know how your company's key account managers spend their time?

- Internal versus external activity?
- What kind of internal activity?
- Do you know the balance between short-term and longer-term activity?

9.2 Key account management implementation processes

9.2.1 Strategic processes

The supplier's Board has an important role to play in key processes that crucially address how key accounts as a group are managed in the company. There is a very great difference between suppliers where the Board has recognized what it has to do, has developed the processes for which it is responsible and is operating them, and one in which the Board has pushed all activity down to the key account manager level and is, basically, 'sitting on its hands'. The former will be reaping the rewards of its efforts; the latter will probably be losing key accounts and key account managers as well.

Some key account managers are ambivalent about having their Boards involved with customer management in any way, but excluding them is unwise and passes up invaluable support. Key account managers need the Board to leverage its authority from time to time in order to achieve certain goals. This authority is better operated through a proper process, which is recognized by all and which delivers the right decisions because of the Board's ongoing involvement with key customers. Figure 9.6 shows the main processes attached to senior management.

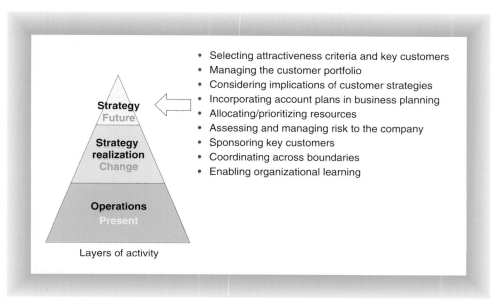

Figure 9.6   Strategic processes in key account management.

Strategic process: selecting attractiveness criteria and key customers

The criteria for evaluating the attractiveness of key customers need to be identified and agreed at the most senior level, since they have serious implications for the company and for individuals within it, and can be quite controversial in their implications. These criteria (see Chapter 2) determine which customers are candidates for receiving special resource and which are not. A multi-step process should be adopted.

1. Agree the criteria (senior management) to reflect the company's strategy and their interpretation of it.

2. Roll the criteria out to key account managers and others in the company with customer knowledge to score the customers.

3. Collect the customers' views of the supplier.

4. Build a portfolio view of the candidates for key customer status.

5. Review the portfolio (senior management), confirm and communicate the selection.

The implications are too important to allow the selection and categorization to be subjected to bias and personal opinion. Take care to obtain objective evidence and the corroboration of third parties wherever possible.

In addition, the original process of selection needs to include a proper process for adding key customers to the portfolio, and also for removing others, or a portfolio can quickly get out of control. Selection and deselection decisions are not easily reversed, so they should not be taken lightly, hastily or on short-term evidence.

Strategic process: managing the customer portfolio

Like a fund manager, someone should be overseeing the performance of the key customer portfolio and making adjustments as necessary. Even where a person has this role, a process of review, response and communication needs to be in place. If there is no single person with this role, then it is even more important that processes exist to:

- enable the performance of these customers to be brought into a single view,

- determine and agree action,

- communicate with concerned parties, and

- implement action.

This is a tough area for companies without a central KAM unit, and the tougher it is, the more important it will be to establish a robust process that is at least sponsored, if not managed, at a very senior level in the company.

Strategic process: considering implications of customer strategies

Key customers do not realistically expect that their suppliers' strategies are entirely driven by their needs, even if they would like it, but they do expect that staff at senior levels will at least know what they are doing and why. However, unless there is a distinct process for conveying customers' strategy to senior managers, it does not happen. Some Boards are out and about in the marketplace and have excellent 'antennae' for sensing customer strategies, and others are very introspective, and will have no such understanding unless it is systematically fed to them. We have observed several processes for this purpose, but you need to decide which one or, better, which combination of them will be most effective in your company. The processes include:

- Monthly reports featuring customer strategy submitted to the Board and discussed as an agenda item.

- Regular presentations of key customer strategies by the key account manager at Board meetings (e.g. two or three per meeting).

- Quarterly or annual forum for presenting key customers and discussing strategic implications.

- Annual/quarterly meetings between the customer's senior management and the executive sponsor (see below).

In developing your process, consider how to use the Board's limited time to best advantage, balancing information input with the time required for it to make a response or decision and communicate it, or you may end up with a one-way reporting process that has no apparent outcome.

Strategic process: incorporating account plans in business planning

In most companies the business planning cycle is already a tortuous series of strategy documents and forecasts whose origins may lie in a supplier's regional organization, production department, finance function or elsewhere. Without a defined step in the business planning process which asks for input from key account plans, they will not make any contribution, and key account managers will feel they have wasted the time they spent on planning. Unless the plans are specifically linked into the process, they will not fulfil the vital function that is an invaluable part of the reason for having key customers at all – their ability to guide the supplier successfully through changing market conditions in partnership with leading customers.

Generally speaking, business plans developed by internal departments will rely heavily on trends mechanically extrapolated from the past. This approach assumes that the future will look like the past, which is a very dangerous assumption these days. Unless strategic key account plans are incorporated into the process, the company could easily find itself underfinanced, or geared up to produce the wrong items in the wrong place, or failing to invest in innovation for new markets, or suffering a host of other unintended consequences of a failure to institutionalize these plans.

Strategic process: allocating/prioritizing resources

The amount a supplier is prepared to invest in a customer marks the critical difference between key accounts and other customers. A company should keep careful control of its resources and which customers receive them, and that demands a proper process of approval at the right level in the company. Some companies still allow significant amounts of resource to be won through key account managers using

---

Case study insight

Investing in R&D with customers in the hi-tech sector

For an innovative hi-tech supplier, co-developing R&D projects with customers was an ideal way of creating new products and the markets for them simultaneously. However, on reviewing the results of its new product development after several years, it realized that it had invested a good deal of time and effort in projects that had been very successful technically, but had failed to yield the commercial returns expected. On further examination, it found that quite a high proportion of these projects had been driven by exciting ideas from rather small companies that did not have the capacity to commercialize the new products when they had been created. From then on, it decided that only key accounts should be offered R&D projects, and introduced a process of approval that ensured enforcement.

their powers of influence and persuasion to elicit resources from department managers and budget holders, which cannot be the right way to manage a company if, indeed, it can be called management at all.

The process should include the following steps, at least:

1. Agree resource available to the key account portfolio.

2. Key account managers submit strategic account plans including requests for specified resources.

3. Approval to commit resources in principle agreed (or not) in line with total budget.

4. At appropriate time, detailed business case submitted for final approval.

5. Approval to spend resource given (or not) in line with forecast outcomes and budget available.

Strategic process: assessing and managing risk to the company

You can assume that if there is no process to manage something, it is not being managed.

Low risk is inexorably related to low returns. While making every sensible effort to reduce exposure to risk, all business activities and all customers involve some residual degree of risk. Companies need to decide on the exposure to risk they are prepared to accept, and then manage towards that level. However, companies talk about risk but rarely measure it and generally do not have a process for managing it. As with everything else discussed in this chapter, you can assume that if there is no process to manage something, it is not being managed.

The process of balancing risk in the portfolio can be included within the overall management of the portfolio discussed above. In addition, though, there needs to be a process for:

● Assessing the riskiness of individual customers relative to other customers and reassessing it regularly

● Supplying the data to the portfolio manager or management process

● Analysing the position and deciding on what action should be taken, if any

● Communicating decisions

● Monitoring their fulfilment.

Many companies only assess the financial stability of their customers in order to establish their ability to pay their bills. There are many more risks involved in KAM which should be properly and objectively evaluated on a regular basis.

Strategic process: sponsoring key customers

Executive sponsorship of key customers is a great idea that needs careful execution. Board members should each be allocated a manageable number of key accounts, somewhere between one and three, in which they will take an ongoing interest and meet a few times per year, somewhere between annually and quarterly. The sponsor gives the key customer a defined route to the supplier's boardroom and a point of final escalation if absolutely needed, which demonstrates to the customer its importance to the supplier. It gives the Board contact with the most important part of its marketplace, and provides support to the key account manager.

Again, executive sponsorship needs a process to make it work properly, one that includes the following elements:

- Matching directors with appropriate key accounts
- Reviewing customer strategy with the key account manager
- Defining and agreeing the role of the executive sponsor and key account manager
- Briefing the executive sponsor on specific aims or occasions
- Providing access on demand to the account plan and current issues.

Case study insight

The Siemens approach to executive sponsorship

Siemens saw that its top management needed to be more involved with its key accounts in order to open doors in the customers and to gain support internally. So the company introduced TERP, its Top Executive Relationship Process, which included an overall plan for TERP meetings and pre-meeting briefings; plus protocols and actions. In Siemens' words, the programme was designed to:

- 'Orchestrate/align the TOP management of Siemens to the TOP management of our customer
- Executive support of account plan projects – key projects and cross selling
- Consistent process of executive meetings and actions (standardized)
- Easy to use systematic information management from executive engagement
  - cross account team portals
  - cross customer
  - cross units.'

The initiative resulted in accelerated growth in Siemens' top accounts and was an important part of a hugely successful KAM programme.

Strategic process: coordinating across boundaries

Key account managers have to work across boundaries, but they normally have to fall back on goodwill and good corporate citizenship to achieve their objectives. At times, that is not enough. Key account managers may encounter internal functional boundaries, and global account managers have to tackle extra barriers from national boundaries in order to coordinate the collection of information and commitment to deals they are trying to negotiate across numerous countries. If each occasion has to be approached as a new occurrence, key account manager talent will wear out very quickly.

These issues are fairly predictable in their nature, if not in detail, so it is quite possible for companies to establish a process to deal with them, although it is not really possible to generalize this process here as much as the others described previously. Several processes are involved: for example, cross-boundary information collection; cross-boundary proposition development and approval; and conflict resolution, on occasion. These processes need to be fitted to each company's structure and managed proactively by senior managers in the interests of the company as a whole, rather than narrow functional or strategic business unit (SBU) interests.

Strategic process: enabling organizational learning

Key account managers develop brilliant ideas, execute fantastic projects, win difficult bids and achieve fabulous results – but not all in the same place at the same time. Imagine how much better the results could be if all of this could be brought together. Sadly, this wonderful experience often stays where it was gained, and is inaccessible to the rest of the company. People are wasting time and resources and failing where others have succeeded, when they could have learned from internal best practice, because there is no process through which their experience can be logged and retrieved when needed.

> People are wasting time and resources and failing where others have succeeded, when they could have learned from internal best practice.

Before a process can be developed, companies must first decide the best way for them to share knowledge. Consider using some or all of:

- Best practice forums
- Communities of interest
- Prepared case studies
- Access to documents like account plans
- Dedicated websites.

> A process should be developed to keep sharing live, easy to access and supplied with fresh material.

When the mix of media has been agreed, a process should be developed to keep sharing live, easy to access and supplied with fresh material. Incentives may be offered for contributing material and for using the system.

Case study insight

IMI promoting sharing globally and across diverse engineering businesses

IMI plc has an extensive list of blue-chip customers across a range of industries and geographies. Key account management is an IMI competency that has supported the delivery of higher added value solutions to this group.

Over the past five years IMI's CEO and senior executive sponsorship of KAM has been active, and high levels of investment have supported skill and behaviour changes. The 'IMI KAM Academy' is coordinated centrally and drives and supports continuous improvements in key account activities and processes across each of IMI's five 'platform' business areas.

The Academy initiates and organizes extensive training activities for key account and line managers. It provides best practice tools and techniques covering areas such as account planning and relationship mapping. There is also a market intelligence service that key account managers from across the globe call on for insights tailored to their needs. In addition, the Academy also coordinates activities to deliver creative concept generation and innovation. An extensive 'best practice' outside network of agencies, consultants and councils, including Cranfield University, is used across these areas.

9.2.2 Strategy realization key account management processes

The majority of the key account manager's time should be spent on the strategy realization processes in Figure 9.7, or how key account management adds value to the organization and to the customer. These are the ones in which he or she plays pole position in managing the inputs to the process, coordinating and driving progress, and managing the outputs from the process.

The word 'developing' appears frequently in the list, which is indicative of the role. Key account managers should be focused on what they are doing to develop and change the relationship with the customer, what value they are adding to the customer's business, and what value they are adding to their own business. That should cover 90 per cent of their time, with no more than 10 per cent, and ideally less, devoted to fire-fighting and problem-solving.

Strategy realization process: analysing key accounts, developing strategy and planning

The key account manager is responsible for most of this process, which explains why Sue Holt found that it took 10 per cent of the key account

The planning process, time-consuming though it is, should not be 'outsourced' to another team member.

Figure 9.7   Value-adding processes in key account management.

manager's time (Holt, 2003). The planning process, time-consuming though it is, should not be 'outsourced' to another team member. Only intimate knowledge of the plan and the rationale behind it can give the key account manager sufficient confidence to discuss it in detail with customers. However, the key account manager can and should work with a team in order to gain a broader range of contributions to improve the quality of the plan.

The key account manager manages this process from start to finish:

- **Setting up:** Identifying, training and briefing the team
- **Analysis and strategy setting:** Development workshops and information gathering
- **Planning:** Producing the plan and planning communication
- **Roll-out:** Get approval, assemble implementation team and communicate
- **Measure and monitor:** Set up and run measurement, review and response.

Strategy realization process: developing relationships with customers

One key account director, when asked if there was a process for relationship development in his company, replied that he did not think so, because people 'just know' how to develop relationships. In fact, he was quite dissatisfied with the state of his company's relationships, and perhaps he should have considered whether a lack of process might be responsible for the situation. Many people know how to develop personal relationships, but not necessarily intercompany relationships, and even the best key account managers would be helped by seeing relationship development as a process. It fits our definition of a process at the beginning of this chapter just as well as many others. Indeed, seeing relationship development as a process, as in Figure 9.8, has a number of advantages:

● Missing out steps is less likely to happen

● Seeing the whole process helps planning, which generally improves speed and certainty

● Other people can see how they can help

● Progress can be monitored

● Progress can be compared with other relationships.

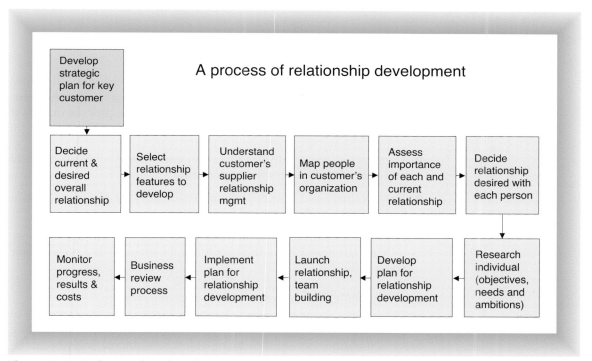

Figure 9.8   Relationship development as a process.

Strategy realization process: developing business, capturing opportunities

Some companies, particularly those involved in markets characterized by very large, infrequent bids, are brilliant at business development. They may track opportunities from the moment they first appear until they are finally won, several years later. There is now plenty of good software available to help the process, so the quality of approach

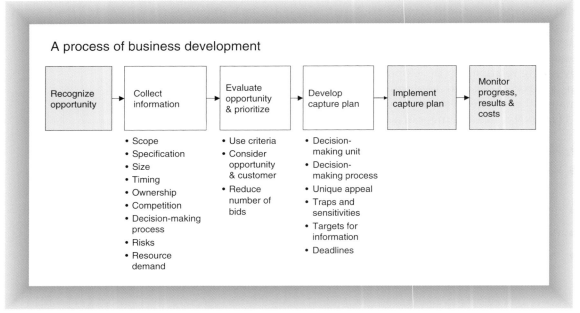

A process of business development

| Recognize opportunity | Collect information | Evaluate opportunity & prioritize | Develop capture plan | Implement capture plan | Monitor progress, results & costs |

Collect information:
• Scope
• Specification
• Size
• Timing
• Ownership
• Competition
• Decision-making process
• Risks
• Resource demand

Evaluate opportunity & prioritize:
• Use criteria
• Consider opportunity & customer
• Reduce number of bids

Develop capture plan:
• Decision-making unit
• Decision-making process
• Unique appeal
• Traps and sensitivities
• Targets for information
• Deadlines

Figure 9.9   Critical steps in the business development process.

should be improving. The trouble is that if everyone is upgrading their game you need to find more ways of being out ahead. Successful companies seem to be better at some of the steps in the process that their competitors may not even recognize (Figure 9.9).

● They collect more information at an early stage so they can fully understand and qualify the opportunity.

● They evaluate and select opportunities objectively according to strategic criteria, and say 'no bid' more often.

● They use formal capture planning – how they will win the business, rather than how they will execute the business – to develop their approach.

Strategy realization process: selling and negotiating

Selling means managing the sales cycle through to the face-to-face negotiation, but plenty has been written elsewhere about the selling process that does not need to be repeated here. Increasingly, negotiation is conducted remotely, as in reverse e-auctions, which are still new to some sectors while they are diminishing in importance in others. In a reverse e-auction, the customer declares the specification of what it wants to buy, prequalifies a shortlist of suppliers, all of which it considers acceptable. Suppliers then bid for the business through a website over a period of, say, two hours, offering lower prices to beat the competition. Often, prices from other suppliers are visible, albeit anonymously, until the last phase of the auction, which gives the customer the option of selecting the lowest price, or not. It is a brutal process!

Customers have cut the prices they pay dramatically in some cases, which has whetted their appetite to buy more through this route, although some have gained very low prices but suffered poor delivery and are moderating their activity. Nevertheless, suppliers must realize that they are very much at risk of losing their volume or losing their margin in reverse e-auctions if they sell a commodity product.

The customer's procurement department normally runs an e-auction, and they are very clear about the whole process from the issuing of invitations to prequalify to participate in the auction, through to the actual auction itself. You must respond with an equally clear process of preparation and response: a great deal of work needs to be completed before the auction begins.

1. Analyse the customer's expressed needs and implicit wants.

2. Propose a specification that plays to your strengths and challenges competition.

3. Establish the buying process and criteria.

4. Carry out a detailed analysis of costs.

5. Build a cost and pricing model to enable testing of prices and terms.

6. Build a model to test results of winning or losing the business.

7. Respond to and pass the qualification process.

8. Decide on the e-auction team, who does what, who approves the final offer on the day or decides to drop out.

9. Agree pricing floors with appropriate people (e.g. finance).

10. Participate in the auction.

The reverse auction process will probably strip out costs for features or services that the customer does not require, so suppliers that bundle costs together are ill-prepared to participate in e-auctions. Winning prices and terms are very finely tuned and negotiators must be able to work with full cost transparency internally.

> Winning prices and terms are very finely tuned and negotiators must be able to work with full cost transparency internally.

In very big deals the selling process for a key customer is normally carried out by the key account manager, with or without a team. Often, this really amounts to a licence to sell to the customer's sites, rather than a guaranteed volume of business. In many markets, thereafter, orders are facilitated on the ground by the field salesforce in each division or locality, not by the key account manager personally. This is a very different selling process, which still needs to be managed by the key account manager, usually without any direct authority (see Chapters 10 and 12). The key account manager needs to build and participate appropriately in a process of:

● communicating information to the salesforce

● supporting their selling process

- monitoring performance
- tracking the customer's response
- recognizing achievements.

From what we have seen, it is not easy to build a robust process in this kind of very common situation, although it is absolutely necessary. It is hard, time-consuming labour to make it work, and any process available to help should be used. If the key account manager does not succeed, the salesforce will be selling other things to other customers, and the volume from centrally negotiated deals may never materialize.

Strategy realization process: pricing

Key customers do not accept standard pricing, and they have enough buying power to put plenty of pressure on prices. They will also be constantly trying out customized products and customized service offerings in order to gain advantage in the marketplace and optimize what they pay for. The volume of pricing exercises is bound to be high and getting higher. Intelligent suppliers have worked to achieve a good understanding of their own cost base, so that they can respond quickly and appropriately with prices.

Case study insight

Fast, consultative pricing in a global services supplier

In order to establish costs and prices, a global supplier needed to consult numerous national SBUs and service experts every time a global or multinational customer asked for prices. The process involved several iterations and took longer than big customers were prepared to wait. It had to change its process from the safe, sequential one it had always used to one with simultaneous consultation at several stages. It introduced brightly coloured, fast-track covers for critical pricing documents, moved them to the top of any recipient's task list, and enforced the discipline. They executed 6–8 iterations in half the time it had taken before – not every time – but whenever it was really necessary.

> Pricing for key customers demands a very transparent process: mistakes can cost a supplier dear.

Pricing for key customers demands a very transparent process: mistakes can cost a supplier dear. It needs to be absolutely clear who provides input, who needs to be informed, who has final approval, what degree of variance is allowable, and when the customer can be approached. Key account managers should play a pivotal role in pricing. They should know what other costs are affected in the customer's business, how the terms can be made more attractive without reducing margins, on what basis the customer will assess a price, what they are likely to pay and so on.

> Suppliers should look at their short-term volume-based incentive schemes and ask themselves who created this conflict of interest and why.

However, in many companies key account managers are largely excluded from pricing decisions, except as a source of specific information, because they are not sufficiently trusted. To some extent, this mistrust may arise from a feeling that they are not financially competent, but often it is because their objectivity and commitment to acting in the company's interests rather than their own is questioned. Suppliers should look at their short-term volume-based incentive schemes and ask themselves who created this conflict of interest and why.

Strategy realization process:

- Developing new products
- Customizing products and service
- Managing the product mix
- Developing marketing programmes
- Developing the supply chain
- Developing transaction handling
- Providing customer training.

These processes address very different aspects of the customer's business, and it is through these processes that the supplier will fulfil most of the added value it can offer to the customer, which makes them extremely important. As processes, however, they can be considered together, since they will generally consist of a project carried out by the supplier's experts, possibly working alongside customer staff. The key account manager will be involved in the coordination and communication during the project, but particularly at the beginning and the end. Figure 9.10 shows the outline of a typical process for such a project, with the key account manager's role highlighted. Step 4 is deceptive, as the bulk of the work lies in this box, so it may need to be split into greater detail in practice.

Where key account managers have an understanding of supply chain issues, marketing, product development, etc., they are more likely to spot opportunities like this, and are better able to support the project and ensure that it stays on track to deliver to the customer's needs than if they do not. They should not fulfil the role of project manager, generally, as the project and the project team should be driven by the subject expert, leaving the key account manager free to take a more detached view and liaise with the customer.

Strategy realization process: developing internal relationships
The same process and techniques can be applied to developing internal relationships as have been suggested for developing external relationships. Indeed, finding your way round a large organization, even if it is your own employer, absolutely requires as systematic an approach as you would apply to a customer.

Strategy realization process: providing information
A substantial part of the key account manager's job will be about providing information, from and to the customer, from and to people internally. The information will be of all kinds, about strategic account plans, project progress, performance figures, customer positioning,

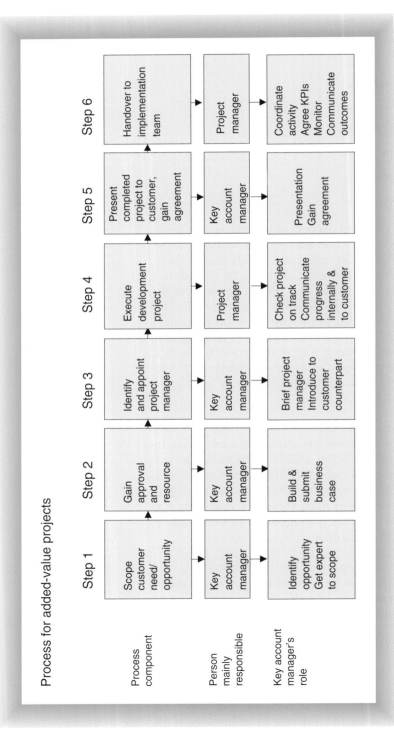

Figure 9.10 Outline of a process for added-value customer projects.

personalities, current issues, etc. So it is not possible to chart a single generic process to provide this disparate collection of information. Wherever it is required regularly, the key account manager should think about developing processes for sourcing and delivering it to its destination in a suitable form in order to avoid a lot of sweat, tears and late nights. If a process has been mapped, it will be possible to clarify the sources of data and the role of other people in providing the information, and hence to delegate some of the work.

This list of processes forms a major part of the key account manager's activity:

- plus his or her contribution to the strategic processes in section 9.2.1
- plus his or her role in operational processes in Section 9.2.3
- plus communication in Section 9.2.4
- plus monitoring and measurement in Section 11.1.

Key account managers have a big job, and they should use all the processes they can.

9.2.3   Operational processes

Operational processes are those that run the day-to-day activity of a company and that actually deliver what the customer has bought. Key account managers need to be involved with them, to the extent that is required to ensure that promises are fulfilled. They must therefore understand the company's operational capabilities; what it can and cannot do, and what is and is not expensive to do. The kinds of processes that we class as operational or transactional are shown in Figure 9.11, and include the regular sales process and transaction and payment handling, as well as production and physical delivery.

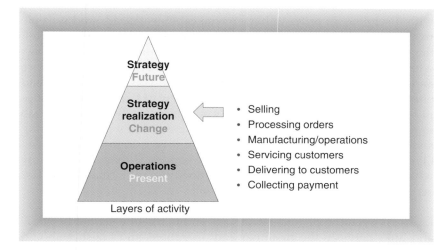

Figure 9.11
Operational processes.

Unfortunately, key account managers easily get sucked into firefighting and problem-solving in this area. Operational people will be more than happy to allow you to take on the role of liaising with the customer and bearing bad news when necessary, and you quickly become a part of the regular mechanism. You are then in danger of being an overpaid customer service executive, and finding yourself with no time or energy to fulfil your own, proper role. Ultimately, the key account manager does take responsibility and communicate with the customer when things are seriously wrong: the issue is balance.

You need to agree with the operational team how you can best work together, so that you supply them with what they need, when they need it, and then let them get on with the job, including talking to the customer. There have been some fabulous relationships built up between suppliers' order processing people and customers' purchasing and supply chain people, which have saved both sides a great deal of trouble. If operational people have been properly briefed and consulted, then they should be trusted to do their job, and to find solutions to issues when required. Figure 9.5 might be a useful way of working out what they need from you, and what you need from them.

CHECKPOINT

Are both key account managers and operations clear about what decisions each can make:

- Without needing to inform the other?

- Informing the other, but after the decision is taken?

- Needing to consult with the other before a decision is taken?

Lines of communication must be open, but they must also be used with discipline, in order to have manageable workloads and sensible working practices. One operations director said, 'You can easily tell the difference between a good key account manager and a bad one: when things go pear-shaped, the good one will bring us the bad news and tell us it's going to happen beforehand, but you won't find the bad one anywhere.' Figure 9.12 illustrates the view of Graham Booth, supply chain director of Tesco, when he said, quite simply, 'It's not my job to work out what we should offer to customers, that's what marketing and sales does. My job, once I know what it is, is to make it happen.' Obviously, operations cannot make 'it' happen if they do not know what 'it' is, and the link between operations and sales/marketing/key account management is notoriously poor.

The link between operations and marketing/sales/key account

Links between the customer and sales and marketing should be good, and links between the customer and operations and logistics should also be good, but links between sales and marketing, and operations and logistics, are often poor. So it could be that while the customer has a full view of what it was offered to match what it received, when

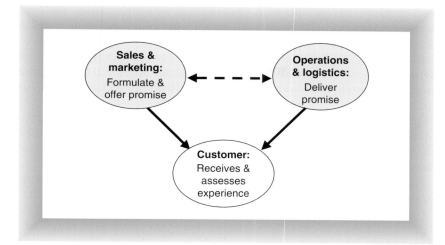

Figure 9.12
Lines of
communication.

nobody in the supplier has a complete picture! This is surely an exposed and perilous position to be in. Key account managers need to strengthen their internal relationships with operations and agree some protocols and processes through which they can work together.

Case study insight

A wasted opportunity in the automotive sector

In companies supplying the automotive industry, contracts are negotiated around each car model, and are agreed quite some time before production actually begins. The key account manager's involvement peaks at contract negotiation, and their attention has normally moved on by the time the goods are actually delivered. As a result, probably, they have virtually no contact with operations and the people do not even recognize each other. The operations manager said, 'I deal with this customer every day, and I think I know a lot about them. But I wouldn't even know who the key account manager is, so I don't pass any of it on. I don't know how or where to call.'

In summary, getting the balance right here is both important and difficult. Key account managers should find it worthwhile to invoke some processes and to start by mapping them to clarify who does what, under what circumstances.

9.2.4   The process of communication

We do not plan to deal with interpersonal communication here, but we do want to make a plea for communication to be considered as a process and dealt with much more systematically than it normally is. As relationships develop, a large part of the key account manager's job becomes communication. Think of all the people with whom you need to communicate inside your own organization, as well as inside the customer organization. If they are not kept fully informed, they cannot make the decisions appropriate to the customer that will allow them to do their jobs properly, and good communication is essential to effective team working. However, communication is often an afterthought, whereas with some forethought, a lot of activities would work much better.

What you want to say is crucial to how and where you say it.

Start by deciding your purpose, why you are communicating. What you want to say is crucial to how and where you say it. What kind of action do you want as an outcome? Do you want someone to give you information? Or do you want to give them information, so that they will do . . . what? Do you want a response? What kind of response? Do recipients know how to make contact, and are you ready to receive it?

Figure 9.13 shows some of the reasons why you may be communicating; and the first step is to decide which.

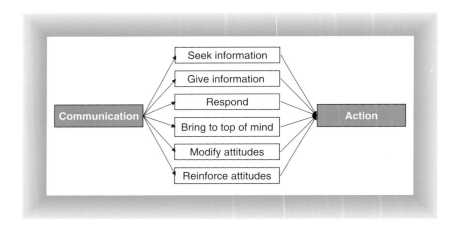

Figure 9.13
Reasons to communicate.

The communicator must take responsibility for directing the audience's attention to the right place and making the meaning readily accessible.

Material sent out is often overloaded and unfocused, so that recipients do not know which part is for them, and may easily miss it. The communicator must take responsibility for directing the audience's attention to the right place and making the meaning readily accessible. Sending out a communication is only the beginning of the process. A communication cannot be considered as effective unless it:

● reaches the intended recipient,

● is absorbed by the intended recipient,

● is understood,

● produces the desired response, and

● is retained (though not always).

These are rather obvious requirements, but if they were taken seriously, plenty of communications would turn out very different. Communication does not achieve these objectives if it is misdirected, incomplete, impenetrable or confusing. It might just as well not have been sent if it does not produce the desired response.

The advertising industry has clearly given a great deal of thought to communication, and we can learn from it. It particularly recognizes the importance of the audience. Just like consumer audiences, business audiences are of different sizes and profiles, speak different languages (finance or logistics or marketing), belong to different cultures that interpret messages differently, and are best accessed via different media. However, business communication often treats them as if they were all identical, which is simply not so. The audience, and the need to communicate, drives the message and the communication of the message, as shown in Figure 9.14.

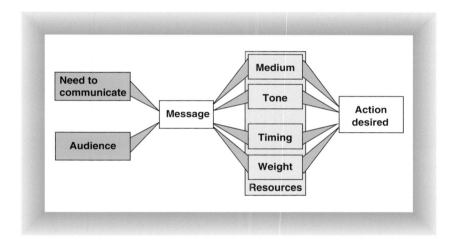

Figure 9.14
Planning communication.

In deciding the most effective way to convey your message, you need to think about:

- **The medium:** Choose email, telephone, videoconference, face-to-face meeting, presentation, special event and so on. Which is most suitable for the audience and most suitable for the message? Use multiple media to reinforce messages.

- **Tone/style:** The audience and the message determine whether the tone should be informative, financial, motivational, humorous or serious and so on.

- **Timing:** At what point in the year should the message be sent – calendar year, financial year, or sales seasons? Should it be timed before, during or after an event, and by how much? Does it need to link with other events or communications?

- **Weight:** Should the message be flagged as very important? How much space should it get? Should it be 'showcased'? Should it be repeated? How often?

These are the elements that begin to take up resources, which may be money in business to consumer terms, but are more likely to be time in business to business. Having no budget at all for communication to or about key customers can be a barrier, but relatively small sums could be used very effectively.

Of course, not all communication requires detailed planning, but certainly strategic account plans, major programmes, initiatives and projects involve a great many people in both the customer and the supplier. Planning them would improve timeliness greatly, and prevent many problems from ever arising. Figure 9.15 gives a planning framework to use based on Figure 9.14. Start by writing all the audiences involved, internally and externally, in the first column, and then complete each row with the specific message for each audience, and the best way of conveying it for them. Clearly identify what response is expected, and consider how the effectiveness of the communication should be measured, whether in terms of response or of attitude, knowledge, etc. Measurement is often not necessary or even possible, but from time to time it will be important to establish whether messages are getting through, and then measurement should be applied at the receiving end.

Need to communicate ....

Audience	Message	Tone	Media	Timing	Weight	Desired action	Metrics/ KPIs

Figure 9.15   Developing a communication plan.

Key account managers struggle with the fundamental requirements of communication.

We have assumed so far that people have basic communication skills but, in reality, key account managers struggle with the fundamental requirements of communication, especially expressing themselves in writing in an appropriate manner and length for business. The strategic account plan is a core item of communication but, sadly, many of those that we have seen fail to communicate clearly or accurately. They veer from the extreme of terseness to the other extreme of verbosity, and fail to do even the essential job of explaining the account in the absence of the key account manager.

Summary

If something has to be done more than once, there should be a process for doing it. As one disillusioned company said, two years after its introduction of KAM, 'We've discovered, the hard way, that it's all about process in the end.' Indeed, process is the way that companies get things done, so that should not come as a surprise. When people like key account managers touch on a great many activities in the company, they can only achieve their objectives by allowing processes to fulfil the tasks. Key customers expect robust and consistent performance across the board, and that can only be managed by good processes.

This chapter is a plea to key account managers to engage actively and positively with their company's processes, because unless they do, they will fail. If the process is rigid and unresponsive, then clarify and discuss the issues with whoever is responsible for it, rather than working round it, so that next time it will work in a more appropriate way. If there is no process at all, and one is needed, then find out where it belongs in the organization and work with those people to come up with a robust solution.

Key account managers who try to do everything themselves will be very limited in what they can achieve – and very tired. In fact, good or excellent processes are fundamental to the success of KAM, and to the success of individual key account managers. If the organization does not make them responsive to the needs of key customers, key account managers will find that they have very little room to manoeuvre in what they can offer, and will be constantly frustrated, fighting 'with one hand tied behind their backs'. If they are good, competent key account managers, they are likely to leave and find an organization that has better processes.

However, if a supplier gets its processes right for key customers, the chances are they will work well for other customers too, and the whole business will benefit. Market-leading customers can teach suppliers a lot, as long as they are able to learn.

Implementation is the graveyard of strategy

10 The role and requirements of key account managers

In order to determine the role of key account managers, suppliers first need to ask themselves what they intend the role of key account management (KAM) itself to be. That should decide what its 'agents', the key account managers, have to do. The objectives for KAM and the route to achieving them should be worked out in some detail.

Normally, the prime driver will be the marketplace and leading customers in it, so the company should have a view on how KAM will work from their point of view. Specifying the role that KAM plays in the supplier's strategy is of the greatest importance, and one often underestimated or misunderstood. Initially, KAM is about making reciprocated commitments to customers, but that quickly needs to be followed by fulfilment of those commitments, so companies should anticipate the issues in operations and adapt. In fact, they will find that adaptation means changing the organization and culture, as well as plans and processes.

The question then arises of 'who does what?' Obviously, key account managers are responsible for a great deal of the activity, but the company is also responsible for supporting them, by providing resources, communicating organization-wide, tackling barriers and making decisions that are beyond the remit of the individual.

The scope of the KAM initiative will highlight the breadth of the key account manager's role. At the simplest level, the key account manager has two roles: *implementation* of a business strategy with the customer, and *facilitation* of that implementation through building the relationship. The relationship is not an end in itself, but should be employed to create and implement strategies that will develop business with the customer. These two roles go hand in hand: success requires both.

Exactly how the key account manager plays these roles depends on the nature of the customer and the overall strategy allotted to it. *Streamline* customers allocated a 'manage for cash' strategy should receive different treatment from *strategic* or *star* customers, so the key account manager's role must be adjusted accordingly. The first require a tough negotiator who will need to manage costs and operations rigorously, while the latter require someone to create a vision of the future and work to make it happen.

The key account team, however, can take on part of the role. The team can apply its expertise to fulfil some elements, though some, like team leadership, cannot be separated from the key account manager. Unfortunately, key account managers' experience of team-working is often very limited, and they make poor team leaders unless they receive proper training and support for this part of their role. To make matters worse, the members of the account team normally do not report directly to the key account manager, but still remain within their function or region. Nevertheless, the key account team should be an ongoing group of people committed to the same objectives for the customer's business, not a project team or other transient group of people. Important customers expect team support and increasingly are getting it from suppliers.

Generally, there are two key account teams that exist simultaneously: the head office, cross-functional team, which is concerned with current delivery of commitments to the customer and also with how to adapt and develop new value; and the regional sales team, which supports customer strategic business units (SBUs) in the field and applies the deals agreed centrally.

Such a broad role demands a wide range of competencies and attributes. Regrettably, in many cases, suppliers have automatically appointed senior salespeople to the role without considering the competencies needed, and then found later that a substantial proportion of them do not have and are unable to acquire them. Indeed, 'selling' is a comparatively minor part of the role, and not one that should be used exclusively for determining the right people for the job.

To make appropriate appointments, suppliers should ideally start by establishing an 'inventory' of their key customers categorized into four types according to the strategy selected for them. Clearly, customers should be managed by a key account manager who is suited to applying the strategy selected for each of them, i.e. an 'entrepreneur', 'business manager', 'customer manager' or 'tactician'. Once the supplier has assembled its customer inventory, it can see how many of each of four types of key account manager are needed.

Different competencies and attributes are demanded by each of these roles, although they also have some in common. Competencies are defined as behaviours required to achieve high levels of performance, whereas attributes are more about the way people think and the values they hold, though they also affect behaviour. Attributes are harder to learn and to change. The competencies and attributes that relate to each of the four roles have been worked out, so that individuals can be profiled and matched to the role they would perform best. Such an approach can be used as a foundation for a conversation with the key account manager to discuss how he or she can develop to achieve personal and organizational objectives, now and in the future.

Introduction

What do you want key account management to do for your organization?

Suppliers often ask us 'Are our key account managers the right people for the job?' At first glance, this might appear to be a reasonable question. A second glance suggests that, before it can be answered, the questions 'What is the job? What do you want them to do?' should be asked. Indeed, even more important is the question, 'What do you want key account management to do for your organization?'

Obviously, companies have different views of what key account management (KAM) can and should deliver. These expectations will drive the investment they make in the initiative; the scope of the change they envisage; the remit they give to key account managers and therefore the quality and capabilities of the key account managers they employ to fill the role.

For example, if KAM is expected to manage customers who are going global, then globally competent, culturally versatile people are required to do the job. If it needs to deliver profitability in an increasingly competitive, mature marketplace, then the company is likely to need people with a strong focus on operations. If it intends to develop and disseminate innovations through its key customers, then it will need people with vision and passion to drive that through.

Clearly, the company should identify its corporate strategy and then consider how its strategy for key accounts will be aligned to and deliver it. After all, if its key customers do not deliver a substantial part of the corporate strategy, the strategy probably will not succeed at all; because it is unlikely that the smaller, follower accounts can do it on their own.

Rather often, suppliers start KAM with incompatible objectives that have in-built limitations. They tend to underestimate the scope of the key account manager's role and the level of competencies required to succeed, and hence they make unsuitable appointments, mostly of senior salespeople, and later discover that some of them are not able to do the demanding job that KAM requires.

10.1 Roles

10.1.1 The role of key account management

The first step in determining the role of the key account manager must be to define the role of KAM itself in the organization. Describing KAM as 'building close relationships between supplier and customer organizations that add superior value to the customer's business as well as to the supplier's' immediately suggests a role in building bridges, defining strategies and delivering them as well. Our research discovered a variety of objectives in developing relationships with key customers:

> KAM is building close relationships... that add superior value to the customer's business as well as to the supplier's business.

- Visibility of key account needs
- Shared customer understanding internally
- Proactive strategies
- Prioritization of resources and investment
- Global coordination
- Increased margins even in very competitive areas
- Profitability
- Growth
- Greater (not guaranteed) security.

When SAP analysed the background for its global account management initiative in 1999, it was very clear about what it wanted the programme to deal with, which contributed to the undoubted success of the programme.

Companies often start out thinking that KAM is just another way of approaching customers that can be left to the salesforce. As you will now realize, it has to be much more than that if it is to succeed (see Chapters 11 and 12). In fact, it should take an important position in corporate strategy, and therefore impacts internally on the organization, culture and operations; and externally on the marketplace, as illustrated in Figure 10.1, which shows four major areas of a company's concerns and activity, highlighting the parts that are core to KAM.

Case study insight

The background to SAP's global account management programme

In 1999, SAP had a number of objectives for its global account management programme:

- To **manage relationships** with our largest, most strategic customers as a long-term business (P&L), rather than an opportunity or sale, and deliver consistent, predictable and repeatable revenues

- To **orchestrate globally** all SAP parties having contact with the account (one face to the customer)

- To **create barriers to entry** for our competitors old and new, protecting our most important asset, our customer base

- To **earn trust** by getting involved at the strategic/planning levels rather than primarily at the transactional levels

- To ultimately **implement account management** best practices in other customer segments.

With a clear focus on the role of global account management for the organization, it launched in 1999 with the full and visible backing of the Board, and in 2000 rolled out what proved to be a highly successful global account management programme.

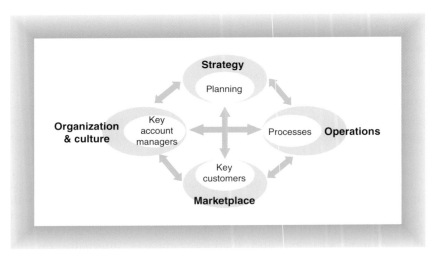

Figure 10.1
The role of key account management internally and externally.

KAM is generally activated in response to a marketplace with key customers at the heart of it. Sometimes the stimulus is a negative event like a large contract that the supplier loses, or expects but fails to win. Most often, major customers demand KAM, rather than suppliers adopting it proactively. The supplier responds by building its strategy and encapsulating it in its plans. The strategy and plans should identify support needed from the organization and culture, which will particularly relate to key account managers and how they do the job. In addition, the strategy should highlight developments needed in the operations side of the business, which will concern the processes that actually deliver commitments to key customers (the focus of Chapter 9).

The role of KAM as identified by a group of practitioners from blue-chip companies is shown in Table 10.1, divided into three of these four areas. These three represent those that drive activity, while the fourth, organization and culture, should support the activity. If this table captures the elements that make up the role of KAM, then it can be divided again into what part the organization should take on, and what part key account managers play. Suppliers should make up their own list, or start with this and add to and subtract from it.

Before it can define the 'job', each company has to work out for itself what it wants KAM to achieve and how it expects it to operate. Consider these lists and check which ones are most important and relevant for your organization.

Table 10.1 The role of key account management

Strategy: Delivering the organization's strategy	*Marketplace: Working with key customers*	*Operations: Effective KAM implementation*
Realizing the strategy and vision	Working together with customers *who want to work with your company*	Offering a single point of contact, internally and externally
Providing market insight and reflecting market changes through leading customers	Developing relationship-led business (not product selling)	Orchestrating cross-functionally, cross-boundary
Identifying and creating new markets	Enabling joint development	Aligning strategy and plans with operations
Defining and achieving value-add for customer and supplier	Leveraging suppliers' range of capabilities and broader portfolio of products into customer	Implementing transactional cost reductions
Providing a route to innovation	Planning and forecasting	Developing effective processes
Integrating route-to-market strategy with marketing and product development	Providing suppliers' credibility with customers	Enabling contact review and control
Managing a major 'source of risk'	Managing resources	Providing tailored reporting

10.1.2 The role of the organization

Some companies seem to have the idea that they will train key account managers to develop relationships with key customers, and then leave them alone with whatever issues arise, using their powers of influence and persuasion to deal with them. It is a curious approach, and one destined to deliver frustration and fury to key account managers, the rest of the company and, worst of all, to key customers. In so doing, senior managers are abdicating their responsibility and, along with it, any hope of success.

Consider the customer pressures and implications for suppliers outlined by Lisa Napolitano, CEO of SAMA (the Strategic Account Management Association in the USA), to which we have added the kind of responses suppliers need to make to stay in business, shown in Figure 10.2. Even the most talented key account managers would

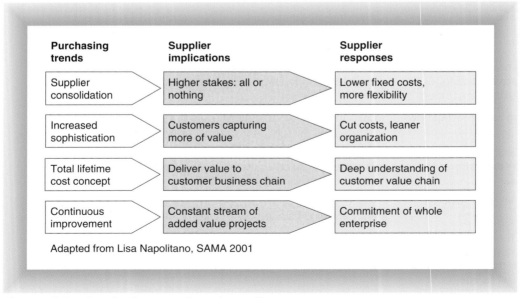

Purchasing trends	Supplier implications	Supplier responses
Supplier consolidation	Higher stakes: all or nothing	Lower fixed costs, more flexibility
Increased sophistication	Customers capturing more of value	Cut costs, leaner organization
Total lifetime cost concept	Deliver value to customer business chain	Deep understanding of customer value chain
Continuous improvement	Constant stream of added value projects	Commitment of whole enterprise

Adapted from Lisa Napolitano, SAMA 2001

Figure 10.2 Purchasing trends and supplier responses.

not be able to deal with these issues alone. They should understand the position and they should be part of creating the solutions, but they do not have a remit to take the critical decisions. The supplier organization must play its role. Only senior management can commit the whole business to customer-driven change or push lower costs through the business and introduce more flexible approaches, like replacing people through outsourcing. Of course, key account managers should have a deep understanding of the customer's value chain, but they will still need the help of technical experts to analyse it and identify how the company can add value to it.

The organization's role in KAM can be broken down into a number of crucial activities (Table 10.2). Without this kind of engagement, key account managers are set up to fail. The worst ones will revert to their old ways and the best ones will simply migrate to a company that is really prepared to back the initiative, and maybe the customers will do that too. People will tolerate a start-up period during which the company finds its way and works out what is needed to support the programme, but after that period of grace has expired, key account managers are thoroughly demotivated if the company does not seem to be matching its own effort with what it is asking of them.

Table 10.2   The role of the organization in key account management

Activity	Expectation
Determines and **communicates** strategy	High-profile commitment from senior management, enterprise-wide communication
Tackles cultural and organizational **barriers**	Removes barriers, develops appropriate culture, polices alignment, rewards collaboration, rejects bad citizenship, mobilizes resources across 'silos'
Provides **resources**	Provides sufficient resource, makes it accessible and usable, exposes talent pool (e.g. account team, training, development, research, technical expertise, marketing intelligence, etc.)
Supports key account managers	Trusts, understands their role, gives visible support, gives authority, promotes their credentials internally and externally
Promotes **sharing**	Of proof of capability, cases, key account plans, ideas, information, knowledge, resources
Makes specific **decisions**	Like resource allocation, approved sources, appointments, marketing responses to competition
Develops the **brand**	Provides pull-through from market, develops positioning and competitor understanding
Monitors results	Identifies measurements, is objective, makes valid comparisons, requires business cases

10.1.3   The role of the key account manager

There are numerous ways in which the role of the key account manager can be expressed. Put very simply, the key account manager has two roles:

● **Implementation:** This means deciding what should happen in an account and making sure it is delivered. Implementation demands appropriate strategies and plans, which depend on a deep understanding of the customer, so all of that can be seen as part of effective implementation.

● **Facilitation:** This involves developing the relationships that will enable the business strategy. It goes beyond the relationship with the key point of contact in the customer, and requires relationships with other functions in the customer, cross-functional relationships in the supplier and possibly relationships with external associates too.

Building relationships is pointless without a business purpose.

The key account manager must maintain a balance between these two roles, remembering that building relationships is pointless without a business purpose, but equally that business strategies are unlikely to be realized unless the right network of relationships is in place.

Not surprisingly, both the supplier and the customer have views on the role that the key account manager should play, which are more or less aligned for a large amount of the role, even though they may be expressed in slightly different ways by each side, as Figure 10.3 suggests.

Implementation roles

● Expert in the customer

● Value developer

● Point of accountability.

Key account managers are often woefully lacking in their understanding of the customer's business and marketplace.

These roles do not seem to be very well clarified and expressed in many supplier organizations, especially that of '**expert in the customer**' and '**value developer**', although they are core to the job. Key account managers are often woefully lacking in their understanding of the customer's business and marketplace, which is why we spend a good deal of our time showing them how to gain this understanding.

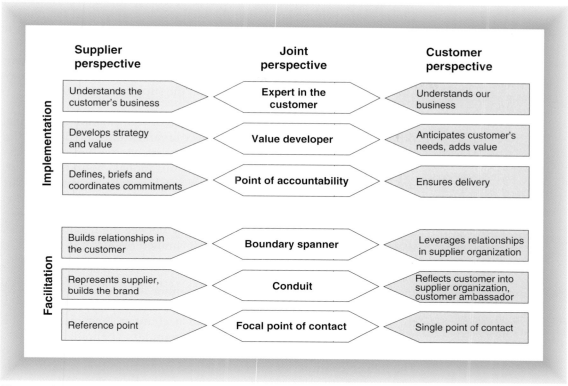

Figure 10.3 Corresponding perspectives on the role of the key account manager.

Without it, they cannot be considered as much of an expert in the customer, nor do they stand much chance of knowing how to add value to the customer, not just as a one-off, but in a continuing stream of added value initiatives.

Both sides seem to be much clearer about what they expect from their **'point of accountability'**. The customer means that whatever the key account manager has promised, he or she is accountable for delivering: not necessarily in person, but by whatever route it takes. The supplier means that the key account manager will deliver the revenue, gross margin or contribution targeted. Both are tough for the key account manager, who very often has not been given the authority to match either the supplier's or the customer's interpretations of accountability.

> The key account manager . . . has very often not been given the authority to match either the supplier's or the customer's interpretations of accountability.

Facilitation roles

- Boundary spanner
- Conduit
- Focal point of contact.

Probably the most disputed role is that of **'boundary spanner'**. Consider a very common situation, in which KAM is introduced into part of a supplier's business on the expectation that it will produce growth.

> Probably the most disputed role is that of 'boundary spanner'.

Closer examination shows that the business is mature and the market is not growing, as in a majority of European markets, so the best opportunity for growth resides in the key customer divisions or SBUs with which the supplier does not currently deal. That means spanning boundaries within the customer organization, obviously, and it may also mean spanning boundaries within the supplier organization.

At the least, there will be a substantial job of coordination to be done, especially between two large, complex organizations. Finding all the information and solving all the issues requires goodwill in parts of the supplier on the other side of organizational boundaries but, unfortunately, goodwill is not always there. It may be because that part of the company feels that it owns the targeted customer division and is not prepared to give it up, or even share it, even if little has been achieved so far. Again, that division may not see the new business as worthwhile and does not want to use its limited resources to support it, even though it may be an unavoidable part of the offer to the customer.

> Key account management, by definition, should be boundary-spanning.

In any event, the role of boundary spanner is fundamental to KAM and therefore to the key account manager. If there are no boundaries to span, a simpler, cheaper form of account management can be applied. KAM, by definition, should be boundary-spanning.

The role of '**conduit**' for information and communication is fairly obvious, though it really goes deeper and means more than the supplier generally anticipates. The customer expects that its strategy will be made known at the highest level in the supplier organization, so that the supplier will give consideration to it in developing its own strategy. The customer also expects to be informed of any changes in the supplier that will have an impact on its business before they become public, such as mergers and acquisitions, key personnel moves, supply chain issues, adverse publicity, etc. Generally, the supplier is seeing the role of 'conduit' more in terms of receiving information about the customer's

---

Case study insight

Seeing communication from the customer's perspective

One supplier caught up in the effects of the 9/11 attack said, 'We didn't call our customers that day or the one after, because we didn't know what was going on. We didn't have any information, as we saw it, and we didn't know what to say. In retrospect, that was a bad idea, and they were frustrated and angry at our silence. Even though we didn't know much, we could have answered a few concerns; for example, we did know that some activities should not be affected because they were driven from somewhere else completely. But by not contacting them, we were effectively placing the obligation on them to call us. We should have just called and told them what we did and didn't know and how we would update them as the situation emerged.'

---

activities, and gives little consideration to the reverse flow and how it should be managed, never mind encouraged and facilitated.

There is wide agreement that the key account manager should act as a **'focal point of contact'**. Unfortunately, this is often called a 'single point of contact', which is not what anyone really means: it implies that the key account manager is the only point of contact, which is not desirable except in some *basic* relationships. The supplier wants robust, reciprocated relationships involving at least several people on both sides, and the customer also wants to know that its business merits support from a team of people, so a single, one-to-one relationship is not the real intention. In addition, as Dr Sue Holt identified in her research (Holt, 2003), the key account manager acts as:

- **A 'single' point of contact** – accepting responsibility for and prepared to be the channel for handling any customer issue

- **An 'escalation' point of contact** – able to take on any contentious issue and work out a solution, with access to the Board if necessary

- **A 'similar' point of contact** – reflecting the seniority of the key people in the customer in terms of his or her own authority

- **A 'strategic' point of contact** – developing the supplier's strategy for the customer and aligning it with the corporate strategy and the customer's strategy.

As if all this were not challenging enough, the supplier has a few more roles it requires of its key account managers.

Internal roles

- **Resource manager:** To make the business case for resource use, apply resource in line with strategies, and control and optimize usage.

- **Risk manager:** To understand the risks in the customer, communicate them to his or her own organization, and minimize and manage them.

- **Team leader:** To lead and enable the account team to bring value to the customer and supplier.

Customer-facing roles

- **Salesperson:** To manage the sales cycle, build deals, present propositions and negotiate.

- **Competition monitor:** To identify competitors and understand their role in the customer's business, and the customer's attitude and perception of them.

- **Lever for full range of capabilities:** To understand the full range of the supplier's capabilities, how they are relevant to the customer, and facilitate their application in the customer.

If you think this looks like a tall order by now, you are right. However, not all customer relationships warrant the full range of roles, or not at full strength. Simple relationships and stripped-down strategies do not require the key account manager to play all these roles. For example, if the customer does not justify an account team, the key account manager does not have to be a team leader. If, on the other hand, the strategy is very demanding, and an account team does exist, members may be able to take up some of the roles required (e.g. competition monitor). The role required of the key account manager and the team is related to the relationship and strategy for the customer, which will also determine the competencies needed, as Figure 10.4 shows.

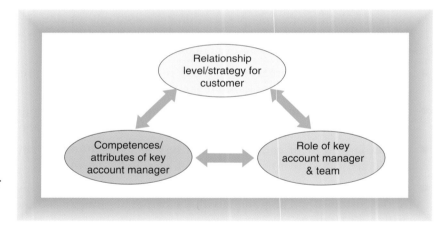

Figure 10.4
Link between customer relationship, roles and competencies.

If the relationship with the customer is not very developed, but it is an attractive customer which the supplier wishes to develop, then a key account manager with an entrepreneurial approach is required (Figure 10.5). Suppliers often call this role a 'hunter', though that implies a search-and-find approach. Normally, the customer has already been found and identified as a key account with potential, and the real need is for an **entrepreneur** who can open doors up to the most senior level, who can hold an appropriate conversation at any level, and who also knows what compelling things to say when the opportunity arises.

If a strategic relationship has already been built with a key customer, then the key account manager has to work closely with it to develop and deliver a variety of business strategies. This role is called '**business manager**' because it requires activities and competencies not very different from those of someone running a business unit. Indeed, some of the most successful key account managers have a general or commercial management background.

Where a key customer appears to have limited future potential, but has a very positive view of the supplier, the key account manager is generally not expected to develop the business. He or she needs to maintain current business proactively, keeping costs in control without stripping away too much value, and keeping a healthy flow of profitable revenue. This role needs a strong operational focus. It suits many people who do not want or would be unlikely to penetrate higher and wider into the customer, but who can manage relationships very well, so this role is called the '**customer manager**' (though all of these roles are, of course, managing customers in one way or another).

Some customers are designated as key accounts because they bring a lot of business, but apply relentless pressure on prices and are not interested in added-value strategies (unless they are free) or strategic development. Suppliers should take a 'manage for cash' approach to them, so the people in charge of this kind of customer also need a strong operational focus in order to strip out excess costs, while they apply tough negotiating skills to counter the customer's assault. The business should be kept as simple as possible, because anything else will eat up resource which will not be repaid, so this role requires a skilful **tactician** who can cope with these gorillas.

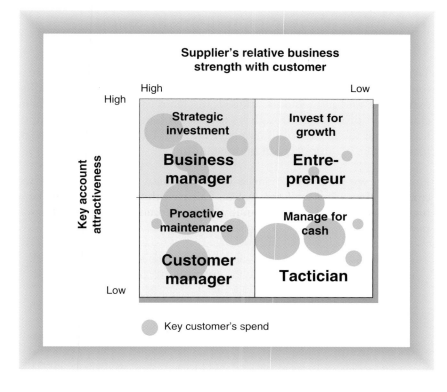

Figure 10.5
Linking roles to the key account strategy matrix.

Objectives, targets, resources, metrics and number of customers per key account manager should be different for each customer type and key account manager role.

If a healthy portfolio should have some customers in every quadrant, suppliers will need a portfolio of different types of people to manage these customers and to play these different roles. 'Key account manager' is not a single role – there are at least four separate roles. It should not be assumed that any particular role is superior to another: each has its part to play in earning the company's current or future profits. However, objectives, targets, resources, metrics and number of customers per key account manager should be different for each customer type and key account manager role. Companies struggle to manage such flexibility.

Every role has its value and its challenges. A 'business manager' with a one-to-one relationship often has less business under management than a 'tactician' handling a small portfolio of customers, but it is usually more complex. A tactician's margins may be very thin, which makes this role crucial to the supplier to make sure it does not slip into a loss-making situation. 'Customer managers' should also be able to handle a small portfolio of customers, and they are vital in maintaining a good quality cash flow from their customers. These customers are probably paying a substantial amount of the salaries of everyone in the company. The volume of business the 'entrepreneur' manages may be relatively small, by definition, but without their efforts to develop the customers of the future, the company will not be sustainable. Each role carries different parameters, expectations and competency needs, and all are important to the supplier.

10.2   Key account management teams

10.2.1   The role of the key account team

Teams get better results than individuals in situations like key customer management.

Teams get better results than individuals in situations like key customer management, which require the combination of multiple skills, experience and judgements. Indeed, the team can play a very beneficial role in providing through its team members some of the competencies that the key account manager may not have: financial analysis, for example, or supply chain understanding.

However, we should first clarify what we mean by a team, before we can talk about key account teams. The defining characteristics of a team are that it has a shared objective and consists of more than one person.

> A team is a group of two or more people who must interact cooperatively and adaptively in pursuit of shared, valued objectives.
>
> (Canon-Bowers *et al.*, 1993)

> Teams are a set of interdependent individuals bound by a collective aim.
>
> (Glassop, 2002)

A key account team is therefore *not* a supplier's collection of key account managers, who are working with different customers and hence with different objectives. Indeed, although suppliers frequently talk about 'the sales team', these definitions show that such a bunch of fiercely competing individuals is not a team at all. This leads to a major issue when key account managers are supposed to lead teams (see Section 10.2.3). Not only have key account managers no experience of leading a team, they have no experience of even being on a team! Teamwork is not part of the average sales environment.

> Not only have key account managers no experience of leading a team, they have no experience of even being on a team!

Key account teams are ongoing groups of people with a consistent membership, working together around a particular customer or a very small number of customers. Normally, most of the members give a significant part of their time to the team, but not all of it. They are called 'virtual teams' as they continue to report to their head of function, and only indirectly to the key account manager. In addition, if they are spread out geographically, they may rarely be in the same place at the same time.

So a key account team is also *not* a collection of people who just come together to deliver a specific project and then break up and go their separate ways, even though they had a shared objective for the project at the time. The composition of project teams changes, as the next project for the customer will involve different people possibly from a different pool.

> A key account team is also not a collection of people who just come together to deliver a specific project.

CHECKPOINT

Does your company operate key account teams?
Try this litmus test: Imagine all the staff in your company are in one big room together, and someone in a corner shouts, 'Key account team for Customer X, come and stand over here!' Would a specific number of people identify themselves, collect at that point and recognize each other as fellow team members?

As we said in Chapter 3, an *interdependent* relationship is probably the most common aspirational level for strategic key accounts, and this naturally implies the existence of team working. *Basic* relationships may or may not require team support, depending on the size, spread and complexity of the customer. In an *interdependent* relationship the key account manager has to manage the relationship through and with others, as Figure 10.6 suggests, because there is more to do than he or she can achieve alone.

The team has the same high-level roles as the key account manager (i.e. implementation and facilitation). The operational part of the team may take the major share of responsibility for ensuring the efficient implementation of commitments, but everyone takes on the role of building more links with the customer, to make the relationship itself more robust and to support facilitation.

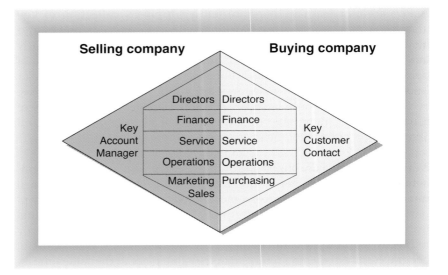

Figure 10.6
A model of an interdependent relationship.

Those people who are regularly involved in dealing with the customer should become part of the key account team. Where the customer interacts frequently, as in customer service or accounts, for example, suppliers should consider directing contact through designated department members who understand the contract with that customer and know how to deal with that customer's issues. These people then also become part of the key account team.

Allocating specific people to customers is often resisted because departmental and call centre managers assume that designating staff to key customers in this way reduces efficiency (i.e. allotting part of their time to a specific customer or customers, but generally not all of it), and that the 'next in the queue' approach is a more efficient use of staff time. In fact, companies are increasingly realizing that dealing with an issue 'right first time' is more efficient still, and that it is best done by someone with an ongoing appreciation of the customer's issues.

Case study insight
Cutting costs through key account teams

Xerox carried out a major exercise to assess the profitability of its key customers. The company had already allocated all or some of the time of specified staff to manage activity with key customers where there was a substantial amount of interaction with the customers. The profitability exercise picked up these costs and compared them with situations where customers were dealt with on the traditional 'first come first served' basis. Xerox found that it saved up to 6 per cent of sales, administration and general costs by working with customer-designated staff.

Key customers expect to have a team working on their business. While they want to know who their focal point of contact is, they want more than the efforts and expertise of just one person applied to their business. Key customers expect excellent performance without having to explain themselves over and over again to different members of the supplier's organization, and they expect consistent performance as well.

Key customers expect to have a team working on their business.

Consistency can only be achieved by people with experience of working together, who have learned about the customer and the value proposition for it and know how to implement it. Research in the airline industry, while admittedly in a different environment, shows what teams can achieve compared with collections of people just assembled for an immediate purpose.

Case study insight

Findings from the airline industry

Researchers studying the effectiveness of flying teams found that:

- Seventy-three per cent of all incidents occur on a crew's first time of flying together.

- Fatigued crews made far fewer errors than did crews of rested pilots who had not flown together before.

- The experience crews gained working together as teams more than overcame the debilitating affects of individual fatigue.

Source: Hackman (2002)

10.2.2   The nature of the team

Teams can work much more successfully if the organization formalizes its role and membership. Given that the members do not report direct to the key account manager, without some formalization the whole idea can get lost. The organization needs to make members' roles on the team clear to them, and also to the rest of the company, especially to the head of the function to which they belong. Otherwise, a situation that is hard enough to manage, even in theory, can become impossibly difficult.

If the team has formal recognition, members will be prepared to invest more in it, and the organization should then see some of the outcomes associated with team working:

- More favourable employee attitudes

- More comprehensive pool of knowledge

- Enhanced productivity

- Improvements in product/service quality

- Improved overall organizational effectiveness
- Delivering superior value.

Along with formal recognition, team members should have roles assigned to them, so they know what they are responsible for and what they are expected to contribute. One may take responsibility for reporting on customer performance, for example; another may track and capture personnel changes in the customer and contact details; another may collect and analyse market information, and so on. Given the complex situations in which theses teams operate, it is important to remove as much ambiguity as is reasonably possible.

Case study insight

Key account team development in a European manufacturing company

A supplier set up pan-European key account teams to manage its key customers, especially those whose business crossed national boundaries. A year later it conducted a survey of the teams, with the following findings:

- A third of the teams had made progress and were working quite well, but had improvements to make.

- Another third of the teams were working to a rather limited extent, but not well.

- The last third were not working, and the members contacted had forgotten that they were supposed to be on a team at all!

Key account teams have a different make-up according to the nature of the customer and the supplier, and what they are trying to achieve. They often split into two in suppliers:

- The cross-functional, head office team
- The geographically based sales and/or support team.

These teams normally exist simultaneously, but for practical reasons, such as opportunities to get together, they tend to be managed separately by the key account manager. These two types of team interface with another type of team, their equivalents in the customer. The key account manager plays a pivotal role in linking the teams and overseeing their interactions with the customer's teams, as Figure 10.7 shows.

The cross-functional team

The nature and operations of the cross-functional team depends a great deal on the supplier's set-up. The team has two aims: the smooth running of current business and the development of new initiatives,

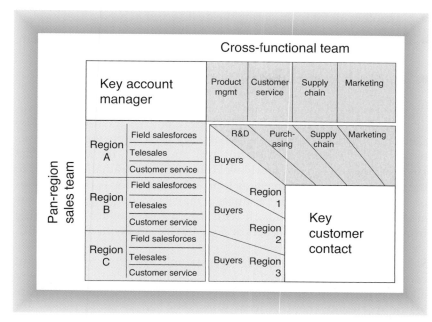

Figure 10.7
Cross-functional and sales teams in key account management.

which may be customizations or innovations that are part of the strategy for the customer. Often, there will be a core team of people from functions that are regularly involved with the customer, and they will coordinate projects to which other parts of the company are contributing.

At first sight, these teams would be expected to have a better chance of meeting each other and bonding together than the geographical sales team, as they are more likely to be concentrated in one place. However, each member has a different technical expertise and a different background related to that expertise, and they have their line manager's demands on their time to consider as well, so getting them to work as a team is still rather challenging. The culture of the company makes a big difference: some have embraced the view that 'One of the values emerging as a requirement for business success in the new and demanding environment is teamwork over individualism. In fact, the team approach must become a management philosophy' (Deeter-Schmelz and Ramsey, 1995), and some have not. Where team working is not a mainstay of the company culture, key account managers have a tough job on their hands.

> Where team working is not a mainstay of the company culture, key account managers have a tough job on their hands.

The geographical sales or support team
Normally, the appointment of a key account manager does not remove the need for local sales and support teams to work with the customer, although the customer's central purchasing function may decide that it only wants operational interaction, not sales interaction. Without the local sales team, the customer's SBUs would feel isolated and neglected. However, the role of the salesperson changes, and this creates an issue. In the new role, they should be:

- promoting and implementing the deal agreed at head office level,

- keeping the customer informed of developments specific to them, and

- removing barriers to ordering and fulfilment.

> The attention that key customers receive at local level often falls off dramatically as local salespeople focus their energies on 'their' customers.

As salespeople, this is not what they mostly want to do. They are 'programmed' to make deals and sell products, both by themselves and by their managers, so, if the deal has already been done, the other tasks tend to fail to capture their enthusiasm. As a result, the attention that key customers receive at local level often falls off dramatically, and to the detriment of the business, as local salespeople focus their energies on 'their' customers. This produces a major and ongoing contentious area for many suppliers, both with the customer which is suffering from such intransigent pockets of poor service, and with the local SBU.

Sales-driven bonus schemes for salespeople are often to blame, but companies have a blinkered belief in sales incentivization, in spite of all the evidence of the negative behaviours that they induce, and are loathe to change them. If local salespeople make more money for themselves by selling to their local customers than they do by spending time with key customers, that is what they will do. If the local SBU is similarly targeted and bonused at SBU level and therefore at senior management level, this behaviour will be driven from the top and reinforced to an insurmountable degree.

Companies have tried to get around the problem by making sure that sales and profit from the local operations of key customers are credited to local SBUs, in recognition of the fact that the business needs local service and support, and it has worked well in some companies, but is still uphill work in others. If, however big the customer is globally, it is relatively unimportant in a particular territory, then gaining the level of service committed by head office is a relentless task for the key account manager.

CHECKPOINT

Securing support from the local team

- Does your company have a clear policy on who is incentivized for what in selling to and servicing key customers at local level?

- Is that policy aligned with:
  - the global deal for the key customer?
  - local SBU objectives?
  - local salespeople's targets and preferences?
  - key account manager targets?

This ambivalence in implementing centrally agreed deals is one of the most common and the most intransigent issues that key customers and key account managers face in KAM. The problem is largely self-induced by the supplier, but it strikes at the notion of territory and ownership that is ingrained in many companies. As a result, many suppliers fail to decide and enforce a clear policy that would resolve it. They suffer the consequences as a company, and the key account manager most of all.

The customer's teams

A large relationship is likely to need a team of people on the customer side as well. As Figure 10.6 suggests, customer teams often mirror the supplier teams, with the make-up of the cross-functional team being appropriate to each business and the relationship goals. Fewer people are probably involved than on the supplier side, but they still constitute a team and the key account manager should see them as such.

If the people on the customer side act as a team, the key account manager should consider:

- What the team's goals and priorities are
- Who makes decisions, and how they are made
- Who communicates with whom and how
- Who influences whom and how
- How team effort can best be engaged and leveraged.

Indeed, if you have developed the skills of leading 'virtual' teams (people who do not report directly to you) in your own business, then perhaps you can use those skills to lead teams of people one step further removed, in the customer's business. With a more proactive, politically sensitive approach, inclusive of your key contact, of course, you could achieve a great deal through leading the customer's teams as well as your own.

10.2.3   Leading the team

Leadership is a big subject, which we can only touch on here, although it is an essential part of the key account manager's role. Some companies, disappointed with the performance of their key account managers as leaders, have speculated on whether someone else could be appointed to carry out that part of the role. Ultimately, abdicating team leadership does not seem to be a viable option. Although team leadership may be a specific competency to learn, leadership positions are given to staff to signify seniority and authority. Giving the job to someone else could only send the wrong messages about the quality and position of the key account manager to the customer and, equally important, internally. The key account manager has to be the leader, and must learn how to lead in this environment.

In a sales environment, leadership is interpreted as 'winning'. Here, 'winning', whether as an individual or even as a team, is not the goal. Indeed, it is likely to lead to inappropriate behaviour on a personal or team level where key customer support and teams are concerned.

The team leader needs to consult, to listen and also, ultimately, to make decisions.

Leaders should set appropriate goals and help the team to achieve them, by showing the way forward and helping to remove obstacles, rather than achieving the goals themselves. As key account managers have very limited direct authority, they are rarely able to give orders to a team member, so they will have to adopt an appealing and appropriate approach, which may be supportive or participative, according to the maturity of the person. The team leader needs to consult, to listen and also, ultimately, to make decisions.

In fact, leadership that encourages team participation is generally associated with greater team member satisfaction, although it is not always associated with higher productivity. Nevertheless, it fits with the matrix mentality and is probably more successful in complex and changing situations where more than straightforward productivity is required, and team members need to be empowered to make decisions and responses to the customer.

Key account managers should consider what makes teams successful in the quest to lead one. Research has identified eight factors of specific importance in KAM teams, as shown in Figure 10.8. The list of these success factors in Table 10.3 explains how team members interpret each of them, and hence what the key account manager needs to clarify for them. Team members also need to contribute to the development of the customer strategy. It will be a better, more rounded strategy that is more likely to be implemented if the team understands it and accepts it.

'Virtual' teams may rarely get to meet. With modern communication technology, this may not matter very much most of the time. However, in our experience, a team must get together physically from time to

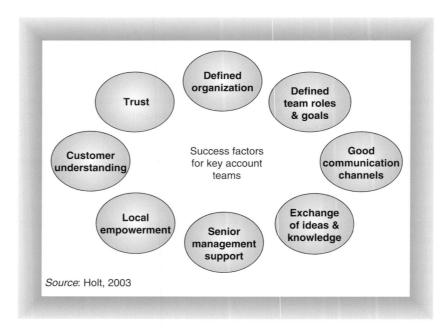

Figure 10.8
Success factors for key account teams.

Source: Holt, 2003

Success factor	Team member's interpretation
Defined organization	Who is doing what?
Defined team roles and goals	What am I doing, what am I trying to achieve?
Good communication channels	How do I find out what is going on?
Exchange of ideas and knowledge	How can we pool our expertise?
Senior management support	Is the rest of the organization behind us?
Local empowerment	What decisions and action can I take?
Customer understanding	How can I get to know the customer?
Trust	You can rely on me, can I rely on you?

Table 10.3
Interpretation of success factors for key account teams

time, in order to gain any real team feeling and synergy. Members need to meet at the outset and then at least once per year, ideally more. It is important that everyone is included, especially in the inaugural meeting. People who are left out at the beginning never really seem to become properly recognized and integrated.

Good communication is crucial, and the leader must consider how good and effective communication will take place, and when. In fact, communication is one of the key account manager's core roles, and he or she needs to think about it systematically and implement it efficiently and effectively (see Section 9.2.4). Not nearly enough conscious thought and effort is given to communication, and many team failures lie at the door of poor communication.

> Not nearly enough conscious thought and effort is given to communication.

In summary, the average key account manager has minimal understanding of how teams work and less of what to do about it. When they get a poor response to their poor leadership, they tend to blame team members and lapse into trying to do everything themselves, which is inefficient and unsustainable. Leadership is a competency which should be learned.

10.3 Requirements of key account managers

10.3.1 Matching roles and requirements

Suppliers asking, 'Have we got the right people?' should really start with the question, 'Have we got the right customers?' or, better still, 'How many of each type of customer do we have?' Start with taking a systematic 'inventory' of your customers and constructing a portfolio view of them, as described in Chapter 2. The portfolio shows how many of each kind of customer your company has, and therefore how many of each kind of key account manager you need.

You may not use exactly the same ratios as the example shown in Figure 10.9 and, indeed, you would want to check out the results with real customers in mind to make sure that it makes sense on the ground, but you should apply some such differential ratio of key account managers to customers in order to optimize your resources.

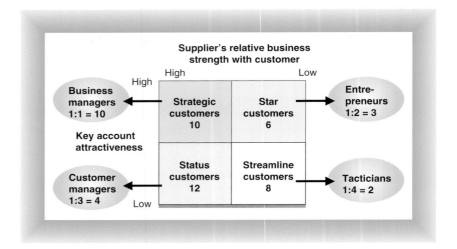

Figure 10.9
Example of how to allocate key account managers to customers.

Most suppliers' portfolio analyses will show that they need considerably more business managers than tacticians.

Smaller companies with less business per customer may not feel they can afford a 1:1 ratio even for their *strategic* customers, but they should still ensure that they have done the analysis and apply a higher ratio than they do for, say, *status* customers. Most suppliers' portfolio analyses will show that they need considerably more business managers than tacticians, though they probably have many more tacticians than business managers, currently.

Rather than make assumptions about the nature of their people, companies would do well to apply a systematic profiling approach such as KAMScope© (a competency and attribute framework for KAM developed by the author specifically for this purpose). This is a detailed 360° review of competencies and attributes (see Section 10.3.2) modelled against the requirements of the four key account manager roles. KAMScope enables key account managers and line managers to focus on the role to which they aspire and identify specifically the competencies that they need to develop to fulfil that role. It leads to a clarity of conversation that is hard to achieve without some such foundation for it.

Suppliers should be matching key account managers with customers according to their ability to play the role required, but traditionally they have been allocated according to:

● Geographical location

● Product expertise

● Industry expertise

- Historical relationship with the customer

- Variety or mix.

Although the key account manager's competency set is taken into consideration intuitively, in practice, these other factors normally outweigh it in making allocations. However, geographical location and product expertise are becoming increasingly irrelevant, and an existing relationship with the customer might or might not be a good thing. The fallacy of variety or mix is demonstrated in this case study.

Geographical location and product expertise are becoming increasingly irrelevant.

Case study insight

Encouraging schizophrenia in the pharmaceutical industry

A pharmaceutical manufacturer described its key customer segments as divided into:

- 'visionaries' – whose strategy looked at the industry in 5–10 years' time

- 'strategists' – who considered developments on a 2–5 year timeframe

- 'operations' – who 'couldn't see beyond breakfast'.

Based on this clear segmentation, we presumed that the supplier had identified those of their key account managers who had vision and matched them with the visionaries; those who took a strategic view and matched them with the strategists; and matched the tactical ones with the 'operations' customers. In fact, they had given all their key account managers a mix, for the sake of 'variety'.

Giving key account managers a mix of customers has two outcomes:

- either key account managers worked according to their preferred style, which would always be inappropriate for some of their customers

- or they tried to change their style every time they dealt with a different customer, several times per day, which would be stressful and probably impossible.

Not surprisingly, the key account managers were finding it difficult to cope.

Whether companies use KAMScope or something else, line managers should find a way of making the role clear to key account managers, and also how they are expected to fulfil it. This means being clear and consistent about it themselves, without falling into the trap of standardizing. With key customers, standardization does not give consistency: indeed, it is inconsistent with joined-up thinking about the customer.

Where the supplier has different kinds of key customers it should have different expectations of their requirements, responses and performance, which should begin to demand different roles from the key account manager. It should also begin to challenge instinctive and cherished ideas about the role. Most sales directors would insist that key account managers should have a sales background. However, we have asked several groups to analyse the role in detail, and they have consistently agreed that only 5–10 per cent of the role is selling (i.e. managing the sales cycle and bid closure).

Only 5–10 per cent of the role is selling.

Table 10.4 shows the breakdown of time that one group of practitioners from different sectors thought ideal – which was certainly not how their key account managers were spending their time currently! In fact, they agreed that there were three activities which should take up more time than selling:

1. Developing relationships (internal and external)

2. Operational implementation

3. Developing knowledge and strategy.

Table 10.4
Practitioners' view of the ideal breakdown of key account managers' time

Activity	Share of time
Developing relationships	20%
Implementing deal operationally	15%
Developing industry knowledge, strategy and planning	10%
Selling	5–10%
Ensuring internal alignment for deal commercially	5–10%
Understanding of internal capability	5%
Solving internal day-to-day problems	5%
Promoting brand/business	5%
Reporting/providing information	5%
Training and education	5%
Managing the team	5%
Other	10%
Total	100%

The big question is, 'Why do suppliers insist on appointing salespeople to the role of key account manager, when their background fits only a small part of the role?

In other words, the selling part of the role is less important than any of these, and not much more important than several others. Needless to say, selling is not a part of the role that customers value, as research has confirmed.

So the big question is, 'Why do suppliers insist on appointing salespeople to the role of key account manager, when their background fits only a small part of the role? And why are they so reluctant to appoint people with other backgrounds, which may equip them to fulfil a larger part of the role?' Either group will need support and development to take on their roles fully, but training non-salespeople to sell might actually be easier than training salespeople to understand the operation of other internal functions, strategy, finance, marketing, etc.

10.3.2   Competencies and attributes

Clearly, key account managers need a wide range of capabilities, which may be seen as 'competencies' and 'attributes'.

- **Competency** is normally defined as the behaviours that employees must have, or must acquire, to input into a situation in order to achieve high levels of performance. Competencies represent what people can do. They can be developed in various ways; by work experience, observation of others, and through training delivered in a number of ways. They can be assessed through the demonstration of task completion, the production of evidence of different kinds and through observation of the key account manager's activity in the workplace. Generally speaking, everyone is more comfortable with developing and talking about competencies than with attributes.

- **Attributes** are individual qualities that differ from competencies in the difficulty of acquisition or change. Attributes represent what people are like, which has an impact on how they do things. They relate more to the underlying values and beliefs that influence the way people think, the way they do things and the way they deal with other people. Attributes are more difficult to develop than competencies. Acquisition depends more on the desire of the individual

---

Case study insight

The importance of attributes as well as competencies in the hi-tech industry

The customer, a huge global corporation, had already rejected one global account manager, so the supplier, also a huge global company, was careful to select a highly competent person to put forward to succeed the previous incumbent. Unfortunately, this global account manager was also rejected after a few months. In spite of his many undisputed competencies, the customer did not appreciate his approach to the relationship. Every time something went wrong, he produced some minor clause in the contract, buried item of information, or obscure communication that 'proved' that he was not at fault. The customer called him 'Mr Teflon', because nothing stuck to him! His competencies did not outweigh this almost legalistic approach and refusal to accept responsibility or ever be 'in the wrong', which were driven by his underlying values and beliefs. (The next global account manager was a great success and stayed in the post for five years.)

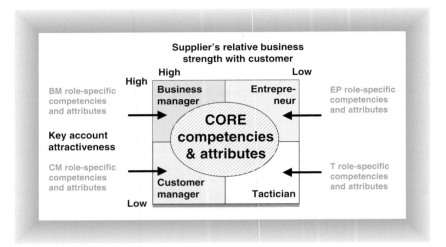

Figure 10.10 Roles and core competencies and attributes.

to make such a change personally, rather than the more externalized acquisition of a competency.

The availability of courses gives a clue as to whether a characteristic is a competency or an attribute. There are plenty of courses to be found for competencies, because they are much more teachable than attributes. 'Selling' is a competency, for example, as is 'financial awareness and analysis': there are plenty of courses in both to be found. In contrast, 'integrity' and 'vision' are attributes, both frequently requested by key customers, but few courses, if any, are offered because they do not respond to that kind of intervention.

Each of the four roles in Section 10.3 (i.e. business manager, entrepreneur, customer manager, tactician) can be described as a set of competencies and attributes. There are a few that are specific to a particular role, but many of them are the same, as you would expect. The latter can be called the core competencies and attributes, as shown in Figure 10.10. In fact, the area of core competencies and attributes is probably even greater than that shown but, in some roles, although the competency is needed to some extent, it is not required to the same degree as in other roles.

The business manager and the entrepreneur have a lot in common. They both need a wide range of competencies and attributes developed to a high degree. This comes as a surprise to many people who see the entrepreneur as a foot-in-the-door encyclopaedia salesman or 'hunter'. While there are, indeed, particular characteristics of robustness and persistence that this role requires, winning over a customer big enough to become a key account is a complex and highly skilled job, which needs as much understanding of the customer and what it would value as the business manager has, achieved from a disadvantageous position on the outside, rather than the inside. However, the level of competencies and attributes required by the customer manager and tactician is lower by a significant amount, as their jobs are less complex. These positions can usually be filled from the supplier's existing pool of account managers.

Finding enough business managers and entrepreneurs will always be difficult – these people have a lot to offer and are in great demand. There is not one 'killer' competency that marks out business managers and entrepreneurs, because that concept is too simple to reflect a job that has so many facets. People who can play these roles should be recognized against a range of competencies and attributes specifically selected to reflect the requirements of key account managers.

KAMScope© is based on a set of competencies and attributes assembled from research interviews with key account managers, line managers and customers in a diverse range of companies and sectors; other research studies; competency profiles collected from a number of blue-chip companies; numerous key account manager development projects with national, regional and global companies; and practitioner workgroups exploring this area.

Key account managers and their organizations receive from KAM-Scope© a reflection of the key account manager's and others' views of his or her existing level of competencies and attributes (Figure 10.11). It also compares their profiles with a model of their current role (business manager, entrepreneur, customer manager, tactician) and the role to which they aspire. The models incorporate the importance of each competency and attribute to the role, and the level of performance required. The key account manager receives a view of which competencies and attributes are already sufficient for the role he or she currently performs, and which need development to reach the level

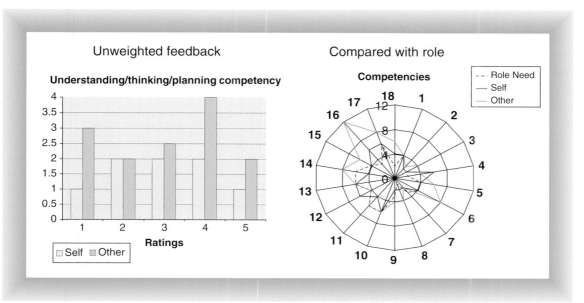

Figure 10.11 Examples of KAMScope© feedback.

required for that role. Output also shows what would need to be developed to fulfil the role he or she would like in the future, which may or may not be different from the current position.

Any such approach which specifically describes expectations of key account managers will be valuable in shedding light on this area, where there is a shortage of clarity at the moment. The real value for both key account manager and employer lies in the conversation that follows any form of profiling.

Summary

The role of key account management itself should drive the definition of the role of the key account manager. What is required of the people will be determined by what the organization wants and expects to achieve, but suppliers generally need to do more to clarify their objectives and strategies, and also their responsibilities to support their key account managers.

Key account managers have a very demanding role to play, and finding the people to play it is not easy. Organizations can, however, deploy their resources more effectively by:

● Operating account teams which can provide some of the competencies that are needed to manage the customer relationship, rather than expecting the key account manager to fulfil it all.

● Identifying the relationship required for each customer and hence which of four roles the key account manager needs to play, and making sure that those with the widest competency range are allocated to customers who need them.

Suppliers need to operate some intelligent talent management to ensure that they have the people to fulfil these roles, both through identifying the competencies and attributes they already have, and then through putting in place programmes to develop what else is needed.

11 Performance and rewards in KAM

Fast track

Clearly, performance is a crucial issue in KAM, or any business initiative for that matter, but what kind of performance, and which or whose performance, is not at all clear in many conversations. In this chapter we look at different kinds of performance, and their measurement, divided into two types: either based on results or on behaviour, and considered at the level of the key account; the key account portfolio; and/or the key account manager.

At the level of the **key account**, expectations of performance need to be adapted to take account of the position of the key account in the selection/categorization matrix (see Chapter 2). A range of results of outcome-based metrics gives a more balanced view of performance than just sales revenue or even customer profitability, such as:

- Sales revenue
- Customer profitability
- KAM input
- Customer retention
- Business extension
- Risk measurement
- Shareholder value
- Customer satisfaction
- Customer attractiveness:
- Relationship.

For the **key account portfolio** as a whole, which can also be equated to the performance of the KAM programme, senior managers should be looking at higher level metrics such as:

- Profit
- Return on investment

- Asset value
- Risk
- Opportunity.

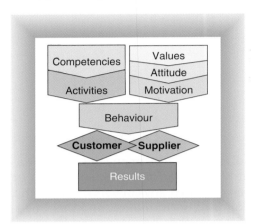

The performance of **key account managers** can be evaluated by the results of the accounts they manage, or by their behaviour. Suppliers are often concerned about the behaviour of their key account managers and recognize the major impact it has on the outcomes from the key account. Key account managers can reasonably be held accountable for their behaviour, but there are intervening factors originating in both the customer and supplier that also have a substantial impact on the outcomes – strategy changes, launching new services, delay in launches, product availability, etc.

Suppliers often have reward schemes traditionally aimed at incentivizing short-term sales, and there are many reasons why they need to change to align their schemes with KAM and with the performance they seek. They must be clear about the purpose and the practicalities of any scheme they devise, since most have negative as well as positive effects, and both sides should be fully understood and assessed before they commit. Sadly, the quality of line managers seems to be a serious limitation on the schemes that can be used: often the scheme is selected because managers will find it easy to apply, rather than because it will be powerful; appropriate to the individual customer and/or key account manager; and drive the right behaviours. Companies can use a variety of rewards, and may use a mix:

- Cash bonus
- Salary increase
- Recognition through non-financial rewards.

The main questions a supplier has to answer when setting up a reward scheme are 'What is to be rewarded?' and 'What is it to be rewarded with?' Then the 'architecture' is constructed from nine elements:

1. Objectives
2. Participants
3. Compensation balance

4. Performance

5. Reward

6. Rates and targets

7. Measurement

8. Timeframe

9. Budget.

Targets probably cause the biggest problems and side effects, and are the most difficult to get right, so it is worth thinking about whether they are really necessary. Indeed, reward scheme issues can be so difficult that it is worth thinking about whether key account managers should have a reward scheme – most of the rest of the company works without one, after all.

Introduction

Curiously, although performance in KAM is a hot topic of conversation, what is meant by 'performance' is often not at all clear. Is it the return on investment, or profit, or simply sales? Or some other expectation? Is it about how the KAM programme works internally, or is it about the outcomes of the whole portfolio of key accounts? Is it focused on the KAM function, the key account manager or individual customers? In fact, the individual's position in the company often determines the kind of 'performance' sought: directors and senior managers are more concerned with the profit of the overall programme and portfolio of key accounts, while line managers and key account managers are more focused on their individual performance and that of each of their customers.

Performance and rewards are frequently linked together. If current reward schemes were delivering the required performance in KAM, there would be no need to change them, but there is a growing feeling that change is needed. An increasing number of suppliers have come to realize that a key account manager is not just a super sales job and therefore that traditional rewards, designed to drive imminent sales, may not be the best approach for key account managers. However, they struggle to define and commit to an alternative interpretation of performance that suits the role better. For some people, performance means behaviour in the role, but while suppliers may say that they are looking for specific behaviours, actually rewarding behaviour is a real sticking point with senior managers. Really, the minimum requisite of a reward programme is that the company should be clear about *why* it wants a reward scheme and *what* performance should be rewarded, but such clarity and consistency are rare.

In our earliest research we found that the reward system was one of the adaptations to KAM that organizations were most reluctant to change. It was not clear whether their reluctance to change was owing to a deep-seated conviction in the efficacy of the approaches they had, which were largely traditional sales incentives, or whether they just did not know what changes to make. However, most people equate what they are rewarded for with what the company really wants from them – it is 'putting its money where its mouth is' – and they often see the rest as 'just words'. So poorly focused reward schemes are not merely an unfortunate detail that will need to be sorted out at some stage – they can be a major driver in the wrong direction. We have often seen the reward scheme frustrate the KAM development that companies hoped to establish, while they seemed to be quite unaware of how it was undermining their plans. Reward schemes entail complex issues and effects that have an impact not only on key account managers but also others with whom they work.

In this chapter, we will consider what performance means in KAM, and then how rewards are linked to it. While there are no unequivocally correct answers to the question of what a good approach to rewarding KAM looks like, the discussion should help companies to understand the issues and design a scheme that will deliver their objectives.

11.1   What is performance in KAM?

11.1.1   *Performance measurement*

Performance is meaningless without measurement, but different purposes drive different measurements, so you should be clear that you are trying to quantify and evaluate performance before specifying and applying your measurement set. Performance in KAM can be aligned with the three levels of the company described at the beginning of Chapter 9. At the top level, the Board will want to know quantitatively what KAM is contributing to its strategic objectives, to enable them to 'steer the ship'. At the next level, questions will be asked about how KAM adds value to the company, and at the operational/transactional level, which is mostly about improving efficiency and productivity, KAM can also have an impact, positive or negative.

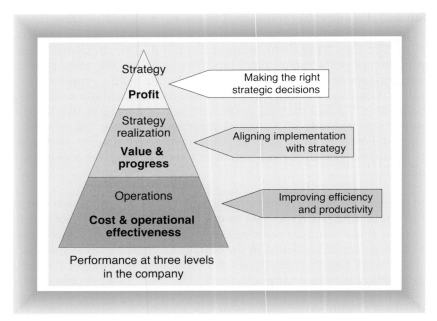

Figure 11.1
The purpose of performance measurement at different levels in the company.

Performance measurement should consist of a set of metrics for KAM at each level in the company, to enable appropriate decision making from top to bottom (see Figure 11.1):

- **Strategy level: making the right decisions:** Performance measurements should be about results/yield from key customers and aligned with the Board's profit focus. They facilitate objective assessment of account strategies and enable senior management to make evidence-based decisions.

- **Strategy realization level: aligning implementation with strategy:** These measurements are designed to track the progress of changes: of implementation against strategy; of progress against plan; and of supplier and customer. They can encourage motivation and pinpoint underlying problems. Measurements should focus on the value that KAM adds to the business.

- **Operational level: improving efficiency and productivity:** The focus is current operational fulfilment of customer expectations, allowing objective monitoring and highlighting opportunities for performance improvement. Measurements will relate to cost and the key performance indicators (KPIs) used to monitor activity.

Table 11.1 shows how a measurement framework for KAM can be built up from these three levels of activity and interest.

Performance in KAM can be related to three entities: the key account; the key account manager; and the key account programme. As for any other part of the business, companies should aim to establish a set of measurements for KAM that are purposeful (matched to desired outcomes), necessary (likely to provoke a response) and sufficient (enough and no more). They should be monitored and reviewed, and acted upon.

Table 11.1   Summary of measurements of key account management

Company level	Strategy	Strategy realization	Operations
Who cares	Directors Shareholders	Key account managers Functional heads	Operations line managers Buyers Key account managers
Focus Measurements	Profit Return on investment Customer asset value Risk Opportunity Key account portfolio contribution growth	Value and progress Customer attractiveness Customer profitability Risk measurement KAM input Customer satisfaction Sales/margin Business extension Customer retention	Performance Cost/price Volume Service levels Failure rates
Benchmarks	Performance against business plan Growth in shareholder value	Customer expectation Portfolio contribution plan	Performance against previous period Performance against agreement
Length of view	Long term Short term	Medium term	Short term

11.1.2   Key account performance

Assessing key account performance should be simple, if success equals the fulfilment of an expectation. It requires you to work out what success means to you, but often the performance expected of the relationship is not explicit, internally or externally. Some suppliers are disappointed in the performance of their key accounts but, on enquiry, it appears that they have never checked out their expectations with their customers. Talking to the customer seems a simple and important step to take, but how these customers were supposed to respond had never been discussed with them and, indeed, they may never have been able or willing to make the desired response.

> Some suppliers are disappointed in the performance of some of their key accounts but . . . they have never checked out their expectations with their customers.

In our early research, we used the following elements of performance as criteria to establish 'success' at account level:

● Financial return

● Operational efficiency

● Strategic alignment

● Ease of doing business together

● Sustainability

● Ultimate judgement: CEO's satisfaction.

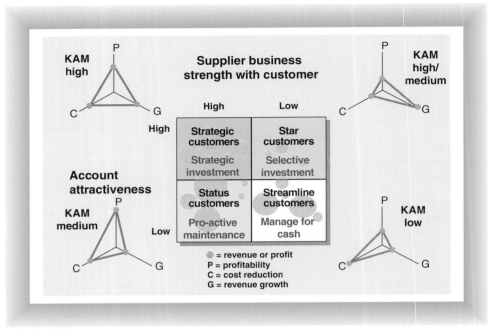

Figure 11.2   Differences in performance of key accounts.

Obviously the same level and kind of performance from every key account is not to be expected. Suppliers should anticipate a different kind of financial performance from customers according to where they have been placed in the key account categorization matrix described in Chapter 2. Effectively, the categories to which customers have been assigned are linked to potential performance, as illustrated in Figure 11.2. Four core measures are pivotal in the account's financial performance (for the supplier):

1. Yield – revenue or profit (shown as disc area in Figure 11.2)

2. Profitability

3. Growth

4. Cost reduction.

Suppliers probably do not want a *streamline*, 'manage for cash' customer to grow, and they do not expect that a *status*, 'maintain pro-actively' customer can grow, or it would probably be rated as more attractive than it is. In these customers the focus should be cost reduction and managing profitability, whereas in *star* 'invest for growth' customers far higher growth rates should be targeted, but not cost reduction at this stage. Cost reduction is not a winning path to growth in a new customer. In *strategic* customers, a strong performance and healthy balance of all performance metrics might be expected

It is entirely inappropriate to judge all key customers (and key account managers) on the same metric, or the same change in that metric. It is nonsensical to target all accounts on growth and at, say, 10 per cent. A *star* customer may easily grow much faster, whereas a *streamline* customer may not grow at all – which could be exactly what you want and expect. However, companies often ignore these critical differences under the pretext of simplicity.

Position in the matrix should also determine how much KAM each account receives, in alignment with the anticipated return on investment (ROI). Suppliers would, no doubt, hope to see greater outcomes from greater inputs and, conversely, should expect lesser outcomes from lesser inputs, so there should be a way of measuring how much 'key account management' the customer actually receives. Ideally, that would be recorded as a financial cost/investment, but many companies are not set up to capture that information, even though they would benefit hugely from a proper financial understanding of their key customers (see Chapter 6), which would give them the information needed to make a sound input to decisions about investing in the customer – or not investing, as the case may be. Failing that, suppliers could use a simple measurement scheme that at least identifies which customers get more KAM and which less. Table 11.2 shows such a scheme that measures KAM input on a points system, which at least quantifies the view of what the customer is receiving and enables it to be compared with other customers.

This measurement scheme implies that the application of KAM is not black or white: in practice, it is likely to be applied to varying degrees. Companies tend to assume that all key customers are receiving 'full-on' KAM when, in fact, some are not. There might be all kinds of reasons why delivery is not living up to what was planned, but without some such measurement scheme, the customer's response, or lack of it, is in danger of being misjudged.

> It is entirely inappropriate to judge all key customers (and key account managers) on the same metric, or the same change in that metric.

Case study insight

Financial services: failing to recognize cause and effect

In the strategic planning and approval round a key account manager gained agreement for a dedicated customer service line and support for her account, which was an important part of achieving the service levels promised to the customer, an ongoing issue with the account. Increased business was forecast if service level targets were reached. However, resources were cut in the supplier, including the customer's service department, and the dedicated line did not happen. At the strategic planning session the following year, directors pointed out that the account was underperforming against the growth target set the previous year, and failed – indeed, refused – to relate the shortfall in input with the shortfall in output.

Table 11.2 Measuring key account management input

Indicator	Score			
	0	1	2	3
Designated key account manager	Key account manager's time: 10%	10–50%	50–100%	100%
KAM team	Non-existent	Exists but ad hoc, reactive, unclear membership	Proactive, internally focused	Externally focused, formal ways of operating, clear membership
Relationship governance in place	Ad hoc	Unconscious, asymmetrical	Conscious, asymmetrical Medium: meets customer	Formally defined, joint
Executive sponsorship (Board or equivalent)	None	Low participation (e.g. once per year)	2/3 times a year, calls for reports on issues, responds on request	High: meets customer regularly, knows account issues, actively promotes, solves problems, accepts brief
Customized offer	Standard offer only	Minor adjustments, superficial	Major adjustments, not exclusive	Major adjustments, exclusive
Organization-wide	Nobody knows	Everyone in sales and customer service knows	Everyone in supplier division/ country knows	Everyone in supplier awareness of status division/ country knows plus top to bottom in customer division
Joint three-year strategic	Budget and annual plan review	Annual review, action plan and budget	Annual review, joint input to one-year action plan and budget	Analysis of customer and strategy, validated and jointly developed, agreed strategies for three years, predicted outputs and measures
Extra resource allocation	Standard	Ad hoc	Defined but short term	Regular and frequent resource input, valued by customer
Evaluation of results				
Level of KAM input	None[a]	Low	Medium	High
Score	0–4	5–11	12–18	19–24

[a] A customer not being subject to KAM may score on one or two parameters, but cannot be considered to be receiving real KAM

Financial 'lag' indicators are not the most illuminating measures. A range like those below, which should be monitored at the level of individual accounts and at the overall portfolio level, will give a more balanced and insightful view of performance.

Financial 'lag' indicators are not the most illuminating measures.

- **Sales revenue:** Almost inevitably, companies consider sales as a measure of performance, but it is not a safe measure of the customer's (or the key account manager's) real contribution to the business.

- **Customer profitability:** This is a better measure than sales, and should be considered as both cash and percentage. The supplier should make an effort to measure both accurately at the level of an individual key customer, and the key account manager should manage them.

- **KAM input:** Although how much KAM input a key customer receives will obviously have a direct impact on customer profitability, and also on most other metrics, it is often not measured. See above and Table 11.2.

- **Customer retention:** The measure for customer retention should be based on share of wallet or relevant spend, defining a retained customer as one where the share is the same or better, and counting the customer as lost if share is declining. Again, volume or margin measurement does not reflect whether a key customer is retained or not: business can continue for quite a while even when a customer has been effectively lost to a competitor.

- **Business extension:** This is defined as business gained from new products or lines of business taken by the customer, or sales to new parts of the customer's business. Volume and margin can rise or fall from swings in the customer's own business, irrespective of KAM effectiveness, disguising this important perspective on KAM performance.

- **Risk measurement:** Absolute measurement of risk is difficult, but by considering the sources of risk in customers in the supplier's sector, and assessing customers against each of these, a composite risk measurement can be calculated and used to compare key customers against each other. If the risk is quantified, it is much more likely that it will be managed.

- **Shareholder value:** Combining customer profitability (return) and KAM input (investment) with risk will yield a measure of shareholder value (see Chapter 6). Key account managers should be managing their accounts to ensure that they create shareholder value relative to the supplier's required risk/return expectations. It provides a useful comparison with other key accounts (Figure 6.15)

- **Customer satisfaction:** This is an obvious measurement, but it needs to be measured properly, addressing the views of decision makers in the customer on their issues, not on standardized operational KPIs. Best conducted by a third party, depth is more important than frequency.

- **Customer attractiveness:** The measurement of customer attractiveness is described in Chapter 2. It needs to be monitored to ensure that the company's strategy is correctly aligned with the customer's attractiveness. It would be good if the sum total of customer attractiveness of the portfolio increased, and cause for concern and action if it declines.

- **Relationship:** Companies measure relationship in a number of ways, taking into account the number of contact points, quality of the relationship, and importance/relevance of the contact. Again, it is advisable to use a third party to avoid bias: several research companies offer an established approach. Relationship is an appropriate measurement of the facilitation element of KAM, which should be regarded as a 'lead', or advance, input indicator rather than a 'lag' or outcome indicator.

Lastly, there are operational performance measurements to take into consideration, which are the KPIs on which both suppliers and customers tend to focus. The customer, not surprisingly, retains its interest in the quality of what it receives and the service that goes with it, and therefore so must the key account manager, although it is the key account manager's responsibility to be aware of and to review this kind of performance, rather than to collect the data him/herself. Operational metrics are benchmarked against a previous period or against the service level agreement with the customer, but it is the agreement which represents its expectations, so the latter is the right benchmark to use. Suppliers need to consider who takes ownership and responsibility for operational performance internally.

Case study insight

False economies

A key account manager negotiated a major contract with one of the biggest hospital trusts in the UK. It was a tough and complex deal that kept the customer's inventory costs to a minimum through just-in-time delivery – in effect, daily. Orders would be placed by an agreed time the previous day, when the hospital was clear about the next day's demand.

A few months into the contract, the supplier's regional distribution manager decided to restructure delivery routes and frequency to cut costs and improve functional performance. Without consulting or even informing the key account manager, he reduced deliveries to the trust's area to twice per week, which meant that hospitals would have to completely revamp their workflow planning processes to cope with the new schedule. The trust, understandably, objected vociferously and treated the change as a breach of agreement.

Customers are clear about this: while they understand how companies work, they also see the key account manager as the person the supplier has put in place to represent it, and that person must, almost by definition, carry the ultimate responsibility for performance. However, it seems that the key account manager generally carries this responsibility without any authority: in most suppliers the operations managers have sole authority in performance matters. While the best work closely with key account managers, others see them as peripheral to their activity, and communication and consultation is poor. These issues must be resolved, and developing a process that specifies how the two interact and what is required of each is probably the best way to do it.

The strategic account plan sits at the heart of KAM and performance measurement. It should contain account performance forecasts for a minimum of three years, according to the key account manager's analysis of the customer and the supplier's situations and potential (see Chapters 7 and 8). The plan provides the benchmark against which actual performance should be judged. It also sets out the measurements that indicate that progress is on track, and using this set of metrics is the most effective way of demonstrating the specific commitment of inputs, activity and outputs: to the supplier's senior management, to the key account manager and to the customer (see Figure 11.3).

The strategic account plan can, in theory, become a contract between all three parties, with performance measured against the particular account objectives. If strategic plans were regarded as contracts in this way, we suspect there would be an immediate improvement in the effort

> The key account manager carries the ultimate responsibility for performance, generally without any authority.

> If strategic plans were regarded as contracts . . . there would be an immediate improvement in them, and . . . the attention they would command in the business.

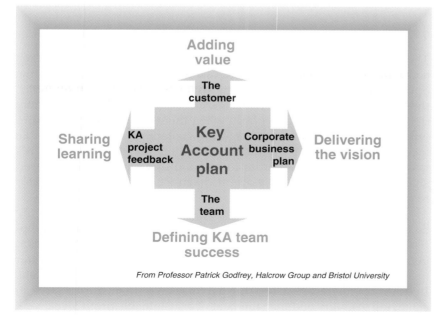

From Professor Patrick Godfrey, Halcrow Group and Bristol University

Figure 11.3
The role of the strategic key account plan.

invested in them, and hence their quality, and the attention they would command in the business. Ideally, the company would look at the strategic account plans and identify the performance it requires based on the account objectives in the plan. That could be, for example, a mix of outcomes from the account, milestones for significant tasks or activities, customer satisfaction evaluation and account team management. Performance would be very clearly defined around real, specific needs.

Account objectives-based performance remains the ideal for relevance for everyone concerned, but regular usage is still some way in the future. It depends on good quality strategic account plans and good quality line management understanding and capability, neither of which is in abundant supply. Some companies now include the quality of the strategic account plan as one of their performance measures, so there is hope of improvement at some point.

> Many companies ask for strategic account plans and then disregard their contents by setting account targets . . . by a completely different process.

Many companies ask for strategic account plans and then disregard their contents by setting account targets 'top-down' according to the supplier's overall performance aspirations, by a completely different process that takes no account of the account analysis, strategy or plan. Key account managers are understandably angry and demoralized by this cavalier and destructive attitude to their account plans and, not surprisingly, cease to put much effort into the plans in future years. Alternatively, if the original total of the forecasts for key accounts produced by key account managers does not add up to the corporate requirement, then at least the key account managers should have the opportunity to identify together the customers and strategies to reach the overall target, rather than having arbitrary targets handed to them by people who know much less about the accounts. Better by far is a business planning process that starts with a clear understanding of this major part of its marketplace, as encapsulated in the key account plans.

11.1.3 KAM programme/portfolio performance

The Board's interest is normally centred on the performance of the key account portfolio represented by a few headline measures: given the opportunity to receive a full diagnostic dashboard for key accounts, most prefer to stick to an overview. Occasionally individuals may delve into the detail, particularly when there are troublesome issues with the largest and most demanding customers, but otherwise the focus is on high-level performance, usually in financial terms. Boards take a long-term view in order to respond to demands for increased shareholder value, but they are also sensitive to City and investor reactions in the short term.

So the emphasis is generally on sales, which the Board expects to represent profit. However, as Chapter 6 explains, that can be a very dangerous assumption in KAM: obviously, profit itself is a much better measure, and some companies are now geared up to collect that data. In addition, there are a few further measures that are valuable in achieving visibility and management of a sustainable profit level.

Profit

Ultimately, profit is the Board's main concern, and the profit (pounds, dollars, euros, etc.) from key accounts should increase in a strong programme. Actual performance should be compared with a benchmark, e.g. competitors or industry forecast rather than last year. Many companies fail to understand their performance because they have not taken a declining market into account.

Profit should not be confused with profitability (profit as % of revenue), which is a management tool, not actual cash. Key customer profitability is quite likely to be lower than for the rest of the customer base, because key customers often tend to reward suppliers with more business, rather than with better prices. Individual key customer and portfolio profitability should certainly be monitored, but profitability targets should be applied cautiously in case they become a barrier to taking good business.

> Key customer profitability is quite likely to be lower than for the rest of the customer base.

Return on investment

Boards commonly assess the performance of initiatives and projects on the basis of return on investment (ROI) but, strangely, it is rarely applied to customers. The Board should be making decisions on where to invest in customers, like any other investment decision. Since customer management, especially for key accounts, involves cost and provides income, there seems no reason why they should be exempt from this measure of performance – except, perhaps, that companies traditionally fail to recognize that investing in customers is what they are doing, in numerous ways.

Asset value

The income from key customer relationships should be here today, tomorrow and for years to come: if not, their status as key accounts is questionable. Assuming that a stream of income is expected, then companies should be able to forecast the revenues and costs; work out a discounted cash flow (DCF); and calculate the net present value (NPV) of key accounts individually and as a portfolio. The KAM programme should be increasing the value of the portfolio year by year

(Figure 11.4), just as shareholders expect to gain an increase in the value of their shares as well as annual income from dividends.

In addition to looking at profit, past (ROI) and future (asset value), Boards should see risk and opportunity as fundamental contributors to future performance that should be measured and managed.

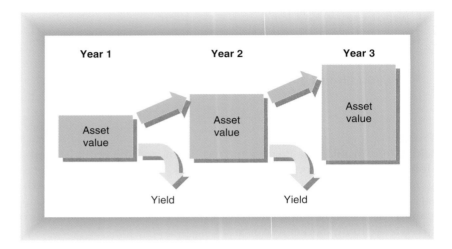

Figure 11.4
Asset growth and yield.

Risk

> Risk in the customer base is a major issue that is rarely reported systematically.

The Board is responsible for the company's stability, so risk in the customer base is a major issue. Nevertheless, it is rarely reported systematically, although customer risk potentially has a major impact on the performance of the key customer portfolio. Suppliers talk about it a lot, but actual measurement and monitoring is rare. A low-risk customer portfolio should entail very different expectations and decisions compared with one containing large amounts of risk: for example, provision for funding and reserves; defensive strategies; action to reduce risk, etc.; and overall levels of return.

Opportunity

The Board may not need to consider individual opportunities, depending on the nature of the sector, but since future performance will depend on a healthy pipeline of opportunities, there should be a quantified view of it with probabilities assigned to levels of business.

Management craves measurement, and not without good reason. Unfortunately, most measurement is unimaginative, and relates only to financial outcomes. Financial results represent the goals that businesses are striving to achieve, but as measurements to manage with they have a huge flaw: financial results are 'lag' measurements – they represent outcomes and, by definition, it is too late to do anything about outcomes, which are the product of what has already happened. The clock cannot be wound back to make different inputs and get a different result, so financial measurements can only be observed and, hopefully, used to provide learning and improvement.

So, measurements that inform, diagnose and track progress need to be found, albeit without losing sight of the fundamental need to measure the financial yield from activities. There is as much danger from measuring too much as there is in measuring too little. Obviously, too little measurement can mean that misleading assumptions and wrong decisions are made; too much, and important information can be lost in a storm of figures. Measurements cost time and money, so they should not be collected unless there is a clear understanding of who wants to know, and what they will do *differently* when they do know. 'Who cares?' is a very good question to ask about measurements.

'Who cares?' is a very good question to ask about measurements.

CHECKPOINT

For each of the measurements your company collects, is it clear:

- What purpose it represents?

- Who wants to receive it?

- Who reviews it?

- Who has the authority and responsibility to respond to it?

- What they will do in response to it (if anything)?

11.1.4 Key account manager performance

Confusion reigns around what key account manager performance is, but we have found two camps of thought:

1. Performance equates to the whole fulfilment of the job: what people do and how they do it.

2. Performance equals results/outcomes (sales revenue, margin or profit) of the key account manager's portfolio of accounts.

The main distinctions between the two ideas are that 'fulfilment of the job' performance is behaviour based and measured by 'lead' indicators, and results performance is outcome based, and measured by 'lag' indicators. 'Lead' indicators equate to inputs to achieving the results, whereas results/outcomes occur following a series of inputs and actions and are therefore 'lag' indicators, only measurable after the event. Differences are shown in Table 11.3.

Behaviour-based versus results-based performance

There are advantages and disadvantages on both sides, but Professor Nigel Piercy's research has shown that suppliers gain more control and better outcomes from focusing their attention on salesforce behaviour (inputs), rather than results (outcomes), and this is probably even more true for key account managers, where the results are likely to be further away in both time and reach. Unfortunately, such best practice has not

Suppliers gain more control and better outcomes from focusing their attention on salesforce behaviour (inputs), rather than results (outcomes).

Table 11.3
Differences between performance as behaviour-based and results-based performance

Focus	Behaviour-based performance	Results-based performance
Defining principle	Input to situation that produces results	Outcome from situation
Relationship to profit	Lead indicator	Lag indicator
Measurability	Qualitative measurement, requires more judgement	Easy to measure, provided by management information system
Management involvement	Potentially high manager involvement	Minimal management required
Positioning with senior managers	Business case more difficult to make, more uncertainty	Easier to fund, 'pays for itself'
Timing restrictions	Not critically time dependent	Pre-set, precise timing, usually company business reporting timelines
Impact on business	Broader, longer-term effect on trading patterns	Can cause distortion in trading patterns (push to reach targets by deadline)
Impact on customer	Positive for customer	Potentially damaging to customer relationship

yet become common practice. Companies should also take note of the well-known potential negative effect of results-based performance approaches on the customer, when key account managers incentivized to meet targets aim to maximize rather than optimize sales. However, the issues arising from using a results-based performance approach may be less about the nature of the performance parameter itself and more driven by the use of targets, but the two usually go together.

The choice of interpretation of performance should come back to the company's purpose for KAM and its purpose for the reward scheme. Regardless of that, it seems, companies still like results-orientated performance for three reasons:

1. Short-term results are what they really want.

2. Results are more easily and unequivocally measured, which makes life easier for managers.

3. Senior managers feel that the reward 'pays for itself' out of the margin on the business won.

However, whether key account managers control results is highly questionable, even more so than for salespeople. Suppliers talk a great deal about the accountability of the key account managers, but it is clear that they do not have, and never will have, the authority to close the gap between their actions (behaviour) and delivery (results). So, for example, a key account manager might win the business for a service line from the customer, and then the customer loses the contract that required that service, and actual sales are considerably less than expected. Or, again, part of the sales expected may depend on a new introduction that is finally launched six months late, or availability is inadequate, so those sales do not materialize. The key account manager is not responsible for either of these events, and is not in a position to control them. Apparently, key account managers do *not* have full control over sales results. In that case, should their performance be assessed on something they do not control, i.e. results, or something they do control, i.e. their behaviour?

Whether key account managers control results is highly questionable.

We can find a clue to what companies really think in the way they react to such a situation. In these circumstances, many would compensate for the consequent low bonus calculated according to the rules of the reward scheme, because they consider the lack of bonus as unfair punishment for things the key account manager does not control. Many companies respond in this way at the beginning of a market downturn, until they feel they can no longer afford to do it.

However, if the key account manager is not responsible for this kind of downside, then he/she is presumably not responsible for the upside either: he/she did not win the customer's contract with its customer or develop the new product in the example above. If it is considered unreasonable to pay key account managers less when things they do not control fail, then it is equally unreasonable to pay them more when things they do not control succeed.

Suppliers can consider rewarding behaviour as something that key account managers certainly can control. Behaviour is something observable, which can be seen as a combination of what is and can be done and the way in which it is done as in, for example, the following behavioural performance elements which have all been cited by suppliers as being important in KAM:

- Client relationships
- Industry knowledge/understanding
- Developing strategy/planning
- Understanding company capability
- Promoting brand
- Training and education
- Team management
- Selling

- Manage risk
- Opportunity
- Manage resource/deal alignment
- Implementing deals
- Problem-solving
- Reporting information.

Behaviour-based performance can be seen as very simple or rather complex. Table 11.4 shows the contributing elements that drive observable behaviour, which relate to the 'back story' of the mostly internal contexts around behaviour. In addition, role requirement is an external driver that sets the scene: it, and the key account manager's perception of it, can have a major impact on behaviour. Besides, behaviour appropriate to one role is not necessarily appropriate to another. Of course, all these personal drivers have an impact on results too, but by then many more external drivers are involved.

Table 11.4
Performance drivers

Performance driver	Description
Role	The external context to individual performance, including relationship with the key account team
Values	As held by individuals, but fit with business values is important. Emphasis can change over time. Accessible by observable behaviours but over a longer time than competencies
Attitude	Mindset founded on personal values
Motivation	A state of mind which companies believe to be positively driven by incentives
Competencies	Capabilities to input to implementing tasks, which can be learned and tested. Minimum standard set for the job
Activity	Series of actions or operations. Being active, energetic, diligent

These elements are linked together in Figure 11.5, which shows a range of input or 'lead' factors on which a company trying to improve performance might hope to have an impact. Competency development can be one of the most powerful levers to pull to gain behavioural performance increases: values and attitude are harder to access. Performance becomes more observable and more measurable as the view progresses from inputs towards outcomes, values being the most difficult to observe, probably, and results the easiest.

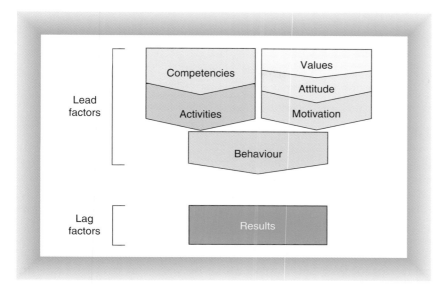

Figure 11.5
Drivers of behavioural performance.

Figure 11.5 shows a gap between the input elements of performance and results, which in many sectors can be over a year, or even several years. Where cycle times are long, the time lag represents a major stumbling block in the practice of rewarding by results, since the key account manager who reaps the reward may easily not be the same key account manager who made the inputs that achieved the result, given staff turnover in many companies. Neither key account manager is incentivized by the reward, because the former will receive it without making any effort, while the other will not receive it in spite of making an effort.

In fact, the gap is not simply about time: it is about risk as well, which is the source of uncertainty that concerns companies considering rewarding behaviours rather than results. There is no guarantee or simple ratio that can be used to convert behaviour into results. Figure 11.6 shows an additional factor in between behaviour and result: i.e. the customer. Customer factors which have very little to do with the key account manager – like mergers and acquisitions, change of strategy, market trends – can have a major impact on the results, whatever the key account manager does. Furthermore, events within the supplier but outside the control of the key account manager, like production failures, or shortage of technical service staff leading to equipment downtime, can also make a big difference to actual results.

In summary, it is easy to talk about performance in KAM, but what it really is and how you judge whether or not you are getting it is a lot more difficult. In spite of these issues, there is a very strong culture of rewarding performance in sales, and although key account management should have developed beyond this short-term focus on sales, the issue will not go away. So the next section focuses on rewarding KAM, although by the time you have read it, you may wish you had never started any kind of reward scheme at all!

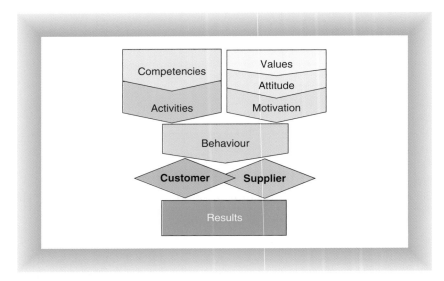

Figure 11.6
The customer element in performance.

11.2 Operating a reward scheme

Companies run reward schemes because they think they have a powerful impact on their people, and indeed they do. However, they can have all kinds of effects, not necessarily the ones desired, so before embarking on a rewards scheme, with all its intended and unintended effects, you ought to go through the process of considering whether you should offer extra rewards at all. Most people do not receive incentives just for doing their job, so why should key account managers?

> Most people do not receive incentives just for doing their job, so why should key account managers?

The answer – though whether it is the right answer is another matter – seems to depend on whether a company generally appoints salespeople to fulfil key account manager positions. If it does, the reward scheme design is likely to hinge on what will keep them happy and motivated, and since they have been schooled to expect cash bonuses for sales results, the company feels obliged to continue with the same approach. However, not all companies have a reward scheme for key account managers, beyond normal career progression for doing a good job, particularly where the key account managers have non-sales backgrounds. On the other hand, such companies often want to introduce rewards to get more proactive and strategic behaviour from their key account managers: but whether they get the change they seek is debatable.

As a start, you should be clear about the purpose of any reward scheme: what you want it to do, and also what you do not want it to do. All too often, companies rush past this critical point and 'just do it', suffering the consequences later. In rewards schemes the 'how' (the devil is in the detail) is at least as important as the 'why', although that is a good place to start.

CHECKPOINT

Before you start to design your rewards
scheme, have you considered:

- Why key account managers should have extra rewards?

- What you want to achieve with a reward scheme?

- What you can realistically expect it to deliver?

11.2.1 Why change?

Suppliers would not be hunting around for ways to adjust their reward schemes if the old ways were fine. Take a look at Table 11.5, which is a checklist of the issues with current reward schemes in a KAM environment, all of which are alive and well in suppliers today. Have any of these issues emerged in your company? Tick any of those you have observed and compare your score with the maximum of 16.

In fact, even if only one issue has appeared in your company, it may still be enough to inhibit KAM and prevent its moving forward with the speed and success the company seeks. If you identify several issues, that makes a compelling case for change. The next and subsequent sections discuss alignment in KAM rewards, and help you to consider important issues before you commit to a specific design.

Table 11.5 Checklist for change

Core issue	Source of issue	Hints and clues	Tick if 'yes'
A. Lack of alignment with KAM	Pre-existing business models	Is continuing alignment with the old business model giving mixed messages?	
	Oversimple schemes	Does applying your current scheme in the context of KAM's complexity have unexpected and unfortunate side-effects?	
	Old skill sets	Does your current scheme incentivize the new KAM skill set and have you clearly identified what that is?	
	Internal functions	Are all objectives aligned – of the key account manager, KAM team, function and account, or is collaboration undermined by conflicting expectations?	
	Territorial conflicts	Do you have potential conflict on ownership of cross-boundary account performance, exacerbated by the reward scheme?	
B. Overemphasis on financial results	Instinctive mistrust	Does senior management mistrust and reject subjective/qualitative assessment, which might lead to difficult conversations, compared with quantitative measurements?	

(continued)

Table 11.5 (*Continued*)

Core issue	Source of issue	Hints and clues	Tick if 'yes'
	Search for security and easy application	Are measurements like financial results seen as more 'true' as well as easier to access and use?	
	Company short-termism	Does your company talk long term but struggle to commit genuinely to long-term objectives, and behave and reward short term?	
	Overuse of financial language	Is the way your company talks about success and expresses itself internally at odds with the language of customers/KAM?	
C. Inappropriate expectations	Recruitment marketplace	Does your company offer packages to attract senior salespeople to the key account manager job, even if they do not really work well in KAM?	
	Salespeople's expectations	Are your key account managers mostly successful salespeople who like selling and sales/results-based rewards?	
	Sales culture	Are your key account managers strongly focused on winning the sale and impatient with a deeper, longer-term approach, with more work and a longer pay-off period?	
D. Inappropriate behaviour	Self-interest	Do manoeuvres to optimize individual gains or disputes over rewards have an impact on customers? Don't make assumptions, check out the real world!	
	Individual short-termism	Do you mostly reward key account managers for behaviour that has a short-term pay-off? Is activity with a longer-term return, like planning and relationship development, unrewarded?	
	Closing deals	Does your current scheme encourage closing deals as early as possible? Even if the customer has other things to talk about?	
	Pre-sales promises	Do your key account managers sometimes make unrealistic pre-sales promises because they want to close deals?	
Total score	Maximum 16		

11.2.2 Aligning rewards with KAM

The reward scheme should obviously support the desired outcomes of the KAM programme itself, and therefore, as a first step, companies should articulate what they want and expect KAM to do for them. Often the purpose of KAM is not plainly stated, or not clearly enough, because if it were clear, companies might see the mismatch between their aim – often for deeper relationships with customers and longer-term security – and their reward scheme – driving short-term sales results and new business acquisition. Interestingly, suppliers are reluctant to move away from traditional, sales-orientated reward schemes' inconsistencies. However, an inappropriate reward scheme can steadily and invisibly undermine KAM and jeopardize the whole initiative.

An inappropriate reward scheme can steadily and invisibly undermine KAM.

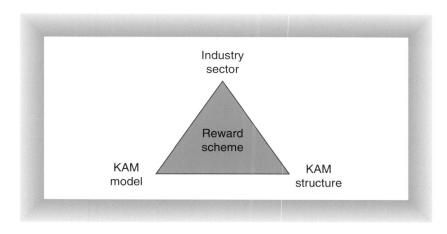

Figure 11.7
Factors linked to KAM model.

Companies operate different reward schemes depending on the industry in which they operate; their purpose for KAM; and how they have organized the function in the company. Indeed, rewards are seen as an important contributor to and outcome of a company's KAM model. Figure 11.7 represents the linkages between these important factors:

● Industry sector: influences common expectations, customer concentration, lead times, globalization

● The KAM model: determines positioning and importance of KAM in the company, its role and expectations, length of perspective, geographical extent

● KAM structure: cross-boundary involvement (function, division, country), team working, positioning of key account managers.

Suppliers change their reward schemes to align with KAM for various reasons, such as those below:

● To develop relationships with key customers

● To keep the best key account managers

● To align individual and account team behaviours

● To differentiate the company for customers

● To achieve a customer focus

● To add value to customers and to the supplier

● To achieve changes in behaviour.

If you want 'different' rather than 'more', then behaviour should be the focus of the scheme.

These kinds of objectives will probably not be achieved by results-based schemes which effectively place the reward on a non-specific 'lag' factor. They often involve high results targets, which generally drive key account managers to deliver 'more' – but probably more of the same – not 'different'. If you want 'different' rather than 'more', then behaviour should be the focus of the scheme.

11.2.3   The nature of rewards

A reward (is) something valued by the recipient, given retrospectively in return for something valued by the giver.

Companies use a working assumption that everyone values money, although industrial psychology has shown that is not necessarily true. A reward may be defined as something valued by the recipient, given retrospectively in return for something valued by the giver. This definition introduces the idea of value to the recipient, which implies that different recipients might value any particular reward to different degrees.

Rewards and incentives are often considered to be much the same thing, but an incentive is the promise of a reward in the future, while a reward may be given without advance notice. Normally, of course, companies use rewards as incentives and announce the level and basis on which they will be given in advance, in the belief that exposing the prospect of extra gain drives extra effort.

Rewards in KAM fall into three main types:

1. Cash bonus

2. Salary increase

3. Recognition/non-financial rewards.

Cash bonus
Cash bonuses may be offered for any period, but in KAM they would usually be for a year, with shorter periods considered more applicable to sales jobs. Companies like cash bonuses because they can pay them out of current earnings, without having to worry too much about sustainability or longer-term parity. Cash has the virtue of simplicity to recommend it, but is this the most important consideration in KAM?

Salary increase
Higher salaries are perceived as indicating greater importance and prestige in the company. Lower salaries, albeit with higher total earnings potential after the bonus is added, are equated with lower value in the company and less influence. So cash may be valued less by an ambitious employee – or simply by someone wanting to buy a bigger house and persuade the bank to increase a mortgage on the basis of secure, sustainable earnings.

A key account manager having done a good job one year might expect to see that effort rewarded by a salary increase, which is the normal mechanism for rewarding good performance in companies. That encourages a wider range of internal and external candidates to apply for key account manager jobs, who might otherwise shy away from the risk of a package with a lower salary and cash bonus. Broadening the appeal of the job beyond salespeople should be seen very positively. However, unlike cash bonuses, salary increases are not adjustable in later years, and companies worry about:

- Affordability, if the company does less well in subsequent years
- Sustainability of performance: will recipients take the increase and relax their efforts?
- Long-term career/salary management: will salary increases on top of salary increases mean that long-stay key account managers are out of line with other positions?

Recognition/non-financial rewards

Recognition involves a wide range of rewards including things that might still cost the company a substantial sum of money, through to things that are more or less cost-free. Below are just a few examples:

- Holidays
- Prizes
- Sporting events/entertainment/dinners
- Invitations to special company events
- Trophies/publicity/profile
- Knowledge development/seminars
- Training/education/educational support
- Mentoring
- Special title/special projects
- Experience/fast-track group.

Some of these are not far from a cash bonus, in that they have a quantifiable value (according to the taxman); and a substantial industry has emerged to help companies with the more expensive items. Others cost very little (publicity, mentoring), but still have great value to the individual. Non-financial rewards can be given to the key account manager as a very personal reward; or to the key account manager and members of the account team, making them more collaborative rewards.

However, different individuals will value some of these and not others, and other people will feel the opposite way about them. For example, a young ambitious key account manager might value opportunities leading to career development, like education or mentoring, while someone later in his/her career may prefer more pleasurable rewards, like sporting events, or more public recognition, like trophies. That means more management empathy and ability to get it right; more management time to create the right package; and more chance of getting it wrong anyway. So while these rewards do have plenty of potential, management enthusiasm for them may be subdued.

11.2.4 Reward management issues

The spectrum of approaches to rewarding performance seems to depend partly on company culture and partly on management capability. At one end of the spectrum is simple 'cash on results' and, at the other end, other forms of recognition with significant management involvement (see Figure 11.8). In the purely cash approach, key account managers are effectively shown where the 'pot of gold' lies, and left to their own devices about how they get to it. In contrast, non-cash recognition plus management involvement demands much more interaction between line managers and their key account managers; developing each other's understanding of the customer situation, coaching, mentoring, developing people and generally supporting them, all of which may be considered highly desirable.

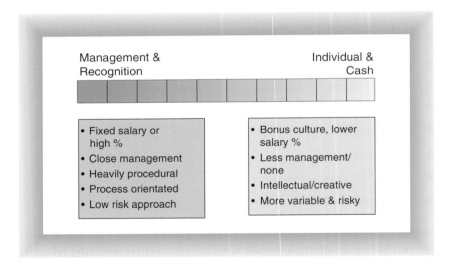

Figure 11.8
Spectrum of approaches to incentivization.

Sadly, adapting to line managers' limitations seems to be a major factor even in the design of reward schemes.

The ability of line managers to manage performance and rewards schemes is critical to their operation. Sadly, adapting to line managers' limitations seems to be a major factor even in the design of reward schemes. Those that require the exercise of management coaching and judgement are quite likely to be rejected in favour of those that depend on minimal management and simple measurements (i.e. results), just because the quality of line managers is not good enough. Schemes that take up much management time are likely to be unpopular too, though that calls into question the role of the line manager itself. Is this not what the management job is supposed to be? Indeed, is 'management by results' really management at all?

The 'less management, more cash' approach represents a focus on individual freedom and responsibility, but that leaves the company open to individual idiosyncrasies and the effects of a heavy engagement of self-interest, which may be to the potential detriment of customer relationships. If the supplier sees these customer relationships as important to the company, they should be owned corporately, and higher management involvement implies more joint responsibility, which is probably appropriate and desirable. The company has to ensure relationship longevity and engage people across the company, in which excessive individualism can cause problems.

KAM is a team activity, and teams are usually cross-functional and/or cross-geography. Members of these teams are rarely fully dedicated to a single customer: they may be involved with other account teams and/or have a 'day' job as well within their home function or area, which could be supply chain, customer service, etc.; or north, south, etc. Clearly, members of the team can have a very powerful impact on the business with the customer. They may be involved in winning bids; in smoothing and expediting deliveries; in handling complaints and claims; in providing information; and a whole host of other business-building or business-losing activities. If they see that key account managers are rewarded for their activity with key customers while they are not, they may, quite reasonably, consider that to be unfair. Potentially, the rewards that key account managers get to incentivize and motivate them run the risk of demotivating the team with which they must work. Team members who are wholly dedicated to an account could, and probably should, be rewarded for their individual contributions where key account managers are similarly rewarded.

> Potentially, the rewards that key account managers get to incentivize and motivate them run the risk of demotivating the team with which they must work.

Fairness, particularly the perception of fairness, is an important concept in any reward scheme, generally related to 'cause and effect': i.e. if someone's input and effort has a traceable impact on the outcome, rewarding them will generally be seen as fair. However, linking cause and effect to part-time team members is difficult: they might be involved with several teams with different levels of contribution and performance. If colleagues in the same function are not involved in an account team at all, they do not have access to such rewards, which is seen as unfair by them and even by account members. If rewards for individual team members mean significant money, schemes must have clear and unambiguous reward bases and proper administration, and that seems to be unattainable in practice for partially dedicated teams. Accuracy, certainty and fairness diminish and administrative complexity escalates. Rewarding part-time teams with a dinner, weekend away or similar event is less contentious and less expensive, and therefore more viable.

> Fairness, particularly the perception of fairness, is an important concept in any reward scheme.

11.2.5 The influence of KAM programme maturity

Organizations generally will have a different strategy and attitude to rewards as the KAM programme matures. In the early stages, they are often hesitant about moving away from traditional sales incentives, but later they should be comfortable with more KAM-orientated approaches to rewards. However, as we have already said, if you do not move on soon enough, you risk undermining the KAM programme. Indeed, suppliers have found themselves perpetuating traditional sales behaviours long after they had hoped to change, partly because they have failed to change their reward system.

As companies develop their KAM programmes, they develop their expectations of performance and their reward schemes. Logically, reward schemes should vary according to the position of the individual account, because some may be in a growth phase while others are in a 'maintain' and cost reduction phase, and the respective key account managers should be rewarded on different parameters accordingly. However, while the principle of reward variation by account makes sense, in practice most companies are not sophisticated enough to manage such flexibility. Good quality strategic account plans are needed to provide the foundation but, sadly, they are not often in place at a satisfactory level. Table 11.6 shows how reward strategies tend to change as the programme develops (see Chapter 13 for a description of these different phases of KAM development).

Table 11.6 Common reward strategies by KAM phase

KAM phase	Reward strategy
A. Scoping KAM	Status quo Cash bonus on sales Non-financial: peer/public recognition of success with important customers
B. Introducing KAM	Cash bonus, re-focused on specific KAM KPIs (targets plus behaviours) for individual Develop rewards linked to appraisal process based on KAM goals
C. Embedding KAM	Likely still to be some 'traditional' form of reward Increase basic salary (though total package may/may not increase) to value the role and attract new recruits, and to increase remuneration certainty Increase other forms of recognition, especially more high-profile encouragement: raise seniority and widen internal remit Institute less individual, more group rewards
D. Optimizing KAM	Reward/incentivize future/lead indicators Senior management recognizes good behaviours through ad hoc rewards More sophisticated processes and measurements, more complex: potentially less clear and compelling Reward wholly dedicated KAM teams

You will recognize the need to be more sophisticated about rewards as your KAM programme progresses, but you will also need to keep a balance kept between fine-tuning and the level of complexity.

11.3 Designing a reward scheme

Having considered everything in the previous sections, the time comes to design the scheme. Any reward scheme should start by asking the fundamental questions:

- What is to be rewarded?
- What is it to be rewarded with?

Both questions should be answered with care. You should first work out what type of performance you want, and what you can measure and evaluate. Taking the merits and demerits of results-based and behaviour-based approaches into consideration, many companies hedge their bets and seek a balance by rewarding both kinds of performance.

11.3.1 Reward scheme architecture

Reward schemes have, at least, nine principal elements:

1. Objectives
2. Participants
3. Compensation balance
4. Performance
5. Reward
6. Rates and targets
7. Measurement
8. Timeframe
9. Budget.

1. Objectives
The first question is 'why'? What should the reward scheme be designed to achieve? Is it aimed at maintaining the business or growing the business, retaining people, developing people, or what? These decisions are fundamental in determining the shape and scope of the scheme, and also in evaluating if it is successful. If the purpose and success have not been defined, how will the company know whether the scheme is working, and in the right way?

2. Participants
The second question is 'who'? The answer is mostly key account managers, but are account team members also included? Account team members who are wholly dedicated to the account may be included in

the reward package, which is tailored to their contribution or to the overall success of the customer/team. For part-time members of account teams financial rewards may be impractical (see Section 11.2.3), but recognition rewards are feasible and desirable. Are key account managers' line managers also part of the scheme? Even if they are not, their reward package still needs to be aligned with the KAM scheme to ensure that everyone is driving in the same direction.

3. Compensation balance

Suppliers need to decide what they believe to be an appropriate balance between base salary, variable cash bonus, salary increase and recognition. Generally, cash bonuses represent a lower percentage of the total earnings of key account managers than for salespeople. Fixed salary for key account managers varies from 100% to 50% of total earnings in practice, but high cash bonuses like 50% are judged by most companies as indicative of a sales job rather than a key account manager role, and actually counter-productive to KAM. For key account managers, about 85% of total package as fixed salary is fairly common.

Case study insight

Driving in the wrong direction?

A US-based hi-tech company that was strongly focused on quarterly performance paid its 'key account managers' heavy cash bonuses on closed deals: generally, their bonus was about 50% of total remuneration. Of course, 50% of their remuneration was also salary, but the key account director lamented that the key account managers were so focused on achieving their bonus that they would not do anything that they did not see as having a direct impact on achieving it: 'They don't bother to build more relationships in the customer, especially with people not directly involved in the purchase decision; they don't spend any time writing their account plans, which are awful; and they don't spend time developing the internal organization or coaching their KAM team members', she said. The balance of the reward scheme would need to be changed in order to make any change in their approach to KAM.

---

4. Performance

The basic structure of a reward scheme depends on what performance is to be rewarded, so the company needs to decide what performance it seeks, which should obviously be based on the objectives of the **scheme**:

- Results: Sales volume in terms of revenue or margin, a lag indicator not entirely controlled by the key account manager.

- Behaviour: Personal competencies and activities, within the control of the key account manager, representing inputs to the situation and therefore a lead indicator of potential outcomes.

- Account objectives: Inputs, milestones or results/outcomes as identified in the account plan, therefore depending on the quality of the plan.

- Business objectives: Overall performance (probably results) of a relevant group or unit, like the account portfolio/key account manager group, to which the key account manager contributes.

Performance in terms of results or behaviour has already been discussed in Section 11.1. Specific account objectives and business objectives should be added to them as further options.

Account objectives

As with KAM itself, 'one size does *not* fit all', and it makes sense to recognize the different kinds of performance that might be expected from key accounts in different positions in their lifecycle with the supplier (see Figure 11.2). The place to go for the information is obviously the key account plan, but that depends on having:

- Good quality, rigorous, strategic account plans

- Robust and flexible measurement systems

- Good quality line management to judge plans and respond appropriately.

The strategic account plan should capture what the organization will put into the situation (resources, products, projects) as well as what the key account manager should input and what outcomes should be achieved. The plan then equates to a three-way performance contract between the individual key account manager and his/her organization: it encapsulates the expectations the supplier has for each of the other two parties, key account manager and customer, and their expectations of the others too, as Figure 11.9 suggests.

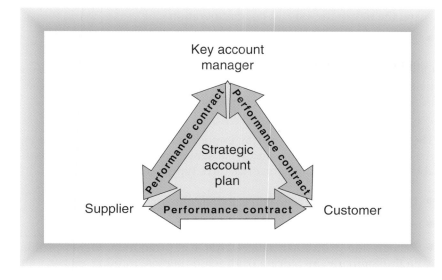

Figure 11.9
The strategic account plan as a three-way contract.

Sadly, these plans are often of poor quality, and the quality of the process of review and validation of the plan on which such an approach would depend is also poor, as it lies in the hands of line managers who are not always capable of such assessments. So, although this is the ideal, real-world, customer-focused base for judging performance, unfortunately, not many companies are able to do it. Nevertheless, it should remain an aspiration because, when you get it right, you can develop a reward scheme with the best possible and most powerful fit of rewards to reality.

Business objectives

Companies sometimes reduce the emphasis on individual performance and replace it with some kind of collective performance from key account managers. They aim to reward cooperative behaviour, at a meaningful level somewhere between the individual and the whole company. Since rewarding part-time account teams is difficult, the KAM unit or group of key account managers is seen as a positive alternative. Performance would then focus on the key account portfolio as a whole, and therefore probably on results rather than behaviour, since results can be aggregated more easily than behaviour. The idea has a number of virtues:

- Balancing anomalies and protecting key account managers from individual customer risk
- Linking to corporate goals better than individual customer objectives
- Sharing best practice between key account managers and learning from each other
- Accommodating accounts at different stages of their lifecycle, including maintenance
- Supporting appropriate resource allocation rather than resource competition
- Allowing more mobility of key account managers between customers
- Enabling recruitment from the rest of the company through lowering the risk in the job and its remuneration
- Fostering better corporate citizenship.

Obviously group performance does not reflect the differences between personal contributions and therefore it is normally used in combination with individual performance measures.

5. Reward

The nature of the reward is also an important decision, usually driven by the culture of the company and what senior management finds acceptable. Of course, a combination of all three types can be employed:

- Bonus: Cash at end of fixed period: month, quarter or year
- Salary: Permanent salary increase, not retractable
- Recognition: Non-financial rewards, e.g. promotion, higher profile in the company, mentoring from senior person, training, prizes.

Companies feel they can afford cash bonuses where they are awarded against sales results and paid out of gross margin. This kind of cash bonus is effectively a profit share, limited to the current year, so that managers do not feel worried about whether it can be repeated in subsequent years. Some companies take reward by recognition very seriously, particularly those in professional services, but for others it is 'the icing on the cake', but definitely not enough to be 'the cake' itself.

6. Rates

You will need to consider:

- Ratio of reward to performance
- Targets and trigger points, where higher or lower rates apply
- Capping and underpinning.

Sales targets are in common use as a benchmark for performance, so bonuses may be paid only on results that fall beyond or within a specified range of the target: companies are mostly averse to paying a bonus on 'what we would have got anyway'. However, it is very difficult to set targets at the right level, and unforeseen circumstances can push the performance and the rewards outside anticipated limits. Furthermore, targets can promote all kinds of inappropriate behaviour, which often run counter to the interests of the customer and, indeed, the supplier too. For example, customers may be pressured to buy more than they need at that time so the key account manager can reach target by bringing sales forward, which can cause cost and resentment in the customer, and depressed sales later on. Another negative effect kicks in when key account managers cut back their efforts on reaching their target or upper limit of their bonus to avoid receiving a bigger target the following year. If you must set targets, be very, very careful how you do it.

> If you must set targets, be very, very careful how you do it.

There is a view that key account managers influence results within a 'bell curve' of expected levels of business. Beyond those limits results are considered to be outside their control, because they are seen as representing an upside windfall, or a downside disaster. Schemes are often capped at the top, therefore, and compensated at the bottom (though the latter may not be published). You should decide in advance the upside and downside levels, if any, that will trigger your contingency plans.

7. Measurement

Robust and accurate measurement is essential, especially where cash bonuses are paid. You may want to reward against customer profitability, but if your measurement of it does not stand up to scrutiny, pick a measurement that does. Quantitative, results-based metrics are not the only measurements that can be used. Qualitative measurements, or quantified judgements, have also been used very successfully by companies: agreeing scores for 'soft' measurements is less contentious than managers fear. For example, some companies pay rewards against the quality of strategic account plans, scoring them on a scale of 1–5 against explicit criteria, without much difficulty.

8. Timeframe
Clarity around timing is always important, so you need to specify:

- The performance reference period
- Point of assessment/review
- Payment/delivery of rewards.

The performance reference period is less critical for qualitative measurements which do not change greatly over short periods of time, compared with sales results, which are much more time dependent. You also need to be clear about whether bonus is awarded against orders received in the period, goods/services delivered in the period, or invoices paid, since there can be significant differences between them. Lack of clarity detracts from the positive impact of the reward, and rule ambiguity will be seen as unfair.

9. Budget
The cost of the reward scheme has to be worked out, and the source or sources of funds identified. They will probably come from different places according to the nature of the reward:

- Cash bonus: Paid from product/service sales or, better, customer gross margins
- Salaries: Paid over a longer span into the future, from the salary/establishment budget, not against product/service sales
- Non-financial rewards: Can still have significant costs (ceremonies, dinners, weekends away, etc.) which are drawn from different budgets in different companies.

The financial justification for the scheme will depend on whether it is seen as an investment in people, an operational cost, an overhead, or a profit share. However, it should be justified and justifiable financially.

11.3.2 Assessing the reward scheme

Reward schemes have a difficult job to fulfil. They need to be effective in promoting KAM and, at the same time, fit into the corporate culture; be aligned with customer needs; manageable and fair; and answer to a number of other requirements too. A set of desirable characteristics for reward schemes is shown in Table 11.7. If you use the table to assess a scheme you have implemented or formulated, you should weight each factor to reflect the importance of each to what your company wants to achieve with its scheme (make sure the total adds up to 100).

If you have more than one proposal in front of you, this is a useful way of comparing them. Otherwise, look for a high score from any scheme that you plan to introduce, or think again.

Table 11.7   Assessing a reward scheme

Desired characteristics of reward scheme	Weight	Scheme rating 0–10	Score = weight × rating
Alignment with company culture and strategy			
Alignment between required, rewarded and measured activities			
Alignment with customer needs and market			
Alignment with individual expectations			
Strength of impact on key account managers			
Match with management time and ability			
Objectivity and fairness			
Perceived cost			
Impact on others			
Total	100		

Whatever the scheme, the rules should be clear and unambiguous, not only from the point of fairness, but also because if the rules do not make clear what needs to be done to gain the reward, individuals will do what they have always done, and the scheme will simply be ineffective and poor value for money.

Reward schemes are notorious for having both positive and negative effects, and it is difficult to avoid all the pitfalls and achieve a fair, transparent and motivating approach. It is especially difficult for companies embarking on a KAM programme for the first time, having to move on from existing schemes whose workings and effects are familiar to them.

The possible permutations of performance and rewards are represented (in Table 11.8) in terms of what kind of performance base could

Table 11.8   Checklist of rewards scheme application effects

Performance	Reward					
	Cash bonus		Salary increase		Non financial recognition	
	Positive	Negative	Positive	Negative	Positive	Negative
Results: sales volume, revenue or margin						
Behaviour: personal objectives						
Account objectives						
Business objectives						

be used and what reward might be given. Use it as a checklist to collect the views of a wide range of the people concerned on both the valuable points and also the untoward consequences of your reward scheme, in advance of launching it. If you are considering the adoption of a scheme giving, say, salary increases based on performance on behaviour, you need to think through all the advantages and disadvantages it might have. Make amendments to negate any unintended and unfortunate consequences and find combinations of performance and reward that could offset the disadvantages.

Summary

Designing an effective reward scheme is not easy, and companies should focus clearly on the purpose of KAM and therefore on the rewards. You should make sure that whatever is proposed delivers to that purpose, rather than to expectations that fit other business models, and may even undermine KAM. Beware instinctive, traditional, sales-based approaches.

The two main elements of any scheme are the performance sought and the type of reward to be given, so be particularly clear about what you mean by performance and exactly how the scheme will have an impact on it – positively and negatively. Performance means behaviour and/or results (sales revenue, margin or profit): behaviour is an input to the account situation, whereas results are an outcome from the account. However, the point at which the scheme can have an influence must be alongside the inputs rather than the outcomes, when it is too late: so 'managing by results' is something of an oxymoron.

The quality of line managers (often not good enough) has serious consequences for the range of schemes that companies can use, but it is much more serious than that. If line managers cannot offer the time and management capability to deliver an appropriate reward scheme, they will not be able to coach and support key account managers anyway, and should not be in those positions. It may be that KAM and key account managers are wrongly placed in the organization and should be reporting to higher level, higher quality line managers like directors.

So, taking all these considerations into account, what does the perfect reward scheme look like? Of course, there is no single answer, and you will need to work out what is appropriate for your company and your marketplace. However, the authors should not duck the question altogether. In our opinion, the following scheme is practical and has merit:

- A good basic salary to give seniority and credibility to the position

- Eighty-five per cent of total package anticipated as salary: high percentage of salary recognizes the multi-faceted and long-term nature of the role

- Maximum 5% of total: as cash bonus for desired behaviour recognized in terms of the quality of the strategic account plan

- Maximum 5% of total: as cash bonus or other form of recognition for some other specific behaviour or activity development, may change each year

- Maximum 5% of total: as cash bonus based on sales or margin, representing a profit share and not attached to a target.

It is important that suppliers acknowledge that the key account manager's job is different from sales, and that means changing the reward scheme. Most companies opt for a balance between the various performance parameters and a balance of cash, salary and non-financial rewards as well, in order to reflect the complexity and longer-term nature of the job.

12 Organizing for key account management

Fast track

Key account management (KAM) is essentially a boundary-crossing initiative. Many of the benefits accrue from crossing boundaries, whether they are internal ones or those in the customer's organization.

- More interesting and powerful propositions with hard-to-match competitive advantage can be achieved by integrating offers from different parts of the supplier organization.

- Substantial growth can be won by developing business with new parts of the customer's organization.

Companies need a clear organizational structure, understandably, especially as they become bigger and more complex, but the structure should be used positively to enact the company's strategy, not to frustrate it. Any structure has its advantages and disadvantages, which can be offset by a genuine will to work across the structure, whatever it may be. Unfortunately, structures and their boundaries are often reinforced by a culture of ownership and defence of a territorial power base, which is not helpful in KAM. Suppliers need to be aware of how the structure can operate to produce 'blind spots', such as an inability to aggregate customer information that will obscure the identity of potential key customers; the ways in which they are organized; and how they make their decisions.

The supplier's structure is not the only consideration in deciding how to organize for KAM. Obviously, the customer's structure must be taken into account as well. For example, whether the supplier is a global or local organization, and whether its customer is global or local, produces a number of different forms of KAM.

In a traditional, country-based organization, the key account manager and hence the customer is several layers away from the top of the company, so communicating their strategies and gaining attention for their needs at a high level is very difficult, and not what key customers expect if they have been invited to participate in a strategic relationship. This form of organization also makes the management of key customers as a portfolio more or less impossible. In fact, if there is no clear process which brings them together in the same framework and authorizes the same person or people to make decisions about them, then portfolio management is not happening.

The ultimate form of organization for KAM is a central unit which has its own resources, with a director of key accounts who reports direct to the main Board rather than a national or divisional Board. Key account managers in a central unit should have the authority to make central or global deals, albeit in consultation and with a defined approval process. In all forms of organization, however, the local company or region will have to support and service the deal on the ground, so it is always important that they back it. Successful suppliers employ various mechanisms to deal with this tricky issue.

In fact, it is the company's targets that are often responsible for many of the conflicts that arise between different parts of the organization. Suppliers that can properly align their targets will avoid many of the problems frequently encountered in KAM, just by resolving that single issue.

In this chapter

Introduction

Restructuring is a favourite occupation of organizations, although it is hard to understand why in terms of business logic. Every few years – indeed, as little as two years in many companies – staff are thrown into a melting pot from which they emerge confused and demoralized, after a prolonged period of distraction and resentment which generally means that attention to customers has suffered, along with a substantial number of other business activities. Competitors may only have to reduce their number of restructurings in order to achieve an advantage over the rivals who cannot resist constantly reshuffling the pieces on the board. In many cases, they still have the same pieces on the board when they finish as they did when they started.

Normally, the driver behind all this activity is the appointment of new directors or other pressures on the Board. Restructuring is easy for Boards to do, though painful for the participants. A Board that is genuinely concerned to improve its customer focus and performance should understand that key customers dislike frequent changes in their interface with their suppliers or in the smooth running of the support teams and activities that underpin their relationship with the supplier. Restructuring generally means that any information the organization may have about its performance is dislocated from previous periods, so that whether or not the organization is increasing or decreasing its effectiveness is obscured.

Suppliers should therefore consider very carefully the impact on customers before they change their structure for any purpose. Incremental

Suppliers should consider very carefully the impact on customers before they change their structure.

and therefore constant changes are inadvisable, which means that some deep thought should be put into deciding the best possible structure rather than compromising on short-term options. The Board should consider whether the new structure delivers significant benefit to customers, as well as to its costs, because the change in itself means that anything less will be decidedly unpopular. They should also consider what they believe to be the proper structure, get there quickly and stay there for a good while.

Having said all that, we need to accept that no structure is perfect and that all involve issues which need to be solved – but by an alternative route to another restructuring. Fostering a willingness to work across boundaries for the good of the customer and the supplier is at least as important, if not more so, than any formal structure.

> Willingness to work across boundaries is at least as important, if not more so, than any formal structure.

12.1 Drivers of organizational structure

12.1.1 Crossing boundaries

Key account management (KAM) is an intrinsically cross-boundary activity. If, in your company, KAM does not cross boundaries, you are probably wasting money on an approach that has been prevented from giving you the return you imagined you would get from it. As Figure 12.1 shows, KAM and key account managers are obliged to cross:

- Internal, functional boundaries
- 'External' boundaries like the supplier's divisions or country management structures, which might be considered internal as they belong to the same organization
- Genuinely external boundaries in the customer's organization, which may be its own divisional or geographical structure.

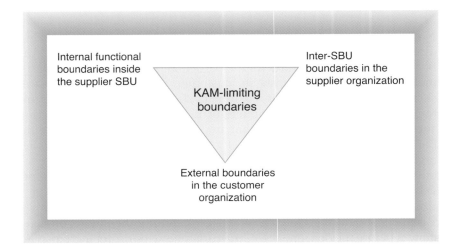

Figure 12.1
Boundaries limiting key account management success.

Internal functional boundaries inside the supplier strategic business unit (SBU)

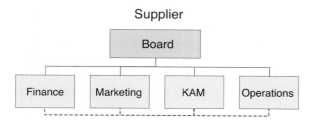

We established in Chapter 4 that customers enter a key relationship in the reasonable expectation that they will get something different from the supplier's standard offer. New, added value for leading customers is likely to require the support of several other functions. These functions may be involved on an ongoing basis, if they have regular and frequent input (see Section 10.2 on key account teams), or on a project basis. In order to engage successfully with other functions in the supplier, the key account manager needs to have an acknowledged and accepted role that allows him or her to assemble the resources needed to implement the plan for the customer.

Too often, key account managers are left to beg, borrow or steal the resource they need, which they may have been allocated in theory, but for which, in practice, they have to battle with functional heads who see the resource as part of their 'territory'. Some companies, although they believe they are implementing KAM, have failed to tackle the issues of the ownership of resource that is determined by structure, and, as a consequence, key account managers are left with little hope of delivering what they know the customer wants and feels it has been promised. In that case, KAM cannot deliver and the company should withdraw promises of innovative approaches and revert to a sound, standard, less expensive sales structure.

> *Too often, key account managers are left to beg, borrow or steal the resource they need.*

Inter-SBU boundaries in the supplier organization

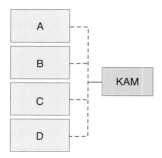

Large suppliers often have several SBUs, determined either by product or by geography, selling to large customers, with the sales effort organized independently by each division effectively operating as separate companies. Customers deal with suppliers according to their differentiation and strategic importance to their business (see Chapter 5), and if each individual division is offering products/services that are seen as undifferentiated by the customers, which can easily happen, each division is then addressed with a 'leverage the volume' strategy from the customer which leads to price competition and hence margin erosion.

However, although the supplier may have strong, comparable competition in each of its divisions, taken separately, together they might be able to offer a combination of goods and services that no other competitor can offer. Suddenly, not only does it achieve differentiation, but its aggregated sales mean that it is much more important to the supplier and worthy of its attention.

Similarly, a supplier that competes on a country-by-country basis will probably find a strong body of competitors in each country. If, however, it makes a pan-region offer to its key customer, the majority of these competitors will be excluded automatically from competing on the same basis because they do not have establishments in the same range of countries.

Increasingly, integrated offers actually create a supplier's differentiation.

Increasingly, for key customers, which are likely to be expanding their own businesses and want suppliers which can expand with them, integrated offers are interesting and actually create a supplier's differentiation. However, integration needs to be real, not just 'lip-service', which means that suppliers must work hard to coordinate across their internal boundaries to ensure that a seamless offer is delivered in reality.

Case study insight

When 'division' really means division

A company had a lot of business and an excellent relationship with a key customer. The customer asked to buy a product made by the supplier's sister division, which the supplier was happy to arrange. However, when the key account manager rang the sister organization, they said, 'We can't supply your customer: we only sell through distributors.' This did not seem important to the key account manager, but he said, 'OK, we'll buy it from you and sell it on.' Astonishingly, the reply was, 'We can't do that: you're not one of our distributors!' Eventually, the key account manager resorted to physically buying the product from a retailer, at a consumer price, and selling it to the customer at trade price. That day, he learned that organizational structure is more important than serving customers in some companies.

Suppliers may feel that the customers' divisions are just as obstructive as theirs, and they may be right, but that does not prevent customers being scathing about supplier 'silos'. In our research, customers clearly stated that they saw supplier's internal boundaries as:

- confusing and time-wasting

- causing extra work and administration

- resulting in areas of low service levels and high irritation
- resulting in inconsistent pricing
- preventing consolidation of deals
- preventing consolidation of information
- hindering forward development generally.

Failure to integrate the customer interface and the customer offer across divisional and country boundaries and across internal functional boundaries stops suppliers from bringing new and innovative value to customers in a world of mature markets where differentiation is hard to find. Such suppliers are effectively turning their backs on one of the few opportunities many of them have and opting for continuing commoditization, with the poor returns that normally yields. And why? Because battling against internal 'turf wars' is just too hard and too dangerous.

Battling against internal 'turf wars' is just too hard and too dangerous.

External customer boundaries

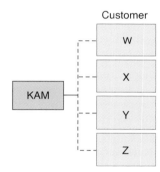

While some of an organization's KAM is dedicated to prospective key customers, most is focused on existing customers. These are often customers with whom a substantial amount of business is already transacted, but who have scope to offer more because they are a large multidivision or multinational company. In many cases, the relationship with one particular part of the customer is excellent, and so the business has reached saturation there, or is approaching it. The supplier should logically choose one of two strategies:

- **Proactive maintenance:** Set targets at current levels, and work on margin and contribution rather than volume and development.

- **Development strategy:** Set targets for growth, by definition with other parts of the customer, and work on opening up the relationship and the business in these new areas.

If the supplier is seeking growth from this customer, it must sell outside its familiar part of the organization. This is neither comfortable nor easy. It normally takes a great deal of effort, persistence and ingenuity in working out how the existing relationship can be used to deliver benefit to the new part of the customer, given that it will already have an incumbent supplier.

It seems really strange, then, that suppliers very often give their key account managers no incentive at all for this effort. Why not? Because, however underdeveloped the relationship is, the territory 'belongs' to someone else in the company even though the customer may not have consented to this ownership.

Case study insight

The price of 'principle': how to prevent growth

A supplier's company in Germany had a wonderful relationship with the German operation of a large multinational. The key account manager, and his counterpart in the customer, thought the relationship could potentially be extended into the customer's French operations, where it was dealing with a French competitor at the time, but not receiving the kind of benefits that the German partnership had achieved.

Exploratory contact with the supplier's French subsidiary established that it would be pleased to accept the introduction and approach the customer's French operation: but also that France did not pay rewards to key account managers from other countries, and was firmly opposed to setting any such precedent. The key account manager passed on the information requested, but he had no confidence that the business would be gained without his involvement to factor in all the benefits that had been set up in Germany – as so it proved. France handled the customer as a new lead, and nothing came of it.

In theory, extra reward drives extra effort. So, presumably, no reward generally gets no effort. Salespeople have traditionally been paid bonuses in addition to basic salary, which are intended by companies to steer them towards delivering the required results (although that is not always what happens). So it seems curious that when suppliers want key account managers to achieve something particularly difficult and time-consuming, for example, penetrating a new part of the customer's business, they are not prepared to incentivize it by even as much as they reward normal business.

Very little cross-boundary business development actually happens, in spite of the vast amount of talk about it; but often, it is only talk. Suppliers need to realize that if they do not follow through a cross-selling strategy to its logical conclusion, and take action to facilitate it at all points, it will fail to happen. If organizational boundaries get in the way, there are two choices: get rid of them, or identify the barriers and create an effective work-around.

CHECKPOINT

Crossing boundaries in your company

- Do your company's key account managers have resource from other functions unarguably allocated to their customers?

- Do you know what and how much each of your key customers buys from any part of your company/group?

- What percentage of your company's sales go to customers buying from other parts of your company/group?

- Do you know how much your company/group has of each of your key customer's total relevant spend?

12.1.2 Considering the customer's structure

Before designing an organizational structure to support KAM, it makes good sense to consider the customer's structure and behaviour. Ideally, the supplier's structure should mirror that of the customer. If it does, then it will be easier to align contacts, negotiate deals, match up information and so on. Figure 12.2 represents four variations of the ways in which supplier and customer SBUs might do business together, which will depend to a great extent on the degree of centralization in their structures. Each lettered box represents a different SBU, defined either by geographical location or division, or both.

A: Decentralized and autonomous

In situation A both sides have decentralized structures and act autonomously in their dealings with suppliers or customers. As both sides operate in the same way, this sounds appropriate, and if they work together exclusively as in the simple version of A, it could be. However, it quickly becomes inappropriate when SBUs start to interact with additional parts of their counterparts' business, as the alternative version shows. This demonstrates how easily autonomous forms of organizations can cause expense, confusion and waste.

B&C: Asymmetric organization and power balance

In approach B, the customer has decided to reap the benefits of being a large customer and leverage its size, rather than behaving like a collection of small companies, as in situation A. The supplier, however, is still behaving as if it consisted of unconnected small companies, and is suffering in negotiations from the inequality of power. In the third situation, C, the organization has reversed, and the supplier is approaching the customer through a unified structure, which should increase its power and interest to the customer.

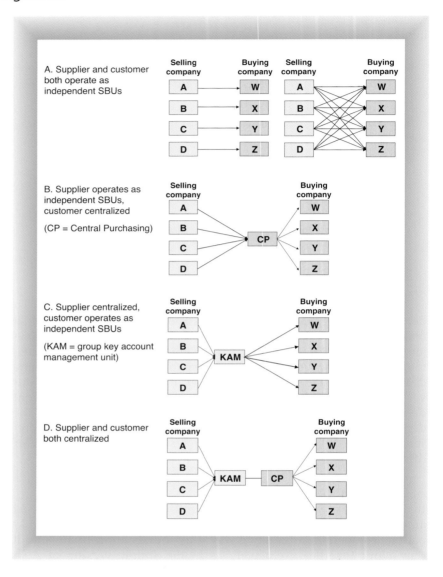

Figure 12.2
The interaction between different supplier and customer organizational structures.

D: Centralized coordination

Situation D shows a comparable structure on both sides in which both organizations have central interfaces that can develop a relationship together, and still acknowledges the existence of the individual SBUs behind both. Through this approach they can deliver what many customers require from KAM (i.e. an efficiently managed, consistent, transparent offer). It can also deliver what most suppliers want (i.e. more business).

The organizational structure and its underlying philosophy drive the structure for KAM rather than any market-orientated strategy. Group Boards who operate by giving total responsibility to the chief executives or managing directors of their SBUs, along with a big reward for performance, and an equally big threat for failure, feel unable to intervene in those businesses in any way in case their intervention is held responsible for poor performance. This philosophy hinders corporate initiatives, including cross-boundary KAM.

CHECKPOINT

How is your company organized for key account management?

- Draw boxes for each of the SBUs in your company and name them, as in Figure 12.2. Then do the same for your customer's organization. Link them up according to how they relate to each other.

- Does your company offer the customer key account management through a single point of contact with appropriate authority?

- Does the customer offer central purchasing through a single decision-making point?

- Is your company organized to maximize its leverage with the customer?

Not only does the corporate structure affect the implementation of KAM, it even affects the identification and recognition of the customer. Look at all the potential relationships in the first situation in Figure 12.2, where both sides are decentralized. If you are in supplier SBU A, do you count the various customer SBUs as one customer, or as four? Presumably, supplier SBU B also thinks it has four customers, and so do the others. The group may easily believe that it has 16 customers, whereas, in reality, it has no more than four, or even just one. Should there be a different key account manager for each relationship? Should each relationship have a different strategy and a separate plan as well? That is the logical outcome that suppliers should confront before setting up their KAM organizations and hence allocating 'ownership' of customers.

Case study insight

The mystery of the most important customer

A supplier in the construction industry had several divisions focused on different areas of expertise. Its key customers were prime contractors and heavy-spending government departments like the Highways Agency and the Environment Agency. Traditionally, it analysed its results by project rather than customer. When it changed its management information system it found that its biggest customer across the group was the Ministry of Defence, because although it was not the biggest in any division, it did business with all of them, whereas most customers were heavily involved with one or two at the most. This discovery was a surprise to everybody, including the Board!

It is exactly the issue of uncoordinated viewpoints that prevents suppliers from answering the simple but crucial question, 'Which is your group's biggest customer?' This very important question takes some companies weeks and months to answer, and they are often surprised at the outcome. (Look out for customers who have different names in different places or in different markets: you may fail to recognize their importance to you if your management information systems do not pick up and aggregate all their data.)

In summary, the customer's structure is a major factor in how the supplier should structure itself. Since any supplier has not one but many customers, it will need, at least, a flexible structure in order to approach each in an appropriate way. Companies tend to like tidy organograms that people with a helicopter view can get their heads round, but suitability rather than tidiness should not be the first consideration in dealing with key customers.

12.1.3   Global versus local

The assumption is often made that global accounts must automatically be key accounts, but this is not necessarily so. In some businesses, most large customers operate globally and require global management, but not all of them qualify to be key accounts. According to Professor George Yip:

> Global account management is an organizational form and process by which the worldwide activities serving a given multinational customer are coordinated by one person or team within the supplying company.
>
> (Yip and Madsen, 1996)

Note that this definition does not say that the customers are necessarily strategically important to the supplier, which is an intrinsic part of the definition of KAM. For example, probably the majority of customers of freight forwarding and logistics companies shift goods all over the world, but they are too numerous all to be counted as key.

On the other hand, where most of a supplier's customers are geographically limited, it is often those who have pushed their business out round the world that provide the most opportunity and the greatest challenge. So for these suppliers, being global or at least multinational is a mandatory criterion for their key accounts. Really, it is the growth and strategic importance of these customers rather than their global reach, as such, that makes them a key account.

The real difference between key account management and good account management is the amount of investment the supplier will make.

The real difference between KAM and good account management is the perceived size and potential of the relationship, and hence the degree of commitment and amount of investment that the supplier will make. There is no intrinsic reason why substantial, stable relationships should be key accounts, even if they are global: but if being global means bigger business then the two may converge in practice.

Again, the customer's structure has to be taken into account, as in Figure 12.3, which charts the kind of KAM that should apply according to the geographical spread of supplier and customer.

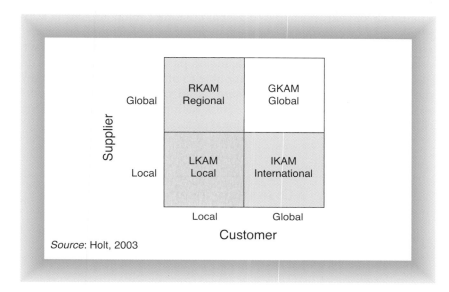

Source: Holt, 2003

Figure 12.3
Matching local and global structures.

For a local supplier with a local customer, local – probably national – account management is fine. A global supplier with a global customer might have a lot to do to manage the relationship, but the match is good and it should work well. The more challenging issues arise from situations in the other two boxes, which represent mismatched organizational structures.

If the customer is global while the supplier is still organized locally then, at least, the supplier needs to institute some kind of international KAM to respond to it. This can work provided that the key account manager has a clear position in the company's structure and a strong remit for the role, and that senior management deal decisively with the territorial issues. Where authority is still vested entirely at local level, it is often exceedingly difficult to get the agreement of all the countries that need to buy into the deal. International account managers have to negotiate internally with individual country managers at the same time as they are negotiating externally with the customer, and may find themselves in a very difficult position, with maximum responsibility and minimal authority.

If the customer is a multinational rather than a global company, in other words it is still making decisions on an individual country basis, then a global supplier can address it at regional level. Regional KAM is probably easier to control and manage than truly global relationships, which involve an additional level of complexity. The countries in the major regions of the world obviously have their distinctive characters, but they also share features in common with other countries in their region, and dealing with them at this level may allow a supplier to leverage scale and achieve economies of scale, while stopping short of the complexity of global relationships.

The major barrier, perhaps, to global customer management is suppliers' fear of customers' demands for globally harmonized prices, which they anticipate being the lowest price paid anywhere. In fact, organizational structure plays a major part in creating barriers to global pricing. Suppliers are better able to offer global pricing, if they must, where they have set up some kind of an overarching global structure for managing key customers with genuine decision-making capability and authority over regional or local SBUs.

> Organizational structure plays a major part in creating barriers to global pricing.

Case study insight
Compensating for a mismatched organizational structure

In one 'global' supplier, different countries not only had different costs, but also different margin expectations and even different cost models. Its global customers used their negotiating power to win very competitive prices, so it was quite possible that the price agreed in the global deal delivered below local target margins in some countries. This then showed as low-margin or even loss-making business on the country's books so, not surprisingly, country managers were not keen to agree to this kind of price level. In order to gain local approval, which was needed before the deal could go ahead, the country had to be compensated for apparent 'losses'.

This was achieved by setting up a global profit and loss account that was owned by the global account manager, alongside the country profit and loss account, and transferring compensation to a pre-agreed level to the country's account, to make up the deficit. This approach, although rather tortuous, was more successful than earlier alternatives.

Generally speaking, suppliers' country-based SBUs still 'own' the income and the costs of business that are delivered to parts of the customer within their territory, even if the deal has been negotiated at a global level. However, customers tend to prefer in-country billing as well, because of issues like local VAT and tax, and their own accounting systems. If pricing were not resolved to the satisfaction of the country as well as the customer and global account manager, it could have major impact on the service support received by the customer on the ground. Indeed, poor support for global customers in countries where they are a minor player is problematic anyway, where the structure allows autonomy to SBU heads. There are three main options to solve the problem:

- Coercion: pulling authority on the country manager, if it can be done.

- Central billing: taking the business away from the country (the ultimate threat).

- Combined business development and compensation: driving more business out of the deal for the country where possible, compensating for losses or low margins where necessary.

Combined business development and compensation is the best choice, since only this solution is likely to result in real cooperation and an adequate level of service for the customer. On the plus side, global account managers who have demonstrated the potential achievable by bringing business to the country from their customer have gained some stunning results from the country's subsequent cooperation.

In summary, there are complex and subtle issues with important consequences that should receive very careful thought when the structure for global, regional or local KAM is developed.

12.2 Organizational structures and their implications

12.2.1 Key account management in traditional structures

We suggested at the beginning of this chapter that, in KAM, the willingness to work across a structure is at least as important as the structure itself. Without contradicting that view, it is true that some organizational structures are distinctly KAM-unfriendly, and are a major cause of failure in KAM initiatives. It must be the responsibility of those at the top to set up an organizational structure with the minimum of barriers to KAM inherent in it, if they genuinely support this approach to customers. Since KAM is essentially a cross-boundary activity, it will frequently encounter barriers, foreseen and unforeseen. If the key account manager is not to be overwhelmed, the amount of obstruction needs to be kept to a minimum.

Some organizational structures are distinctly KAM-unfriendly.

Sadly, ambivalence is as common as wholehearted support from the senior management team. KAM often starts with a single champion, who does not alone have the power to make the structural adjustments necessary for success. The rest of the Board may sit on the fence, passing resolutions stating that, if the initiative 'proves itself', consideration will be given, at some unspecified time in the future, to formalizing its position in the structure with a wider remit.

The organizational structure through which KAM is delivered has a major effect on the supplier's ability to implement strategies like global pricing, or standardized service offerings, or consolidated information management, for example. It also has a significant effect on suppliers' costs. Resources are wasted through duplicating effort, and cost savings fail to materialize if they require a critical mass, because they cannot consolidate activity or amass the volume from several geographies.

With a traditional country-based structure, the supplier is more or less incapable of having a unified view of the customer, so it is very often alarmingly ignorant of this customer's position in the marketplace; how it is changing; how much business it gives the supplier and hence the supplier's dependency on such customers; and how much this customer costs the supplier as well.

Consider the structure in Figure 12.4. It shows a traditional country-based organization which is led by the country managing director, reporting to a regional director who may or may not be on the main Board. The managing director has a number of directors reporting to him or her, one of which is the sales director: key account managers then report to this position. In some cases, key account managers report to a key account director, who reports to the sales director.

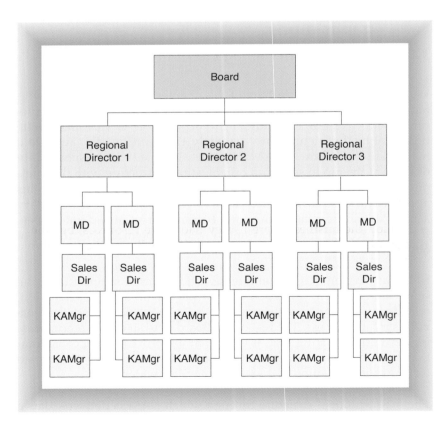

Figure 12.4
Traditional country-based structure.

You can see that in a structure like that in Figure 12.4 the key account managers, and the customers they represent, are anything from four to six levels away from the Board. It is most unlikely that the Board will know anything about the strategies of these customers, or even those of their own company for these customers. The decisions they make will not be informed by this crucial part of the marketplace, so they run the risk of being out of alignment with the leaders in it.

This is not what key customers sign up for when they enter into a relationship with a key supplier. Indeed, it is not unusual for key customers to insist on proof that their key account manager has access to the group Board when they commit to the relationship. However, it is most unlikely that a key account manager in a structure like that in Figure 12.4 would get anywhere near the Board. In this kind of set-up the key account manager can normally only draw on the resources of his or her own country, which may not be suitable or sufficient for the purpose. Any activity of the customer outside the geographical boundary is problematic, often so much so that it is denied or ignored, if at all possible. It is certainly not considered as an opportunity.

Case study insight

How a regional structure masked the real identity of a key customer

Among the customers of a supplier to the luxury goods industry were two companies owned by the same parent. However, they had different names, operated in different parts of the world and, while there was some overlap in activities, one was largely a retailer while the other's main activity was manufacturing and wholesaling. For various reasons, but particularly because the headquarters of the two companies were in diametrically different parts of the world, they were managed by two different key account managers. Both customers were treated as borderline key accounts, and both key account managers felt they could develop the business more if they had more resources, but the business case for neither customer individually justified greater investment.

In fact, these two companies were really the upstream and downstream activities of the same business. Regardless of what they were called or where they operated, they should have been managed by the same key account manager. He would have been able to draw up a more comprehensible and comprehensive view of the customer's operations, and make a strong business case for supporting them at a key account level.

12.2.2 Centralized key account management organizations

The importance of key customers is made clear by their proximity to the Board.

In an alternative form of organization better suited to key accounts, a dedicated unit is created which is independent of country or division. Dedicated, independent KAM units will focus on a consolidated view of the customer in a way that country-based structures do not, and probably do not want to either. Such units generally have resources of their own, such as market experts and financial analysts, and buy in additional services from the rest of the organization, as they need them. The importance of key customers is made clear by their proximity to the Board, as Figure 12.5 shows.

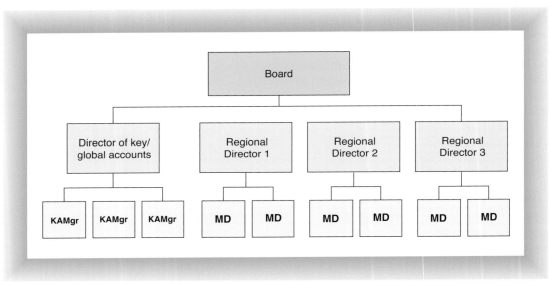

Figure 12.5 Structure with dedicated, independent key account management unit.

This kind of structure is often driven by the need to deal with global customers (though not exclusively), as companies recognize that they have issues like global consistency of service and global pricing that nation-based organizations do not handle well. The chances of identifying appropriate strategies for key customers, agreeing them with the customer, and monitoring them are much higher within a dedicated unit than when key accounts are owned by country or product units and dispersed through the company.

One of KAM's main wins is growth gained by extending a good relationship with a customer into new areas of its organization.

One of KAM's main wins is growth gained by extending a good relationship with a customer into new areas of its organization. This route to growth alone offers major rewards. The strategy for a key account managed by a dedicated, independent unit should give a great deal of attention to such opportunities. However, in key accounts managed from a country or division home base these kinds

of opportunities are often not addressed for a whole variety of reasons, including lack of knowledge, mismatched culture and a narrow
interpretation of self-interest overriding the company's interest, and
so on.

Customer profitability should be easier to observe overall from a
dedicated unit. In this form of organization measurement of cost
to serve is easier, and hence understanding and management of
customer profitability is also potentially better. Inconsistencies can
be seen and addressed; synergies can be spotted and the consequent opportunities explored. However, it is still not always
easy to coax systems and countries into providing the necessary
information.

In the end, however, regardless of who handles the development side
of the relationship with the customer, ultimate success or failure
depends on what is actually received, and delivery on the ground is
still the province of the operational side of the traditional organization.
While the key account manager strikes the high-level deals centrally
with the customer, it falls to the local organization to make it work,
and that is likely to include the local salesforce as well as operations,
logistics, customer service and so on. As one key account manager
said, 'We have to get them (the local organization) happy. It's all about
service in the end, and they deliver it.'

We cannot stress too highly the importance of understanding the different targets set by different people in the company who have various
and diverse goals and agendas, which will impact on the development
and execution of the customer's business. Suppliers that have put several target-setting mechanisms in place find they collide horribly with
each other around key customers. Unless targets are clarified, simplified and aligned, the supplier will probably succeed only in frustrating
its own ambitions.

> Unless targets are
> clarified, simplified
> and aligned, the
> supplier will
> probably succeed
> only in frustrating
> its own ambitions.

As a compromise between local ownership of customers, as depicted
in Figure 12.4, and a dedicated unit divorced from any particular affili-
ations, as depicted in Figure 12.5, suppliers sometimes implement a
structure that gives account leadership to one particular part of the
business on a customer by customer basis, as illustrated in Figure 12.6.
So, for example, the French SBU may lead on a customer that has its
headquarters in France, while the Italian SBU leads on key customers
based in Italy. The decision on who will lead may also be based on the
location of the bulk of the customer's business with the supplier.
In other words, a customer that spends most with the supplier in
Germany will be managed from Germany, even if the customer's head
office is in Rome. This approach can be applied on a divisional basis as
well as geographically. If the freight-forwarding part of a supplier
sells more to a customer than its logistics and assembly division,
the lead key account manager for this customer will be in the freight-
forwarding division.

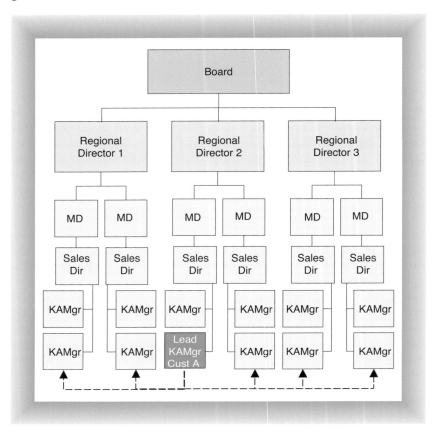

Figure 12.6
Compromise structure
with designated lead
key account manager.

Some customers apply a similar policy in their buying structures so that, in a manufacturer of cars, trucks and buses, for example, the lead buyer for valves may be in the truck's SBU, in which case the supplier might choose to lead its approach for this particular customer from the SBU that has the best relationship with the customer's truck division.

These approaches
are awkward
compromises that
should be seen as
transition stages
towards a
dedicated,
independent unit.

Though they may not be recognized as such at the time, these approaches are awkward compromises that should be seen as transition stages towards a dedicated, independent unit. They are, nevertheless, rather popular. They are believed to have the advantages of the dedicated unit in terms of the consolidation of views and of strategies. However, as Figure 12.6 suggests, the supplier has not made any radical changes to the pre-existing structure, and therefore it works in much the same way as it did before. The key account manager is somehow supposed to make the 'dotted line' links work, in spite of the very mixed and unclear mandate they have been given.

In fact, after some initial progress that may come from ironing out anomalies, further business development often fails to materialize. The SBU hosting the key account manager still exerts a strong gravitational pull, which has several unfortunate effects:

- The host SBU requisitions resource that was meant for the relationship, to apply it to its own purposes.

- The key account manager remains in a familiar 'home', and is then not forced to learn and offer to the customer the capability of the supplier as a whole.

- Trying to reconcile the conflicting demands of the host SBU and the group as a whole from this position is a no-win situation that causes wear-out in key account managers.

These compromise structures arise from a mixture of concerns, which are real if not necessarily praiseworthy or valid:

- Perceived loss of territory or importance for country or divisional managers

- Concern that key account managers become distanced from the 'real' business

- Reluctance to add to central costs in decentralized businesses.

If the Board accepts the overriding importance of achieving the right form of customer management for each customer, none of these are insuperable, but the first – concerns about territory and power – is undoubtedly the strongest. In the case below, global KAM won in the end, but if the customer backlash had not been so clear, the internal forces might have won the day, to the long-term detriment of Citibank's business.

Case study insight

Pitched battle: country managers versus customers

Citibank has many global customers, and it was one of the first companies to recognize that customers wanted joined-up, consistent service wherever in the world they dealt with Citibank. It introduced global account management, and the customers really liked and responded to the programme. However, the country managers were deeply opposed to it, because they felt it challenged their sovereignty. They fought back so effectively that Citibank felt it had to concede, and the programme was shelved. The country managers had won!

However, there was such a wave of protest from customers threatening to take their business away, that the Board decided it had to reinstate the approach (Buzzell, 1985).

Overall, traditional and compromise structures are really inadequate to deliver anything like the full benefits of KAM. Unless a structure is set up that genuinely unites the view of the customer and the approach to it, then the outcomes will be disappointing, not because the principle is wrong, but because suppliers have failed to grasp the nettle and really organize themselves appropriately.

So far we have discussed the structural sources of difficulties in handling each key account, but the structure also has an effect on whether the supplier is in control of the whole portfolio of its most important customers, which is considered in the following section.

12.2.3 Portfolio management

The portfolio overall should perform to expectations, not necessarily any particular customer.

A supplier's key customer portfolio should be managed like a share portfolio (Figure 12.7 and Chapter 2). Some customers are there for growth, and others for current income. Some customers are high risk, but may pay off with high returns: they should be balanced by others that are low risk, which then offer lower, more secure returns. The customers in which investment is appropriate should be carefully selected against a business case for each that takes at least the next three years into account, and if a customer is not responding well, investment may be switched to a more promising customer. The portfolio should be varied and well balanced, and the portfolio overall should perform to expectations, not necessarily any particular customer.

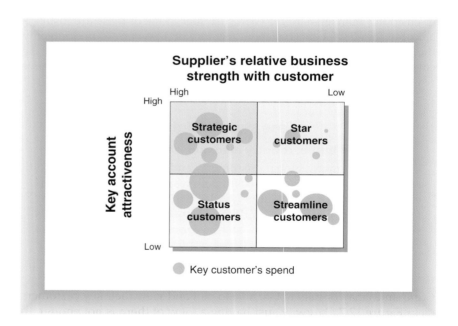

Figure 12.7
A supplier's portfolio of customers.

Where a separate KAM unit exists, so that key customers can be recognized and managed as a group, this kind of approach is possible. Valid comparisons and carefully calculated trade-offs are made to optimize the use of the supplier's resources of time and money. However, in the traditional or compromise structures shown in Figures 12.4 and 12.6, this is more or less impossible. Funds allocated at country or divisional level will be applied by the SBU managing director. Each may have a different view of how much to invest in customers against their other priorities, and how to invest it.

The company below had taken management of its key customers as a portfolio very seriously by having the KAM unit report to the Board via the finance director.

Case study insight

Managing key customers as an investment portfolio

A supplier acknowledged a distinction between key account management and normal sales activities by creating a separate department for it reporting to the finance director, rather than the sales and marketing function. This positioning helped key account managers to get the support they needed with financial information and financial modelling, and establishing that the numbers checked out. This reporting structure was driven by the recognition that a decision in this area could add or wipe off £millions in profits for the company.

Resource allocation and management are an integral part of KAM. Suppliers need to apply the following elements as working concepts all the way through the important chain of decisions that finally agrees which customers are fully backed with resource and which receive less:

> Resource allocation and management are an integral part of key account management.

- **Customer categorization:** A view of key customers as a group, sub-categorized according to their potential.

- **Forecasting:** An ability to forecast outcomes and model the responses to different levels of resource, given the customer's position in the portfolio.

- **Value-based prioritization:** A process that compares the potential values of customers, and agrees customer priorities based on strategy and balance in the portfolio.

- **Resource allocation:** A process of allocating resources in line with strategy and the optimization of the portfolio.

Companies may or may not be able to plot and view their key customers as in Figure 12.7. Anyway, just having a view of them is not enough to qualify as effective portfolio management. In fact, if there is no specific supra-SBU mechanism for approving and controlling the application of resource, you can take it that there is no control. Such mechanisms generally sit alongside dedicated KAM units, and we do not find them in devolved SBU-based structures. As a result, in many cases nobody in the company has control over the most important single group of customers and, potentially, source of income.

> If there is no specific supra-SBU mechanism nobody in the company has control over the most important single group of customers.

In fact, there are three levels at which suppliers make decisions that have an impact on key customers: at the level of the contract, at the level of the customer and at portfolio level (Figure 12.8). At contract

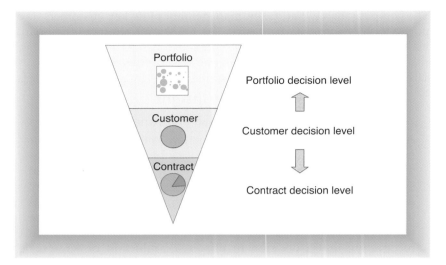

Figure 12.8
Decision-making
levels.

level, most companies have in place reasonably clear decision-making processes for approving which they will bid for, although most could and should use better and more explicit evaluation criteria. However, the customer dimension is often omitted and decisions are made based only on the contract. You should be asking more than just 'Does this look like a profitable contract in its own terms?' when it may consume resource that would be better applied to another customer and more aligned to the overall portfolio strategy. You should be asking 'Is this contract profitable and does winning it further our strategy?'

CHECKPOINT

Do you check all three levels to make decisions on contract acceptability?

1. Contract decision level:
   – Will this contract be profitable for us?

2. Customer decision level:
   – Does this contract fit customer strategies?
   – Is the plan for the customer valid in their terms and viable in ours?

3. Portfolio decision level:
   – Does the plan for the customer fit with portfolio strategies?
   – Can it be resourced?
   – Does it make an appropriate contribution to portfolio objectives?

Using a matrix like that in Figure 12.9 might help you see that you should at least consider less attractive contracts with attractive customers, where you want to develop the relationship, for example. You might also want to reconsider taking an apparently attractive contract with an unattractive customer, as experience shows that these often do not turn out well, or even profitably in the end, and may divert scarce resources from the use intended for them.

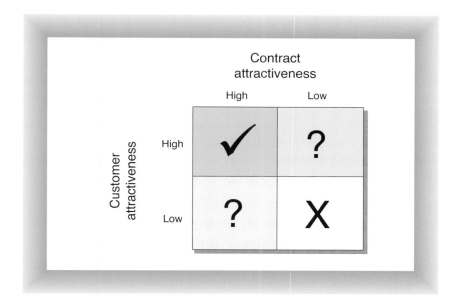

Figure 12.9
Assessing opportunities.

Both the broader, portfolio-level view and the narrower, contract-level view should be operated, but the customer should be the pivotal decision-making level that informs decisions at the lower and higher levels. Furthermore, suppliers' decisions at contract level and at customer level should be linked together and guided by decisions taken at port-folio level. Our research showed that such processes are frequently absent, and without the processes to implement it, real portfolio man-agement does not exist.

Without the processes to implement it, real portfolio management does not exist.

12.2.4   Target alignment

Target alignment or, more commonly, target misalignment is one of the most difficult issues in implementing KAM. Targets, and who sets them and how, epitomize all the unresolved issues around customer 'ownership', profit and loss responsibilities, rewards and more. Mis-aligned targets bedevil implementation, but however obvious this is from an external perspective, companies clearly have real difficulties about putting coordinated targets into practice, since conflicting tar-gets seem to be the norm.

Misaligned targets bedevil implementation.

Conflicting targets that are problematic for KAM are set at all levels in the organization:

- SBUs/divisions

- Internal functions/departments

- Individuals, key account managers and others.

'I don't focus on overhead contribution. When I'm incentivized on it, I'll do it.'

It is fairly common to make national companies and other internal service delivery units into profit centres, and hence set profit targets for them. Targeted, profit-seeking divisions and internal support departments cause real issues in managing key customers, for example by trying to claim parts of the key customer's business as 'theirs'; or by spending more time on 'their' customers (lower tier customers with less business and simpler needs); or worse, by pushing up prices to achieve their profit targets. In effect, part of the profit has been detached from the customer and kept by the division or department. If the key account manager cannot secure a price premium, which is tough when competing for key customers, the profitability of the account appears worse than it really is, leading to misinterpretation of the situation and potentially bad decisions.

Case study insight

Manufacturing company removes barrier to competitiveness

A European manufacturing company had several production units in Europe, which made different products that were sold through its national sales and marketing companies. In an effort to focus efficiency and cost-cutting measures, it made its production units into profit centres. The production units priced their products on a cost-plus basis at a level that allowed them to reach their profit and loss targets. Based on these prices, the national companies were losing bids too often, especially with key customers, because they were uncompetitive when they priced to meet the additional profit targets they also carried.

Volumes went down. So the production units raised their prices to cover their heavy overheads on the lower volume but, obviously, this situation could not continue. The directors reinstated the production units as cost centres rather than profit centres, and kept the national sales companies as profit centres. They were now able to work with transparent pricing that could meet the needs of key customers.

There are numerous drivers of misaligned targets, as shown in Table 12.1, together with the effect each can have, so perhaps the fact that they conflict so often should come as no surprise.

Driver	Effect
Aspirations	A supplier may set a high-level target for its business overall, roll it out to all customers and apply pressure to achieve it to everyone, even where it is inappropriate for specific customers
Ownership	Targets are given to individuals or groups of individuals: the emphasis on their responsibility for meeting their targets also means that they do not take any responsibility for meeting anyone else's target
Time span	Key customer targets should be medium/long term, which is often at odds with the short-term targets normally applied to salesforces, or to demands on SBUs, especially those closely watched by investment analysts
Customer definition	Ambitious targets for key customers as a whole may mean nothing to SBUs with only a small part of the customer which expect to fulfil their ambitions through other customers
Business mix	Suppliers can set production targets according to the needs of their manufacturing/operating units, which apply pressure to sell what they produce that may be at odds with what the customer wants to buy
Metrics	Targets may be set in terms of volume, revenue, gross margin, costs or contribution in different parts of the business: different metrics implies different behaviour
Target-setting processes	Target-setting may be started at the top or the bottom: top-down generally aligns itself with corporate ambition, but has no guarantee of feasibility, while bottom-up is aligned with market forces but may fall short of corporate requirements

Table 12.1
Drivers of misaligned targets and their effects

Targets are taken to represent the ultimate manifestation of strategic intent, so they act as the guidelines for those who implement strategy; and when they are mismatched with strategy, implementation will be compromised. Staff believe that their targets indicate what the company really wants them to do, in a way that any amount of rhetoric does not. If they are also rewarded on achieving those targets, then that clinches any argument: fulfilment of targets, if at all possible, is what the company will get. If those targets, taken across the organization, point in different directions, then confusion and conflict are what the company will get. Only if they are aligned will it make the progress it seeks.

Targets act as the guidelines for those who implement strategy.

Summary

Key account management is essentially a boundary-crossing initiative. If it fails to cross boundaries, both external ones in the customer and internal boundaries in the supplier organization, then it is probably an unjustifiable expense. It is certainly a wasted opportunity.

However, suppliers seem to lack the conviction and confidence to remove the barriers to make KAM work effectively, and leave it to individuals to use their powers of influence and persuasion to overcome them. In fact, key account managers will need all their reserves of influence and persuasion on legitimate targets anyway. For the supplier to duck the issues that it alone can address, such as alignment of targets, is an abdication of its responsibility that sets a poor example throughout the organization.

Although the customer's organization clearly plays a part, the most difficult problems in KAM are caused by the supplier's own organization. You would think that such issues could easily be solved if the solution lies in the supplier's hands, but their persistence shows clearly that is not the case. Suppliers might be able to resolve the issues either by adopting a more appropriate structure, or by installing processes that work across the existing structure, but very often they do neither. If they find it difficult to retain key account managers working under a burden of organizational misalignment, they should not be surprised.

13 Transitioning to KAM

KAM is not an easy or simple business initiative: it involves exten-sive organizational and cultural change, and will undoubtedly take time to implement and overcome the inevitable resistance. How-ever, strong internal and external factors, particularly customer demand or customer defection, drive suppliers to adopt the approach. Bringing all key stakeholders in the company to the same understanding of what KAM is and what it is not constitutes an important first step, because many companies think that they are already doing KAM when, in fact, it is account management or even thinly disguised selling in reality.

Working with experienced practitioners in large companies, we identified five stages of KAM development, culminating in best practice:

A. Scoping KAM

B. Introducing KAM

C. Embedding KAM

D. Optimizing value

E. Best practice KAM

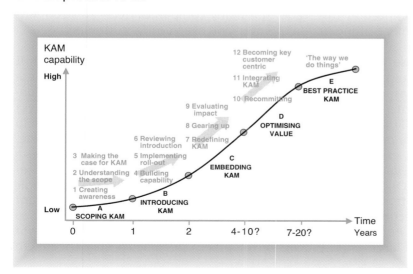

This chapter describes the first four phases, since the rest of the book is focused on best practice. In each phase, decisions and action will be required around:

● Strategy and planning

● Organization and people

● Processes

In Phase A, Scoping KAM, the supplier needs a champion to research KAM and what it would look like in the company. The champion appoints a team, if possible, to help with the considerable amount of work that it takes to collect the information, especially from external sources, and to construct a business case for KAM. The case will never be as strong as the company would like, because it has to cover a wide-ranging initiative whose extent is uncertain, and predict outcomes beyond five years. Nevertheless, the more issues that are brought to the surface at this point, the fewer unpleasant surprises the company will get. For example, adopters should know that KAM regularly takes two years to introduce and considerably longer to become really operational, although small and medium companies with very strong commitment and dedication to the change may be able to move faster.

Phase B, Introducing KAM, can be a chaotic period, which can be mitigated by anticipation and coordination which would prevent wasted costs; premature and unsupported promises to customers; and internal confusion and non-cooperation. Building capability, particularly in key account managers, needs to occur neither too early nor too late, but be closely followed by launch and roll-out. Suppliers often make the serious mistake of appointing all their senior salespeople as key account managers, only to discover the pain of unpicking that decision later when they realize that a majority will not make the grade. KAM teams should also be appointed at this stage: too many companies delay this commitment, resulting in disappointed and even cynical customers.

Phase C is where the company really begins to operate KAM. It should learn from the launch and make early adjustments where necessary, especially working on the quality of some of the elements that were kicked off during introduction, but are not yet really fit for purpose. For example, strategic account plans should have been produced in Phase B but, typically, they are incomplete, lack explicit strategies, are operationally focused and only cover a one-year period at this stage. They should be upgraded to a three-year view with a strong push towards better insight, more strategic content and more clarity on resource requirement. Key account selection and categorization criteria should also be improved to ensure that they identify responsive and productive customers, not just large ones. Process development becomes a major focus, to operationalize KAM as far as possible without removing the flexibility and adaptability that KAM also requires.

Arrival at Phase D, Optimizing value, can be assessed by a quick litmus test for the company and another for key account managers. At this point the supplier can truly be said to be operating KAM, but there are still developments which will make the company genuinely key customer centric, and comfortable in so doing. Phase C should include a thorough review of the way the company operates KAM and the opportunities for gaining even more from the approach: some companies become stuck in their suboptimal ways and are overtaken by others. For example, all senior managers, not just sales and commercial, should vocally and visibly recommit to KAM and proactively explore ways in which their functions can better serve key customers, rather than trying to force KAM to adapt to functional priorities.

Eventually, when the supplier's worst fears about working more closely with key customers have proved unfounded, and it has successfully negotiated riskier areas and gained positive outcomes, the company can embark on making the deeper changes it was unwilling to implement earlier.

With confidence in its own experience of KAM, suppliers can achieve best practice KAM through whole-heartedly embracing the concept of the importance of key customers.

In this chapter

Introduction

For quite a few years we focused on painting a picture of how KAM should look, based on our research into best practice. However, as increasing numbers of companies ceased to challenge the vision, they began to turn their attention to implementation. They were looking for a route map that started at the beginning, and showed how to change to reach best practice KAM. Having bought into the idea of KAM, they were asking, quite reasonably, 'So how do we get there, because we're somewhere quite different right now?' We therefore started to investigate how companies made the transition and to map out the journey, working with experienced practitioners who had endured the pain and the gain.

Much of the material in this chapter was discovered and developed through practitioner workgroups drawn from global and national companies at different points in their KAM development. Some were still in the early days, others had gone a long way but felt they were stuck on a plateau, and others had made great progress already and were still developing. It became clear that KAM is a journey that is not achieved quickly: it typically takes two years to complete introduction, so if you thought your company could launch in six months (as many do) you should think again: plan for a longer process and set your and others' expectations to a realistic timescale.

Small and medium sized companies with a relatively simple business and more cohesive management group have an advantage over large companies here: they should be able to move faster and still maintain the flexibility that is so important in dealing with key customers. However, just as much as large companies, they need a clear understanding of what is required and what the journey looks like, to make sure that they do not shoot themselves in the foot or waste time by unconsciously taking KAM-unfriendly action. Large companies have the same issues in developing KAM as they will with any other major change. First, they need to recognize that it is a major change, and treat it accordingly. In large companies the actions to implement the change described in this chapter are likely to be more difficult to execute and more contentious than in smaller ones, with a greater danger of recidivism. Nevertheless, the actions required to adopt KAM are essentially the same for all.

KAM is, in fact, a long and possibly never-ending journey as suppliers continue to develop the ways they work with their key customers. Development post-introduction is rarely linear, and can go backwards as well as forwards, so timing is also much more variable than in the early phases. It is dangerous to assume continuous improvement: constant pressure is needed to maintain forward momentum. You should not underestimate the effort required – the more you have already done to develop KAM, the more there is yet to do because, as it develops, it touches more people and processes in your company and in the customer too. This chapter describes the journey and some of the potholes to avoid along the way.

> The more you have already done to develop KAM, the more there is yet to do.

13.1   Ready to change

13.1.1   Drivers of KAM

Organizations rarely make the effort to adopt KAM unless there is a powerful driver behind it, usually triggered by a particular event. Often that event is a symptom of an underlying trend or need that has not gained credibility or urgency until the event drew attention to it. The event may be the loss of a major contract, a public brawl between companies or other adverse publicity, or unexpectedly bad results, or a variety of other unfortunate circumstances.

Organizations usually contain a potential champion for KAM who has observed a worrying trend, or an opportunity, and is convinced that KAM is the route to dealing with it. Champions who have not yet gained the attention and support of the company to take action can grasp untoward events and wield them as sharp sticks to goad their companies into action.

Although it seems to be the negative issues that provide the 'tipping point' for action, drivers for KAM may be divided into positive and negative factors, which may originate from inside or outside the organization. The most powerful drivers are often the negative ones,

	Internal	**External**
Positive	• Desire for growth • Capitalizing on broad product/service offering through cross-selling • Accessing same customers through multiple channels • Desire to join useful bandwagon? • Better MIS systems	• Customer demand – one company, less time, spent better • Customer demand for strategic partnership • Globalizing/cross-boundary customers
Negative	• Pressure on margins • Pressure on resource • Organizational change/low internal cohesion • Need for cover for failing offer	• Mature market • Embarrassment in the marketplace • Customer loss/ potential loss/pre-loss feedback

Figure 13.1
Drivers of KAM.

particularly the external drivers, but there are also positive drivers that may be leveraged to promote the initiative or to make it possible. Figure 13.1 shows some typical drivers.

> The company needs to be constantly reminded of the compelling reason why it opted for KAM.

At an early stage, KAM champions should identify the most powerful drivers and decide how they can best be employed. Even if there are clear reasons for change, there will also be strong resistance from internal forces: from people who simply do not like change; or who consider any new approach to be a criticism of what they have done to date; or who see the new way of working as eroding their territory or power base. The company needs to be constantly reminded of the compelling reason why it opted for KAM, as the champion meets the inevitable resistance.

Customer demand for KAM treatment should be one of the strongest drivers, but companies can fail to recognize it if they are not looking for it. Table 13.1 represents a simple 'litmus' test which can quickly indicate whether the customers are ready for KAM. Look out for the resistors' argument, 'But not all of our customers want it.' This argument is totally fallacious even if it is true: you will not be planning to offer KAM to all your customers, nor do you have to force it on those who do not want it. Crucially, is a significant amount of your business tied into customers who *do* want to be treated differently?

CHECKPOINT

How much of your business lies with important customers who would respond positively and productively to KAM treatment?

Ask around your customers and the people who manage them currently, and see if they are showing an interest in working more closely with you. If they are not, you might still like to check whether that is genuinely how they feel, or whether your communication channels are blocked for any reason. Then take a look at Table 13.1: you do not require all of the indicators to be positive to make the case for KAM – any one of them could be sufficient.

Are customers . . .	Answers
1. Communicating opportunities and initiatives and involving the supplier in their strategies?	Yes/No
2. Expecting an understanding of their business: inviting the supplier to meet a wider range of people in their organization and giving a broad range of information about their business and marketplace?	Yes/No
3. Wanting to explore joint projects involving more commitment?	Yes/No
4. Wanting to talk longer term and develop strategies together?	Yes/No
5. Asking for a more senior account manager with more authority and/or competency?	Yes/No
6. Wanting a transparent or integrated approach and a single point of contact, dealing with them as a single entity?	Yes/No

Table 13.1
Litmus test for KAM-ready customers

Blocking from the opposite, internal direction, opposers tend to say, 'But we're already doing KAM, we don't need to do anything different.' They are probably confusing KAM with account management: Table 13.2 shows some of the main differences. Account management can and should coexist alongside KAM, for customers that are still important and valuable, but not key to the supplier. You may continue to operate traditional selling alongside these other approaches, for smaller and new customers.

In strongly sales-driven companies, KAM may be competing with an ingrained traditional sales approach rather than account management. In fact, KAM may be seen by many in the company as a sales job, especially if the people recruited for it have sales backgrounds. However, we have asked numerous experienced KAM practitioners and companies for their views on how much of the job is selling, and the result is almost invariably the same: only 5–10% of a key account manager's time should be spent on selling (when defined as converting specific opportunities to wins, i.e. managing the sales cycle, gaining bid sign-offs, pitching and closing the deal). It certainly is an important element of the KAM job, but only one of several.

Only 5–10% of a key account manager's time should be spent on selling.

Table 13.2   Account management versus KAM

Account management	Key account management
Coordinated overview of account based on current year	Holistic, helicopter, longer-term view
One-year plans, mostly action plans	3–5 year explicit business plans representing all of supplier's interaction with customer, not just sales and marketing or personal activity
No investment, or not much	Investment, in line with strategy
Opportunity-focused understanding	Deep understanding of customer's business
Managed by account manager alone	Managed by key account/business manager and ongoing key account team
Works within normal organization	Cross-boundary sharing and activity
Largely 'business as usual'	Emphasis on growth or change

You must tackle the positioning of selling at an early stage in this kind of company, or the key account managers themselves and their line management are likely to revert to familiar sales behaviour and frustrate any chance of change. Understanding why people revert to selling rather than KAM activity helps to identify strong influences that should be addressed at an early stage of transitioning to KAM. We have found both obvious and hidden selling drivers in numerous companies:

● Strong, even relentless, business focus on the bottom line

● Reward systems designed for sales (see Chapter 11)

● People like it (they feel successful when they close a deal)

● Security and familiarity ('we know how this works')

● Confidence in outcomes (clearer cause and effect linkages).

If your company does not change its own behaviour or communicate the change in its expectations clearly and with conviction, because in reality it is ambivalent about moving from a sales approach to KAM, you must expect that the people concerned will reflect that ambivalence and be slow to respond, or not change at all, until they are convinced that the company is serious about KAM.

13.1.2   Making the change

KAM is not easy to implement because it is a cultural change, more than a straightforward business initiative. Successful cultural change starts with an exploration of the gap between the current situation and the desired situation and a stage of 'unfreezing' to allow people to move on. Successful change programmes demand sensitivity, political awareness, clarity, consistency, translation into practicalities, energy and stamina from the people determined to make the change happen.

Using all these attributes, the KAM champion will have to convince senior management and the salesforce of the imperative for change. At least some of the salesforce, if not all, will lack much of the skill set required to fulfil key account manager positions, which presents potential personal problems that cannot be dismissed if the current salesforce needs to be won over. You need to recognize their need for development and offer training and learning opportunities at an early stage, rather than later, but still make the requirement to adapt very clear.

> Some of the salesforce, if not all, will lack much of the skill set required to fulfil key account manager positions.

There will be others around the organization who are also threatened by the change, both in reality and in their imagination, and their issues need to be recognized too. Overlaying the corporate culture are all the functions such as sales, supply chain, service, marketing, etc. which all have their own subcultures to be understood and considered and, of course, national cultures too. Furthermore, underlying the corporate culture in all companies are the informal networks and links, the 'underculture'. All these need to be understood and addressed in order to align them with a significant change like KAM. People who currently feel comfortable and in control will have to move to situations that they cannot yet visualize and where, honestly, their control and comfort is likely to be diminished. Others will find their power and influence increased, and be uncomfortable with that too.

Case study insight

Changing to KAM

A company took the decision to introduce KAM, but was concerned about how a number of constituencies inside the company would respond. It conducted workshops focused on cross-functional ways of working to make the requirements concrete rather than abstract, working with the functional business language in use. In these sessions, participants were offered KAM scenarios and then developed their own projections and conclusions.

At the same time, the champions pinpointed where existing language was unhelpful, and where new language would be helpful and powerful. A new, carefully chosen vocabulary was introduced, which was readily adopted by workshop participants. The process was very successful in promoting the change to KAM.

The champion should create a common vision of what KAM means for the organization, since the supplier organization will have either no concept or understanding of KAM, or will contain several different interpretations of it. In particular, senior management support and engagement must be gained for sustainable KAM, in order to achieve cross-functional support for major change and for serious investment. To quote the Global Accounts Director of 3M Electronics, 'A firm commitment from senior-level management won't ensure a program's success, but the lack of commitment can seal a program's failure' (Stevens, 2009).

> KAM champions are not always entirely frank with senior management in explaining the extent of change required!

The 'hearts and minds' of senior management will have to be won, but to what? Interestingly, KAM champions are not always entirely frank with senior management in explaining the extent of change required for successful KAM. Quite frequently, they describe an intermediate, transition stage of KAM to senior managers, in order not to alarm them and risk an adverse reaction. 'We decided not to "spook" senior management early on', said one KAM champion in a global supplier. If the CEO or MD is also the KAM champion, this strategy may not be necessary, but often it is.

The KAM champion or core team will need to:

● Articulate what KAM is and how it differs from existing approaches

● Agree KAM's priority versus other initiatives

● Specify the effort and supporting action required from senior managers.

Table 13.3 seeks to describe KAM by listing 'what it is' through its purpose and requirements, and also identifying misconceptions in terms

Table 13.3
Description of KAM

KAM is . . .	KAM is not . . .
Tool to grow business	Magic wand
Tool to maintain business	Cure-all for problems
Aligning the customer's strategy and ours	Reactive
Increasing contact points for customer retention	Customer 'liking', e.g. old boys' club
Cross-silo	Automated system or process, or off-the-shelf
Structured approach	Regular sales process
More focused on the customer	Free
New and joint opportunity identification	
Adding value to the customer	
Innovation	
Investment	

of 'what it is not'. Investment in specific customers is one of the most important differences between account management, which many companies already have, and KAM. Investment in a key account implies funding the customer relationship over and above the ongoing cost to serve, where there is no direct or immediate recovery of costs. Suppliers can be uncomfortable with the idea of investing in customers, even when they are doing it. However, you really need to understand that, for example, key customers expect innovation in a strategic relationship, which is just one of the elements that will require investment. If suppliers refuse to understand and respond to such expectations, there will be a negative impact on development of the relationship and, indeed, being prepared to invest in customer relationships is a key indicator of KAM (see Table 13.10).

How fast can the change be made? Suppliers are commonly inconsistent on this point: they always want speed but equally they seem to have little appetite for the 'big bang' approach, usually owing to fears that the 'big bang' will be followed by a high profile 'big splash' as the initiative is rejected by the company (not by the customers), and its champions with it. Suppliers are often nervous about a full-on KAM implementation, and want to find a way of progressing gradually and testing KAM as they go along. So an incremental approach to KAM, changing by gradual degrees, may seem attractive, but likely to be less successful than a step change, for the reasons in Table 13.4.

Incremental approach to change	Step change
Cautious approach, seen as safer	Good where powerful/urgent driver exists
Culture-dependent, matches companies with risk averse profile	Shorter time to result
Possibly partial implementation, applied in one sector	Creates urgency
Where parent company not bought in to KAM	Creates 'problems'
Greater risk of fizzling out	Gets to critical mass
	Gets noticed, highlights need for action

Table 13.4
Comparison of incremental and step changes to KAM

Even step changes take time – and always more than expected – so anything deliberately slowed down further is probably not even noticeable, and therefore stands a greater risk of failure. Revolution is not recommended – few companies seem able to cope – but aiming for a step change is advisable, because implementation is inevitably slower than planned. Suppliers who are still nervous can trial KAM in one area or sector, provided that they recognize that:

- Gaining experience of how to execute KAM is the aim of the trial

- The trial cannot yield results to prove whether KAM is worthwhile as a business case, because KAM is a medium-/long-term strategy that cannot be properly judged over a short period

- Limitations in scale, duration and commitment mean that the trial may not throw up important issues, especially those caused by crossing boundaries, so it may be deficient as a microcosm of eventual reality

- A trial is fine if the supplier is not under pressure in the marketplace and can afford to wait for a sensible period before evaluating the trial and deciding how to proceed. Competitors may not be prepared to wait, however!

> Introducing KAM needs to be a management decision based on analysis and strategy rather than trial.

Suppliers can also start KAM with a few customers and roll it out to more later. Indeed, it is important that the company does not take on too many key customers when it does not really know how many it can handle. This kind of small trial runs the same risks as the incremental approach; if it fails to gain attention and gets lost, or if the rest of the customers move on and begin to defect. Really, introducing KAM needs to be a management decision based on analysis and strategy rather than trial.

13.1.3   The transitioning curve

Working with KAM practitioners from major companies, we have put together a view of how development proceeds in most organizations. Every company takes a wrong turn at some point and heads into a cul-de-sac from which it will have to extricate itself at some point, but the transitioning journey we have assembled from common experience omits these excursions. However, there are still stages that are suboptimal because most companies seem to pass through them, and these have been included. The transitioning curve shown in Figure 13.2 therefore represents a realistic picture, neither idealized nor peppered with mistakes, organized into five principal phases in KAM development:

A. Scoping KAM

B. Introducing KAM

C. Embedding KAM

D. Optimizing value

E. Best practice

This chapter will focus on the first four phases, since the rest of the book discusses 'Best practice KAM', which we define as the kind of approach that would be a beacon of achievement to other companies. Phases A and B, which together take a company to the point of having introduced KAM – no more – consistently, take about two years, but

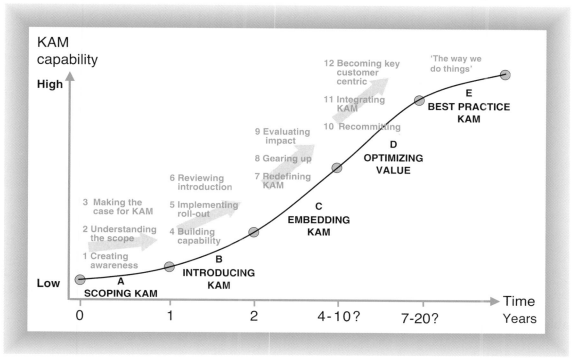

Figure 13.2   Transitioning to KAM.

can take longer. Shorter periods seem rare, so suppliers new to KAM need to adjust their expectations accordingly.

The time required for Phases C and D seems less consistent. We would estimate anything from a further two years to complete Phase C if a supplier were a fairly small or simple company and united in its determination to make progress in KAM, and had a good understanding of what needs to be done. However, Phase C often takes much longer, especially in larger and more complex organizations. Indeed, many companies get stuck in Phase C and never reach Phase D, Optimizing value, because deep down they are not ready to take on some of the organizational changes and power shifts that are involved. Phase D takes at least as long if not longer than Phase C, because the changes to the organization are more radical, although by now the company's commitment to KAM should be beyond question, which should allow change to become easier and faster. Some companies have been implementing KAM in various forms for 20 years, but still cannot say they have reached best practice.

Each phase is divided into three periods or subphases following on from each other chronologically, in which different actions are executed: these are described in more detail in Sections 13.2 and 13.3. However, there will undoubtedly be considerable overlap between the periods, so any sequence of actions should not be taken as set in stone: some will be proceeding simultaneously.

A wide range of action is involved in implementing a KAM programme, which can be organized into three coherent streams of activity observable across all KAM development phases. Suppliers will, at most times, have some activities running that address:

● Strategy and planning

● Organization and people

● Processes.

Obviously, the balance of activity will differ in different phases. A heavy focus on strategy and planning would be expected at the outset in the exploratory phases with little, if anything, developing in processes at that point: action on processes begins to increase later on, as the focus is rebalanced from strategy towards implementation. Development activities can be further grouped within each broad stream of the initiative, as in Table 13.5. At some points, there will be critical milestones to pass, such as the point when a company decides whether or not to adopt KAM, or to recommit to KAM at a later stage.

Table 13.5 Activity streams in KAM development

Stream of activity	Contributory streams	Description
Strategy and planning	Goals and strategy	Vision and overall aims
	Planning and objectives	Specific planning activities and quantified forecasting
	Research	Finding out information needed from internal and, importantly, external sources
Organization and people	Key account managers	Changes in the role, rewards and development of and for the individual
	KAM teams and the KAM community	People consistently working on a key account or the KAM programme
	The wider organization and senior management	Addressing the rest of the company
Processes	Key account manager activities	Processes engaging individual key account managers and generally their responsibility
	Other KAM activities	Processes involving the KAM community, typically customer service, monitoring and review
	Core processes	Implementation processes run by the rest of the organization, not specifically for KAM

Each phase is explained in the next sections. Section 13.2 deals with the early phases, i.e. A: Scoping KAM and B: Introducing KAM: while Section 13.3 describes the later phases, i.e. C: Embedding KAM and D: Optimizing value.

13.2   The early stages

13.2.1   Phase A: Scoping KAM

This first phase is a crucial one. Falter at this point and the organization might never embark on KAM at all. Champions of KAM would be wise to look outside at the marketplace for their justification, at what their most important customers are saying and doing, and at what approaches their competitors and other leading companies are taking. Too many companies are entirely absorbed by their internal world and take important decisions with insufficient reference to external reality. Finally, the KAM champion should define what success in KAM would look like for the company and describe the journey towards that success, taking into account outcomes for both the company and the individuals involved. Phase A may easily take up to a year, and involve a good deal more effort, discovery and political activity than anticipated. 'Scoping KAM' can be divided into three periods, as Table 13.6 shows.

Table 13.6   Phase A subphases in Scoping KAM

Subphase	Key actions
1. Creating awareness	Identify a powerful driver, which could be positive but is generally negative
	The KAM champion (often self-appointed), who recognizes the possibility of KAM as a solution, works to generate awareness of KAM
2. Understanding the scope	Appoint a KAM programme team to work with the champion
	Get to grips with how KAM will address the issues through research, putting it in context, and communicating with stakeholders
	Begin to look at which customers would be involved
3. Making the case for KAM	Clarify specifics of strategy, objectives, costs and customers
	Assemble the business case with what KAM will look like in the organization and expected outcomes
	Position and define the job of key account manager
Milestone: senior management approval	Critical decision point: stakeholders should have been identified and the hearts and minds won over

The end of this phase is marked by a breakpoint: will senior management give its approval to proceed with KAM, given the information now in its possession, or will it back out? The champion and core team will have found that they needed to go into much greater depth earlier than they anticipated originally, just to get the go/no go decision to proceed. Putting together the business case for a major change is very difficult, because of the range of implications and the uncertainty associated with assessing a complex position in the future, and KAM is no exception. Most organizations will look for strong justification before taking on KAM but, in spite of the KAM champion's efforts, the extent of the development and the difficulty of quantifying the outcomes may still mean that they have in order to take their decision with less than cast iron proof. Having said that, you should still gather as much insight as possible to make sure that the decision is the right one, and that you are adequately prepared for the journey.

'Corporate wobble' ... can become apparent with disastrous effects on key account managers and customers.

Even so, suppliers quite often embark on KAM on a false premise, entering as a short-term initiative from which they can readily disengage. When they fail to get a quick and unequivocal payback, wavering in their commitment to the KAM programme, or 'corporate wobble' as one company described it, can become apparent, with disastrous effects on key account managers and customers who have committed to KAM.

It is dangerous to start a KAM programme on a promise to senior management of cost savings that will probably not materialize.

For this reason, it is important to be as clear as possible about the reasons why the company is adopting KAM, and at least to attempt to model the business case for it in an appropriate timeframe, i.e. as a medium- to long-term strategy, probably about five years. The investment required should be identified, and any cost savings that may be made from KAM ways of working, but it is dangerous to start a KAM programme on a promise to senior management of cost saving that probably will not materialize, for two reasons:

- KAM generally increases the cost of running the customer interface for key customers. Companies often find those resources by withdrawing them from other, smaller or less important customers, but there may not be a cost saving.

- KAM is more likely to increase volumes or maintain business that might be lost, rather than save cost.

The business case needs to be assembled with great care and with neither undue optimism nor undue caution. Business cases can look misleadingly unattractive if the wrong baseline is used, i.e. assuming that current levels of business would be maintained if the supplier does not adopt KAM, whereas in a KAM-ready marketplace a failure to change the approach to key customers ('doing nothing different', not 'doing nothing') is likely to cause a decline in business. This decline should be applied as the most probable baseline underlying the case for KAM.

Making the business case will be easier if you have a culture of investing in customers, which implies that such funding has a return. Investment would involve spending on things like extra people on the account; specific market development; customization; and IT systems, e.g. an extranet dedicated to the customer. Anything that is funded specifically by the customer is effectively purchased by them, so costs of any such items or projects is not an investment, and nor are entertainment expenses and normal sales activity.

13.2.2 Phase B: Introducing KAM

The launch phase can be a chaotic period in which the organization finds that it is still 'making it up as it goes along', depending on the amount and depth of scoping carried out in the first phase. It is

Table 13.7 Phase B subphases in Introducing KAM

Subphase	Key actions
4. Building capability	Finalize goals and the plans to meet in greater detail, highlighting specific, actionable requirements
	Appoint competent key account managers with high priority
Milestone: launch	Coordinated launch: though capability building and roll-out are likely to merge in practice
5. Implementing roll-out	Build specific internal support rapidly so that key account managers can function effectively
	Inform the rest of the organization about the new approach
	Adopt feedback and progress monitoring processes
6. Reviewing KAM introduction	Review the introduction and make adjustments to structure and ways of working at an early stage (too soon to review revenue or profit)
	Publicize good practice and actively discourage bad/old practice to make the commitment to change clear: identify issues

difficult to coordinate such wide-ranging changes. However, once certain elements are put in place, others need to be implemented within a fairly short space of time (see Table 13.7), not least because of the cost implications. For example, from the time that key account managers are appointed they will be costing the company money and anyway they will want to get on with the job. So they are likely to start developments with customers, often before important support elements are in place inside the company. To make sure that customers are not given promises and then let down, it is worth getting a grip on which actions belong to each of the subphases, to understand the timing and sequence of changes required and plan to implement them in good time.

The *appointment of key account managers* is a crucial action at this stage. Unfortunately, many companies make a huge error that they will regret bitterly later, making all their senior salespeople (sometimes the whole salesforce!) into key account managers, and 'divvying up' the customers between them according to existing relationships. In fact, while you can call everyone a key account manager, you cannot just make them into one, and eventually you will realize that two-thirds or more will not make the grade. To avoid this issue, the job should be carefully described together with the competences and attributes required to fulfil it, and then key account managers recruited, internally but also from other functions within the company and even externally, from candidates who match the profile. It causes a great deal of trouble and bad feeling to remove people from positions later on, when it becomes obvious that they cannot meet the requirements of the job.

> Many companies make a huge error that they will regret bitterly later, making all their senior salespeople . . . into key account managers.

As early as possible, the company should set up *key account teams* to work with and be led by the key account managers. Delaying team

408 Key Account Management

involvement is dangerous, because customers will quickly respond to the new initiative and expect to see significant changes, which are probably more than the key account manager can deliver alone. Some suppliers have decided that they will set up account teams 'next year, when we understand better what we're doing', but by that time the customer is likely to have concluded that the whole thing was just sales talk and empty promises, and withdrawn their commitment, which will be much more difficult to regain once disappointed.

> The biggest single issue . . . is the cooperation of team members, given the conflicting demands of their functional head and the key account manager(s).

KAM teams are tasked with the *long-term management* of the customer, so there should be at least a consistent core of team members, who form a fundamental part of the relationship. KAM team members are almost always only partially dedicated to the key account and in most cases they have 'dotted line' reporting to the key account manager, and 'solid line' reporting to their functional head. Commonly, team members have other key customers with which they work and/or they also have objectives set by their 'home' function. As a result, the biggest single issue in the effective operation of KAM teams is the cooperation of team members, given the conflicting demands of their functional head and the key account manager(s), as Figure 13.3 suggests.

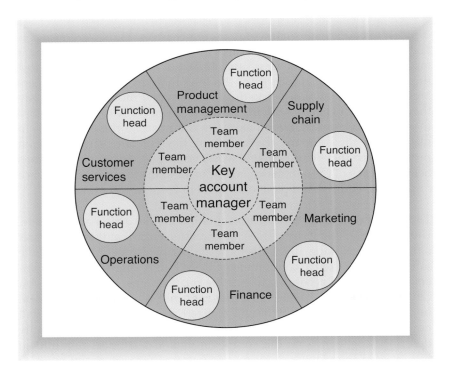

Figure 13.3
Cross-functional key account teams.

How you set up, facilitate and support these teams is critical to KAM success. *Training*, both for key account managers and for team members (who often receive none at all), needs to be relevant and timely, so that people are ready for the job they have to do in time for the change, rather than later when they have settled into other ways. Communication to the rest of the business also needs to be relevant and timely: some companies have never thought of telling the rest of the company anything about KAM, and then are surprised when their staff take intuitively sensible but actually anti-KAM action.

At the end of the introductory phase, some of the organizational issues that might cause friction and disruption will begin to emerge. Be mentally prepared for them, so that they can be acknowledged and tackled, rather than denied and left to fester. Cross-boundary issues (whether national, divisional, cultural or just departmental) will undoubtedly arise. If left unattended, they sow the seeds of poor performance against high expectations that will eventually undermine and potentially destroy the whole KAM approach.

Even at this point there will be people who are already asking for evidence of the value of KAM in terms of increased revenue, margin or profit, but this should be resisted: as we have already said, KAM is a medium- and long-term strategy and should be judged accordingly. That does not mean, though, that specific examples of how KAM has helped the business with customers should be ignored, but that such examples should be used anecdotally for the purpose of encouragement rather than evaluation.

13.3 Continuing and developing KAM

13.3.1 *Phase C: Embedding KAM*

When you reach the end of Phase B, Introduction, you see that KAM is not quite as simple as first envisaged, and there are a number of elements that need to be reconsidered and respecified. Indeed, the organization needs to recognize that it has only reached the end of the

> Organizations who get KAM all 'right first time' do not exist.

Table 13.8 Phase C subphases in Embedding KAM

Subphase	Key actions
7. Redefining KAM	Tighten up some elements, like customer criteria and account plans, in terms of both specification and quality of execution
	Relax other elements to allow more flexibility in response to customers and circumstances
8. Gearing up	Invest seriously in KAM; in the key account managers, support, feedback and more
	Develop processes to operationalize KAM; to manage it more professionally; and to ensure alignment of KAM strategy with application
9. Evaluating impact	Clarify expected outcomes of KAM
	Evaluate results versus expectations and impact internally and externally, reviewed by senior management
Milestone: review commitment	Decision on whether and how to continue with KAM now the organization understands what it is and what its outcomes can be: agree to commit to decision

beginning, and expect to make further, substantial developments, or it is in danger of ploughing on with an inadequate model. Organizations who get KAM all 'right first time' do not exist.

So there should be a period of redefining various elements of the programme, such as the customer categorization criteria, roles and rewards, followed by a period of intense activity to 'gear up' to the new perception of the requirement: see Table 13.8. The quality of elements that were put in place in Phase B at a basic level now needs to be brought up to a much higher standard.

So, for example, in Phase B the *selection criteria* for key customers usually emphasize current volumes of business, but the limitation of this approach becomes clearer with experience of working with those customers who take large volumes but remain uninterested in closer collaboration. In addition, as suppliers recognize the amount of resource absorbed by key customers, they understand the importance of ensuring that only those who will respond at a satisfactory level should receive such expensive treatment. The criteria for selecting those customers need to be more sophisticated, and the process for applying them.

Again, *key account plans* should have been produced in Phase B, but commonly they will be incomplete, lack explicit strategies and have a short-term focus, whereas they need to be genuine strategic account

---

Case study insight
Achieving high quality strategic account plans

A new global accounts director reviewed the plans and performance of all key accounts in his first week after appointment. He was disappointed with both. Performance was mediocre and key account managers were only acting at an operational level. They were not using the account plans or keeping them up to date, and most had dropped the three-year strategic view that was originally part of the requirement. He immediately insisted that all plans be rewritten and upgraded, including the case for any resource. He made it clear that he would allocate his entire budget for the year based on the business cases in the plans, taking into account the short-term and the longer-term perspective too. Any late requests would not and could not be approved, since the budget would be fully committed elsewhere. Some key account managers responded, some continued in the same way – until they discovered that, indeed, they did not get any response to ad hoc requests for resources. Eventually, even the laggards also delivered plans at the required level of quality for the next planning round. Key account planning and performance both improved significantly.

plans with at least a three-year vision (and one year action) in whose development the customer has been heavily involved. In this phase, the plan format is upgraded, more training on producing strategies and plans is delivered to key account managers (and teams, ideally), and the requirement for quality is clarified and followed through, for example, as in the following case.

In this phase, *process development* becomes a major focus (see Chapter 9). Processes should be designed to facilitate the implementation of strategies with key customers, whatever their nature, with the emphasis on maintaining flexibility. It is an enduring feature of KAM that key customers will always be pushing the boundaries to achieve new and better approaches, so companies developing processes to help them work more efficiently should beware of building in counterproductive rigidity and insisting on conformity. Effective processes designed to deliver to KAM needs should replace standardized 'rules', which are driven by a fear of loss of control. The company and the individuals involved should both be able to behave like responsible, expert adults rather than raw adolescents in need of vigilance and control, and expect that of each other as well.

> Companies developing processes . . . should beware of building in counterproductive rigidity and insisting on conformity.

By the end of this phase, the supplier should have a fully functioning KAM approach that is valued by customers, is properly embedded in the organization and is producing results. Even though the supplier can still improve its approach to KAM and get more out of it, senior managers should now take a step back, reflect on the journey the company has taken and consider the value that KAM gives. Expectations should be revisited, as they will probably have changed substantially since the launch, when the company did not really understand what KAM would mean for it, either in terms of investment and involvement, or what it could take from it. The company should take the opportunity to:

- Complete a thorough review

- Check that the decision to operate KAM is still valid

- Gain the unequivocal commitment of all senior and middle managers to KAM and their role in it, at least

- Prepare to revise, upgrade, reconfigure and take all elements to another level.

Assuming that the company confirms the decision to operate KAM, it should now have sufficient confidence in the approach and the individuals it has made responsible for it, to allow KAM to be delivered with the flexibility and variety that it requires.

13.3.2   Phase D: Optimizing value

By the end of Phase C, Embedding KAM, a supplier should be genuinely operating KAM. There are some telling indicators that seem to be valid across a broad range of sectors, which can be used as a quick-dip

Table 13.9 Litmus test for the organization

Questions	Answers
1. Do *all* senior managers talk openly and frequently about key customers and their key account managers?	Yes/No
2. Is the company prepared to *invest* in key customers (against a business case with returns expected beyond one year)?	Yes/No
3. Do strategic account plans play a major part in the *corporate* planning process?	Yes/No
4. Do you measure the *profitability* of key customers (beyond gross margin)?	Yes/No
5. Are key account managers paid at the same level and on a *similar basis* to strategic business unit directors (rewarded on company rather than personal performance)?	Yes/No

'litmus' test to confirm or refute whether KAM is really embedded in the company, or is actually shallow and inconsistently implemented. The first test concerns the organization (Table 13.9), and the second concerns the key people who apply KAM, i.e. the key account managers (Table 13.10). Unambivalent answers of 'yes' would be required on four of the five questions on both tests if an organization were to be considered as truly operating KAM, albeit with opportunities for development in Phase D.

Table 13.10 Litmus test for key account managers

Questions*	Answers
1. Can you identify *all* the account team members and define their roles in the relationship with the customer?	Yes/No
2. Is your *strategic* account plan written for at least three years, complete, live and up to date?	Yes/No
3. Do you have a business-focused relationship with at least one of the customer's Board Directors?	Yes/No
4. Would your customer rate your understanding of their business *and* their marketplace at or over 8/10?	Yes/No
5. Can you define and quantify the *added* value you brought to the customer in the last year?	Yes/No

* Repeat for all customers for key account managers with more than one customer

Phase D represents the opportunity to increase the benefits from KAM, capitalizing on the company's greater knowledge and comfort with the approach (see Table 13.11). By this stage, it is to be hoped that the supplier's worst fears have proved unfounded, and that it has successfully negotiated riskier areas and identified positive outcomes. With a more confident mindset, the company can embark on making some of the changes that it was unwilling to implement earlier, even when it saw the logic of the idea behind them. It will probably mean accepting

Table 13.11 Phase D subphases in Optimizing value

Subphase	Key actions
10. Recommitting	Senior managers recommit to KAM very publicly and re-energize the programme
	KAM is accepted as a permanent part of the culture and operations of the organization
11. Integrating KAM	KAM and key customers are represented in all major forums and plans
	The needs and operation of KAM are integrated into all relevant business processes
12. Becoming key customer centric	Information is seen as central to proper management and is not subservient to traditional metrics
	KAM's strategic position and contribution is recognized and accepted

that finding the best way to supply and support key customers is more important than standardizing processes for maximum efficiency, for example. Internally, operations and management might become more complex, but if that complexity allows the supplier to offer customized solutions for key accounts, then managing that complexity is a valuable capability.

In Phase B, the mediocre quality of the account plans meant that they were probably not good enough to make a contribution to the *business planning* cycle for the whole organization, but if the quality of the plan has been lifted in Phase C, they should now take up this role. Strategic account plans show the supplier how a very significant part of its business will develop over the subsequent three years: where its key customers are heading; which strategies it needs to support and invest in; what resources it will require; what outcomes it can expect; and whether the overall direction is aligned with its own strategies. These plans are an invaluable source of information that should be linked into the process for developing the corporate business plan. Suppliers should have worked out good processes for producing the plans, and now they should develop another for securing their input to the business planning process. Unless you can point to the process for doing it, it will not happen and the contribution will be missed, which is a terrible oversight.

Any processes that are intransigent, inflexible and unhelpful to key customers should be investigated with a view to making them more KAM-friendly. All *senior managers and function heads* should reverse their way of thinking about KAM, i.e. normally how KAM fits into their function's priorities and ways of working, and be proactively exploring what their function can do for KAM. They should acknowledge the needs of key customers in any of their plans and be vocally

Senior managers and function heads should acknowledge the needs of key customers in any of their plans and be vocally and visibly supportive of KAM.

and visibly supportive of KAM. Only through consistent and continuous communication about what KAM and key accounts mean to the supplier's business can the whole company achieve best practice KAM. Companies must put an end to ideas lingering in any part of the company that KAM is a fad that has been temporarily grafted onto the surface of the organization, and may be shed again at some stage.

Ultimately, companies struggle to act effectively and to gain the full benefit from KAM when resources are distributed across the company, whether they are divided up by country or division or on any other basis. The really integrated customer management that many key customers want finally becomes possible through a *central KAM/GAM* unit that is simultaneously able to maintain strong links with the rest of the business.

KAM should be *fully integrated* into the working of the organization at all levels. It now holds a permanent and appropriate place in the structure, the planning cycle, budgeting and resourcing, career development for key account managers, etc. The focus shifts from how to install, communicate and operationalize KAM to how to manage and implement the exciting raft of key customer programmes and projects that are enabled through KAM. KAM is accepted as the normal way of working: 'why' and 'how' are no longer challenged, and are replaced by a focus on 'what' in terms of the business with customers.

Key account managers should be fully competent and trusted to take over as the 'Managing Director of the customer'.

With confidence in its own experience of KAM, suppliers should be able to improve performance further through whole-heartedly embracing the concept of the importance of key customers. This also means that, having developed the people to manage them, key account managers should be fully competent and trusted to take over as the 'Managing Director of the customer' in terms of the supplier's business with them, backed by a suite of management information that readily and accurately represents the position with each customer individually. The company is now ready for best practice KAM.

13.3.3   Phase E: Best practice KAM

In effect, the rest of the book deals with KAM as it can and should be, i.e. best practice, so we will not go into further detail here. Of course, your KAM approach should constantly be reviewed, revised and kept fresh and up to date. Competitors catch up, customers want more innovation and newly appointed directors arrive with the clarion call of 'back to basics' at regular intervals. There is always a danger of complacency and slippage, and of companies becoming so used to KAM as 'the way we do things round here' that they forget what made it successful. You may relax your vigilance and lose vital ground if you restructure, reinvent strategy, reallocate resource and dismantle the progress you have made in KAM.

Case study insight

Destroying hard-won best practice

A global company organized its operations into four regions of the world, and ran its KAM programme in line with that regional organization. However, it observed that most of its key accounts were themselves global companies, and most of the difficulties that it encountered internally in dealing with them were cross-boundary issues that arose when two different people managed them in different regions, and when terms and conditions, service support, etc. varied according to where in the world the customer business unit was located. Eventually, a GAM champion convinced the company that such customers should be managed centrally as global accounts, to put an end to all the disputes and negotiations involved in managing them regionally. The change was not easily made, but it was very successful, and results improved markedly. After several years of much smoother customer managements, however, the fairly new supplier CEO decided to realign KAM with the company's regional structure, overriding why and how the programme had evolved to become global, and deciding that internal structure was more important than supporting strategic customers!

Uniform and standardized approaches and processes will, by definition, not meet the expectations of all key customers.

Summary

Making the transition to KAM is not easy or quick. Eventually, it will touch almost every part of the company and people at all levels in the organization, and make changes in the way they work and with whom they work. The early stages, in which suppliers research and explore what KAM will mean for them, are very important in making the smoothest possible transformation: at least, issues can be anticipated and planned for in advance. That is not to say that there will be no resistance to the change because, in our experience, resistance from some quarters is inevitable. KAM champions need political skills, robustness, persistence and the backing of senior management.

The transition requires action across strategy and planning; the organization and people; and processes. Several areas will need to be revisited as the company learns more about KAM, and the original approach reworked with increasing sophistication and subtlety. KAM is not simple: it is predicated on treating key customers individually and differently according to their needs (and yours), and uniform and standardized approaches and processes will, by definition, not meet the expectations of all key customers. Suppliers start by making fairly superficial adaptations for key customers, but go deeper as they learn from their customer partners and reap the business benefits.

Key account managers that start out as salespeople also have to transform themselves to play their role as leaders. Sensible companies help them in every way to achieve the required level, both through training and development and through removing barriers and supporting them as much as possible. Companies that have strong functional and divisional structures with weak customer orientation are asking key account managers to execute a high-pressure job in a generally hostile environment, inevitably with limited levels of success.

KAM teams have become a very important part of the offer to key customers: their broad and mixed skill set and specialized knowledge provide a great deal of the value a customer receives from the supplier. These are mostly virtual teams, only partly dedicated to any one customer, so both the organization and the key account manager that leads the team need to make substantial and continued efforts to give and gain recognition for the team; communicate objectives and ways of working; and attract buy-in from team members and their functional heads.

Suppliers with mature KAM programmes generally come to the conclusion that the only way they can achieve the business synergies they seek is through a centralized unit of key account managers working with key customers across all geographies and products, not attached to a local or specialist structure. They recognize, however, that this approach still requires major efforts to keep operational delivery links close and realistic. Whatever the structure, successful KAM requires a willingness to share and to work across boundaries in teams, for corporate rather than territorial objectives.

Ultimately, companies need to recognize that transitioning to KAM is a long haul, but very worthwhile, and probably even obligatory in some markets.

Further reading

General

This is a list of publications and research reports from the authors which address numerous aspects of key account management. As we have drawn on them in several chapters they are noted here and not repeated in the additional references under each individual chapter.

McDonald, M. and Rogers, B. (1998). *Key Account Management – Learning from Supplier and Customer Perspectives*. Butterworth-Heinemann.

McDonald, M. and Woodburn, D. (1999). *Key Account Management – Building on Supplier and Customer Perspectives*. Financial Times Prentice Hall.

McDonald, M., Millman, A. and Rogers, B. (1996). *Key Account Management – Learning from Supplier and Customer Perspectives*. Cranfield School of Management Research Report, Cranfield University.

McDonald, M., Rogers, B. and Woodburn, D. (2000). *Key Customers: How to Manage Them Profitably*. Butterworth-Heinemann.

Woodburn, D. and McDonald, M. (2001). *Key Customers. World-leading Key Account Management: Identification and Development of Strategic Relationships*. Cranfield School of Management Research Report, Cranfield University.

Woodburn, D., Holt, S. and McDonald, M. (2004). *Key Customer Profitability – Making Money in Strategic Customer Partnerships*. Cranfield School of Management Research Report, Cranfield University.

Chapter 1: The crucial role of key account management

Hancock, S. (1998). Fair's fair. *Purchasing and Supply Management* 5 November.

McDonald, M., Ryals, L., Dennison, T., Yallop, R. and Rogers, B. (1994). *Marketing, the Challenge of Change*. Cranfield University.

Porter, M.E. (1980). *Competitive Strategy*. The Free Press.

Porter, M.E. (1985). *Competitive Advantage: Creating and Sustaining Superior Performance*. The Free Press.

Wilson, C. (1998). *Profitable Customers: How to Identify, Develop and Keep Them*, 2nd edn. Kogan Page.

Chapter 2: Selecting and categorizing key customers

Fiocca, R. (1982). Account portfolio analysis for strategy development. *Industrial Marketing Management* 11: 53–62.

Zolkiewski, J. and Turnbull, P. (2000). Relationship portfolios – past, present and future. *Proceedings of the 16th Annual IMP Conference*, University of Bath.

Chapter 3: Relationship stages

Christopher, M. (2005). *Logistics and Supply Chain Management*. Prentice Hall.

Dunn, D.T. and Thomas, C.A. (1994). Partnering with customers. *Journal of Business Industrial Marketing* 9(1): 34–40.

Maslow, A.H. (1943). A theory of human motivation. *Psychological Review* 50(4): 370–396.

Millman, A.F. and Wilson, K. (1996). Developing key account management competences. *Journal of Marketing Practice: Applied Marketing Science* 2(2): 7–22.

Scott, C. and Westbrook, R. (1991). New strategic tools for supply chain in management. *International Journal of Physical Distribution and Logistics Management* 21(1): 23–33.

Chapter 4: Developing key relationships

Dunn, D.T. and Thomas, C.A. (1994). Partnering with customers. *Journal of Business & Industrial Marketing* 9(1): 34–40.

Håkansson, H. and Snehota, I. (1995). Analysing business relationships, in Håkansson, H. and Snehota, I. (eds) *Developing Relationships in Business Networks*. Routledge, pp. 24–29.

Millman, A.F. and Wilson, K. (1996). Developing key account management competences. *Journal of Marketing Practice: Applied Marketing Science* 2(2): 7–22.

Morgan, R.M. and Hunt, S.D. (1994). The commitment-trust theory of relationship marketing. *Journal of Marketing* 58: 20–38.

Scott, C. and Westbrook, R. (1991). New strategic tools for supply chain management. *International Journal of Physical Distribution and Logistics Management* 21(1): 23–33.

Chapter 5: The buyer perspective

Anderson, J.C., Hakansson, H. and Johanson, J. (1994). Dyadic business relationships within a business network context. *Journal of Marketing* 58: 1–15.

Buzzell, R.D. and Gale, B.T. (1987). *The PIMS Principles: Linking Strategy to Performance*. The Free Press.

Ellram, L.E. (1991). Supply chain management. *International Journal of Physical Distribution and Logistics Management* 21(1): 13–22.

Krapfel, R.E., Salmond, D. and Spekman, R. (1991). A strategic approach to buyer-seller relationships. *European Journal of Marketing* 25(9): 22–37.

Millman, A.F. and Wilson, K.J. (1994). From key account selling to key account management. In *Tenth Annual Conference on Industrial Marketing and Purchasing*.

Olsen, R.F. and Ellram, L. (1997). A portfolio approach to supplier relationships. *Industrial Marketing Management* 26: 101–113.

Perrien, J., Ricard, L. and Landry, C. (1999). *Proceedings of the Ninth Biennial World Marketing Congress*. Sage Publications.

Porter, M.E. (1985) *Competitive Advantage: Creating and Sustaining Superior Performance*. The Free Press.

Turnbull, P.W. and Valla, J.P. (1986). *Strategies for International Industrial Marketing*. Croom Helm.

Williamson, O.E. (1985). *The Economic Institution of Capitalism: Firms, Markets, Relational Contracting*. The Free Press.

Chapter 6: Key account profitability

Davidson, H. (1998). *Even More Offensive Marketing*. Penguin.
Haigh, D. (2005). Brand finance. *Marketing Magazine* 1 April.
McDonald, M. (2009). The future of marketing: brightest star in the firmament or fading meteor? Some hypotheses and a research agenda. *Journal of Marketing Management* 25, 5–6.
Millman, A.F. and Wilson, K.J. (1994). From key account selling to key account management. In *Tenth Annual Conference on Industrial Marketing and Purchasing*.
Pascale, R.T. (1990). *Managing on the Edge: How Successful Companies use Conflict to Stay Ahead*. Viking.
Peters, T.J. and Waterman, Jr, R.H. (1982). *In Search of Excellence: Lessons from America's Best-Run Companies*. Harper & Row.
Reichheld, F.R. (1994). Loyalty and the renaissance of marketing. *Marketing Management* 12(4): 17.
Reichheld, F.R. and Sasser, Jr, W.E. (1990). Zero defections: quality comes to services. *Harvard Business Review* September-October, 105–111.
Ryals, L. (2002). Key account profitability. PhD thesis, Cranfield University.
Storbacka, K., Sivula, P. and Kaario, K. (2000). A strategic perspective on the most valuable customers. *Velocity* Q2.
Wilson, C. (1998). *Profitable Customers: How to Identify, Develop and Keep Them*, 2nd edn. Kogan Page.

Chapter 7: Key account analysis

McDonald, M. (2007). *Marketing Plans: How to Prepare Them, How to Use Them*, 6th edn. Butterworth-Heinemann.
Porter, M.E. (1980). *Competitive Strategy*. The Free Press.
Robinson, J., Farris, C.W. and Wind, Y. (1967). *Industrial Buying and Creative Marketing*. Allyn & Bacon.

Chapter 8: Planning for key accounts

McDonald, M. (2003). *Marketing Plans: How to Prepare Them, How to Use Them*, 7th edn. Butterworth-Heinemann.
Millman, A.F. and Wilson, K.J. (1994). From key account selling to key account management. In *Tenth Annual Conference on Industrial Marketing and Purchasing*.
Pascale, R.T. (1990). *Managing on the Edge: How Successful Companies Use Conflict to Stay Ahead*. Viking.
Peters, T.J. and Waterman, Jr, R.H. (1982). *In Search of Excellence: Lessons from America's Best-Run Companies*. Harper & Row.

Chapter 9: Achieving with processes

Bonoma, T. (1985). *The Marketing Edge: Making Strategies Work*. The Free Press.
Holt, S. (2003). The role of the global account manager: a boundary role theory perspective. PhD thesis, Cranfield University.

Chapter 10: The role and requirements of key account managers

Canon-Bowers, J.A., Salas, E. and Converse, S. (1993). Shared mental models in expert decision making teams, in Castellan, Jr, N.J. (ed.) *Current Issues in Individual and Group Decision Making.* Erlbaum pp. 221–246.

Deeter-Schmelz, D.R. and Ramsey, R. (1995). A conceptualization of the functions and roles of formalized selling and buying teams. *Journal of Personal Selling and Sales Management* 15(2): 47–60.

Glassop, L. (2002). The organizational benefits of teams. *Human Relations* 55 (2): 225–249.

Hackman, J.R. (2002). *Leading Teams: Setting the Stage for Great Performances.* Harvard Business School Press.

Holt, S. (2003). The role of the global account manager: a boundary role theory perspective. PhD thesis, Cranfield University.

Homburg, C., Workman, Jr, J.P. and Jensen, O. (2002). A configurational perspective on key account management. *Journal of Marketing* 66 (April): 38–60.

Chapter 11: Rewards and performance in key account management

Woodburn, D. (2008). Rewarding Key Account Management: Issues and Pitfalls in Rewarding the Performance of Key Account Managers. Cranfield School of Management Research Report, Cranfield University.

Chapter 12: Organizing for key account management

Buzzell, R.D. (1985). *Citibank: Marketing to Multinational Customers.* Harvard Business School.

Homburg, C., Workman, Jr, J.P. and Jensen, O. (2000). Fundamental changes in marketing organization: the movement toward a customer-focused organizational structure. *Journal of the Academy of Marketing Science* 28(4): 459–478.

Jones, E., Chonko, L. and Cannon, J. (2005). Key accounts and team selling. *Journal of Personal Selling & Sales Management* 25(2): 182–198.

Yip, G.S. and Madsen, T.L. (1996). Global account management: the new frontier in relationship marketing. *International Marketing Review* 13(3): 24–42.

Chapter 13: Transitioning to key account management

Stevens, M. (2009). Sprouting a strategic account management program: how to build one from the ground up. *Velocity* Q3&4, 25.

Woodburn, D. (2006). *Transitioning to Key Account Management: How to Get your Organisation from Where it is to Where it Ought to Be on KAM.* Cranfield School of Management Research Report, Cranfield University.

Integrated fast track

For those who want to start or finish with the complete helicopter overview, we have compiled all the 'Fast tracks' of the essentials of each chapter into this rapid reprise of the content of the entire book. However, to understand more, or to find out what to do about these issues, you will need to read the chapters themselves.

The crucial role of key account management · CHAPTER 1

For over 15 years, the authors have been researching global best practice in the domain of account management, sponsored by many of the world's leading companies. The following topics in particular have been the focus of our research:

- **Key account selection:** Only a few selected customers can be included in the key account programme.

- **Classification of key accounts:** Derogatory labels like A, B, C, or gold, silver, bronze should be avoided at all cost.

- **Key account profitability:** The power of customers and their increased purchasing power has led to greater demands on the services of their suppliers. Unfortunately, many traditional accounting systems are incapable of accurately capturing all of the associated costs of dealing with major customers. Consequently, many suppliers are acting in ignorance of which customers make or lose them money.

- **Key account needs analysis:** A deep understanding of the customer's business is essential to success.

- **Strategic planning for key accounts:** Just as a three- to five-year strategy is essential for any business, so strategic plans for selected customers, signed off by the customers themselves, are also critical to success.

- **Roles and skills of key account managers:** Selling and negotiation skills are no longer sufficient on their own.

- **Other issues:** Information technology, organization structure and internal marketing all contribute to creating successful key account programmes.

The challenges that all organizations face today are:

- **Market maturity:** In most sectors, mature markets have transferred power from suppliers to customers, as suppliers compete for a share of a decreasing number of customers.

- **Globalization:** Market maturity has led to an increasing number of industries in which only a handful of truly global companies dominate the landscape. Hence, any supplier who cannot offer a seamless service in every part of the world where the customer operates will not win the business.

- **Customer power:** With their new-found power, customers are increasingly looking to selected suppliers to give them competitive advantage by product and process development.

All these developments mean that suppliers have to be much more stringent in their key account selection criteria. They must allocate their scarce resources intelligently across their customer base, taking account of the risks associated with different kinds of customers in order to build continuous shareholder value added.

CHAPTER 2   Selecting and categorizing key customers

Choosing the customers that your company wants to treat as key accounts ought not to be too hard, certainly when compared with some of the difficult cultural and structural issues that arise from key account management. However, many companies approach the task in a rather casual fashion first time around, and only later realize how many onward decisions are driven by their selection of key customers, and how awkward it may be to unpick inappropriate choices.

The key customers you seek should be those that are aligned to your corporate strategy and will therefore make a major contribution to its achievement. If they do not, who will? So your portfolio of key accounts should contain these customers, and only these customers. If you dilute it with customers with dissimilar agendas, which will not respond particularly favourably to your strategies, you will be unable to demonstrate sufficiently positive results from the key account management programme, and you risk sinking the whole initiative. Undoubtedly, there will be pressures to include unsuitable accounts, but they must be resisted. Counter such pressures by adopting an objective criteria-based process, and applying it rigorously.

Whatever the size of the organization, there seems to be an almost universally appropriate number of key accounts, which is probably between 15 and 35, with 5 and 50 as the outer limits. Certainly, anything with three digits is too many. In fact, the process of selection and categorization starts with deciding, more or less, how many key accounts your company can handle.

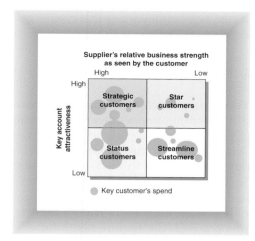

The identity of the customer deserves careful attention. It not only determines how the customer will score against the criteria, and hence how much resource it should receive, but it also has implications about how it should be managed. Customers should be identified in their terms, not carved up according to the supplier's structure, unless it is well matched with the customer's.

Selection criteria should be chosen and their importance weighted by a senior management group, and then rolled out to be scored to people who know the customer. These criteria are applied to assess the customer's attractiveness to your company, and the data are then used on the vertical axis of the key account selection/categorization matrix to build a picture of your portfolio of customers.

To complete the picture, you need the customer's view of you as a supplier, in their terms. Obviously, that will be different for each customer, and you must resist the urge to apply a standard set of criteria on the horizontal axis. If you did that, it would only be a reflection of what you think of yourselves, and would not represent their views and differences at all. You would also, in effect, be saying that these customers are all the same and all want the same things, which is contrary to the whole philosophy of key account management, apart from being patently untrue.

The matrix identifies four kinds of key customers, to which it is appropriate to offer four generic strategies that should guide the specific strategies that are developed for each customer individually:

1. Star key customers – investment for growth

2. Strategic key customers – strategic investment

3. Status key customers – proactive maintenance

4. Streamline key customers – management for cash.

The systematic assessment approach described in this chapter enables suppliers to build a portfolio view of their customers that drives many further insights, decisions and expectations about them, which is much more realistic and powerful than the key customer lists that many suppliers use. We will refer to it frequently in the rest of this book.

CHAPTER 3   Relationship stages

Key account management (KAM) is very much concerned with managing the relationship with the customer, but remember that the relationship is a means to an end, that is, business development, and not an end in itself. Nevertheless, it is important to understand these relationships, which vary from simple, transactional forms to intimate and complex liaisons. There is a distinct hierarchy of relationship levels which describes the progression from the simple trading stage right up to a configuration that is only a short step away from a merger. Whatever level of relationship is reached, the requirements for efficient fulfilment of basic transactions remains, although a good relationship might allow a greater period of tolerance and assistance with poor performance than a simple, easy-to-exit relationship. Ultimately, however, a customer will have to buy from the supplier who gives them the offer they need, however good the relationship.

Both the key account manager and the supplier organization need to know what kind of relationship they have with each customer, and therefore what they can and cannot do with it. Suppliers generally have delusions of intimacy with the customer, and believe that they are one stage closer than the customer does. Since the essence of a relationship is reciprocation, then the supplier can only work with the level of relationship that both parties agree on.

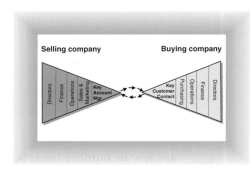

Exploratory relationships

Suppliers need to recognize potential key accounts from the outset and treat them as such. The bigger the customer, the longer it takes. Be prepared to be patient and manage internal expectations. Monitor the signals sent out rigorously.

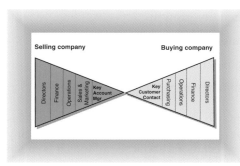

Basic relationships

This simple, transactional relationship has benefits of efficiency, clarity and resource control alongside its disadvantages of vulnerability to competition, fragility to change, potential for bias, limited understanding of each other and limited opportunity.

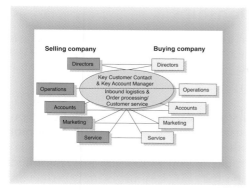

Cooperative relationships

To be regarded as a transitional stage, this stage is hard to control and likely to be losing money. It may be a necessary rite of passage, but not a stage to prolong. Key account managers are still 'out in the cold' and 'in the dark', and the supplier is not yet trusted, so the more positive feel has yet to be translated into real advantage.

Interdependent relationships

This is the stage to which suppliers developing KAM normally aspire with the right kind of customer. These relationships involve trust, much more exchange of information, proactive strategies based on a much deeper understanding of the customer and opportunities for joint strategic planning leading to substantial business growth.

Integrated relationships

These relationships are just short of a merger. Boundaries between the two companies are dissolved, since a high degree of trust eliminates the need for protection. *Integrated* relationships are few in number because they take a lot of dedicated resource, are not easy to put together, and tend to repel other customers in the same marketplace.

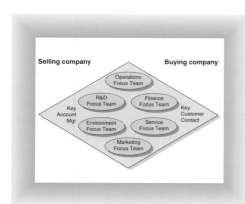

Even close relationships do not necessarily last forever, although there are some that have worked for decades. Disintegration may be driven by changes in the ownership or market position of either company, or by the supplier's failure to develop the relationship. Ultimately, the supplier has to be able to offer the customer what it wants, so a relationship, however good, cannot compensate if the supplier's product or service fails to meet the customer's needs.

CHAPTER 4 Developing key relationships

Most companies embarking on key account management (KAM) are hoping to develop their customer relationships. We hope you will do so having first decided, very carefully, which ones are suitable for development – because some are not.

But what does deciding to develop a relationship mean? How do you know where to start? Charm has very limited leverage in corporate purchasing today and, indeed, the procurement department will make sure that it does not count for much. If you want to be a key supplier, much more tangible value is expected.

In fact, the way to a customer's heart is through its business – not your business. As a minimum, the customer expects its key suppliers to understand:

- Its marketplace
- Its strategies
- What its customers want
- How it adds value in its business
- Where it makes its money.

There are no shortcuts that are likely to last, so Chapters 7 and 8 give you a systematic process to gain the deep customer understanding you need, plus a process to help you come up with strategies that add value to the customer's business. Added value (for the customer, not necessarily for you) is what gains commitment. Your company is expected to bring an ongoing stream of value propositions to the customer, and you cannot possibly do that without a real understanding of what adds value and why, where and when.

Customers classify suppliers according to the potential they have to bring value to their business, in terms of the supply-side market risk and their purchasing power. If what you have to offer is, in the customer's eyes, a commodity product delivered in a commoditized way, you are wasting your time trying to build a relationship. What would they gain? Customers, like suppliers, have a limited capacity for intimacy, and they will use what capacity they have where it gives them most advantage.

Given a strong foundation of customer understanding, relationship development can be accelerated through doing a good job of mapping the people inside the customer who matter to you, and deciding with whom you want to have your relationships. You should also decide who, in your organization, will be the 'owner' of that relationship – no key account manager can or should 'own' them all. Rather, it is the key account manager's job to encourage and build a balanced set of relationships from top to bottom of both organizations, supporting the supplier's staff in working out strategies to help their counterparts in the customer organization. Rather than responding to purely personal needs, ideally, they will be adding value to the contact's working life and area of the business, which is a more robust way to build a relationship anyway.

Many people seem to believe that relationships 'just grow', but if you have good business development strategies and adopt a process of applying them through good relationship development strategies, you should really be a winner with your customers. Try picking the features of an *interdependent* relationship and working on those alongside your business development strategies. The synergistic effect of the two together should give the relationship and its outcomes some real acceleration. Having achieved the relationship your company wants, there are a few traps to be avoided. They may seem obvious when simply stated but, sadly, they appear quite frequently:

- complacency
- lapses in integrity
- leaking profitability.

Relationships with key customers can and should be developed with purpose and with process (see Chapter 9). These relationships are too valuable and too risky to leave to any less focused approach.

The buyer perspective   CHAPTER 5

As buying companies seek new routes to competitive advantage and value for their customers, they now look to key suppliers to help them. Naturally, customers are far more likely to act according to their own perceptions and aspirations than to any view or objective that selling companies might wish to impose on them. A buying company has its own set of strategic decision support tools to help it select the suppliers who are important to the fulfilment of its aspirations.

First, a selling company needs to understand whether it has the opportunity of being a key supplier. The chances are small if it is one of many competitors, or it is in a weak position relative to the customer, or it supplies a product or service which does not contribute to the customer's critical path. If analysis reveals that this is the selling company's situation with this customer, the supplier should look elsewhere for its own key relationships or possibly reposition itself through developing its offer. It should not waste money and effort on trying to develop a relationship that is unlikely to succeed and bear fruit.

At the same time, the supplier should decide what this customer can contribute to its own strategic objectives, using the methods described in the following chapters. These methods require an in-depth understanding of the customer's situation, needs and strategies and, indeed, successful key account managers are those who really know how their customers operate and why.

Generally speaking, only if buyer and seller strategies are complementary in terms of products, their approach to business and to the relationship between them will it be possible to develop the relationship beyond a fairly simple level towards an interdependent or integrated stage. However, if all these elements are in place and closer involvement is achieved, the flow of benefits to both parties can be very exciting.

At less-developed stages of the relationship the cost of nurturing the relationship can easily outweigh the benefits. The range and extent of cost savings increase on both sides as trust between the two parties grows and barriers are reduced. In some situations, reducing risk by working with a known partner can allow costs to be cut, for example by eliminating duplication of processes. In other situations, reduction of costs may increase risk, for example by moving to just-in-time supply and eliminating buffer stocks. Clearly, reduction of costs and reduction of risks are closely linked and need to be managed jointly from a foundation of a thorough understanding of the partner and its concerns.

Trust is a mediator through which most interactions pass and activities will be interpreted. Care should be taken to manage the partner's perceptions, as reserves of trust may be crucial in carrying a supplier through any difficult patches in performance or in the relationship. In the end, powerful customers still call the shots.

CHAPTER 6   Key account profitability

Marketing as a discipline has failed during the past 60 years by concentrating on promotion rather than on developing world-class marketing strategies. The result is that in most companies, marketing has been relegated to running promotional campaigns and designing T-shirts and does not deserve a place at the high table, that is, the Board of Directors (McDonald, 2009).

The result of this sad lack of marketing leadership is the demise of many of our erstwhile famous organizations. Most of the highest earning return on investment plcs during the decade up to 1990 have gone into liquidation or were acquired in desperate circumstances, while many of the leading companies in different sectors up to 2000 also got into financial difficulties or were acquired.

At the time of writing, it is too early to complete a comparable analysis of performances of top companies for the first decade of the twenty-first century, but even a cursory glance at what happened in many of the world's top financial institutions such as Lloyds Banking Group, Lehman, Merrill Lynch, AIG, Freddie Mac *et al.,* is sufficient to indicate that things have not improved.

All of this happened against a background of three major challenges that industry was facing during this period and still faces – market maturity, globalization and customer power.

The most dramatic challenge has been the massive shift of power to customers away from suppliers. Today, customers are destroying old make/sell business models, while technology has empowered customers to have more information about their suppliers than they have about them. Meanwhile, a new wave of business metrics and new pressures from institutional shareholders to report meaningful facts about corporate performance, combined with demands from other stakeholders for exemplary corporate behaviour, have resulted in a need for strategies other than downsizing and cost-cutting as a route to increased profitability.

Never before has the need for real marketing professionalism in relation to key account management been greater.

This raises the question of what marketing is. It is a function, just like finance, with its own professional institute and body of knowledge. The challenge is to understand the needs of customers, then to formulate strategies for meeting these needs in a way that enables the company to create long-term net free cash flows which, having taken account of the associated risks, represent a financial return over and above the cost of capital, thus creating shareholder value. This strategic imperative is quantitatively measurable using the body of existing marketing knowledge and CEOs must demand of their chief marketing officers that their strategic forecasts for their key account performances are subjected to the same rigorous due diligence as other initiatives, such as acquisitions.

Some key accounts will inevitably reduce shareholder value, but providing these are managed to increase net free cash flows and to reduce risk, this is acceptable. Overall, as long as the aggregate of the net forecast value from all key accounts is positive, having taken account of the risks and the cost of capital tied up in servicing them, then it is possible to prove to the Board and to shareholders that the key account performance is creating shareholder value continuously.

Key account analysis   CHAPTER 7

Correct market definition and market segmentation are essential prerequisites of successful key account management. A market is the aggregation of all goods and services that can satisfy a particular need or set of needs. Drawing a map of how goods and services flow through the value chain helps a key account manager understand the customer's business, as well as revealing ways in which you may be able to add value as a supplier.

Market segmentation is the process of breaking a market down into smaller groups of customers who share the same or similar needs. It is important at two distinct levels. First, key accounts in one segment may have different needs from those in another segment. Second, understanding how your customer's market is segmented provides much potential for helping them to succeed.

The total process of preplanning prior to producing a strategic plan for your customer is shown in the following diagram.

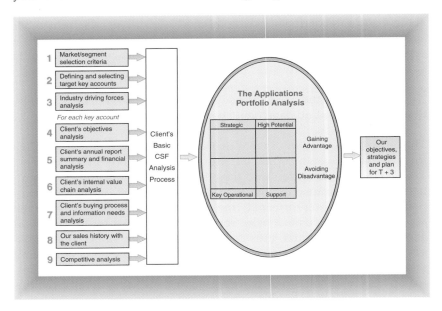

Steps 1, 2 and 3 should, ideally, be completed centrally to avoid duplication of effort by key account managers. Step 3 is about understanding in depth the forces that are being brought to bear on competitors in an industry. These are: customers, supplies, substitutes, potential entrants and, of course, industry competitors. A PEST analysis (political, economic, sociological, technological) is also an extremely useful way of understanding more about the customer's trading environment.

Each key account manager can now use this information to delve further into each customer's specific business processes. This includes understanding the customer's objectives and strategies, their financial ratios, how their business processes work, their buying processes, their sales history and their dealings with competitors.

One extremely useful vehicle for summarizing much of this is the traditional SWOT analysis (strengths, weaknesses, opportunities and threats), completed as if it were the customers themselves completing it.

All the CSFs (critical success factors) for the customer can now be sorted into those categories that merely help them to avoid disadvantage and, crucially, those that can create advantage for them, for clearly it is this latter group that will encourage a key customer to prefer dealing with you rather than with one of your competitors. You now have everything you need to approach the customer with your proposals for how you can help them increase sales, reduce costs, avoid costs or add value in other ways. They are usually so impressed that they are prepared to give you additional confidential information. You are now ready to prepare a strategic plan for the customers.

Planning for key accounts   CHAPTER 8

Marketing planning is a logical sequence of events leading to the setting of marketing objectives and the formulation of plans for achieving them. The sequence is:

1. Mission statement

2. Set corporate objectives

3. Conduct marketing object

4. Conduct SWOT (strengths, weaknesses, opportunities and threats) analyses

5. Make assumptions

6. Set marketing objectives and strategies

7. Estimate expected results

8. Identify alternative plans and mixes

9. Set the budget

10. Establish first-year implementation programmes.

The plan itself contains:

1. Mission statement

2. Financial summary

3. Market overview

4. SWOT analyses

5. Portfolio summary

6. Assumptions

7. Marketing objectives and strategies

8. Forecasts and budgets.

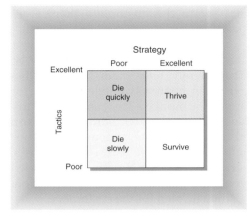

All companies need to have a longer-term (strategic) marketing view as well as a short-term (tactical) marketing operation. Often the most potent short-term tactic is the use of the salesforce. These can combine as shown in the matrix alongside.

From this it can be seen that being good at implementation of the wrong strategy can lead to a very quick death!

Exactly the same philosophy must be applied to planning for key accounts, as sophisticated customers will only build integrated relationships with suppliers who understand this business and can help them to increase sales, reduce costs, avoid costs and create value for them on a continuous basis. As this involves committing resources to such suppliers, they insist on well-researched strategic plans which are agreed jointly.

Even in cases where suppliers do not enjoy integrated relationships, it is still essential to prepare strategic plans designed to capture the inherent value planned for customers.

In this chapter a template is provided for preparing a strategic plan for a key account. Finally, a format used by customers for preparing strategies for their key suppliers is provided.

CHAPTER 9   Processes – making key account management work

Today, the delivery of superior customer value is as much about a company's business processes as it is about the core product or service, and yet implementation gets nothing like as much attention as it needs. If something has to be done more than once, and almost everything does recur, then there should be a process for doing it. A process can even be mapped for relationship development and, indeed, relationships might develop a lot faster if such a process were followed.

A process may be defined as 'A continuous and systematic series of actions performed in a definite manner directed to some end'. It should represent the most effective and efficient route to converting inputs into outputs. Suppliers' processes are generally designed to deliver to many customers in a standardized, replicable manner, which is good for costs but often not good for key accounts. Start by 'auditing' your processes to see which perform well for key accounts and which, from their point of view, are too slow, inflexible, unreliable, opaque, uninformative, uncosted and unsuitable for integration with the customer's processes.

While, at first sight, you may think that there are only a limited number of processes which impact on key customers, on closer examination you will see that there are far more. They can be divided into:

- **strategic** processes that involve senior management, to which key account managers contribute,

- **strategy realization** processes that add value to the supplier and customer through realizing the agreed strategy, with which the key account manager spends most of his or her time, and

- **operational/transactional** processes concerned with the delivery of what has been promised.

The key account manager plays a different role in each and has different levels of 'ownership' of the process. For example, key account managers need to understand operational processes and be alerted to deviations from expectations, but should not be part of the daily machinery or they will never do anything else.

Each process should be broken down into its component steps, and the role of the key account manager and others identified at each stage. This exercise demonstrates how the process works, and also builds up a picture of what their job should be.

Senior management is responsible for a number of processes in successful key account management, and if they are not aware of that at the outset, the requirement and the means to fulfil them should be identified for them at an early stage. The key account manager's role is mostly provision of information to these processes, so he or she needs to be aware of them, how they work, and what should be contributed. The strategic processes include:

- Selecting attractiveness criteria and key customers
- Managing the customer portfolio
- Considering implications of customer strategies
- Incorporating account plans in business planning
- Allocating/prioritizing resources
- Assessing and managing risk to the company
- Sponsoring key customers
- Coordinating across boundaries
- Enabling organizational learning.

Key account managers have another set of processes with which to work. 'Developing' occurs frequently in this list, because their job is to add value to both organizations by managing change:

- Analysing key accounts, developing strategy and planning
- Developing relationships with customers
- Developing business, capturing opportunities
- Selling and negotiating
- Pricing
- Developing new products
- Customizing products and service
- Managing the product mix
- Developing marketing programmes
- Developing the supply chain
- Developing transaction handling
- Providing customer training
- Developing internal relationships
- Providing information.

Below is a simplified list of operational processes, which run day in, day out. Key account managers, whether they like it or not, are held responsible by the customer for the delivery of what they have promised, so they need a process of two-way communication with operations by which they can brief operations with information they get from the customer, and operations can brief them as appropriate, about good and poor performance.

- Selling
- Processing orders
- Manufacturing/operations
- Servicing customers
- Delivering to customers
- Collecting payment.

A good deal of sales activity belongs at this operational/transactional level, and may be carried out by the field salesforce or telesales, rather than the key account manager.

CHAPTER 10 The role and requirements of key account managers

In order to determine the role of key account managers, suppliers first need to ask themselves what they intend the role of key account management (KAM) itself to be. That should decide what its 'agents', the key account managers, have to do. The objectives for KAM and the route to achieving them should be worked out in some detail.

Normally, the prime driver will be the marketplace and leading customers in it, so the company should have a view on how KAM will work from their point of view. Specifying the role that KAM plays in the supplier's strategy is of the greatest importance, and one often underestimated or misunderstood. Initially, KAM is about making reciprocated commitments to customers, but that quickly needs to be followed by fulfilment of those commitments, so companies should anticipate the issues in operations and adapt. In fact, they will find that adaptation means changing the organization and culture, as well as plans and processes.

The question then arises of 'who does what?' Obviously, key account managers are responsible for a great deal of the activity, but the company is also responsible for supporting them, by providing resources, communicating organization-wide, tackling barriers and making decisions that are beyond the remit of the individual.

The scope of the KAM initiative will highlight the breadth of the key account manager's role. At the simplest level, the key account manager has two roles: *implementation* of a business strategy with the customer, and *facilitation* of that implementation through building the relationship. The relationship is not an end in itself, but should be employed to create and implement strategies that will develop business with the customer. These two roles go hand in hand: success requires both.

Exactly how the key account manager plays these roles depends on the nature of the customer and the overall strategy allotted to it. *Streamline* customers allocated a 'manage for cash' strategy should receive different treatment from *strategic* or *star* customers, so the key account manager's role must be adjusted accordingly. The first require a tough negotiator who will need to manage costs and operations rigorously, while the latter require someone to create a vision of the future and work to make it happen.

The key account team, however, can take on part of the role. The team can apply its expertise to fulfil some elements, though some, like team leadership, cannot be separated from the key account manager. Unfortunately, key account managers' experience of team-working is often very limited, and they make poor team leaders unless they receive proper training and support for this part of their role. To make matters worse, the members of the account team normally do not report directly to the key account manager, but still remain within their function or region. Nevertheless, the key account team should be an ongoing group of people committed to the same objectives for the customer's business, not a project team or other transient group of people. Important customers expect team support and increasingly are getting it from suppliers.

Generally, there are two key account teams that exist simultaneously: the head office, cross-functional team, which is concerned with current delivery of commitments to the customer and also with how to adapt and develop new value; and the regional sales team, which supports customer strategic business units (SBUs) in the field and applies the deals agreed centrally.

Such a broad role demands a wide range of competencies and attributes. Regrettably, in many cases, suppliers have automatically appointed senior salespeople to the role without considering the competencies needed, and then found later that a substantial proportion of them do not have and are unable to acquire them. Indeed, 'selling' is a comparatively minor part of the role, and not one that should be used exclusively for determining the right people for the job.

To make appropriate appointments, suppliers should ideally start by establishing an 'inventory' of their key customers categorized into four types according to the strategy selected for them. Clearly, customers should be managed by a key account manager who is suited to applying the strategy selected for each of them, i.e. an 'entrepreneur', 'business manager', 'customer manager' or 'tactician'. Once the supplier has assembled its customer inventory, it can see how many of each of four types of key account manager are needed.

Different competencies and attributes are demanded by each of these roles, although they also have some in common. Competencies are defined as behaviours required to achieve high levels of performance, whereas attributes are more about the way people think and the values they hold, though they also affect behaviour. Attributes are harder to learn and to change. The competencies and attributes that relate to each of the four roles have been worked out, so that individuals can be profiled and matched to the role they would perform best. Such an approach can be used as a foundation for a conversation with the key account manager to discuss how he or she can develop to achieve personal and organizational objectives, now and in the future.

CHAPTER 11 Performance and rewards in KAM

Clearly, performance is a crucial issue in KAM, or any business initiative for that matter, but what kind of performance, and which or whose performance, is not at all clear in many conversations. In this chapter we look at different kinds of performance, and their measurement, divided into two types: either based on results or on behaviour, and considered at the level of the key account; the key account portfolio; and/or the key account manager.

At the level of the key account, expectations of performance need to be adapted to take account of the position of the key account in the selection/categorization matrix (see Chapter 2). A range of results of outcome-based metrics gives a more balanced view of performance than just sales revenue or even customer profitability, such as:

- Sales revenue
- Customer profitability
- KAM input
- Customer retention
- Business extension
- Risk measurement
- Shareholder value
- Customer satisfaction
- Customer attractiveness:
- Relationship.

For the key account portfolio as a whole, which can also be equated to the performance of the KAM programme, senior managers should be looking at higher level metrics such as:

- Profit
- Return on investment
- Asset value
- Risk
- Opportunity.

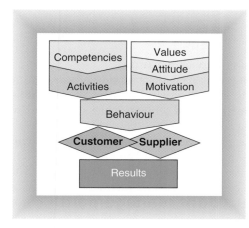

The performance of key account managers can be evaluated by the results of the accounts they manage, or by their behaviour. Suppliers are often concerned about the behaviour of their key account managers and recognize the major impact it has on the outcomes from the key account. Key account managers can reasonably be held accountable for their behaviour, but there are intervening factors originating in both the customer and supplier that also have a substantial impact on the outcomes – strategy changes, launching new services, delay in launches, product availability, etc.

Suppliers often have reward schemes traditionally aimed at incentivizing short-term sales, and there are many reasons why they need to change to align their schemes with KAM and with the performance they seek. They must be clear about the purpose and the practicalities of any scheme they devise, since most have negative as well as positive effects, and both sides should be fully understood and assessed before they commit. Sadly, the quality of line managers seems to be a serious limitation on the schemes that can be used: often the scheme is selected because managers will find it easy to apply, rather than because it will be powerful; appropriate to the individual customer and/or key account manager; and drive the right behaviours. Companies can use a variety of rewards, and may use a mix:

- Cash bonus
- Salary increase
- Recognition through non-financial rewards.

The main questions a supplier has to answer when setting up a reward scheme are 'What is to be rewarded?' and 'What is it to be rewarded with?' Then the 'architecture' is constructed from nine elements:

1. Objectives
2. Participants
3. Compensation balance
4. Performance
5. Reward
6. Rates and targets
7. Measurement
8. Timeframe
9. Budget.

Targets probably cause the biggest problems and side effects, and are the most difficult to get right, so it is worth thinking about whether they are really necessary. Indeed, reward scheme issues can be so difficult that it is worth thinking about whether key account managers should have a reward scheme – most of the rest of the company works without one, after all.

CHAPTER 12 Organizing for key account management

Key account management (KAM) is essentially a boundary-crossing initiative. Many of the benefits accrue from crossing boundaries, whether they are internal ones or those in the customer's organization.

- More interesting and powerful propositions with hard-to-match competitive advantage can be achieved by integrating offers from different parts of the supplier organization.

- Substantial growth can be won by developing business with new parts of the customer's organization.

Companies need a clear organizational structure, understandably, especially as they become bigger and more complex, but the structure should be used positively to enact the company's strategy, not to frustrate it. Any structure has its advantages and disadvantages, which can be offset by a genuine will to work across the structure, whatever it may be. Unfortunately, structures and their boundaries are often reinforced by a culture of ownership and defence of a territorial power base, which is not helpful in KAM. Suppliers need to be aware of how the structure can operate to produce 'blind spots', such as an inability to aggregate customer information that will obscure the identity of potential key customers; the ways in which they are organized; and how they make their decisions.

The supplier's structure is not the only consideration in deciding how to organize for KAM. Obviously, the customer's structure must be taken into account as well. For example, whether the supplier is a global or local organization, and whether its customer is global or local, produces a number of different forms of KAM.

In a traditional, country-based organization, the key account manager and hence the customer is several layers away from the top of the company, so communicating their strategies and gaining attention for their needs at a high level is very difficult, and not what key customers expect if they have been invited to participate in a strategic relationship. This form of organization also makes the management of key customers as a portfolio more or less impossible. In fact, if there is no clear process which brings them together in the same framework and authorizes the same person or people to make decisions about them, then portfolio management is not happening.

The ultimate form of organization for KAM is a central unit which has its own resources, with a director of key accounts who reports direct to the main Board rather than a national or divisional Board. Key account managers in a central unit should have the authority to make central or global deals, albeit in consultation and with a defined approval process. In all forms of organization, however, the local company or region will have to support and service the deal on the ground, so it is always important that they back it. Successful suppliers employ various mechanisms to deal with this tricky issue.

In fact, it is the company's targets that are often responsible for many of the conflicts that arise between different parts of the organization. Suppliers that can properly align their targets will avoid many of the problems frequently encountered in KAM, just by resolving that single issue.

CHAPTER 13   Transitioning to KAM

KAM is not an easy or simple business initiative: it involves extensive organizational and cultural change, and will undoubtedly take time to implement and overcome the inevitable resistance. However, strong internal and external factors, particularly customer demand or customer defection, drive suppliers to adopt the approach. Bringing all key stakeholders in the company to the same understanding of what KAM is and what it is not constitutes an important first step, because many companies think that they are already doing KAM when, in fact, it is account management or even thinly disguised selling in reality.

Working with experienced practitioners in large companies, we identified five stages of KAM development, culminating in best practice:

A. Scoping KAM

B. Introducing KAM

C. Embedding KAM

D. Optimizing value

E. Best practice KAM

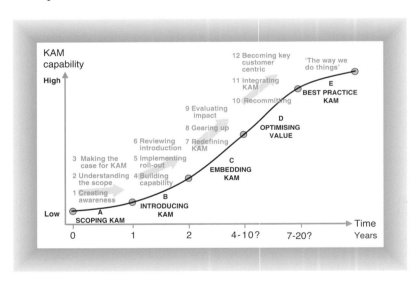

This chapter describes the first four phases, since the rest of the book is focused on best practice. In each phase, decisions and action will be required around:

● Strategy and planning

● Organization and people

● Processes

In Phase A, Scoping KAM, the supplier needs a champion to research KAM and what it would look like in the company. The champion appoints a team, if possible, to help with the considerable amount of work that it takes to collect the information, especially from external sources, and to construct a business case for KAM. The case will never be as strong as the company would like, because it has to cover a wide-ranging initiative whose extent is uncertain, and predict outcomes beyond five years. Nevertheless, the more issues that are brought to the surface at this point, the fewer unpleasant surprises the company will get. For example, adopters should know that KAM regularly takes two years to introduce and considerably longer to become really operational, although small and medium companies with very strong commitment and dedication to the change may be able to move faster.

Phase B, Introducing KAM, can be a chaotic period, which can be mitigated by anticipation and coordination which would prevent wasted costs; premature and unsupported promises to customers; and internal confusion and non-cooperation. Building capability, particularly in key account managers, needs to occur neither too early nor too late, but be closely followed by launch and roll-out. Suppliers often make the serious mistake of appointing all their senior salespeople as key account managers, only to discover the pain of unpicking that decision later when they realize that a majority will not make the grade. KAM teams should also be appointed at this stage: too many companies delay this commitment, resulting in disappointed and even cynical customers.

Phase C is where the company really begins to operate KAM. It should learn from the launch and make early adjustments where necessary, especially working on the quality of some of the elements that were kicked off during introduction, but are not yet really fit for purpose. For example, strategic account plans should have been produced in Phase B but, typically, they are incomplete, lack explicit strategies, are operationally focused and only cover a one-year period at this stage. They should be upgraded to a three-year view with a strong push towards better insight, more strategic content and more clarity on resource requirement. Key account selection and categorization criteria should also be improved to ensure that they identify responsive and productive customers, not just large ones. Process development becomes a major focus, to operationalize KAM as far as possible without removing the flexibility and adaptability that KAM also requires.

Arrival at Phase D, Optimizing value, can be assessed by a quick litmus test for the company and another for key account managers. At this point the supplier can truly be said to be operating KAM, but there are still developments which will make the company genuinely key customer centric, and comfortable in so doing. Phase C should include a thorough review of the way the company operates KAM and the opportunities for gaining even more from the approach: some companies become stuck in their suboptimal ways and are overtaken by others. For example, all senior managers, not just sales and commercial, should vocally and visibly recommit to KAM and proactively explore ways in which their functions can better serve key customers, rather than trying to force KAM to adapt to functional priorities.

Eventually, when the supplier's worst fears about working more closely with key customers have proved unfounded, and it has successfully negotiated riskier areas and gained positive outcomes, the company can embark on making the deeper changes it was unwilling to implement earlier.

With confidence in its own experience of KAM, suppliers can achieve best practice KAM through whole-heartedly embracing the concept of the importance of key customers.

Now you should have a good idea of the whole content of the book, either to whet your appetite before reading it, or to remind yourself of the entirety of what you have just read in much greater depth. Try reading it again at a later date.

Mini-cases

The following mini-cases are offered to readers as a way of considering just some of the complex issues that face all organizations who are serious in their intentions to build profitable and lasting relationships with customers. Please 'role-play' the characters in the mini-cases, but also consider what would happen in your company if it were faced with the situation described, and how you think your customer would react. We have also included some case studies from the customer's point of view, which may be used as training scenarios for 'boundary spanning'.

Each of these mini-cases is based on real cases, but the names and some of the circumstances have been changed. Any name similarity with existing companies or people is entirely accidental and unintended.

We have included a brief discussion at the end of each mini-case. We stress that these are not answers, as there is never a perfect answer to any problem in life. Please compare our thoughts with your own, and discuss them with colleagues, as this is the best way to learn.

These mini-cases are reproduced with kind permission from Beth Rogers, author of *Rethinking Sales Management* (published by Wiley and Son, Chichester).

Case 1 – Diversification dilemma

SNT, a medium-sized IT services provider, implemented a 'turnkey' information systems solution for a major government department five years ago, which they continue to support. Relationships between the Board of SNT and the senior professionals in the department are very positive. However, the key account manager absorbs most of the stress inherent in the business relationship. He has had to mediate in disagreements between SNT and government technical staff on a few occasions when the system has not met user expectations. In addition, the system now needs a major upgrade, which has been delayed because of budget constraints. The perceptions of users are that the SNT system is creaking at the seams and SNT are not responding to their needs to squeeze more out of it.

The government has now decided that it wants to contract out all the IS operations of this department, which will mean any bidder taking on all the civil service technical staff in the unit, as well as being given the challenge of upgrading the system and keeping it up to date. The opportunity will be advertised in the *European Journal* and subject to all the usual public sector tender approval procedures, designed to ensure fairness and objectivity.

As an existing supplier, SNT are invited by the senior civil servants in the department to a meeting, to be informed of the new situation (the grapevine had already got to the key account manager). The meeting involves the managing director and the key account manager from SNT, and, from the customer, the head of department and head of IT (the latter will probably be transferred to the employment of whoever wins the bid). Officially, the department staff are only one small part of the decision-making procedure for the new contract, but they can influence the brief. Meanwhile, SNT have concerns about whether it is strategically appropriate for them to bid for an 'outsourcing' contract, and whether they can compete with big international players in public sector outsourcing. However, they do not really want to lose this flag-ship customer . . .

How should they conduct the meeting?

What did they decide to do as a result of it?

SNT have clearly had problems integrating their operations with the customer's, and have not developed the network of contacts seen at the cooperative-KAM stage. Consequently, they are starting at a disadvantage. Nevertheless, at the meeting, both representatives from SNT should show real enthusiasm for the proposal and should act as if they were extremely keen to proceed with this outsourcing opportunity, and put the relationship on a new footing. The objective should be to collect as much information as possible about overheads, including salaries, terms and conditions, and details of all fixed and variable costs. Crucial to any potential bid will be a deep understanding of all the tasks undertaken by the customer's information systems department. The purpose of this is to establish whether there is likely to be sufficient margin in such a contract to warrant starting what will, in effect, be a new business venture.

Having done these calculations, the company should decide how it is going to respond to the trend towards outsourcing of information systems work. There are three options:

1. Ignore it, and continue to be a software house

2. Form alliances with outsourcing specialists

3. Diversify into outsourcing.

In order to be an outsourcing company or even an alliance partner of one, SNT would have to invest a great deal in relationship building in and understanding of how to manage in different company cultures.

In the event, even the 'one-off' opportunity was considered to be such a radical departure from SNT's core business that they decided to forego the opportunity. They worked with the large consultancy that won the bid, and were eventually taken over by them.

Case 2 – Taking a key account for granted

Product design consultancy EPP was spun off from a large manufacturing conglomerate six years ago. The former parent, GLOSS, is still the dominant account in the EPP portfolio, representing 40 per cent of business.

Old loyalties are beginning to break down. The financial controller of GLOSS has recently complained to the purchasing director that he has had to allocate senior staff to spend days sorting out EPP invoices. Apart from being arithmetically inaccurate, which is just pure sloppiness, they are presented in a way which makes it very difficult for people approving the invoices to reconcile them to services that they know have been received.

The purchasing director himself is aggravated because he perceives that the new key account manager his senior buyer is dealing with is inexperienced in comparison with his predecessor, and cannot always make decisions without referral to the sales director. There is no doubt that the services of EPP are first class and good value, and he does not want to seek an alternative supplier. However, the company is making itself difficult to deal with, and he wants to take a relatively hard line to ensure that they improve.

He decided to request a one-to-one meeting with the sales director, but discovers that he is on holiday. The purchasing director is in no mood to wait, but refuses the offer made by the sales director's PA of a meeting with the key account manager. He does not say so, but he does not believe that the key account manager could initiate the changes he wants.

The sales director's PA informs the key account manager for GLOSS that the purchasing director has tried to contact the sales director. The key account manager has had little contact with the purchasing director, as his main contact is the senior buyer.

> **What should he do to resolve the immediate need to identify the purchasing director's concerns?**
>
> **What ought to be done in the long term to improve relationships between EPP and GLOSS?**

EPP has obviously made one of the cardinal mistakes in key account management. Putting a comparatively junior manager into such a pivotal key account in the mistaken belief that old loyalties will see the relationship through is irresponsible in the extreme. Major accounts must know that their business is in the hands of a senior person who can take decisions as and when necessary.

In this particular case, no doubt EPP's key account manager for GLOSS by now understands some of the reasons for the purchasing director's concern. His pressing task must be to reassure GLOSS, probably by getting another EPP director to visit the purchasing director immediately, so that the operational concerns may be attended to as a matter of urgency. This will at least allay fears until the return of the sales director. The more difficult issue concerning the nature of the relationship and representation issues can then be tackled by EPP. Clearly, however, the status of the key account manager for GLOSS needs to be raised.

Besides this, there is a need for involvement of more EPP staff to resolve process issues. For example, a focus team of EPP sales ledger and GLOSS bought ledger staff must be set up to sort out the invoicing problems. The key account manager must ask the sales director to support him and apply pressure to other functional managers to support such initiatives. The sales director must also lobby the managing director to ensure that the key account manager has a permanent team of named functional professionals who will have some objectives placed on them related to his account. Those objectives must be set by the key account manager, so that he has authority to get things done for the customer.

There are some other issues that you might have picked up:

- Is it prudent to have one dominant customer? Should EPP be doing more to diversify their customer portfolio?

- Does the sales director have a hidden agenda to withdraw resource from GLOSS because their customer profitability is dropping? Is this why they have a less experienced key account manager?

- Have GLOSS tested the market since EPP were spun off? What is the purchasing strategy here?

(You may think that this case is far-fetched, but it is based on a real situation!)

Case 3 – Demanding flexibility

All Components PLC is a key target for Special Raw Materials Limited. Although they are not the biggest company of their type, since they have been dealing with Japanese motor companies in the UK, All Components have been looking to replicate the partnership agreements they enjoy with customers with their critical suppliers. This means that some suppliers will be assured of 100 per cent of their business for five years at a time (assuming excellent performance). All

Components declaration of interest in 100 per cent partnerships has meant considerable competition among the suppliers who might be eligible.

A key account manager, Damon Riley, was appointed two years ago, and he has worked very hard, at significant cost to SRML, to convince All Components that they would be their best partner for strategic raw materials. The effort included pilot deliveries at special prices which demonstrated the quality of SRML products. Now, 18 months later, the big opportunity to gain 100 per cent of All Components' business is on the table.

However, All Components are looking for terms and conditions which are not common in the business. For example, they want to be able to choose their own key account team, including technicians, they want SRML to manage the raw materials stocks on a consignment basis, and they want up to 40 success criteria to govern the ongoing relationship.

They also want extended credit from SRML. Damon quickly assures them that consignment stock and their 40 success criteria are acceptable. He tells All Components that he must take their other requests to the Board. SRML takes equal opportunities very seriously, and the Board would be worried about allowing a customer to choose their own key account team. While accepting that a good personality fit is important, normally team members would be chosen by SRML on the basis of their career development, not a customer's preference. Changes would only be made if a team member made a mistake which caused serious customer discontent.

SRML is also reluctant to extend more than 30 days' credit, even to the most strategic of customers, due to effect on cash flow and the cost of working capital.

Of course, the Board will be expecting Damon to make a recommendation.

What will Damon's recommendation be?

Damon recommends to the Board that SRML offer All Components a team somewhat more highly skilled and experienced than the account might expect. Their request to choose the team might well come from insecurity, and the offer of a top team should diffuse it. If the team are introduced to their opposite numbers by an SRML director at a social event, this will be an opportunity to build up mutual liking and respect with their opposite numbers, and will show high level endorsement of the people chosen for the account.

On the credit issue, SRML could hide behind proposed UK legislation to ensure prompt payment, although the partnership is also likely to operate in countries where extended credit is not only legal, but business as usual. An alternative would be to make an exception, provided interest were paid. Nevertheless, since the volume of business that could flow from the partnership is substantial, All Components would doubtless be disappointed with such a compromise. Damon recommends that 60 days' credit is formally agreed with them for an initial 12-month period. SRML should reserve the right in future years to vary credit terms in line with exceptional economic conditions or local legislation.

He also recommends, assuming his recommendations are acceptable to the Board and to the prospect, that Board members become involved in the formal signing of the partnership agreement with directors of All Components. Assuming it is agreeable to both companies, the trade press could be invited. Both companies would gain favourable publicity for their flexible, partnership approach.

Case 4 – Learning to look a gift horse in the mouth

Jo Young, who works for Punch Financial Services, is key account manager for Clover Inc., an innovative fertilizer company. Punch is well known for its coordinated approach to customers' risk management – key account teams consist of a variety of specialist underwriters.

She is approached by Brian Dale, the finance officer of a very large local government authority. He has heard about Punch, and Jo herself, from someone he knows at the golf club who was at university with her. His authority has a myriad of suppliers of financial services, and he would like to start consolidating with fewer suppliers as contracts come up for renewal. Because of public procurement procedures, he cannot promise a full partnership, and he makes it clear to Jo that Punch must compete with incumbent suppliers on price.

Jo listens politely, thanks the finance officer for his interest, and says she will come back to him to suggest how they might proceed.

Punch operates very proactive prospect targeting, and one of the key criteria used is that companies of strategic interest to Punch are likely to be in high risk businesses. Punch has never done any work in central or local government. Although the company has never turned 'bluebird' business away in the past, Jo is not entirely sure that it would do either party any good to do business on a transactional basis. The local government authority would never be 'key' to Punch, whereas it might be 'key' to another financial services company.

Then she considers that the nature of the public sector has changed significantly in recent years, and there are new opportunities for shared risk. Perhaps Punch ought to rethink its aversion to public sector business?

What does she decide to do?

It is always very flattering to know that a contact has recommended you to another organization, and instinctively we want to do a good job for the person who is approaching you on this basis. Jo could treat this as a test case, to explore whether opportunities really do exist for building some kind of profitable partnership with public sector organizations.

However, difficult choices do have to be made in key account management. Punch cannot afford to be all things to all people, and must be pragmatic. This local government authority is likely to be in the bottom right hand box of Punch's account portfolio matrix. The reason is that the profit opportunities are likely to be minimal, and Punch's strengths compared to others are also likely to be minimal. While Jo might indeed want to do a good job for Brian Dale, he is working in a political environment where his professional judgement could be overruled. Learning the formal and informal decision-making structure of a big local authority would be a major challenge.

Jo decides to supply the minimum information necessary to ensure Punch is included on the tender list. If invited to tender, she would submit a standard proposal, but would make no allowances for Brian's warnings on price. In fact, she would probably have to include a substantial contingency to compensate for the risk to Punch of taking on non-core business. This means that she keeps faith with Brian and the contact who recommended her, while also keeping faith with Punch. In the unlikely event of the tender being successful, the business would be treated as incremental and transactional, a one-off. It could generate useful cash for Punch, without having to tie up too many scarce resources chasing low margin business. Punch has a special department to look after tactical business.

Had an invitation to tender been received without the personal contact and apparent keenness of the finance officer, Jo would definitely have decided not to submit a proposal.

The situation would have been quite different had it been a food or chemical company (i.e. high risk). Punch would have seen an opportunity for at least a 20-year relationship and would have invested considerable resource and effort into learning about the prospect and their risk management challenges. They would have ensured a highly competitive, value-based proposal was presented to them.

Case 5 – A family feud

LogFast is a division of logistics conglomerate Singh & West. The company distributes extremely high volumes of low value products for mail order company XMT. XMT is exceedingly entrepreneurial in style, which has caused one or two culture clashes with the more conservative LogFast. However, the relationship seems to thrive on the challenge, and both supplier and customer demonstrate significant commitment to each other and work very closely together. Focus teams involving personnel at all levels from both companies have been formed to examine ways in which mutual cost reduction and quality improvement can be achieved.

Singh & West has a number of other divisions. One (HighShift) is the market leader in the distribution of high value goods.

XMT deals in high value products as well as low value products, although volumes of high value products are quite low. The distribution director of XMT wants to do business with HighShift on the same basis as LogFast.

To date, LogFast's key account manager has been avoiding the issue, as the internal rivalry between LogFast and HighShift within Singh & West is not something he particularly wants to, or is able to, explain. The sales director of LogFast has been pleading with his counterpart in HighShift to join the very positive business relationship they have with XMT, but without success.

The distribution director of XMT is getting impatient, and the key account manager and sales director of LogFast know that they have to make a case to the main Board of Singh & West. Even if they succeed, the sales director of HighShift might be infuriated and obstructive, which might not help the customer.

What case do they make, and what happens next?

This is a fairly typical problem that customers have with their suppliers. Indeed, what emerged clearly from our research was that the customer is intolerant of internal conflict within the supplying organization, so this issue needs to be resolved quickly.

It is clear that Singh & West run the risk of losing the XMT business unless their own group's internal divisions can be resolved.

The issue has to be escalated to Board level in a purely objective way. A cost/benefit analysis is required, so that no one is in any doubt how much business will be lost unless HighShift cooperates with LogFast. Furthermore, the same document should raise the general issue of how the group should deal with customers requiring one policy.

One possible solution would be the creation of a key accounts division, which can be seen as independent of the functional divisions. Of course, key account team members would still have to be drawn from other divisions. They must have objectives placed on them which relate to achievement for the key account. In practice, this often leads to the erosion of divisional 'tribal' rivalries, which delivers benefits for the customers and the company overall.

The situation described here can be encountered as companies internationalize their account management, as well as in extensions across divisions. Country managers may not see the benefit of engaging in global contracts that include customized service levels and pricing negotiated beyond their control. However, global account managers have frequently opened the door to high levels of business for subsidiaries that they would not otherwise have got. Company power struggles will always exist. Account managers have to be wise about dealing with internal political situations, but senior managers must also back them up, to ensure that the company achieves its growth objectives and strategic customers are satisfied.

Case 6 – Practise what you preach

The VP sales of Workwise Uniforms has just had a meeting with the key account manager for their top client and her identified successor, who announced that they were both leaving to join a top competitor.

They complained about lack of status and authority, a situation which the VP sales has known about for some time, but has been unable to convince the chief operating officer that key account managers and key account teams should be more empowered. (He also knew that the key account manager had been disappointed because the market position of her client had slipped from number one in their sector to number three, and she had wanted him to move her on to a client on the way up their league. This the chief operating officer had also blocked because of her popularity with the company's top account.)

The irony is that Workwise Uniforms encourage empowerment, among other positive employment practices, in their clients. It would be hugely embarrassing if their competitor was able to boast about the defection of key staff because Workwise did not practise what it preached. It was the sort of story that certain business magazines might be delighted to get their hands on.

Needless to say, the VP sales would also have to deal with the client. The top decision makers would be devastated to lose not only their popular key account manager, but the team member who had been presented to them as her eventual successor. It would be difficult to match someone else to their exacting requirements at short notice.

What should the VP sales do next?

The VP sales has two issues to address here. First, there is the immediate problem of the defection of the key account manager and her No. 2. Here, the only solution would appear to be for the VP sales to take on the account personally until staff can be recruited to replace them. He should also be totally honest with the client, explaining what has gone wrong and informing them that any future key account manager will be given more reassurance about their status and authority.

The second issue is, of course, the issue of empowerment generally in Workwise. They need to establish general principles, a framework for decision making within the company. Consultation should take place with staff and key accounts to find an optimum solution to which they will provide all-round satisfaction.

Case 7 – Jealous partners

Ideally, Jellox SA would like to ensure that their partnership suppliers do not work with their competitors. However, since competition law precludes them from being able to enforce such a demand, they have placed on their suppliers the burden of convincing them that no possible cross-fertilization can take place between what they do for Jellox and what they do for their top rival, NV Inc.

How should the suppliers respond?

As has been explained, competition law in the UK and Europe states that anything offered to one customer by a supplier must theoretically be offered to all. Key account strategy offers the opportunity to tailor products and processes so closely to an individual customer that no key account would get the same formula. They would get what offers them best value.

Professional services companies faced with this challenge from customers are careful to ensure that key account teams are specific to particular customers. Confidentiality agreements are signed, which include the pledge that no member of the designated team will work in the competitor's team, even for a certain period after their duties have changed. However, in other sectors, such as process manufacturing, the customer's demand would be unreasonable, as operationally most staff have to work on most orders. Confidentiality could be ensured at a strategic level, so that account managers were specific to major customers, and project teams on activities such as joint product development were also specifically assigned to them.

Case 8 – Healing wounds

Winston James is the Technical Manager for HighRisk Products. The company has just installed new processes and received training from ProcessMaster. While the new processes are still parallel running with the old, something goes terribly wrong with them. The operatives claim that they have been following ProcessMaster instructions to the letter.

The failure attracts top management attention. Winston calls in the consultant who delivered the training, who, in front of the human resources director, accuses the operatives of sabotaging the new processes because of their resistance to change. Winston, fuming, asks her to leave the premises and declares that the purchasing director will have to sort out some compensation with the key account manager while he concentrates on making sure that the customers of HighRisk Products get what they have ordered using the old processes. However, he is worried that the human resources director might just have seen some justification for the accusation of resistance to change.

A large post-mortem meeting is called, involving all interested parties from HighRisk and ProcessMaster. Meanwhile, Winston works all the hours he can to keep products flowing to customers while also finding out more about the failure of the new processes. He concludes that there had been flaws in the delivery of the training, but it also seems to be the case that one or two 'opinion leaders' on the shopfloor have been fomenting discontent.

Winston knows that, whatever the outcome of the meeting with ProcessMaster, he has a huge problem on his hands restoring the morale and motivation of the workforce, but it is one that he feels very unwilling to admit to anyone else.

What happens at the meeting?

What *does not* happen is the trainer repeating her accusations, and there is no 'banging of the table' which will ensure ProcessMaster is blacklisted forever more . . .

What *does* happen is that the key account manager of ProcessMaster has to be empowered to offer compensation and training alternatives. He needs to secure the opportunity to talk to the HighRisk workers to find out what their problems are, and try to arrange more training for them. He can probably second-guess Winston's anxiety, and needs to ensure that technical expertise is available to him full-time to offer support and make sure that he comes up smelling of roses!

The directors of HighRisk Products know that they need the new processes, and are unlikely to chuck ProcessMaster off-site, unless they are offensive. If they demonstrate appropriate humility and a genuine desire to put things right, they are likely to be given the chance to do so.

Ironically, it is often in the context of putting problems right that stronger relationships can be forged between suppliers and customers. Problem accounts have been transformed into reference accounts!

Case 9 – Pride comes before a fall

John Uplook, general manager of 234 Services Europe, a market leader in office services, thinks that they have a very good record on key account management. In fact, he thinks that they are masters of best practice in key account management.

One of 234's prize accounts is Telephony International. The managing director of Telephony International, Rod Lines, has appeared in 234's national magazine advertisements, praising their services. Privately, however, he is irritated by what he perceives as a cultural fault – their market leader arrogance – and a tendency to quote prices which they then lower when he challenges them.

The public closeness of 234 and Telephony has not stopped 234's nearest rival, Green and White Limited, from targeting Telephony International, and Rod Lines in particular. They are offering him better prices first time, without time-consuming negotiation. They display eagerness for his business, rather than condescension, and their products are just as good. Rod feels obliged to let them pitch for his business, but he does not welcome the hassle that changing supplier would cause. He would prefer 234 to be more like Green and White in their approach. He knows that the culture of 234 comes directly down to the key account teams from the very macho general manager.

> **What can he do, short of changing supplier, to convince John Uplook that he ought to change?**

The first action that Rod Lines should take is a thorough analysis of the value that his company receives from 234, rather than concentrating solely on price. If the same value can be achieved from Green and White at a lower price, then it is his duty to change suppliers. Before doing this, however, he should insist on a bid from both companies for a 100% partnership arrangement, not to help him decide on price, but to help him decide on value.

If he really prefers to keep 234 from doing this, he should have a frank meeting with 234 on the basis of total value and the nature of the desired relationship. In this case, he was reassured that they would respond to his requirements.

If, after this, he had still been unsure about 234's cultural capability to adopt a partnership approach, he would have had two options:

- Switch 100 per cent to Green and White
- Manage the status quo.

Many purchasing decision makers feel the need to ensure some degree of competition for their business, because they associate risks with single sourcing, such as the complacency of the supplier.

Case 10 – Going global

XYZ Global have announced to the world their plans to reduce their lines to a few global brands and to reduce their supplier base from

500 000 to 50 000. All existing suppliers have to bid for the global business. ION Services will no longer be able to serve XYZ separately in the UK, Belgium, Brazil and the USA. ION has no problem in demonstrating a presence in all the countries of the world that XYZ operates, but whether they can offer a consistent standard of service globally is quite another matter.

ION has to be a front-runner for XYZ's property services, they already have a majority share by being their supplier in four out of the 20 countries in which they have major plants. Most of the competitors do not have offices in other countries, just alliances with other independents.

XYZ have given their potential suppliers three years to build up to the global bid. ION has to win. The company might not stand the shock of losing a key account in four countries at once. Apart from that, it is obvious that achieving the global coordination required by XYZ will stand them in good stead for winning business with other global companies.

What sort of plan do ION's strategists start to put into place?

This is a problem faced by most global suppliers today, as more and more of their global customers seek to reduce the complexity of decentralized, multi-supplier contracts.

Fortunately, ION have all the pieces already in place. What ION must do is call a meeting of subsidiary principals and relevant headquarters personnel to deliver a strategy for global key account management, as many of their potential problems will stem from ethnocentric attitudes in the subsidiaries. The authors ran such a conference for a decentralized, country-based supplier of services, using a business game to test out the decisions which would be made by delegates in respect of a hypothetical global key account. The results were surprising to all and hammered home to all the need to subjugate local interests to the good of the global account. More importantly, it changed attitudes and paved the way for constructive teamwork across national organizations to support global customers.

ION have to address the following challenges:

- Process excellence
- Cross-cultural management
- Thorough and effective communications, internally and externally
- Attention to detail over a huge scope of work
- Ensuring the whole team can see the whole picture (there may be hundreds of people devoted to a key account worldwide).

Case 11 – The power of persistence

Jeanne Étoile, general manager of Étoile Consulting, has just awarded the trophies in the annual Étoile & Clients' doubles tennis tournament. She has been extremely proud to see the Étoile/customer doubles teams playing together – a mirror of the way her company works together with clients. It was particularly pleasing this year to see 26 nationalities represented in the tournament.

Étoile spends her next day in the office thinking deeply. She is recognized as the best practitioner of key account management in its sector. The company could be finished if it lost that accolade.

How can Étoile keep up the momentum?

Étoile needs to keep abreast of developments in their industry and continuously to seek to provide solutions which provide superior value to their clients. Apart from this, however, Étoile could join a Best Practice Key Account Management Benchmarking Club at one of the leading postgraduate business schools such as Cranfield. This way Étoile will always be at the leading edge of key account management best practice.

The company will also invest effort in the following activities:

● Process integration

● Continuous communication with clients in between projects

● Recruiting specialist skills

● Strong marketing communications and promotion.

Case 12 – The frustrations of a 'basic' relationship

Peter Piper has been the account manager for DeepDiscount Retail Stores for three years. DeepDiscount keep all suppliers of goods and services at arm's length. All business is bid for on a one-off basis. Social invitations from suppliers are rebuffed. Account managers are very unlikely to meet a purchasing manager regularly, let alone a decision maker in another department.

Peter works for Contract Employees Limited. The company has been successful in regularly supplying temporary staff to DeepDiscount's warehouse. Recently, a few vacancies were filled by another agency, who undercut Contract Employees' price. In fact, the warehouse manager was furious with purchasing because the staff supplied by the competitor were incompetent.

Peter is keen to persuade his managing director to take DeepDiscount out of his portfolio and give the company to a junior account manager.

Then word gets back to Peter from one of the temps who had done an assignment at DeepDiscount about the dispute between the warehouse manager and purchasing.

Should it change his mind?

This knowledge should probably not change Peter's mind. Deep-Discount is clearly not the kind of key account with which a value-creating relationship can be built. It would be in the bottom right hand box of the account portfolio matrix. There isn't much potential for profit growth here and the relationship is poor. Accordingly, the relationship should remain transactional, with each transaction done on the basis of generating cash.

Peter may decide to stay just long enough to discover if the warehouse manager wins his argument with purchasing and gains higher level support for preferring Contract Employees Limited. This could establish a special status for CEL within the account which might enable the account to be reclassified in the account portfolio matrix. Peter could then move on to his next account having achieved some progress in difficult circumstances. The reclassification of the account would influence the choice of the skills required in the new account manager.

Case 13 – Surviving market testing

Components GmbH has won a contract to supply newly developed sealants to a European manufacturing consortium, KFG. They are the only supplier of these parts to KFG. The entry costs were high, due to the unique customer requirements, but it is now unlikely that any competitor could follow. The sealants are performing very well, and Components GmbH has the opportunity to demonstrate more of its products. More importantly, the customer is very interested in the company's keenness to set problem-solving targets, to be jointly addressed and met.

In the course of reviewing how the sealants are working, the Components GmbH account manager has uncovered one of KFG's operational problems – an expensive, inefficient and dangerous cleaning method has to be changed. Components GmbH have recently acquired a services company which has just the right expertise to solve the problem. He recommends their high technology cleaning system, which fulfils all the customer's needs.

KFG insist that they must search the Internet for alternative suppliers and conduct an online reverse auction.

How can both parties proceed?

It is not clear why KFG need to run an online auction, but if it is company policy then they must do it, and they must be very specific about their requirements. They can of course encourage Components GmbH to respond.

Components GmbH need to proceed as follows:

- Use their special expertise to influence the specification
- Use their existing knowledge of KFG to ensure they meet all the common requirements
- Provide extra, convincing information and analysis which should establish edge over any other tenders submitted
- Establish a price floor and stick to it – doing the job unprofitably is not an option.

Many selling companies with a partnership approach are averse to customers going out to tender in this way. Nevertheless, they must remember that the customer will be required to market test their performance from time to time, and, if they truly are offering the best solution, an objective tendering process should recognize it.

Case 14 – Disaster recovery

You are the key account manager for customer XAN. XAN have ordered 100 per cent of their requirement of an essential raw material (Zippo) from your company (SZM) for some years. The business is moderately attractive to SZM. XAN's enthusiasm for SZM is, unfortunately, taken for granted.

XAN has recently taken over QES. The purchasing manager of XAN has discovered that one of your colleagues has been giving QES a lower price than he has been getting. You try to retrieve the situation, but the financial director of your company blocks the lower price and compensation package that you propose. The purchasing manager of XAN, who is now the chief executive of the merged group, punishes you by giving 20 per cent of the business for Zippo to your main competitor (BLK). He has also told you that he has discovered that BLK have a new product that he wants to pilot.

Despite everything, communications with the ex-purchasing manager (now chief executive) are still cordial. The new purchasing manager is more sceptical. You are determined to rescue the situation.

What steps are you going to take to re-establish the company as a 'partnership' supplier to the XAN/QES Group?

First, the key account manager, with the key account team, should review the positioning of the account in the relational development model and consider the high risk of disintegration. The candidate should identify 'breach of trust' and 'complacency' as reasons for disintegration. They should also identify that there were aspects of 'delusion' about the relationship – the strategic intent of seller and buyer were not aligned. XAN thought they had a partnership, but the breach of trust on price and the attitude of the financial director indicates that, corporately, SZM was not managing the account as an 'interdependent' partner.

Second, the key account manager must re-examine the positioning of XAN/QES in the customer portfolio analysis. The indications are that the attractiveness of XAN and QES together is greater than XAN alone. Unfortunately, the customer's perceptions of SZM versus the competition have deteriorated, and investment will be required to restore their confidence. So, the candidate might describe the movement of the account from the 'maintain' box to 'selectively invest'.

Third, if communications are still cordial, the customer will probably be willing to explain what they want SZM to do. The key account manager must prepare a strong case for the SZM chief executive to meet the XAN/QES chief executive to hear his views. If SZM is committed to key account management and XAN/QES is strategic to them, the chief executive must put his commitment behind a joint strategic plan to jointly innovate and add value in the supply chain.

Give yourself extra marks for suggesting a reconfiguration of the value that SZM is delivering to XAN/QES to get away from directly comparable prices; such as managing stock for the customer, managing the use of the product in the customer's processes, reducing quantity needed by improving quality, etc.

Case 15 – Promise unfulfilled

RDT is a glamorous brand name in fast food catering, and is regarded by your company (UYT) as a key account. It has a high profile and commands management attention. The company has bought some of its equipment from you in some European markets, but at very low prices. The promise to open the door for global supply has never been fulfilled.

You have just found out that RDT is losing market leadership and is planning to close hundreds of branches worldwide. The expected announcement is causing panic in the industry, and a trade journalist tells you that she expects all companies to be running around looking for lower grade equipment.

You are the key account manager for RDT. How do you respond?

RDT's intentions towards UYT are 'basic', since they promised wider scope in return for lower prices and never delivered. Therefore RDT ought to be managed in a tactical way. Its elevation to 'key account' has more to do with status than profit potential.

The key account manager would check any rumour about his or her account. He or she would usually check with the customer if the relationship is strong, but in this case, checking with industry sources might be more successful. Attention should then turn to the customer portfolio matrix. RDT's position should be reassessed on the basis of a decline in status and volume potential. The account is clearly less attractive than originally thought. The key account manager should be proposing a 'demotion' of the account to 'maintain' or 'manage for cash'. Candidates should present the arguments they would use to justify that to the Board of UYT and members of the key account team.

Give yourself extra marks if you also considered where new business is going to come to replace the RDT volume. Some might consider the lower grade products that seem to be attracting attention. Others might suggest going up-market to avoid price competition.

Case 16 – Parochial pains

You are the manager of the global accounts division of a worldwide information systems supplier (WHIZZ). The national account manager for a famous American retail company (G-Stores) sends you an e-mail. He comes from the same home town as the chief executive of G-Stores, and they both still live there. G-Stores' headquarters is in their home town. Apparently, G-Stores is planning pilot stores in South America and Europe, and he cannot persuade the relevant country managers to give the new stores any local support.

How do you work with him to maximize the opportunity for WHIZZ?

The creation of a global accounts division is one of the ways of overriding local variations in service. Candidates might discuss the different ways in which companies can organize themselves in order to 'go global' with relevant accounts.

The answer should also discuss the nature of the relationship with G-Stores. It sounds like the relationship is at least cooperative, but it may be rather overreliant on the personal relationship of the key account manager and the chief executive, rather than WHIZZ company capabilities.

Next, a consideration of the global attractiveness of G-Stores to WHIZZ and their perceptions of WHIZZ's global capabilities should be undertaken. The customer portfolio matrix is likely to show G-Stores as a 'selectively invest' global account.

The national account manager seems to realize that he is 'out of his depth'. The manager of the global accounts division needs to appoint someone with international experience to make sure that WHIZZ business growth is closely interlinked with G-Stores' expansion. Also, in the short term, he is likely to have to organize intercompany payments to the countries in which G-Stores has pilots in order to ensure that the proper service levels are provided.

Award yourself extra marks for considering how a joint strategic plan might move the supplier/customer relationship forward to maximize mutual benefit and potential for 'integration'.

Case 17 – Driving change

You are the financial director of a multinational chemical company (ChemCo) with manufacturing plants in Belgium, Argentina and India, and sales units in 60 countries. Competitors have been publicizing the cost advantages they have gained from concentrating on a few key suppliers who can service them globally and offer a global price. You have known for a long time that this is the only way forward for your company, but have been hampered by a hierarchy that allows country managers and plant managers to buy locally. Although the company has a worldwide purchasing policy, it is largely ignored. You have just had a heated conversation with the plant manager in Belgium who has bought some 'dumped' supplies from a company with a poor quality record. He was only interested in making his short-term profit objectives.

This has prompted you to check on insurance cover, and you realize that there are too many different levels of cover with different companies in different geographies. You feel that the company's risk is not being handled consistently, and the company may be highly exposed in the event of major claims. You telephone the company that deals with insurance matters for corporate headquarters. The voicemail system asks you to wait if you do not know the extension and plays you some Vivaldi. After an irritatingly long wait, you ask for the name that is on the system as a main contact. He has left the company. You ask for whoever is dealing with your account. You are transferred to his mobile. Over a very crackly line you ask about global cover. He doesn't know the answer, but thinks they may not have global scope.

Where do you go from here?

When you have done your research on potential global service providers and when you have a business case for supplier rationalization, then you can approach the CEO. You can show him the article about your main competitor and their supplier rationalization and global purchasing programme. You must also show him, on one sheet of paper, a list of quantitative and qualitative reasons why your company should follow the trend and go further than the competition, rationalizing suppliers of services as well as raw materials. You can cite the example of the dodgy raw materials in Belgium and the subsequent insurance issue. You can show him a list of potential service suppliers who claim that they have global scope.

The CEO will probably be convinced that it makes sense, but concerned that people who currently have purchasing power around the company will not give it up to a central department. Even if they did, does the company have the capability to manage the change.

This is where you can test out the mettle of the service companies who claim to have global scope. Make contact with them and ask them what their customers are doing and how. They may be able to introduce you to non-competitive companies who are globally sourcing their services and can give you some ideas for a way forward.

Case 18 – Homework failure

You are the IT director of a fast-growing UK-based mail order company (MoCo) that is in the process of implementing a new customer relationship management system. CRM was needed because of Internet-based sales that have vastly increased the number of customers and varied the location of customers. Your senior systems analyst rushes into the office to tell you that the new system has hit another glitch. She expresses concern about the skill levels of the software engineers who have been supplied by XYZ Limited. XYZ Limited is a 'business partner' of ABC Computing Plc, whose brand of hardware they use. An ABC consultant introduced XYZ to you. (The hardware is installed by another 'business partner', MNO Limited, also introduced by ABC.)

ABC don't know it, but you are about to take over your nearest rival, a German company (who uses PQR systems), which will give you a significant market share in Europe, and form an alliance with a US company. What they should know is that your Internet-based business is doubling every month and has driven sales up 20 per cent overall. ABC is still treating you like small fry. Since IT is absolutely crucial to your business, you need something more sophisticated from your preferred brand.

You call a named contact at ABC, who is responsible for your account and dozens of others. He visits about once a year, usually with the MNO account manager. A gatekeeper tries to put you off speaking to him – surely MNO or XYZ could deal with your query?

How do you respond?

Clearly, your contact/rep has a short-term approach to your business and has not bothered to learn anything about your company. A sale is made and then the installation is chucked 'over the wall' to a third party. While consortium solutions can be appropriate, you expect the brand you trusted to take charge of owning the relationship, even if they don't own the day-to-day technical details.

Unfortunately, you are stuck with the systems that you have bought and have to find a way of leveraging some power to ensure that you get the value you need from them. Because the supplier is treating you tactically, you will probably need to escalate the matter above the contact/rep to a senior manager, using your Internet success as a carrot. A threat to tell your story to the computer press could be the stick!

In the long run, since the systems are strategic to you, a more cooperative relationship is desirable. However, should you really invest time and resource in trying to develop the supplier? Find out what you can about PQR!

Case study 19 – Telling isn't selling

You are the operations director for a major European manufacturer. You are sitting in a room with the managing director and the purchasing director, waiting for a presentation from a supplier of an important subassembly. There are four of them fussing over a personal computer and projector, trying to get the best focus. There's the key account manager, the production engineer, a customer service specialist and someone new. Eventually, they announce that they are ready and the key account manager flashes up the title of the presentation: 'Pushy Plc and Key Plc – Partnership Plan 2000'.

He starts to talk.

'Excuse me.' You say. 'I'd just like to do some introductions, just so that everybody knows everybody.' It turns out that the new person is an account management trainee, who looks nervous.

The account manager raves on about the increase in demand for this sort of plant around the world, and how their subassemblies can be used in virtually any model you might have thought of making, and how the future looks bright for both companies. The slide show has mesmerizing animated cartoons and sound effects. You try to ask a few questions, but the account manager does not seem keen on straying too far off the script. The engineer occasionally interjects a few wise words on their technical excellence. The customer service person offers a few platitudes about good relationships between the two companies. The trainee continues to look nervous.

> **The account manager finishes his presentation with a flourish. What is your response?**

You thank him and get up to respond. You have one humble black and white overhead with a few bullet points.

'It's true that we have made the right choices about market segments and are doing better than most manufacturers of heavy plant and machinery. It's true that we could use your subassembly in some of our new models. We could use someone else's just as easily. So what do you say to:

- our engineers auditing your shopfloor processes
- joint work scheduling
- joint R&D
- online data sharing and transactions
- oh – and after we've helped you save money on all of that – how about a price reduction?'

Case 20 – Turf wars

You are the HR manager for SDY Ltd, a relatively small company serving some very big powerful customers. The managing director met a few key accounts a year ago and they expressed a wish for wider contact within SDY, so he set up a number of departmental contacts for them, and asked the account managers to brief the contacts for their accounts monthly. The key accounts seem to like their departmental contacts very much, in some cases, more than they like the account manager. You are observing a 'team meeting' called by the account manager of the biggest accounts, PUG Retail. She talks about how much volume the customer wants for the next few months: 'Great news! PUG want 100 000 extra units next month for a special promotion in their new hypermarkets in France.'

The factory manager folds his arms and sucks air through his teeth. 'That'll be difficult with the big order from Hollo due any day.' He looks to the cost accountant. 'Will you authorize overtime?' She shrugs. 'I suppose I'll have to.' She looks at the account manager. 'You do realize that agreeing this volume with PUG will make the Hollo job less profitable? You know we always give them priority at this time of year because it is their high season.'

'We'd all be out of a job if it weren't for PUG!' She retorts. 'I slog my guts out to keep them loyal to us and you're all supposed to support me. I get the orders. I'm not here to sort out your departmental difficulties.'

'They're loyal to us because they get a silly price. They may keep the factory running, but do we actually make any money out of this account?' The cost accountant mumbles.

The account manager bangs the table. 'I hope you don't say that sort of thing to their accountants when you're reconciling the invoices with them?'

'Of course, I don't! Anyway, what else do you have to brief us about?'

'They want regional delivery instead of central warehouse delivery. So I said that would be all right.'

Suddenly the logistics manager leaps into action. 'You did what? Whereabouts in France do we have to get to? It's a big country you know. Do they want an artic every time or a seven tonner?'

'You have a contact in their logistics department – talk to them directly.' The account manager replies.

'Never mind that – how much extra is it going to cost?!' The cost accountant fumes.

After a pregnant pause, the customer service manager pipes up: 'Did anybody sort out the new labels? There was a translation mistake. I did send the new copy to the print room.'

What is the role of HR in such a situation?

Setting up key account teams may not be enough to make sure that they flourish. Hostility has even been known to break out between different functions in one department, even in quite a small company. This is probably a job for specialists. Team members need to be confronted with the effect of their behaviour and attitudes on others as individuals, and on the company and its customers. In addition to the training cost, you need to be aware that rebuilding the team will take time.

Case 21 – Plunging into the unknown

You are the Managing Director of a medium ranking US advertising agency. Your relationship with a fast food chain that grew from being a kiosk in a poor town in Virginia to being a national flagship is a famous case study in what a supplier/customer partnership should be.

You are playing golf with Ol' Joe Dollopin, the founder of 24hrBreakfasts, when he says he has made the decision to go into South America and Europe and asks if you can provide advertising services for their pilot stores in Argentina and Holland. You have no idea, and you have no idea if any of your colleagues have any idea.

Ol' Joe says he can see you need some time to come back to him with a proposal. He'd be really sorry to lose you and have to go to a bigger agency that is already established worldwide, so he hopes you can do the business. The truth is, without the 24hrBreakfasts account, your agency will probably become a takeover target.

You discuss the matter with the other four directors who agree to come forward with well-reasoned arguments to support their proposals for the way forward.

Two argue for going global with 24hrBreakfasts because:

- It makes the company competitive with the big boys
- 24hrBreakfasts will provide some security
- Alliances can be formed with local agencies that want some exposure to the US market
- It is a big growth opportunity
- Profit will follow, eventually

Two argue for selling up to an existing global player because:

- The market has already got as many global advertising agencies as it can support
- You can use the growth of the 24hrBreakfasts account as leverage in the negotiations
- Each director can take a wad of money from it and start rediscovering leisure time
- It is easier to do.

You have the casting vote. What do you decide?

Taking a plunge into unknown territory on the basis of the requirements of only one customer is very high risk. The rewards could also be very high, but it would require very strong motivation plus bought-in expertise to realize them. It seems that not all your team are very highly motivated. It may be more appropriate for you to seek a sympathetic global player to take your company over. The potential of the Dollopin account will ensure a good price and you and your colleagues could either take early retirement or pursue a career in the new company.

This selection of mini-cases has presented just a small part of the myriad of problems that result from an organization's efforts to become more customer focused. We hope that you enjoyed thinking about these problems and are better prepared as a result for dealing with the challenges inherent in your key account relationships.

Index

Compiled by Indexing Specialists (UK) Ltd